AF600317

MIND, BODY, MOTION, MATTER

Eighteenth-Century British and French Literary Perspectives

Mind, Body, Motion, Matter

Eighteenth-Century British and French Literary Perspectives

EDITED BY MARY HELEN MCMURRAN
AND ALISON CONWAY

UNIVERSITY OF TORONTO PRESS
Toronto Buffalo London

Toronto Buffalo London
www.utppublishing.com

ISBN 978-1-4426-5011-4 (cloth)

Library and Archives Canada Cataloguing in Publication

Mind, body, motion, matter : eighteenth-century British and French literary perspectives / edited by Mary Helen McMurran and Alison Conway.

Includes bibliographical references and index.
ISBN 978-1-4426-5011-4 (cloth)

1. English literature – 18th century – History and criticism. 2. French literature – 18th century – History and criticism. 3. Philosophy in literature. 4. Materialism in literature. 5. Vitalism in literature. 6. Aesthetics in literature. I. Conway, Alison Margaret, editor II. McMurran, Mary Helen, 1962–, author, editor

PR448.P5M55 2016 820.9'384 C2015-908168-8

University of Toronto Press acknowledges the financial assistance to its publishing program of the Canada Council for the Arts and the Ontario Arts Council, an agency of the Government of Ontario.

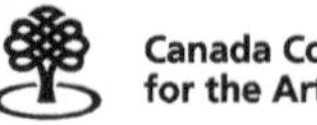

Funded by the Government of Canada
Financé par le gouvernement du Canada

Contents

Illustrations

Acknowledgments

We gratefully acknowledge the University of Western Ontario and the Social Sciences and Humanities Research Council of Canada for their support of the publication and the workshop in which these essays were first presented. We also thank the contributors for their collaboration, our editor, Richard Ratzlaff, the anonymous readers for University of Toronto Press, and, finally, Emily Sugerman, for her fine proofreading.

MIND, BODY, MOTION, MATTER

Introduction[1]

MARY HELEN MCMURRAN

The essays gathered here represent recent approaches to eighteenth-century literature and philosophy. Beginning in the 1980s, Foucauldian criticism, among other theoretical currents, transformed the study of philosophical ideas into analyses of "knowledge."[2] Early modern and Enlightenment philosophies, in particular, were subsequently interpreted as cultural constructions and assessed in terms of their historical effects. The literary works of the long eighteenth century were taken, in large part, as representations of the same social and political domains in which knowledge operated, even as they performed distinctive cultural work.[3] The twenty-first century has brought about a critical shift from the study of knowledge-making in our period to natural philosophy. Natural philosophy is a capacious field of inquiry that traditionally encompassed both the natural world and human nature, and during the seventeenth and eighteenth centuries witnessed major revisions of its three core concepts: matter, or what the world is made up of; motion – not simply as a spatial phenomenon, but as an account of why things come to be and how things change; and the nature of humans as "thinking things."[4]

This volume builds on current scholarship in eighteenth-century natural philosophy and literature, cognitive humanities, and the history of science, which take up these fundamental concepts. Because scholars' interests branch out in many directions, we have not solicited contributions focused on just one theme.[5] Our essays discuss such diverse topics as artisanal aesthetics, religious toleration, pneumatology, thinking matter, and theories of judgment. The contributors consistently attend to aesthetics in their arguments and rely on literary-critical methods, yet some of us bring philosophical ideas to interpretations of literary works or literary tropes and others direct their studies more broadly to theory and the history of ideas. Despite these dissimilarities, we all engage with the re-grounding of human experience that resulted from early modern materialist and mechanistic tenets. This is not to say that there is only one philosophical school that informs eighteenth-century writing. The premises of materiality and motion are not stable, nor do they unilaterally commandeer the period's intellectual developments. On the contrary, they are significant for us because they posed difficult questions: Can matter and motion account for all being, be it the generation of a new biological life or human will and desire? Is matter inert and motion external to matter in living things, or is activity inherent in animate matter? If the human being is both material body and consciousness, what is the nature of their interaction? How do the motions of sensation and feeling mediate bodies, minds, and their environments? Concepts elicit debate, of course, but it is the curiously conjunctive natures of matter and motion, body and thinking that exercised the era's theoretical imagination.

The topics we address would appear to invite interdisciplinary analysis, yet our essays are premised instead on the eighteenth century's pre-disciplinarity. As we show, silos of learning were rare despite the growth of expertise in the period, and transnational conversations as well as transhistorical ones were commonplace.[6] This pre-disciplinarity is also highlighted by the pansophism of several authors featured in the volume: the third Earl of Shaftesbury, who is treated by David Alvarez and Vivasvan Soni, aggregates politics, ethics, religion, and aesthetics; Denis Diderot, who appears in the essays by Sarah Ellenzweig, Kate Tunstall, and Joanna Stalnaker, not only directed the *Encyclopédie*, but expounds on epistemology, biology, and aesthetics, while writing novels and plays. Laurence Sterne, who appears in Jonathan Kramnick's and Tunstall's essays, and William Hogarth, who is discussed by Ruth Mack and Kramnick, are as important for their theories of mental operations as for their literary and visual works. The cross-fertilization of ideas enabled by the eighteenth-century's pre-disciplinarity is also evinced, as Sara Landreth shows, in Daniel Defoe's overlap with Cambridge Platonism, and, as Ellenzweig demonstrates, in Samuel Richardson's alliance with philosophical materialism.

Rather than attempt to outline the complex ideas pertaining to materiality and motion, and how they cross various fields of inquiry in the eighteenth century, let us begin with one of our recurring motifs – the concept of form. Although form is a term that largely dropped out of philosophy in the eighteenth century, its absence helps explain the abundance of speculative energy around matter and motion, body and mind, as well as the imbrication of these concepts with aesthetics. It is often remarked that modern philosophy was inaugurated by rejecting such metaphysical superstitions as form inherited from Aristotelianism, and that the new philosophy relied instead on clear perception and reasoning. The standard view of form's elimination has obscured the fact that closely related notions of organization or structure are central to understanding everything from living beings to sensory perception to visual diagrams and narrative plots in the eighteenth century.

In Aristotle's system, which was later translated into Scholastic philosophy, form is one of the four causes; the others are material, efficient, and final (telos). For Aristotle, substance, which is to say anything that exists, is composed with both matter and form. Matter is undifferentiated, though it has the potential to be a specific thing. Form is actuality, by which matter becomes individuated. At the same time, form provides for the thing's belonging to a kind or species.[7] Martha Bolton explains: "The form of horse, for example, is shared in that one form is individuated by union with the (quantified) matter of many individual horses."[8] Similarly, the soul in Aristotle's philosophy is the form or actualizing principle of all living things (plants, animals, and humans) that endows living things with both individual essence and species essence. Thus, form provides a systematic explanation of the otherwise inert material world. Although formal cause is distinct from final cause, it is nonetheless closely allied with telos, that is, the idea that everything must aim towards some end already embedded within it. In the early modern era, the notion that all substances are a composite of matter and form is subjected to radical revision. Philosophers like John Locke deny that matter and form come together to individuate things and to identify species. Instead, matter is its own substance, and its changes in state can be attributed to mechanical motion, not different forms.[9] Locke also helps dismiss the concept by arguing that the "substantial forms" were not knowable: "Those therefore who have been taught, that the several *Species* of Substances had their distinct internal *substantial forms*; and that it was those Forms, which made the distinction of Substances into their true species and genera, were … set upon a fruitless inquiry."[10]

If form, as a causal principle, becomes a mere figment in eighteenth-century thought, this ought to be reckoned with the many circumlocutions for form on offer. Locke, to take one influential example of the trend, explains that what sustains a (living) thing as itself, that is, what makes an oak still an oak though it changes and grows over time, is its "fitness of organization." In his chapter on identity in the *Essay Concerning Human Understanding*, Locke writes that the oak is "fit to receive and distribute nourishment, so as to continue, and frame the wood, bark, and leaves, etc. ... in which consists the vegetable life." The identity of an animal also consists in its "fitness of organization and the motion wherein life consists," though unlike the plant, fitness and motion "begin together, the motion coming from within."[11] These statements explicitly negate the Aristotelian principle of form, and yet, connecting the "organization" with "fitness," which is a necessary condition of life, retains some idea of form as a blueprint for things. Locke simply does not require further explanation of what makes "fitness of organization," or how it relates to the motion in which life consists. Although Locke's minimization of form is influential, many seventeenth- and eighteenth-century writers resisted the mechanistic thesis that organization alone could support life, and further, that it could support immaterial thinking. Questions regarding the nature of organized structures and what they could bear continued to vex.[12]

Form has a second, but no less important, conceptual role in Aristotelian philosophy, which is also reworked in the early modern period. In addition to being the principle of change, form is also the principle that governs how the external world is mediated by the mind. By definition one cannot have a materialized object as such in an immaterial thought, and thus the object must be in the mind in some other way. For Aristotle, the object is in one's mind as form without its matter or material attributes. We come to know forms by a process of abstracting the object from these particulars. In this way, the mental form relates essentially to the object, and the act of cognition is no less than an identity with or becoming of the forms of things in the mind.[13] Considered as something in the intellect, rather than in things, form predicates the mind's acceptance of the material world.[14] Certain aspects of this Aristotelian-Scholastic view were already undergoing a shift as early as the fourteenth century when philosophers like William of Ockham began to argue that objects *caused* intuitive and abstractive notions in us. Later, the empiricists developed the causal thesis by claiming that objects make impressions on a tabula rasa and that the subsequent ideas are not forms in the mind, but resemblances of objects' qualities. This empiricist view negates the principle of form, but replaces it with the mental imprint. Like organization, this form-like alternative of mental image is not a transcendent idea. Nonetheless it connotes a whole with a particular composition and shape, which predicates cognitive activity, just as organization predicates life-force. I am not arguing that form endures, but rather that the early modern philosophers who wish to evacuate its scholastic meaning substitute other terms that we now recognize as synonymous with form.

Form was not so assiduously avoided in eighteenth-century non-philosophical writing, and, as our essays reveal, the meanings and uses of form may even have gained ground. Hogarth, for instance, devises a theory of mental form in his aesthetic treatise, *The Analysis of Beauty*: he posits that a visual object in our mind is like the thin shell of a material object that remains after scooping out its contents.[15] Ruth Mack argues that Hogarth's shell is not merely a virtual representation of a real thing. Since the inner and outer surfaces of this empty shell coincide in the mental object, the form rematerializes. Jonathan Kramnick also emphasizes the materialization of form in Hogarth's idea of the scooped-out shell, noting that the observer and artist now inhabit the entire object, and view the whole form as if from within. If Hogarth signals the emergence of form's materialization, this demystified idea of form is not characterized by rigid constraint, static structure, or singular purpose. Several of the concepts featured in our essays, including the serpentine line, the aesthetics of presence, and Dionysian ritual, among others, register this new notion of form, which connotes both shape and flux. And many of us discuss the formalizing endeavour of literary writing as a similar kind of structured vibrancy. Sara Landreth demonstrates that form both solidifies and evaporates in Daniel Defoe's *The Consolidator* and *Vision of the Angelick World*. In her reading of Samuel Richardson's *Clarissa*, Sarah Ellenzweig notes that motion is crucial to the novel form's open-endedness. Kate Tunstall's interpretation of entomological metaphors in Laurence Sterne's *Tristram Shandy* and Diderot's *Le Rêve de d'Alembert*, and Joanna Stalnaker's interpretation of Diderot's *Éléments de physiologie* reveal a productive tension between the generative workings of the mind and the form of writing. Other literary forms discussed here – metaphor, comparison, and personification, as well as structured patterns of action (artisanal work or religious ritual), and habitual structures of feeling and thought (enthusiasm and judgment) – are complicated by tensions between dynamism and regulation. Form has a special pertinence for the eighteenth century, which a return to the era's philosophical questions promises to illuminate, and which, in turn, will enable new genealogies of literary formalism.

The full story of form in premodern philosophy, early modern thought, and its subsequent reappearance as literary formalism in the twentieth century, is too lengthy to examine here, but the need for such a history was noted long ago by the philosopher and intellectual historian of the Renaissance and Enlightenment, Ernst Cassirer. In his essay, "The Problem of Form and the Problem of Causality," Cassirer argues that the early modern denial of form created a gulf between the humanities, which cannot do without forms, and the sciences, which pursued the denunciation of form. This lasted until the early twentieth century when form returned as a concept of vital wholeness, or "organic becoming," in natural science. Cassirer explains that this concept of wholeness, which alluded to form, but without form's purposiveness, gave "unexpected aid" to the humanities to reconsider "its own forms and its own structures."[16] The essays in *Mind, Body, Motion, Matter* reveal that vital wholeness was already permeating philosophy, science, and aesthetics in the eighteenth century. Despite the decline of metaphysical form's causal role, it was not reduced to powerless shape, but became as we know it now – difficult to disentangle from things and mysteriously endowed upon them.[17]

Form is emblematic of many other conceptual re-significations facilitated by scrapping old philosophical principles. For our present purposes, the tenuous relation of form to life and mind is important because it pulls into focus philosophical dilemmas regarding matter and motion, and body and mind. A brief orientation to the general course of these unsettled questions from Descartes and Hobbes to Diderot will fill out the background of our diverse studies. Hobbes, as is commonly known, claims that all human and non-human being is only matter, and that motion is the sole cause by which matter is moved or changed. Matter, being inert, requires external actions of contact or collision. On the assumption that human bodies are subject to the natural laws of motion that govern other bodies, Hobbes asserts that thought begins with the motions of objects on the sense organs, which produce like motions in the mind corresponding to the object; the passions are motions internal to the body; actions are the motions of willing. Motion is not simply an observable phenomenon for Hobbes; it belongs to first philosophy, or an account of causes.[18] Descartes also espouses mechanism as it relates to material objects and bodies, but where Hobbes is a substance monist, Descartes is a substance dualist, that is, he claims that materiality and immateriality, and body and mind, are distinct by definition.[19] Dilemmas are endemic to both systems. If matter is inert and motion a passive principle, the cause of originating motion and the cause of the conservation of motion become difficult to explain, even if God's will is taken for granted. Monists must also explain how the motions of corporeal bodies on the sense organs become dephysicalized ideas in the mind. Dualists, for their part, need an account of how the immaterial and material coincide and interact. If collapsing the material and immaterial into monism seems inadequate to some explanatory tasks, the mediations required by dualism seem equally difficult.

Despite Locke's call to recognize the limits of human knowledge on such questions, accounts of matter, motion, and mind flourished in the long eighteenth century. An initial reaction against Hobbesian materialism took up the problem of "senseless" matter and the counterintuitive claim that a living sensitivity could emerge from inert matter. Ralph Cudworth defends the idea of an immaterial principle behind inert matter, and proposes "plastick nature" as the formative and originary force, which also functions as an intermediary between God and matter.[20] His contemporary, Henry More, defends the existence of immaterial substance, which he defines in opposition to inert matter: active, penetrable, but indivisible. Matter is defined as *res extensa* from Descartes onward, but for More and Cudworth both material and immaterial substances are extended, that is, they occupy space. The positions of these two seventeenth-century Cambridge Platonists – somewhat misnamed because their interests range more widely than Plato or Neoplatonism – reiterate that God and mind are ontologically prior, but by positing spirit as itself extended, they attempt to solve the problems of adhering to either substance monism or to dualism.[21] In his discussion of embodied soul, Henry More writes: "It is plain therefore, that this Union of the Soul with Matter does not arise from any such gross Mechanical way … but from a congruity of another nature, which I know not better how to term then *Vital*," which, he goes on to claim, is "in the Matter" (emphasis added).[22] Samuel Clarke, John Toland, and Isaac Newton all acknowledge the problem of denying or separating immateriality from materiality, and respond by generating translative forces, or by increasing pressure on the concept of immanence. As Richard Baxter put it: "In the flux of forms emanating from God … who can say where immateriality ends and materiality begins?"[23]

Over the course of the eighteenth century, philosophers continue to search for ways to incorporate impulses and life into matter. As evinced in theories of vitalistic monism and of preformation (in which the ovum contains the whole adult in miniature), they hold to materialist tenets while trying to modernize Aristotelian hylomorphism in the wake of the dilemmas found in Hobbes's and Descartes's philosophies. At the same time, the materialist standpoint inflects the body-mind issue: some eighteenth-century theories of mind emphasize sensation, and theories of the body's sensitivity as its vital, comprehensive sense are put forth. Diderot, for example, returns on several occasions to the difficult relations of matter to life and mind. At one point, he responds to the dualist-mechanistic view that the soul is the cause of the body's action: "What a difference there is, between a sensitive and living watch and a watch made of gold, iron, silver or copper!"[24] In the *Essay Concerning Human Understanding*, Locke uses this same metaphor of the watch with its machine-like and replaceable parts to explain in what precisely the identity of the animal consists. In that passage, he confuses the metaphor's meaning by supplementing the bodily mechanism with "fitness of organization" for life, as noted above, and consequently, commits neither to pure mechanistic materialism, nor to immaterial forces. Diderot recycles the metaphor, and in the simple gesture of figuring a "sensitive, living watch," exposes the conundrum of deriving vitality from a mechanistic framework.

Vitalism, which was on the ascent in the eighteenth century as mechanistic accounts proved dissatisfactory, is often seen as a proto-scientific movement due to its association with medical, biological, and chemical experiments in the period.[25] Diderot, among others, reminds us that such inquiries should not be cordoned off as purely scientific. Studies of vitality ought to include its close association with earlier compromises of mechanistic claims, as in Henry More's hypothesis. And, just as mechanist materialism is applied to mental as well as physical operations, it should be acknowledged that vital materialisms are as relevant to embodied thinking as to biological reproduction. Vitalisms are spurred by a search for wholeness that exceeds strictly scientistic application; their conceptualization is often poised at the threshold of description, formal logic, and the craftwork of imagination. Our interests, which coalesce around the materiality of experience during this segue in the history of thought, privilege expansive concepts of vitality and activity, not least by attending to sites of contiguity between the body and mental or spiritual states, as well as those between bodies and objects. In pursuing these lines of investigation, we contribute to a re-evaluation of the standard accounts of thinking and feeling in the empiricist eighteenth century. The constitution of a self-conscious, individualistic subject may be an important and lasting contribution of early modern and Enlightenment philosophy, but turning towards materialist, mechanist, and vitalist theories not only unveils generative dilemmas, it challenges the over-emphasis on the disjunction of the self from materiality. To reflect again on the contestations over materialist premises reveals a being-of-the-world rather than a subject receding from it.

The first four essays focus on embodied experience as differently situated in visual aesthetics and religion. It is usually assumed that the empiricist understanding of visual perception, in which objects produce mental images, puts us at a distance from the object realm in ways that are reinforced in eighteenth-century visual art and visual description. In Ruth Mack's and Jonathan Kramnick's essays, visuality is reconceived as contact. In "Hogarth's Practical Aesthetics," Mack investigates the object-centred experience of visual design in *The Analysis of Beauty*. Drawing on Hogarth's own artisanal modus operandi and his investment in the everyday object, which run counter to neoclassical high art, she not only repositions our understanding of Hogarth's themes of corporality, but also demonstrates the materiality rather than the representationality of Hogarth's visual aesthetic. Key to this aesthetic is the "serpentine line," which is of a piece with the tactile motions of the engraver's body as well as the customary lines and motions of the social body in casual gestures, dancing, etc. Hogarth articulates an experience of shape that is quotidian rather than extraordinary and belongs not only to the individual subject, but also to the collective body's habits.

Kramnick's "Presence of Mind: An Ecology of Perception in Eighteenth-Century England," also discusses eighteenth-century visual aesthetics. Kramnick counters, first of all, the representational model of visual perception found in Hobbes (that objects reach the mind through our sense organs as mental images of the qualities of those objects) with a theory of direct perception patterned on touch. Citing contemporary work on active, embodied, or haptic perception that is now putting pressure on the representational model, Kramnick argues that these alternatives have their roots in the eighteenth century. Our ability to see with our whole bodies as if to touch the environment is a skill of shaping "presence." Readings of several passages of poetry and prose demonstrate how this model was worked out in eighteenth-century literary description. Kramnick also retraces the shift from Hobbes's mechanistic account to Thomas Reid's theory of direct sensation, but shows that philosophy lagged behind literature's capacity to bring things to life and train readers in the skill of perceiving presence. The bridge between seeing and touch is completed with a reading of Sterne's kinetic unfolding of sensation in *Sentimental Journey*, which forces us to reconsider feeling as perceptual.

The next two essays continue the themes of feeling and motion, but shift from visuality to eighteenth-century religion. They complicate the accepted view that during the Enlightenment, religiosity was considered antithetical to thinking and to the liberation of individual subjects from the bonds of custom. In "Reading Locke After Shaftesbury: Feeling Our Way Towards a Postsecular Genealogy of Religious Tolerance," David Alvarez undertakes a careful reading of the affective politics of Shaftesbury's *Letter Concerning Enthusiasm* and Locke's *Letter Concerning Toleration* to demonstrate that religious differences were not quelled by the exercise of rationality. Shaftesbury does not seek to control religious enthusiasm, but invites an alternative system of "mood management." Recognizing that tolerance itself can threaten, Shaftesbury's ideal magistrate recasts Christianity as a "good humoured and witty religion" that will in turn establish the grounds of sociability among his subjects. Because of its apparent emphasis on "dispassionate judgment" and "mutual recognition," Locke's *Letter* has been a hallmark of modern liberalism's theories of religious toleration. In Locke, however, sentiment, not the skeptical-epistemological critique that privatizes belief, allows us to endure the acts of tolerating and being tolerated required by religious pluralism. Alvarez thus revises the origins story of secularism, not least by attending to late seventeenth-century embodied religiosity.

"Rethinking Superstition: Pagan Ritual in Lafitau's *Moeurs des sauvages*" provides another exploration of pre-conscious religiosity, but focuses instead on the externalized motions of rites. I demonstrate that early eighteenth-century ethnographies of religious customs did not simply derogate them as habitual motion-machines of bodies and sentiment. Rather than condemn pagan ritual practices (ancient or native) as idol worship rooted in fear or awe, many writers admitted that all humans are naturally capable of knowing the divinity, and thus that divine presence can attend the performance of rites. Focusing on Joseph-François Lafitau's comparative ethnography of pagan ritual, I argue that his method is not, in fact, comparison but analogy. Lafitau is not a precursor to modern thought, not least because he resists empiricist observation and description. His most significant analogy, which is that all pagan religion is nothing other than the obscure and formless Dionysiac mystery rites, provides a conjectural unification of diverse forms of religion and functions as a denial of the separation of bodily or material aspects of religious experience from immateriality. For Lafitau, the bacchanal's frenzied motions synch human consciousness with imperceptible being as nature's religion.

The next group of four essays is similarly concerned with preconscious states, but here explicit engagements with philosophical materialisms frame focused readings of literary texts. Sara Landreth's "Defoe on Spiritual Communication, Action at a Distance, and the Mind in Motion" refers us back to seventeenth-century contestations of Hobbesian materialism. Landreth homes in on pneumatology, "the science, doctrine, or theory of spirits or spiritual beings" that was traditionally part of metaphysics, but later became a psychological term, as well as a theological, and a scientific term.[26] The eighteenth-century pre-disciplinary polysemy of pneumatology serves Landreth's investigation of Defoe's *Consolidator* and his *Vision of the Angelick World* well. For Defoe, the mind/soul is a thing that moves and feels, an idea that reveals his link to Henry More and the hypotheses of air as a quasi-material substance. Landreth is also concerned with the repercussions of materializing immaterialist principles for the act of reading and the printed text: she shows how reading and textuality become less concrete and discrete in Defoe's writing, sustaining what Jay David Bolter and Richard Grusin call the "double logic" of immediacy and hypermediacy. This double logic, Landreth observes, allows us to become aware of the "medium as a medium"– the experience of reading as "an intermingling of multiple representations, both mental and physical."

Materialist-mechanist concepts of motion engender another innovative close reading in Sarah Ellenzweig's "The Persistence of *Clarissa*." Ellenzweig begins with Hobbes's view that motions of physical bodies persist, and that human *conatus*, or appetitive motion, like the motion of all matter, persists unless interrupted. She then argues that the persistence and perseverance of the eponymous heroine of Richardson's novel does not present us with the disembodiment of Clarissa's person in opposition to Lovelace's materialist pleasure-seeking. Rather, the argument draws together the characters' pursuits of desires – ones they both know and yet which escape their grasp – as the same persistent motions in all life forms. Lovelace and Clarissa can be understood as similarly underestimating the power of materialism's vitality: Lovelace because he can only imagine one script for it, and Clarissa because she believes in the power of her will over her motions even when she cannot move. Clarissa, rather than willing her own destruction, merely "swerves" as all of nature necessarily swerves – a prospect more terrifying for Richardson's heroine, perhaps, than the idea of her own culpability. Her death drive shows her, paradoxically, "to be a desiring, aspiring participant in the natural world, embedded in its order of things."

Kate Tunstall's and Joanna Stalnaker's essays complement these discussions of the motility of matter by introducing a Continental perspective. In "The Early Modern Embodied Mind and the Entomological Imaginary," Tunstall analyzes the insect metaphors for mind in Laurence Sterne's *Tristram Shandy* and Diderot's *Le Rêve de d'Alembert*. She offers a fresh look at *Tristram Shandy*'s appreciation of the body's "cognitive and creative capacities," and, focusing on the figure of the Momus glass, shows how its image of "frisky maggots, gamboling about inside a dioptrical beehive" enables the author's self-satirization of his own mental misconceptions. Tunstall then contrasts Sterne's figure with the bee swarm in Diderot's *Le Rêve de d'Alembert*. This dialogue, which begins as a debate between Diderot and d'Alembert about materialism and dualism, continues in a dream-conversation with multiple characters. As Tunstall shows, Diderot's argument that a material body is by its own constitution capable of thought depends on the idea of the whole body's sensitivity to the world and to others; the bee swarm is a metaphor for this unified body and mind (without recourse to an immaterial soul). At the same time, the bee swarm unsettles the idea of subjective consciousness, not least by emphasizing collectivity. Diderot's and Sterne's speculations on thinking matter and creative generation, expressed in witty transgressions and affirmational sensualism, fully implicate aesthetics in the mid eighteenth-century shift from mechanistic to vital materialism.[27]

In "Diderot's Brain," Joanna Stalnaker discusses the *philosophe*'s vital materialism and its aesthetic expression in his sprawling last work, *Éléments de physiologie*. She explicates each of the three sections of Diderot's opus: death, biological generation, and memory. In the first section, Diderot considers theories of animal organization, in which the living creature's parts are both vital in themselves and act in concert with a single sensitivity, to muse on the possibility that the end of life is a gradual process of losing vitality rather than a sudden event. In the second part of the work, Diderot returns to the generation of living beings, and, as Stalnaker argues, this section, usually seen as borrowed from other authors, realizes the very vitality of elements on an aesthetic level that he attributes to living things. In the final section, Diderot, in a departure from the empiricist idea that memory is the locus of a continuous self, claims that the soul is "amid its sensations," and wonders how the memory of a lifetime of both conscious and unnoticed sensations might extend beyond the self in a continued vitality. Stalnaker reveals that Diderot's materialist sensibility finds its proper form in the energies of dialogic and fragmented discourses.

The volume ends with Vivasvan Soni's "Can Aesthetics Overcome Instrumental Reason? The Need for Judgment in Mandeville's *Fable of the Bees*." The invention of the aesthetic in the eighteenth century, Soni reminds us, brought forth a form of judgment that resists the instrumentalization of ends. Yet, he argues, "the distinction between defensible ends and a mere instrumentality becomes elusive." Turning to Mandeville, who appears to embrace instrumentality, Soni argues that the *Fable of the Bees* actually abolishes ends orientation, and replaces it with something that looks very much like the aesthetic in that its purposiveness lacks purpose. The way out of the impasse of ends-orientation is through the labour of judgment, which is not grounded "in Reason," as Soni suggests, but in "the giving of reasons."

Soni's interrogation of the Enlightenment dilemma regarding ends might seem to diverge from others' readings of pre-reflective and materialized experience since it puts thinking, and particularly the active labour of judgment, in the forefront. Yet Soni's point that we must acknowledge that purposes are a kind of fiction coheres with our project of recasting rationalism in eighteenth-century thought. The idea of "fictioning purposes" likewise provides us with another angle on the history of form with which we began: "true" purpose or end, which was assigned to form in the Aristotelian-Scholastic system, is revealed once again to be disrupted by seventeenth- and eighteenth-century philosophers. Yet ends are not altogether nullified, and, like form, they undergo a conceptual deregulation that nurtures aesthetics. On the whole, our volume's detailed inspections of the new philosophies demonstrate the volatility of the core ideas opened up by materialism, and the possibilities of an aesthetic vitalism of form.

NOTES

1 Thanks to Alison Conway for her contributions and editing.

2 A classic work such as Arthur Lovejoy's *The Great Chain of Being: A Study of the History of an Idea* (Cambridge, MA: Harvard University Press, 1936) discovers an autonomous "unit-idea" in canonical texts.

3 Studies of eighteenth-century sensibility and sympathy, which draw equally from philosophical and literary texts to diagnose cultural phenomena, exemplified the trend in the 1990s and 2000s.

4 René Descartes, *Meditations* (1639). *Res cogitans* or thinking substance is distinguished from *res extensa*. Lucretius's materialism has been the subject of several recent studies. See, *inter alia*, Jonathan Kramnick, "Living with Lucretius," in Helen Deutsch and Mary Terrall, eds., *Vital Matters: Eighteenth-Century Views of Conception, Life, and Death* (Toronto: University of Toronto Press, 2012), and Stephen Greenblatt, *The Swerve: How the World Became Modern* (New York: W.W. Norton, 2011).

5 This volume builds on studies of eighteenth-century empiricism, sensation, cognition, and science, including Helen Thompson and Natania Meeker, eds., "Empiricism, Substance, Narrative," special issue, *The Eighteenth Century: Theory and Interpretation* 48.3 (2007); Helen Deutsch and Mary Terrall, eds., *Vital Matters*; Manushag Powell and Rivka Swenson, eds., "Sensational Subjects," special issue, *The Eighteenth Century: Theory and Interpretation* 54.2 (2013); Kevin Cope, ed., *The Sensational Centuries: Essays on the Enhancement of Sense Experience in the Seventeenth, Eighteenth, and Nineteenth Centuries* (New York: AMS Press, 2013); Fiona Macpherson, ed., *The Senses: Classical and Contemporary Philosophical Perspectives* (New York: Oxford University Press, 2011); Jayne Lewis, *Air's Appearance: Literary Atmosphere in British Fiction, 1660–1794* (Chicago: University of Chicago Press, 2012).

6 See Robin Valenza, *Literature, Language and the Rise of the Intellectual Disciplines in Britain, 1680–1820* (New York: Cambridge University Press, 2009).

7 Some standard readings of Aristotelian matter and form can be found in *The Concept of Matter in Greek and Medieval Philosophy,* ed. Ernan McMullin (Notre Dame: University of Notre Dame Press, 1963).

8 Martha Bolton, "Universals, Essences and Abstract Entities," in *The Cambridge History of Seventeenth-Century Philosophy*, ed. Daniel Garber and Michael Ayers (New York: Cambridge University Press, 2003), I, 179. See Nicholas Jolley, "Metaphysics," in *The Cambridge Companion to Early Modern Philosophy*, ed. Donald Rutherford (New York: Cambridge University Press, 2006), 95–135.

9 Edwin McCann, "Locke's Philosophy of Body," in *The Cambridge Companion to Locke*, ed. Vere Chappell (Cambridge: Cambridge University Press, 1994), 56–7.

10 John Locke, *An Essay Concerning Human Understanding*, ed. Peter Nidditch (New York: Oxford University Press, 1975), 3.6.10.

11 Locke, *An Essay Concerning Human Understanding*, 2.27.4 and 2.27.5.

12 See Ann Thomson, *Bodies of Thought: Science, Religion and the Soul in the Early Enlightenment* (New York: Oxford University Press, 2008), chapter 3.

13 Aristotelian epistemology as presented in *De Anima* is largely worked out by Thomas Aquinas. See *Summa Theologica* I, question 79.

14 "Nothing is in the intellect that was not first in the senses" predates empiricism; it is cited by Thomas Aquinas, *De veritate*, question 2 a. 3 arg. 19 from Aristotle.

15 William Hogarth, *The Analysis of Beauty*, ed. Ronald Paulson (New Haven: Yale University Press, 1997), 21.

16 Ernst Cassirer, "The Problem of Form and the Problem of Causality," in *The Logic of the Humanities*, trans. Clarence Smith Howe (New Haven: Yale University Press, 1961), 164–5, 172. As Marjorie Levinson remarks of new formalist literary criticism: "despite the proliferation … of synonyms for form (e.g., genre, style, reading, literature, 'significant literature,' the aesthetic, coherence, autonomy) none of the essays puts redefinition front and center" (8). Marjorie Levinson, "What is New Formalism?," *PMLA* 122.2 (2007): 558–69. She published a longer version, which I have used here: www.sitemaker.umich.edu/pmla_article (accessed 8 June 2014). Also see Richard Strier, "How Formalism Became a Dirty Word, and Why We Can't Do Without It," in *Renaissance Literature and Its Formal Engagements*, ed. Mark David Rasmussen (New York: Palgrave, 2002), 207–15; Caroline Levine, *Forms: Whole, Rhythm, Hierarchy, Network* (Princeton: Princeton University Press, 2015).

17 The "new materialism" has not always fully recognized the historical complexity of active materiality. See, for example, Jane Bennett, *Vibrant Matter: A Political Ecology of Things* (Durham, NC: Duke University Press, 2010); Diana Coole and Samantha Frost, eds., *New Materialisms: Ontology, Agency, and Politics* (Durham, NC: Duke University Press, 2010).

18 See Doug Jesseph, "Hobbesian Mechanics," in *Oxford Studies in Early Modern Philosophy* 3, ed. Daniel Garber and Steven Nadler (Oxford: Clarendon Press, 2006): 119–52.

19 Descartes and other dualists did not deny the common sense proposition of embodied consciousness. Descartes argues that mind and body are substantially united, "very closely joined and, as it were, 'intermingled' with the body" and that sensations arise "from the union and so to speak intermixture of the mind with the body." Quoted in Daniel Garber and Margaret Wilson, "Mind-Body Problems," in *The Cambridge History of Seventeenth-Century Philosophy*, ed. Daniel Garber and Michael Ayers (New York: Cambridge University Press, 2003), I, 834. Locke believed that the ontological status of the union of mind and body, and an explanation

of how thought produces a motion in the body or the body produces motion in the mind, are remote from our understanding.

20 Ralph Cudworth, *The True Intellectual System of the Universe* (London, 1678), chapter 3 and passim.

21 Sarah Hutton, "The Cambridge Platonists," in *Stanford Encyclopedia of Philosophy*, http://plato.stanford.edu/entries/cambridge-platonists.

22 Henry More, *The Immortality of the Soul, so farre forth as it is demonstrable from the knowledge of nature and the light of reason* (London, 1659), 263.

23 Richard Baxter, *Of the Immortality of Man's Soul* (1682) quoted in John Henry, "A Cambridge Platonist's Materialism: Henry More and the Concept of Soul," *Journal of the Warburg and Courtauld Institutes* 49 (1986): 185. Also see P. M. Heimann, "Voluntarism and Immanence: Conceptions of Nature in Eighteenth-Century Thought," *Journal of the History of Ideas* 39.2 (1978): 271–83.

24 Denis Diderot, *Éléments de physiologie*, ed. Jean Mayer (Paris: Marcel Didier, 1964), 60.

25 See, for example, Jacques Roger, *The Life Sciences in Eighteenth-Century French Thought*, trans. Robert Ellrich (Stanford: Stanford University Press, 1997); George Rousseau, "The Perpetual Crises of Modernism and the Traditions of Enlightenment Vitalism: with a note on Mikhail Bakhtin," in *The Crisis in Modernism: Bergson and the Vitalist Controversy*, ed. Frederick Burwick and Paul Douglass (New York: Cambridge University Press, 1992): 15–75.

26 *Oxford English Dictionary Online*, s.v. "pneumatology," def. 1a, http://www.oed.com/Entry/146322.

27 See Natania Meeker's study of Diderot in *Voluptuous Philosophy: Literary Materialism in the French Enlightenment* (New York: Fordham University Press, 2006), 155–6.

PART ONE

Pre-Reflective Experience

1 Hogarth's Practical Aesthetics

RUTH MACK

In *London and Westminster Improved* (1766), John Gwynn observes that in current times the work of the history painter is "less attended to"; "his part," rather, "is usually supplied by a paper hanging maker and two or three workers in stucco."[1] The wallpaper and ornamental plasterwork to which Gwynn refers here is a sign of what Charles Saumarez Smith calls a "change in … perception" of the "material environment," a new focus on the decoration of the interiors of houses and on those interiors as complete wholes.[2] Near the beginning of the eighteenth century, architectural illustrations of buildings began to include cutaway sections, revealing individual rooms.[3] As such images would suggest, design began to matter for all parts of a dwelling: from the arrangement of columns and the layout of rooms, it moved to wallpaper, to elaborate chimney pieces, and to patterned silks on chairs and curtains. While there had for some time been a robust set of manufacturing industries for such luxury goods in France, England lagged behind – at the beginning of the century, severely so. Anne Puetz observes that "in Britain, very little original engraved ornament had been produced prior to the fourth decade of the eighteenth century, and craftsmen had to rely on imports, or copies of designs, from France, Italy and The Netherlands."[4] But, over the course of the century, this state of affairs began to improve. The Nine Years War, with its restrictions on imports, created an incentive for the English to create at home. And the luxury goods that still filled the marketplace, especially those from China and France, put pressure on domestic manufacturers to compete with increasingly high standards of production.[5] When, in the first half of the century, native manufacturing rose to the occasion, silk design flourished as the industry began to separate out designers from weavers; ornamental plasterwork and wallpaper surged in popularity, especially in the 1740s and 50s, losing their status as cheap replacements for textile hangings and becoming fashionable in themselves; and styles of furniture proliferated. As interiors of houses, generally, acquired new importance, architects like the Adam brothers created and popularized what we would now call interior design.[6] By the 1730s, Saumarez Smith observes, "design consciousness emerge[d] in the public vocabulary."[7] By the 1750s, according to Jules Lubbock, "public interest in design rose to fever-pitch."[8]

This public interest in design – that newly visible, interesting, and commercially important aspect of objects that could not be reduced to their materials – involved both artist and artisan, both the "history painter" and the "worker in stucco." For the pressure to create new design quickly opened into an old set of proprietary questions: to begin with, was this the domain of craft or of high art? On the side of the former, numerous private drawing schools were founded across London to educate artisans in the practice that would lead to inventive new design, and the Society for the Encouragement of Arts, Manufactures, and Commerce was founded in 1754, explicitly tying this new English design to economic interests. On the side of high art, The Royal Academy was founded in 1768, formally establishing the polite arts as the source for design, with Joshua Reynolds's idea that such invention would filter down to the world of the artisan.[9]

William Hogarth was intimately connected to several aspects of the new eighteenth-century development and "consciousness" of design. His mentor (and, ultimately, his father-in-law) James Thornhill became famous as a history painter but then began to work outside those strict bounds and is now credited with some of the earliest conceptual thinking on interior design.[10] Hogarth himself furthered the new cultural focus on the interior environment in his conversation pieces, portrait paintings focusing on small groups of people engaged in everyday activities.[11] And, finally, and most important for what I will discuss here, Hogarth straddled the roles of artist and artisan for his entire career. Hogarth was apprenticed to Ellis Gamble, a silver engraver, at 16. To some extent, Hogarth would spend the rest of his career distancing himself from this early work, disparaging the "drudgery of mechanical reproduction" and separating his identity as an "artist" from the early instruction of "a master who was fundamentally an artisan."[12] This is what Hogarth has in mind, for example, when in one of the manuscripts for the *Analysis of Beauty*, he remarks that he "lost a great part of [his] time, in engraving coats of armes on Silver Plate"

(*AB*, 121). But despite such reflections, Hogarth never entirely left artisanal practice behind. The St Martin's Lane Academy, with Hogarth at its head, was full of artists – medallists, engravers, enamellers – whose arts were "useful" or "applied" (as we would now say), rather than "high." And Hogarth's own artistic practice fit well with this world; as Ronald Paulson observes, Hogarth's mature process of engraving his own paintings would have been called "necessary" or "mechanical" by the proponents of "high art" of the likes of Shaftesbury, Hutcheson, and Richardson.[13] And so it was: in the debates over the foundation of an English academy on the model of the French one (in full steam, as the *Analysis* was published in 1753), Hogarth's opponents depicted him as a mere artisan and merchant, committed to the useful arts and to the world of the market.

The history of design generally moves through questions raised by architecture and decorative art, but I would like to take up Saumarez Smith's suggestion that we should consider design history as part of a larger intellectual history.[14] At this moment of an emerging "design consciousness," how was Hogarth thinking about design's relation to the everyday object? And how was he thinking about the relation between design and historical or cultural context? Answering these questions, I contend, leads us to understand Hogarth's aesthetic project as also undertaking a kind of early social theory, one explicitly concerned with discovering how representation might come close to the practices it attempts to depict.

I'd like to turn now to Hogarth's aesthetic treatise, the *Analysis of Beauty*, which has never been taken as seriously as his painting and engraving. Indeed defences of Hogarth's *Analysis of Beauty* frequently falter when they come to the serpentine line – a real problem since the line is Hogarth's definition of beauty (Figure 1.1). While Ronald Paulson and Jenny Uglow, the artist's twentieth-century biographers, defend his turn to the written word and even stress the positive reception of the treatise, they both appear at a loss when it comes to accounting for the basic grounding of the aesthetic theory in a universal "line of beauty." Hogarth's "real mistake," Uglow writes, "was to defy the tyranny of rules by inventing a new rule himself, and insisting that it was an absolute truth." How indeed does one reconcile the Hogarth who, as Uglow puts it, could claim that "the essence of beauty lay in one form, the 'serpentine line'" with the Hogarth who in his visual work "himself acknowledged that ideals of beauty could be local and cultural"?[15] Paulson, in his introduction to the *Analysis*, makes clear, moreover, that

Figure 1.1. *Analysis of Beauty* (1753), Plate 1. Courtesy of the William Ready Division of Archives and Research Collections, McMaster University Library, Hamilton, Ontario. Hogarth's line of beauty is line four (No. 49), near the centre of the top of the plate.

the text of the treatise itself seems conflicted in this way: "Hogarth had introduced 'the Power of habit and custom' in his Preface to beat connoisseurs and their dupes … He seemed unaware that the argument could be turned against his own Line of Beauty, which might be as locally and perhaps as ethnically conditioned."[16]

I would like to approach this problem by reconsidering Hogarth's "practical" aesthetics. Paulson uses this term to describe Hogarth's opposition to the Third Earl of Shaftesbury's "theoretically pure" neoclassical aesthetics, in which "the human body can only be beautiful if divorced from function, fitness, and utility."[17] Indeed, Hogarth makes the term "experience" central to his aesthetic argument, and when he does so he turns away both from Shaftesbury and from classical art treatises, arguing that the artist-viewers, indeed all his readers, should "see with our own eyes" (*AB*, 18). Here, in the first part of the treatise, Hogarth echoes Bacon and Locke, rejecting custom for clear sight. In this domain, the artist, writing from experience, can bring forward a familiar visual metaphor, even as he embraces its literal meaning: Hogarth observes that the majority of artists see through their experiences with art – "the manners in which pictures are painted" – rather than looking directly at the world in front of them. He begins, then, by acknowledging that artists and connoisseurs will have the hardest time reading the *Analysis*, because they will have to unlearn "the surprising alterations objects seemingly undergo through the prepossessions and prejudices contracted by the mind" (*AB*, 20).

In the first pages of the text, Hogarth repeatedly reminds us that this treatise is one written by an artist, rather than a philosopher.[18] Indeed, he says, he is "one who never took up the pen before" (*AB*, 1). Hogarth's written treatise is a straightforward response to the requirements for the mastery of liberal arts on the model of the Renaissance artist;[19] his claim for greater experience with brush than pen is no doubt a jab at the connoisseurs, as well as at Shaftesbury's armchair theorizing. Such claims for the artist also connect the general category of experience to Hogarth's long-standing conduct as an artist and as a teacher of art. In his academy at St Martin's Lane, this meant a style of instruction that opposed the hierarchical French academy style and use of drawing books and casts and instead "urged students to learn expression, movement, and the appearance of things from the model or from general observation."[20] But this is not all Hogarth has in mind in calling attention to himself as a practitioner.[21] He hints at the complexity of his definition of experience when he says that having conceived the idea for a treatise, "I applied myself to several of my friends, whom I thought capable of taking up the pen for me, offering to furnish them with *materials* by word of mouth" (*AB*, 13, my emphasis). We might neglect, or suppose incidental, this reference to ideas as "materials," "the matter or substance from which a thing is or may be made,"[22] were it not for Hogarth's subsequent lines. He describes himself as having instead "thrown it in to the form of a book" before submitting it to the judgment of his friends (*AB*, 13). Here, "thrown" almost certainly means "to put deftly into some other form or shape" (a sense of the word that, in eighteenth-century discourse, can refer to everything from translating language to tilling a field). Given the subject of the treatise, the winding line, it is also hard not to hear "throw" in another contemporary sense: as "to form or fashion by means of a rotary or twisting motion" – descriptive, in the eighteenth century, of the manufacture of both pottery and silk.[23] Hogarth as writer, he seems to remind us, is still Hogarth as artisan, making a treatise as he might a pot or a piece of cloth. But what does it mean, exactly, to make a theory of beauty artisanally?

At the very least, it means to write counter to Renaissance art treatises. As Ann Bermingham observes, such treatises attempted to separate art from craft, establishing "liberal arts" by opposing intellectual to manual labour. Pointing back to Florentine theory and its focus on "disegno" – which Alberti defines as "the ability to abstract ideal beauty from the most beautiful examples of nature and to reproduce them in or as art" – Bermingham shows how writers from Castiglione to Vasari attempt to reduce even the manual act of drawing to a form of intellectual endeavour.[24] Hogarth was acquainted with such formal treatises, of course, and these would have been central to his conception of his own endeavour. But it is important that his terms come, as well, from a much more general thinking about "experience." The terms of the debate over the practical knowledge in craft have a long history that extends beyond this formal writing on art. In her account of the Renaissance division between theoretical and practical knowledge, Pamela H. Smith turns back to Aristotle's separation of *praxis* or experiential knowledge from *scientia* or *episteme*. There, theory was the domain of logic and geometry, certain truth, and practice (*technē*, the kind of practice that concerns us here) the domain of things made by bodily labour: the latter was the realm of custom and habit, and a knowledge "of how to make things produce effects."[25] In tracing the history of this division through the seventeenth century, Smith shows how early modern artisans produce theory through practice and she also demonstrates, near the end of her account, that the separation between the practical and the theoretical lingers even in the seventeenth-century empiricism that, in its focus on experiment and experience, would seem to undo the division. As she puts it, "the new natural philosophers expressed an ambivalence toward the role of the body and the senses … they sought to control the bodily dimensions of empiricism at the same time that they began to distance themselves from artisans and practitioners."[26] For Bacon and his contemporaries, experience is privileged, but the artisan is exiled, and the habitual, sensual quality of artisanal experience is distanced from the experience of the scientist.[27] It is in these terms that we should read Hogarth's intervention: if the *Analysis of Beauty* most obviously claims that "experience" should be the grounds for knowing beauty, it also shows how the line of beauty can offer us a way to know something more about the vexed category of "experience" Smith describes.[28]

Hogarth's turn towards individual experience ("our own eyes") makes clear his debt to the English tradition of empiricism. Such a focus on experience would have come to him directly through Bacon and Locke as well as through seventeenth-century Dutch painting, itself strongly influenced by this English empiricist tradition.[29] If we see both of these influences alongside Smith's account of the earlier period, we can make better sense of the philosophical stakes of Hogarth's insistence on the importance of practical experience. Writers on Hogarth have expressed, in a variety of ways, his embrace of an unusually bodily empiricism: his aesthetics is one committed to beauty as pleasure, going Addison one better and turning aesthetics fully towards the "gross" senses; Hogarth is committed to a "corporeal, sensorial experience."[30] As David Bindman has pointed out (in useful philosophical terms), Hogarth went beyond Locke's model of vision and brought touch into his primary understanding of experience. Bindman notes that Hogarth's take on Molyneux's problem was different from Locke's, and that Hogarth imagined a closer connection between touch and the visual sense.[31] Usually critics stressing the artist's heightened bodily empiricism take as their examples for it the eroticism of Hogarth's visual art, but I will suggest in what follows that this is only one of its manifestations. Rather, we should understand the erotic "corporealism" in Hogarth as one dimension of a larger investment in practical knowledge. When the debate over an art academy again made central the relation between artist and artisan as a way of thinking about the nature of artistic creation, it is perhaps no surprise that Hogarth returned to terms that are close to his Renaissance precursors', attempting to think theory in terms of practice.

The *Analysis* is very much associated with the everyday object: it is often understood as remarkable precisely because it offers as examples of beauty not only the Apollo Belvedere but also stays and smoke-jacks. Presumably it is the presence of such everyday objects that has led historians of design to see the text as important. Puetz claims, for instance, that "Hogarth's *Analysis of Beauty* (1753) first provided a detailed aesthetic discussion of 'design' in its fullest sense," by which she means including its figurative one: as "conceptual control over the production of objects."[32] There is no doubt that Hogarth possesses such a conceptual understanding of design, but his relation to it is more complicated than such a summary lets on. Take, for example, Hogarth's explanation in the introduction to the *Analysis* of how we are to conceive objects in our minds, something he ultimately claims as a strategy for seeing "the *inside* of those surfaces, if I may be allowed the expression" (*AB*, 21):

> In order to my being well understood, let every object under our consideration, be imagined to have its inward contents scoop'd out so nicely, as to have nothing of it left but a thin shell, exactly corresponding both in its inner and outer surface, to the shape of the object itself: and let us likewise suppose this thin shell to be made up of very fine threads, closely connected together, and equally perceptible, whether the eye is supposed to observe them from without, or within; and we shall find the ideas of the two surfaces of this shell will naturally coincide. (*AB*, 21)

Uglow gestures towards the strangeness of this thought experiment when she remarks, "Perhaps late twentieth-century readers find this easier, since it is very like computer graphic modeling, in which an image can be revolved and viewed from within or without and from different angles."[33] And Abigail Zitin has recently focused on this passage in a reading that stresses how "the virtual inhabitation of an object reconceived as an empty shell deprives the object of its quiddity. It becomes a form and nothing but a form, a set of coordinates on a grid."[34] But both descriptions miss something important about – or, rather, abstract something from – Hogarth's description. Hogarth insists that we are to think of this object not only as composed of lines but as having its entire materiality emptied from it; what is left is not mere form at all, but a material shell. Moreover, Hogarth's desire that we imagine the process of emptying the shell (not just its final incarnation) emphasizes a multiplicity of surfaces without relinquishing the material qualities of the object. In this, Hogarth resembles the empiricist Dutch artists of Svetlana Alpers's description, who, to "maximize surface" for the "probing" and "attentive eye," show us lemons as objects by splitting and peeling them.[35] Unlike such artists, however,

Hogarth's ultimate aim lies not so much with the object in all of its particularity as with what the object, in its objectness, can tell us about the idea of abstraction. We are to see lines as made and as materials for making: they are not lines only but "very fine threads." As Hogarth makes this shell, he abstracts only to pull the abstraction into an image and, then, into a hollow thing of thread. Here, he seems to reply to the likes of Joshua Reynolds that even the abstract or conceptual, in Reynolds's terms the domain of high art, must partake not just of the material but of the artisanal domain of habitual action: thinking comes close to weaving, carving, casting – and, hardly incidentally, engraving.

This example is more than just a witty formal rejoinder to Reynolds in the form of a new metaphor for conceptual thought. It is also related to the positive idea of the image that Hogarth works out in his plates for the *Analysis*, themselves the products of his own made, engraved lines. Indeed, at the outset of the treatise, Hogarth makes a point of specifying his aim for the plates:

> And in this light I hope my prints will be consider'd, and that the figure referr'd to in them will never be imagined to be placed there by me as examples themselves, of beauty or grace, but only to point out to the reader what sorts of objects he is to look for and examine in nature, or in the works of the greatest masters. My figures, therefore, are to be consider'd in the same light, with those a mathematician makes with his pen, which may convey the idea of his demonstration, tho' not a line in them is either perfectly straight, or of that peculiar curvature he is treating of. Nay, so far was I from aiming at grace, that I purposely chose to be least accurate, where most beauty might be expected, that no stress might be laid on the figures to the prejudice of the work itself. (*AB*, 17)

Scholars of Hogarth, Paulson included, have tended to concentrate on the first and last parts of this quotation, which suggest that the print points beyond itself, to the real world.[36] We certainly see Hogarth wrestling with the problem of including plates at all in a treatise that discourages copying and argues against the origin of art in representation, instead directing the reader/artist to the direct observation of Nature. But also contained in this remark is the idea of the mathematical figure, important because it is neither illustration nor direct contact with nature. Mathematics should make us think about how exactly it is that Hogarth's image points to nature.

Hogarth's term "figures" brings together geometrical shape with the range of "artificial representation[s] of the human form" (and representations of such representations, in the case of the statues) that populate his plates.[37] In stressing the way in which his engravings might work to "convey the idea of his demonstration," Hogarth uses mathematics to push his own representations towards what Reviel Netz describes for ancient "diagrams." Netz, in his work on Greek mathematics, explains that diagrams are not like pictures. They are, rather, in his terms, "psychological objects."[38] They contain, as Hogarth suggests, a "subset of the real properties of the object."[39] But what Hogarth does not spell out here in the *Analysis* is that diagrams are partial representations that do not emphasize their partiality. If they throw us on the world, they do so not by making us look away from image and towards the world but by teaching us how to think. They accomplish this in a way that (if our minds are focused on artistic representation) will seem strange. In the impossible "perfectly straight" lines (Hogarth) and in the "so-called equilateral triangle" (Netz), diagrams have about them the status of "make-believe."[40] They function with an interesting kind of partial correspondence: they are "functionally identical" to the intended object.[41] Diagrams work on what Netz calls an "ontological borderline" – gifted with a kind of reality that works within a "cognitive process" as the thing it represents.[42] Netz writes, "The diagram is not a representation of something else; it is the thing itself. It is not like a representation of a building, it is like a building, acted upon and constructed."[43]

How does this notion of the diagram work in terms of Hogarth's two plates "illustrating" the *Analysis*? John Bender and Michael Marrinan give us an excellent starting point for answering this question in their book *The Culture of Diagram*, where they offer the diagram as a paradigmatic Enlightenment way of thinking. Following Netz in opposing a diagram to a picture (though this time with the plates of the *Encyclopédie*, rather than Euclidean geometry, in mind) they offer this definition: a diagram is "a proliferation of manifestly selective packets of dissimilar data correlated in an explicitly process-oriented array that has some of the attributes of a representation but is situated in the world like an object."[44] Bender and Marrinan focus, for instance, on the plate from the *Encyclopédie* depicting the pastry-maker's shop: its upper tableau, roughly the top third of the plate, shows a scene from the shop, with objects arranged on tables and shelves and "work stations where each figure performs a specialized task"; the remainder of the plate depicts a set of objects, tools from the shop now pulled out, placed on a white background and shown in views that clarify their "features of use."[45] We do not have to work hard to see a relation between the diagrammatic French plate and Hogarth's first plate from the *Analysis*.

In both cases, the plates offer us "packets of data" without telling us explicitly how to interpret that data. Indeed, the complexity of working between text and plate, and between images in the plate, is part of what Bender and Marrinan argue is characteristic of the diagram's new cognitive model: here (unlike a history painting) the plates offer viewers multiple points of access, just as we might walk around an object and look at it from all sides. In the *Encyclopédie*, this fulfills Diderot's aim to establish "interconnections" and a great "frequency of the cross-references," leading the viewer between tableau and tools, and between the explanatory text and the numbers on the plate.[46] At work here is the "user's active exercise of relational judgment."[47] Certainly Hogarth's plate does this in the way it makes us search for relations between the examples in the frame and the scene in the sculpture yard: a frame here does not contain so much as it offers up additional vectors of inquiry, of experience. Even the seemingly random numbering of Hogarth's images (as the frustrated reader of the treatise can testify within a few pages) moves the eye back and forth, along the way forcing it to encounter relations and resemblances.[48]

Hogarth could not have known the *Encyclopédie* plates (the first volume of which was published in 1762), but Diderot could have known Hogarth's images.[49] My argument here, though, is not about influence; rather, I'm interested in thinking about what Bender and Marrinan's account of the *Encyclopédie* can help us to see about Hogarth's prints and thus about some of the diverse aims and effects of diagrammatic images. In this regard, I am especially curious about the omission of Hogarth's *Analysis* plates from their account of diagram (though they include a more obscure Hogarth engraving on perspective). I'd like to think, then, about why Hogarth's plates in the *Analysis* might offer both a great example of diagrammatic thinking and a bad example of the kind of scientific work that Bender and Marrinan claim diagrams ultimately do.

Considering the obvious similarities between the two diagrams, one striking difference between Hogarth's plates and those of the *Encyclopédie* concerns the tableau. On the *Encyclopédie* plate, we are to imagine the tableau as the home of the objects that lie below it, even as the juxtaposition multiplies possible relations. Bender and Marrinan describe this as the relation between two unlike systems, the visual catalogue and the tableau: "Diagrams align, juxtapose, and contrast two kinds of information: on the one hand, the autonomous bursts of data that characterize visual catalogues; on the other, the uniform flux of homogenous information provided by tableaux."[50] Language, they make clear, cannot specify all the relations between these parts, and "this unspecified interaction of varied components generates kinds of knowledge impossible to infer from any one element."[51]

Hogarth creates two distinct systems, forcing us to ask questions about the connections between frame examples and the scene in the yard, but he also raises additional questions, within the tableau, about where – and how – "autonomous" objects belong. We can see this by considering closely an element in his discussion of "Fitness," the first chapter of the *Analysis*. Here Hogarth's account of beauty's relation to "fitness," to the "use" of an object, is an idea he takes from Xenophon's *Memorabilia*, in which Socrates defines beauty in terms of fitness for use. Hogarth's examples range from "twisted columns," which are "ornamental" but "convey an idea of weakness" to the positive example of the race horse (*AB*, 25). Fitness is a relation of "parts" to "design," as in the proportions of chairs and the "dimensions" in ship-building (*AB*, 26). But at the end of this first section, Hogarth becomes more particular in his presentation of two examples: "The Hercules, by Glicon" and "the leaden imitations near Hyde-park" (*AB*, 27). One example, Hogarth seems to say, is good: what we now know as the Farnese Hercules "hath all its parts finely fitted for the purposes of the utmost strength," requiring irregular proportions. And the other example is bad: the leaden and stone imitations of classical statues, bound for country house gardens, which attempt to "correct such apparent disproportions," resulting in a clumsy regularity (*AB*, 27). But Hogarth's own reference to the figure on plate 1 complicates this opposition. The text reads this way, "The Hercules, by Glicon, hath all its parts finely fitted …" (*AB*, 26). The reference follows this first mention of the Hercules, suggesting that the figure depicts "The Hercules, by Glicon." But what does this mean in terms of the image the viewer then confronts in the plate, with the statues in the sculpture yard? Is this a representation of a good copy (or, even, of the original), as the placement of the textual note would suggest; or is it a bad eighteenth-century copy, as the context of the sculpture yard would seem to demand? In forcing this question, Hogarth uses one of what Bindman describes as "the ideal marble figures, which were, from at least the sixteenth century, treated primarily as aesthetic objects, detached from specific physical or historical settings" to make us wonder about the nature of form and setting.[52] That is, the example of the Hercules makes us wonder whether we are seeing a form embedded in and determined by its context or a pure form that would not be contingent in this way.

Part of what generates this uncertainty is that Hogarth does not use the plate to offer a visual contrast between good and bad form. Hogarth's larger point about the Hercules concerns proportions, the relations between parts and whole. Ships, chairs, and race horses bring together beauty and function in the abstract – presumably, the reason for referring to a race horse, rather than a named, particular, represented race horse, is to maintain this level of abstraction, letting us see relationships more clearly. But in the case of the Hercules this breaks down as Hogarth's example takes on greater particularity. When he mentions the Hercules in the text, Hogarth moves to a particular statue and, at the same time, to visual representation (pointing us to the plate). Then, however, instead of giving us a visual comparison of good and bad form, he juxtaposes the form of the Hercules to the details of the sculpture yard. In this case, the juxtaposition he offers through text and image calls on an additional kind of identification from the reader, as she is asked to recall a place that is part of her everyday, real-world experience. For Hogarth refers here to a very particular sculpture yard (Henry Cheere's) on a very particular corner (Hyde Park). There is something intriguingly excessive in this particularity and something consequently strange about the analogy Hogarth posits: the form of the classical statue; the leaden imitations in Cheere's yard on Hyde Park corner. These descriptions are different in kind. Indeed, it is as though Hogarth moves too quickly through his argument, collapsing teaching us about form with instructing us on where to find it in the outside world. The formulation may be clumsy but the suggestion it raises is an interesting one: that everyday context, the one the reader knows first-hand, could be experienced as she experiences a shape.[53]

Hogarth continues this line of thinking near the end of the treatise in his discussion of "action." In this last section, too, he is concerned with how shape could serve as a special sort of representation of the everyday. Hogarth begins by separating the beautiful from the everyday by thinking of them in terms of two kinds of lines. There are two kinds of movements, he says: "useful" and "graceful," and only the latter express the line of beauty. All "useful and habitual motions, such as are readiest to serve the necessary purposes of life, are those made up of plain lines" (*AB*, 106). As for graceful movements (and their waving lines): "The whole business of life may be carried on without them" (*AB*, 106). But this is a distinction that does not hold. In his account of the graceful movement of the arm in the "habit of moving in the line of grace and beauty," he seems invested (much like Locke is in his treatise on education) in thinking through how such movements become customary: "they by frequent repetitions will become so familiar to the parts so exercised, that on the proper occasion they make them as it were of their own accord" (*AB*, 107). The customary seemed to separate straight and beautiful, but now all is customary. This repetition (not unlike the working on silver or making objects into threads) gets the habitual, the customary, into action – indeed, into the line of beauty itself. What seemed a bit awkward in the example of the Hercules – the equation of details with form in the written text – here acquires a more precise resolution. The everyday becomes a shape.

It is not, however, a static shape. Hogarth works hard throughout the treatise to enable us to see lines as themselves moving. Thus, he describes the line of beauty as "varying" and conveys this through the image of its making: "the hand takes a lively movement in making it with pen or pencil" (*AB*, 42). The serpentine line, yet more varied, is described as "waving and winding at the same time different ways"; it is the line, not the eye, that "leads ... in a pleasing manner along the continuity of its variety" (*AB*, 42). When Hogarth arrives at the topic of "action," then, he is contemplating a way that moving lines can encode – or somehow otherwise contain – motion. As in the example of polite gestures, though, tracing shape means tracing something else: the body's situation in the culture that surrounds it. Hogarth begins straightforwardly: "bodies in motion always describe some line or other in the air, as the whirling round of a fire-brand apparently makes a circle, and the water-fall part of a curve, the arrow and bullet, by the swiftness of their motions, nearly a straight line" (*AB*, 105). But this is not the only way action can make its way into form, as Hogarth makes clear in turning to "*habit* and custom" (*AB*, 105). The lines that "describe" an individual's "gait in walking," for example, stand not just for those actions (of lifting the foot or swinging the arms) but for "the habits [each person has] contracted" (*AB*, 105). Lest we imagine this just as an imaginary line, a line marked in the air, Hogarth fills out the picture by turning us to material lines on a page: for as it is with walking so it is, too, with the "visibly different" handwriting that marks each individual's habitual movements (*AB*, 105). That motion that the line contained when made "with pen or pencil" was never just abstract shape; it was always attached to the body and to habit. It is hard not to think here of Hogarth's taking up the pen and throwing his materials into a book, for writing, handwriting, is also a kind of making associated with the body and indeed the habitual movements that are the domain of the artisan.

Again, though, the individual artisan seems attached here to a kind of cultural making. Angela Rosenthal's account of the fan in Hogarth's treatise shows how Hogarth's minimal descriptions can take for granted, as though part of the body, what we might now call cultural objects: "In early Georgian England, these invisible lines 'formed in the air' by the movement of the hands and arms that Hogarth encourages his reader to image were rarely drawn by the fingertips alone. Those belonging to fashionable society would also sport something in their hands – the gentleman a cane or a snuffbox, the ladies a handkerchief or, more commonly, a fan."[54] What seems like individual gesture is the gesture of "fashionable society," both conventional and completed by that society's favourite commodities. Hogarth makes this connection between the individual and the social explicit when he treats dance. The minuet, he writes, is really an intensification of the "ordinary undulating motion of the body" in walking; moreover, "the figure of the minuet path on the floor is always composed of serpentine lines" – something that can be said, as well, of the very different country dance. Habit, then, is broadened to this shared experience: walking becomes dancing, the shape of which "var[ies] a little with the fashion" (*AB*, 109). And it becomes clear that Hogarth is thinking not just of individual habits but of what we would now call "customs" – and what the eighteenth century sometimes called "manners" – those other-than-conscious practices that tie a community together. Hogarth's moves from the setting of his first plate, the sculpture yard, to that of the second, the country dance, bears this out: as if the social questions raised by individual forms in the sculpture yard should now be thought in terms of a more dynamic, more obvious set of social relations.

To characterize social movement as he does, Hogarth must position a viewer outside the action: a viewer who can see the lines made on the floor by the dancers' movements. To reinforce this aspect of distance, Hogarth relates that "the dances of barbarians are always represented without these [that is, graceful] movements, being only composed of wild skiping, jumping, and turning round, or running backward and forward, with convulsive shrugs and distorted gestures" (*AB*, 111). For Hogarth, it is as though, when you look at society from the outside, you can see that each society, or each kind of society, is understandable as a pattern of shapes and lines. We should not allow this rough caricature of barbarians to distract us from the larger implications of Hogarth's argument. In its treatment of contingent and ideal forms, and in its accounts of action, his demonstration of a universal form of beauty, far from neglecting the social and the contingent (as Paulson and Uglow worry), lays bare a rather sophisticated thinking about the relation between form and habit or custom. This thinking places the *Analysis of Beauty* in dialogue with social theorists of the French and Scottish Enlightenments: Montesquieu on "spirit" or William Robertson on "stages." Yet Hogarth's aesthetic treatise leads him to entertain questions that are less about using structures as a way to compare different societies and more about how shape or structure might be understood to represent society. In this (though he approaches the problem from the opposite direction) he may be closer to twentieth-century cultural anthropology and sociology after the linguistic turn – as in Clifford Geertz's use of literary form or music in order to understand an ethnographic event.[55]

An even better corollary, though, is the vein of twentieth-century thinking about society deeply concerned with the stakes of representing "practice." Take, for instance, Michel de Certeau's *Practice of Everyday Life*, which begins by describing "the signifying practices of consumers," who act with "artisan-like inventiveness."[56] De Certeau encourages us to imagine this inventiveness in terms of Fernand Deligny's "wandering lines" depicting the everyday movements in space of autistic children, what de Certeau calls "indirect or errant lines obeying their own logic."[57] The strange "tracings" that children and caretakers alike mapped onto everyday spaces serve for de Certeau as a way of thinking about how "everyday practices" can be "tactical in character," potentially directed against structures of power.[58]

The connection between Hogarth and de Certeau is not as strange as it might at first appear, and it can help us to see aspects of Hogarth's project that are otherwise difficult to discern. De Certeau's example reminds us, for instance, of the origin of Hogarth's line: both in the rococo style, originating in France but popularized by practitioners at St Martin's Lane (like Hubert-François Gravelot the engraver, who was famous for his book designs), and in graffiti and children's art.[59] Furthermore, these eighteenth-century visual forms were not as culturally distant from each other as we might predict. The rococo line was seen as "errant" – empty, counter to reason – at least partly due to its "perceived origins in the craft workshop"; indeed, even its proponents in Britain were middle-class practitioners, not architects and their patrons.[60] The rococo line, then, stood for design that had emerged through craft, a good example for Hogarth's side of the Academy debate. And it is because of this origin in artisanal practice that the line offers Hogarth an obvious way to think about another kind of practice: customary, everyday experience. Moreover, if we are tempted to read the last part of Hogarth's treatise as an "etiquette manual," this complicated origin for the line should suggest otherwise.[61] Certainly Hogarth describes "grace" not as something innate and inimitable but as something that may be learned by bodily practice. But the strangeness, the movement within the line, suggests an interest in change that goes beyond that familiar middle-class story. For de Certeau the everyday is tactical. The vitality of Hogarth's lines reaches towards this wandering, anti-systematic potential.[62]

For Hogarth the line stands to represent social experience even as it is also a form of social experience. In the course of his treatise – and likely long before its writing – Hogarth encounters something that also interests de Certeau: the problems and possibilities offered by lines as representations. Lines are not perfect representations of practices; once they advocate for the line, both Hogarth and de Certeau spend some time explaining to the reader how lines should be read. Hogarth, as we have seen, first uses geometry to encourage us to think about lines as representations that tip over ontologically, standing for but also working as the things they represent. For both Hogarth and de Certeau, lines are able to do an unusual sort of work: they show habits and customs – practices – not as static things but as movements, forces,[63] and, at the same time, they pull making back into representation. Lines, in both accounts, stand for everyday practices, but they also *are* practice. Hence Hogarth's attention to line as not just a visual language of motion but as itself moving. In this sense, the line is the domain of artisan and of the ethnographer, as a kind of practical analyst.

For Hogarth, and certainly for de Certeau, the point is not just being able to represent – on the page, or through language – the right kind of line. In this regard, it is significant that de Certeau comes to his thinking about the lines not only through perusing Deligny's book on autism but also as a direct response to earlier ideas of representation within anthropology and sociology. Bourdieu had already called attention both to "practice" and to representation as a problem: the trouble, in his words, of "constitut[ing] practical activity as an object of observation and analysis" is also the trouble of the analyst introducing "into the object the principles of his relation to the object."[64] Bourdieu's terms are familiar. In the first pages of *Outline of a Theory of Practice*, with structuralism very much in mind, he observes that the "social world" is the object of "three modes of theoretical knowledge which have only one thing in common: the fact that they are opposed to practical knowledge."[65] In his project to define further what exactly such practical knowledge would entail, Bourdieu casts the relation between the theoretical and the practical in terms of lines: the "logical" relationships are those shown by lines on a "map" and the practical relations, movements, a "network of beaten tracks made ever more practicable by constant use."[66] Like Hogarth, both Bourdieu and de Certeau fight the limitations of representation not by turning away from it entirely but by attempting to find new ground within representation itself. Bourdieu does not want to turn away from structuralism altogether, but he does want to show that structuralism's maps of relations contain additional relations that they do not declare.

Despite his obvious attempt to view social action from the outside, as a shape or line, Hogarth writes against the false distance of outside, theoretical knowledge – and, importantly, without any obligation to tackle the problems of objectivity foisted upon later studies of society by scientific method. We can see one example of this if we return to the first plate. Take the narrative, erotic vectors here as Paulson explicates them. On one side we have the dancing master propositioning Antinous (the lover of the Emperor Hadrian). On the other, Venus (though depicted here as the modest type) exchanges amorous glances with the Apollo Belvedere.[67] The Antinous example is especially interesting. On face, Hogarth presents this as a formal comparison of the two figures: stiff, straight lines as opposed to serpentine form, activating in different terms his argument through stays (no. 53) and table legs (no. 50). But he overlays this formal comparison with an erotic relation,[68] one that does not occur merely on the level of content. Rather, this erotics is an account of relation.

This is also a direct response to the neutral gaze Bender and Marrinan assume, indeed make primary, in their scientific "diagrammatic" thinking, and which they attach to a later discourse of scientific objectivity. Consider first that in explaining the scientific purchase of their "culture of diagram," the authors turn to Lorraine Daston's account of "aperspectival objectivity" – an objectivity that negates the idiosyncrasies of the viewer, a concept Daston historicizes (in an article prior to the book-length *Objectivity*) by turning to eighteenth-century moral philosophy. Daston thus grounds an understanding of perspective that we associate with nineteenth-century science in an eighteenth-century discourse of morality and aesthetics: "Eighteenth- and nineteenth-century discussions of perspectivity agree in both their means (de-individualization, emotional distance) and ends (universal knowledge of one sort or another), but they treat very different objects: moral and aesthetic claims on the one hand, and scientific claims on the other." Her earliest example of such "perspectival suppleness" is in Shaftesbury.[69]

When they attach "aperspectival objectivity" to the plates of the *Encyclopédie*, then, Bender and Marrinan pull in the scientific valence of the phenomenon but ironically leave aside the eighteenth-century origins that Daston gives for this later scientific concept. Put another way, to ground "diagram" in a history of science, they project a concept from nineteenth-century science (i.e., the result of a pointedly teleological historical account) back onto an eighteenth-century phenomenon. In so doing, they incorrectly generalize – and disembody – Enlightenment "experience." After all, one of the central critiques Hogarth (and Addison before him) offers of Shaftesbury's disinterestedness has to do with its ridiculous neglect of desire. For Hogarth seeing is desiring; we understand beauty not by our remove from it, but through our interest in possessing it. Indeed, we might understand desire and artisanal experience to be bound together in their location of the body as the source of experience. Beauty and desire go hand in hand – form and desire go hand in hand – as is evident in the Miltonic quotation on that first title page and the line with its serpent head.

As we have just seen, Hogarth dips into the reservoir of the unseemly, bodily nature of experience to make even relationality seem desiring, as though some of those abstract vectors of diagrammatic thinking could be made into affective ones. But the implications of this sight that entangles itself with its object are not limited to desire per se. Early in the treatise, Hogarth describes the pleasure of motion he has felt as seeing a country-dance: "particularly," he says, "when my eye eagerly pursued a favourite dancer, through all the windings of the figure, who then was bewitching to the sight, as the imaginary ray, we were speaking of, was dancing with her all the time" (*AB*, 34). In the *Analysis of Beauty*, desire lets us think about the way that the eye-beams of vision move as the dance moves, reflecting and becoming part of, its motions.

Let us return to Hogarth's first plate as depicting the objects of everyday life. Bender and Marrinan's analysis allows us to see just how far

Hogarth's commitment goes, and how it sutures the diagrammatic to the everyday by way of design. Bender and Marrinan assume that the diagram's creativity must be new and thus opposed to what they call "habit" and "normal use," which they illustrate by opposing encyclopedic diagram to Chardin's *The Copper Fountain*, which shows the objects' "patina of wear," the evidence of "repeated enactments of ... ritual gestures" of everyday life.[70] But Hogarth's diagrammatic thinking allows for no such opposition. Even if his candlesticks look new, Hogarth works to show us the presence of the everyday within objects by teaching us how to re-envision those objects (to recompose them as threads, or place them in known settings). We should view his attention to the vision that moves with the dance as part of this same commitment to thinking about how the object reaches out to its viewer and its environment.[71] Everyday objects, then, are the perfect way to illustrate design's own role in this reaching out. For Hogarth teaches us, through his theorization of the line, to think of the way an object (a candlestick, or a piece of wallpaper) could be tied to the cultural world – that world of people, of practices – that surrounds it.

Hogarth's response to Reynolds's idea of merely conceptual design, then, is not only that thinking can be understood as a kind of making. It is that if we understand practice in this way, we necessarily take as a given a mind that cannot be separable from its objects. Bourdieu and de Certeau greatly trouble objectivity, showing how the separation of self from object cannot be as complete as Lévi-Strauss (and, of course, many others before him) hoped that it might be. Hogarth, for his part, begins to indicate just how complicated the intellectual history of these problems is. Before nineteenth-century science made its mark, Hogarth understood that Shaftesbury's proto-objectivity was not only a poor fit for the social world but that it would need to be rethought on the very basis of the kind of practical object that world could be.

NOTES

1 *London and Westminster Improved, Illustrated by Plans* (London, 1766), 63.
2 Charles Saumarez Smith, *Eighteenth-Century Decoration: Design and the Domestic Interior in England* (New York: Harry N. Abrams, 1993), 73.
3 See, most prominently, Colen Campbell's *Vitruvius Britannicus* (London, 1715–25).
4 Anne Puetz, "Design Instruction for Artisans in Eighteenth-Century Britain," *Journal of Design History* 12.3 (1999): 220.
5 Saumarez Smith, *Eighteenth-Century Decoration*, 73, 47–8.

6 In *The Prose of Things: Transformations of Description in the Eighteenth Century* (Chicago: University of Chicago Press, 2006), ch. 7, Cynthia Sundberg Wall examines interior design as "arrangement" and suggests the relation between such design and the "individualization" – and "interior" self – of the Enlightenment person (200). In the work of Hogarth, design is a means of getting outside the individual person, offering a way of specifying that person's relation to a larger community.

7 Saumarez Smith, *Eighteenth-Century Decoration*, 136.

8 Jules Lubbock, *The Tyranny of Taste: The Politics of Architecture and Design in Britain 1550–1960* (New Haven: Yale University Press, 1995), 218.

9 Puetz, "Design Instruction," 219.

10 As Saumarez Smith relates, Thornhill "became interested in the surrounding visual context in which his painting would appear" (*Eighteenth-Century Decoration*, 41). Saumarez Smith calls him a "forerunner of the fully fledged interior decorator" (43).

11 Ibid., 78.

12 Ronald Paulson, *Hogarth*, 3 vols. (New Brunswick: Rutgers University Press, 1991–3), 1:47. Hereafter cited as *Hogarth*.

13 Paulson, *Hogarth*, 2:69.

14 Charles Saumarez Smith, *Eighteenth-Century Decoration*, 140.

15 Jenny Uglow, *Hogarth: A Life and a World* (New York: Farrar, Straus and Giroux, 1997), 525, 540.

16 Ronald Paulson, "Introduction," *The Analysis of Beauty*, by William Hogarth, ed. Paulson (New Haven: Yale University Press, 1997), xlvi. This repeats in stronger language an earlier claim of Paulson's in *Hogarth* 3:125.

17 Paulson, "Introduction," xxxi.

18 All citations refer to Paulson's edition of the *Analysis* and will be cited parenthetically (*AB*).

19 Paulson, *Hogarth* 3:58.

20 Ibid., 3:75.

21 Abigail Zitin has recently offered an account of Hogarth's "practitioner's formalism," and her interest in "form as the technical achievement of an artist" is very much in sympathy with my concerns here. But by "technical" Zitin means only the practice of painting (as her terms "context" and "illusion" demonstrate). She thus assumes an immaterial form – something that can be separated from "content" – that is at odds with Hogarth's own terms for the materiality of his lines and with his interest in practice more generally. "Thinking Like an Artist: Hogarth, Diderot, and the Aesthetics of Technique," *Eighteenth-Century Studies* 46.4 (2013): 555–6.

22 *Oxford English Dictionary Online*, s.v. "material, n.," def. 2a, http://www.oed.com/Entry/114923.
23 *Oxford English Dictionary Online*, s.v. "throw, v.1," def. 32b; def. 6a, 6b, http://www.oed.com/Entry/201413.
24 Hogarth, of course, would have known the treatises of Alberti and Vasari, chief among Ann Bermingham's examples. *Learning to Draw: Studies in the Cultural History of a Polite and Useful Art* (New Haven: Yale University Press, 2000), 4–5.
25 Pamela H. Smith, *The Body of the Artisan: Art and Experience in the Scientific Revolution* (Chicago: University of Chicago Press, 2004), 17.
26 Bermingham's account of this part of the history distinguishes between the Baconian approach that privileged vision and the mechanical (as through Boyle and Hooke) and the Society's "more abstract and theoretical turn" at the end of the seventeenth century (*Learning*, 66). Smith's point is further reaching: even Bacon's privileging of the mechanic may attempt to separate out degrees of the "sensual."
27 I pointedly refer to Pamela H. Smith's account here, rather than to Joanna Picciotto's account of early modern labor, which begins in the early modern period and ends in the eighteenth century. Although Picciotto is dismissive of Smith's privileging of Paracelsus (214), Paracelsus allows Smith to capture more fully the divisions that continue to exist within early science – and persist into the eighteenth century. Picciotto's turn to the model of scientific experience in Sprat as the foundation for a general eighteenth-century epistemology, by contrast, suggests a resolution to the problems of artisanal and theoretical knowledge that, as Hogarth evidences, continue to resonate throughout the period – and beyond it. Picciotto, *Labors of Innocence in Early Modern England* (Cambridge, MA: Harvard University Press, 2010).
28 For a general account of Hogarth's relation to empiricism, see Ogée, "Aesthetics and Empiricism," in *The Dumb Show: Image and Society in the Works of William Hogarth*, ed. Frédéric Ogée (Oxford: Voltaire Foundation, 1997), 177–91.
29 On the connection between English empiricism and Dutch art, see Svetlana Alpers, *The Art of Describing: Dutch Art in the Seventeenth Century* (Chicago: University of Chicago Press: 1983); on the connection between Hogarth and Dutch art, see Ogée, introduction to *The Dumb Show*, 12, and David Bindman, *Hogarth and His Times: Serious Comedy* (Berkeley: University of California Press, 1997), 34.
30 Paulson, *Hogarth* 3:69; I take the slight redundancy of Ogée's phrase (the second quotation) to be an attempt to stress this experience that is even

more bodily than that accounted for by ordinary empiricism. "The Flesh of Theory: The Erotics of Hogarth's Lines," in *The Other Hogarth: Aesthetics of Difference*, ed. Bernadette Fort and Angela Rosenthal (Princeton: Princeton University Press, 2001), 73.

31 Bindman describes how this thinking may have come to Hogarth through his friend (and commentator on Locke) Dr Thomas Morell (*Hogarth and His Times*, 54). This "problem" was communicated to Locke by William Molyneux in a letter of 1688 and published by Locke in the second edition of the *Essay Concerning Human Understanding*. Molyneux asks if a man born blind and able to distinguish between a cube and a sphere would, if his sight were restored, be able to distinguish between the two based on vision alone. Locke answered in the negative.

32 Puetz, "Design Instruction," 218, 217.

33 Uglow, *Hogarth*, 532.

34 Zitin, "Thinking Like an Artist," 566. In making this claim about form, she follows, for instance, J. Dobai, "William Hogarth and Antoine Parent," *Journal of the Warburg and Courtauld Institutes* 31 (1968): 364.

35 Alpers, *The Art of Describing*, 91. She describes a still life by Willem Kalf. We might also see Hogarth's penchant for engraving without reversing his images as producing a similar result. As Paulson notes, it means that he shows familiar sculptures "in unaccustomed views and partly in the moment of turning from one pose to another" (*Hogarth* 3:111).

36 An important exception to this is Tom Huhn, who goes straight for the example of geometry as a way of explaining Hogarth's interest in "relations between ideas" (68). But Huhn's central term "mimesis" restricts knowledge in Hogarth's treatise to sight and thus can't accommodate the made, material diagram so necessary to Hogarth's understanding of "practice." *Imitation and Society: The Persistence of Mimesis in the Aesthetics of Burke, Hogarth, and Kant* (University Park: Penn State University Press, 2004). On the limits of vision also see Bender and Marrinan, who argue that diagrammatic thinking (in general) exceeds the visual. *The Culture of Diagram* (Stanford: Stanford University Press, 2010), 12.

37 *Oxford English Dictionary Online*, s.v. "figure, n.," def. 10, http://www.oed.com/view/Entry/70079?rskey=RioXkn&result=1#eid.

38 Reviel Netz, *The Shaping of Deduction in Greek Mathematics* (Cambridge: Cambridge University Press, 1999), 33.

39 Ibid., 35.

40 Ibid., 54.

41 Ibid., 56.

42 Ibid., 57.

43 Ibid., 60. In the final, historical narrative of the book, Netz remarks that Greek mathematicians may have "felt uneasily close to the banausic" (60), and he describes the "mechanical" nature of drawn diagram, its place in the "material world," as revealing an "estangement between the theoretical and the practical," something Hogarth surely appreciated (303).
44 Bender and Marrinan, *The Culture of Diagram*, 7.
45 Ibid., 23.
46 Diderot quoted in Bender and Marrinan, *The Culture of Diagram*, 9.
47 Ibid., 10.
48 As an aesthetic principle, this is not unique to Hogarth. See Paulson on Hutcheson and active viewing (72), as well as on this kind of process and Hogarth's ideal viewer for his paintings (99). *Hogarth* 3.
49 Diderot had read the *Analysis*. For an interesting account of the connection see Zitin. For Hogarth's relations to the contemporary French context more generally, see Robin Simon, *Hogarth, France and British Art* (London: Hogarth Arts, 2007), ch. 3.
50 Bender and Marrinan, *The Culture of Diagram*, 34.
51 Ibid., 52.
52 Bindman, *Hogarth and His Times*, 34.
53 In this, I mean to open up the plate to a set of questions not visible from Paulson's extensive analysis. He reads Hogarth's form as making canonical sculptures into "empty signs" which are filled by a new, contemporary meaning. I am suggesting, rather, that Hogarth's interest in the "empirical sensory data of London" goes beyond this kind of allegory and toward a very primary philosophical question about how meaning is generated in relation to the line. *Hogarth* 3:107.
54 "Unfolding Gender: Women and the 'Secret' Sign Language of Fans in Hogarth's Work," in *The Other Hogarth: Aesthetics of Difference*, ed. Bernadette Fort and Angela Rosenthal (Princeton: Princeton University Press, 2001), 122.
55 See Peter Wagner's complementary assessment of Hogarth's visual art as involving a rich "semantic ambiguity" that showcases Hogarth's rather sophisticated understanding of the "sign systems" of "dancing, ballet, pantomime, and 'Stage-action.'" "Spotting the Symptoms: Hogarthian Bodies as Sites of Semantic Ambiguity," in *The Other Hogarth: Aesthetics of Difference*, ed. Bernadette Fort and Angela Rosenthal (Princeton: Princeton University Press, 2001), 103.
56 Michel de Certeau, *The Practice of Everyday Life*, trans. Steven Rendall (Berkeley: University of California Press, 1984), xviii.

57 Ibid., xviii. Deligny began his project of exploring autistic life beyond the institution in 1967 in the Cevennes at Monoblet. The children were between three and ten and were mute, thus offering the possibility to see experience organized by those "who cannot speak the dominant language." Erin Manning, *Always More than One: Individuation's Dance* (Durham: Duke University Press, 2013), 190.

58 de Certeau, *Practice of Everyday Life*, xix.

59 See Michael Snodin and John Styles, *Design and the Decorative Arts: Georgian Britain 1714–1837* (London: V&A Publications, 2004), 44–6; Paulson, *Hogarth* 3:123. While Paulson claims that the serpentine line was meant to serve a broader "normative function," he acknowledges that "contemporaries associated the serpentine line with rococo forms." *Hogarth* 3:122.

60 Snodin and Styles, *Design and the Decorative Arts*, 44, 46. Snodin describes rococo as a "style without rules" and the *Analysis* as "the nearest rococo ever came to a theoretical justification" (44).

61 K.L.H. Wells describes the treatise thus on the way to her discussion of the serpentine line in furniture design. "Serpentine Sideboards, Hogarth's *Analysis*, and the Beautiful Self," *Eighteenth-Century Studies* 46.3 (2013): 404.

62 This is not an argument about Hogarth's politics, but I do see the connection to de Certeau as a means of elaborating on the democratic Hogarth of the graphic prints championed by Paulson and others.

63 See Paulson's brief connection of Hogarth's treatment of dance with James Harris's description of dance as a "motion or an energy" in "A Dialogue Concerning Art" (1744); Paulson, *Hogarth* 3:112.

64 Bourdieu, *Outline of a Theory of Practice*, trans. Richard Nice (Cambridge: Cambridge University Press, 1977), 2.

65 Ibid., 2.

66 Ibid., 38.

67 Paulson, *Hogarth* 3:106.

68 Here the comparison shares qualities with the line of beauty itself, as James Grantham Turner describes it. "'A Wanton Kind of Chace': Display as Procurement in *A Harlot's Progress* and Its Reception," in *The Other Hogarth: Aesthetics of Difference*, ed. Fort and Rosenthal, esp. 40.

69 Lorraine Daston, "Objectivity and the Escape from Perspective," in *The Science Studies Reader*, ed. Mario Biagioli (Oxford: Taylor & Francis, 1999), 114.

70 Bender and Marrinan, *The Culture of Diagram*, 25.

71 Hogarth thus promotes a way of seeing that is quite different from the one Bender derives from the progress prints. This is especially plain in Bender's use of Michael Fried's theory of absorption to account for how the prints function. After reading the *Analysis*, we might say that no matter how self-enclosed the action of the plates, Hogarth is theorizing a way of experiencing those plates that leaves no room for the kind of separation of the viewer the absorption model proposes. At root is a profound difference between "experience" on the model of Royal Society experimentation that Bender marshals here and "experience" as Hogarth conceives of it in relation to this scientific tradition. *Ends of Enlightenment* (Stanford: Stanford University Press, 2012), 73–4.

2 Presence of Mind: An Ecology of Perception in Eighteenth-Century England

JONATHAN KRAMNICK

This essay explores some connections between theories of perception and varieties of literary form in the long eighteenth century. My goal will be to trace the development of what I call an anti-representational model of perceptual experience during the period, a model that considers perceiving to be an active process – more on the pattern of touch than vision – and that proposes that what the senses do is make the world available rather than hold it at a skeptical remove. The anti-representational view, I'm going to suggest, is a dissident line or countercurrent within the eighteenth century's dominant theory of perception. On the dominant account, ideas or impressions provide an internal picture of an external object or event or state of affairs. "The thing we see is in one place," writes Hobbes, "the appearance in another."[1] I'm going to begin with this theory of perceptual representation (the dominant theory) and then turn to works of poetry, philosophy, and fiction that propose that what minds or works of art do is not so much represent things as make them present to us, or that concentrate on the process rather than the product of perception. My examples of the dissident line will be from the loco-descriptive poetry of John Dyer, James Thomson, and William Cowper, the aesthetic theory of William Hogarth, Thomas Reid's commonsense philosophy, and a few moments from Laurence Sterne. My interest in these examples will be to explore how perception could be understood as direct contact with external objects: as an aesthetics of presence, in other words.[2] With its emphasis on skilled action and its embrace of naiveté, I'll intermittently suggest that the eighteenth-century aesthetics of presence has some bearing on our current critical mood, both with respect to surface reading and speculative realisms close to home in the humanities and ecological or embodied theories of perception further afield in the cognitive sciences.[3] So I conceive of this project as one of historical recovery as well as one of bringing the past to bear on some features of our present.

The Representational Stance

Empiricism is famous for saying that knowledge derives from the senses, but what do the senses actually show us, and how should their relation to the world be conceived? The question emerges across the period, in the manner, eventually, of a debate: is our sensory apprehension of the world direct, reaching out to objects and entities themselves, or roundabout, mediated by internal images of external things? This is Thomas Hobbes choosing the second option at something like the dawn of empiricism and materialism alike. "Concerning the thoughts of man," he writes in the first sentence of *Leviathan*'s first chapter, "they are every one a representation or appearance of a quality or accident of a body without us; which is commonly called an object" (14). The point for Hobbes is that in coming up with our best theories of mental life we ought not to confuse the pictures in our head for the objects they represent. When external bodies "presseth the organ proper to each sense," they create an internal motion whose "appearance to us is fancy" (14). Perceptual experience thus moves through a kind of filter, with motion on the one side producing an image on the other. "Sense in all cases, is nothing else, but original fancy," Hobbes writes, "caused by the pressure, that is, by the motion, of external things upon our Eyes, Ears, and other organs thereunto ordained" (14). Fancy is original on this account because it occurs at the moment of perception, not in a later instance of reverie. To fancy is simply to experience by way of the internal picture Hobbes calls a "phantasm" what is already in one's midst.

So although Hobbes insists that perception should be understood in physical terms, as a motion that joins internal fancy to an external world, he also maintains that one's engagement with this world is always at a distance, always tarrying after its images. "The object is one thing," he writes, "the image or fancy another" (14). Many that followed shared this oscillation between worldly engagement and perceptual seclusion. Consider Locke's celebrated likening of vision to a camera obscura: "Methinks the understanding is not much unlike a closet wholly shut from light, with only some little openings left, to let in external visible resemblances, or ideas of things without; Would the pictures in such a room but stay there, and lie so orderly as to be found upon occasion, it would very much resemble the mind of man, in reference to all Objects of sight and our ideas of them" (2.12.17). Would the pictures in a camera obscura remain in place they would resemble the settled ideas in a person's head. And they would do so because the understanding in Locke's account stands in view of ideas that both represent things and acquire a kind of stability. Or to put matters in reverse, vision furnishes the mind with ideas that shape what we see. Experience tells me that one red voluminous object is an apple, another a tomato; and, after each idea is hung in place, I don't have to guess which is which every time I step into a garden. Viewed either way, however, our senses do not so much reach to objects themselves as bring ideas of objects to mind. Summing up the conventional wisdom some forty years later, Hume writes in the *Treatise* that "'tis universally allow'd by philosophers, and besides is pretty obvious of itself that nothing is really ever present with the mind but its perceptions or impressions and ideas, and that external objects become known to us only by those perceptions they occasion."[4] Or, as he clarifies in the *Enquiry*, "the slightest philosophy teaches us, that nothing can ever be present to the mind but an image or perception, and that the senses are only the inlets, through which these images are conveyed, without being able to produce any immediate intercourse between the mind and the object."[5] Our experience is of the solid world but this world shows up on a screen, as "fleeting copies or representations of other existences, which remain uniform and independent" (2.12.9).

The representational stance seems at first glance to be a kind of soft dualism and so to keep the mind out of the physical picture of the universe preferred by modern science.[6] And yet for Hobbes or Hume (as for Boyle and Newton), the stance followed directly from the discoveries that science had made. Our senses reveal to us an apple or a fly or a rock. At the same time, instruments like a microscope show us that such middle-sized objects are made from smaller bits of matter. So we may conclude on this basis that our perceptual acquaintance is never quite with the ultimate nature of things. And we may further maintain that a science of perception should tell some sort of causal story about events out there and experience in here. In this respect, much of today's mainstream cognitive science of perception follows directly from assumptions put in place during the seventeenth and eighteenth centuries.[7] David Marr's groundbreaking study *Vision* (1982), for example, begins with the observation that "if we are capable of knowing what is where in the world, our brains must somehow be capable of *representing* this information," and so concludes that "the study of vision therefore must include not only the study of how to extract from images the various aspects of the world that are useful to us, but also an inquiry into the nature of the internal representations by which we capture this information and thus make it available as a basis for decisions about our thoughts and actions."[8] The question for Marr as for Hume is how does an organism build a rich three-dimensional set of images that correspond in some fashion to invariant features of the physical surround. Representation in either case is understood to be a structural relation between acts or entities of the mind and properties or features of the world.

Towards a Theory of Direct Perception

Much of today's cognitive science of perception follows in the representational line of Locke and Hume, but not all. In recent years, the representational stance has come under pressure from active, embodied, or haptic theories of perception, themselves a lineal descendant, I want to argue, of some eighteenth-century views of the mind and the senses. On the ecological theory of J.J. Gibson, for example, perception is not an event in the brain but an achievement of the whole animal. Vision should be understood, wrote Gibson, as an "exploration in time, not a photographic process of image registration and image transmission," as a style of tactile engagement rather than optical remove.[9] This account has been important for subsequent criticism of neural reductionism – the dominant approach to the mind today – because it puts the perceiver in touch with an environment instead of focusing on the internal, enabling conditions for perceiving something. The idea is to conceive of perceiving with respect to a creature in motion rather than a single point and to think of what is perceived with respect to potentials for action or dwelling rather than objects in space.[10] "Instead of thinking of perception as a passage from inside to outside, from in here to out there," writes Alva Noë, a contemporary philosopher and cognitive scientist in the tradition of Gibson, we need to account for how "we ourselves (whole persons) undertake our perceptual consciousness of the world in, with, and in relation to the places where we find ourselves."[11] The argument for direct perception and the insistence on ecological analysis go together. "The world shows up for us in experience," Noë says, "because we know how to make contact with it" (2). And we know how to make contact with it because we know how to use our bodies. Perception is a kind of skilled attunement to what the world affords, done by creatures whose eyes move as so or whose paws curve like this.[12]

I'm going to argue now that this idea of making contact with objects and environments in our midst – and in particular the notion that perceptual acquaintance employs a kind of everyday skill or homely style – emerges over the course of the eighteenth century in contrast to the idea that we ought to worry about whether our perceptions accurately capture the precise features of things. I'm also going to argue that literary writing plays an important role in getting this account off the ground. What I'm calling the eighteenth-century aesthetics of presence emerged in part as a way to address an urgent problem faced by the representational view. The problem went something like this: If visual perception moves on a line from the eye to the object, then how does one perceive the distance between here and there? All one should see is the point at the end of the line, and yet we experience visual space in three dimensions. How is this so? George Berkeley begins his 1709 *Essay Towards A New Theory of Vision* with just this conundrum. "It is," he writes, "agreed by all that Distance of itself and immediately cannot be seen," and that is because "Distance being a Line directed endwise to the eye, it projects only one point in the Fund of the Eye, which point remains invariably the same whether the Distance be longer or shorter."[13] These sentences would prove to be very important. Our supposed inability actually to see distance – its existence only on a line directed endwise – formed the problem of depth perception for much of the eighteenth century. On Berkeley's influential account, the space between one point and another is not so much seen as inferred, calculated by means of "an act of Judgment grounded on experience than of Sense" (2). When we handle or bump into something we form "ideas of touch," whereas when we view something we form "ideas of sight." And when we perceive the distance between one thing and another – and so experience the world in three dimensions – we calculate unawares the distance of each from our hands (15). The house across the way looks to be smaller than the tree in between, but since I have touched both a house and a tree at some point I know things appear that way because the one is behind the other. So while "Tis plain that Distance is in its own nature imperceptible," we are able to experience depth and curvature and full surround by abstracting from tactile experience an idea of where something must reside if it appears to be of a certain size (4). Berkeley's new theory conceives of visual perception as indirect and inferential, a product of internal calculations. At the same time, it relies upon the immediate grasping of things by the fingers. After all, he says, we would never understand where anything is located, here or far away, without coming into contact with "the Objects that environ us, in proportion as they are adapted to benefit or injure our own Bodies" (64). The legacy of Berkeley's argument, we might say, is double, as he understands vision alone to move on a line through empty geometrical space and seeing at large to be wound up in ecologies of action and dwelling.

For literary scholars, this legacy is probably most familiar in Addison's notion of sight as "a delicate and diffusive kind of touch," one that "spreads it self over an infinite Multitude of Bodies, comprehends the largest Figures, and brings into our reach some of the most remote Parts of the Universe."[14] This sentence is from the first of the *Spectator* papers on the pleasures of the imagination, a series ostensibly designed to popularize Locke's representational view that sense "furnishes the imagination with its ideas" (411: 536). Addison's notion of tactile vision is and is not a metaphor, however, and to that degree does and does not live up to this view. Sight brings into our reach things we could never actually touch and yet also turns and responds to what it encounters. In keeping with each, the papers that follow toggle between an account of vision that operates at a length beyond the fingers and one that likens seeing to drawing everything close. The papers on beauty tend to set tableaux at a linear distance whereas those on the "new or uncommon" emphasize mobile gradation. Often associated with later ideas of the picturesque, Addison's category of the "novel" might be considered instead as an aesthetic of measured distance.[15] We delight in scenes that are "perpetually shifting, and entertaining the sight every moment with something that is new," he writes, with "such Objects as are ever in Motion, and sliding away from beneath the Eye of the Beholder" (412: 544). We delight in these acts because they turn or adjust as we get closer to the grain, as the line from one object to another bends, rises, or descends according to the motion or sliding of things along the surface of the earth. Addison's tactile vision is in this way distinct from Berkeley's. Whereas Berkeley says that depth perception combines ideas of sight with those of touch, Addison says that seeing is a form of touching. For Berkeley, sight and touch pick out different features of an object then combine them in the internal representation box. For Addison, at least in some of his moods, sight is touch-like because it picks out the same features we might access with our fingers: one thing beneath another, the rise and fall of the ground, the backward curve of a figure.[16]

Touching Ground

For writers after Berkeley and Addison the question of whether visual perception moved on a line through the air or along the uneven grade of the earth's surface remained open. Most followed the geometrical and representational line of thinking proposed and worried over in Berkeley's *New Theory*. For some, however, the project was to make visible the distance between one place and another by filling in and presenting space rather than drawing it on an intangible set of coordinates, by seeing along a receding surface or curved gradient for example, or through a translucent covering or along an occluding edge. Among writers concerned with this filling-in, none are more relevant for my current purposes than authors of loco-descriptive poetry, preoccupied as they were with varied matters of the earth's surface, with the sliding from vale to tree to hill to sheep to fruit and so on. It is this preoccupation, I'll now argue, that leads some poets to work out an aesthetics of perceptual presence in advance of its formalization in philosophy or science: specifically, again, to consider and account for seeing distance along a gradient or through a top layer or behind an occluding surface or edge rather than on a line directed endwise. The "curious eye" of Dyer's *Grongar Hill* (1726), for example, strays "over mead, and over wood, From house to house, from hill to hill," seeing on its way (among other things) "the gloomy pine, poplar blue/ The yellow beech, the sable yew" until "wandering" beyond the "purple grove," it pauses for a moment on the walls of Dinefwr castle:

> Deep are his feet in Towy's flood,
> His sides are cloth'd with waving wood,
> And ancient towers crown his brow
> That cast an aweful look below,
> Whose ragged walls the ivy creeps
> And with her arms from falling keeps.[17]

Responding to these lines almost fifty years later, William Gilpin would complain in *Observations on the River Wye* that Dyer had botched the perspective: "his distances are all in a confusion," Gilpin writes, "and indeed it is not so easy to separate them from his foregrounds … His castle, instead of being marked with still fainter colours than the purple-grove is touched with all the strength of a foreground: you see the very ivy creeping upon its walls."[18] Gilpin's complaint notes a dramatic foreshortening: the ivy-covered walls in Dyer's poem have the clarity of something etched and immediate, not a hazy prospect. This perspective is botched, however, only on the assumption that the poem intends to reproduce one vista from a place that does not move, rather than wind its way along the ground to walls whose presence is sketched by the partial occlusion of ivy. On this reading, Dyer does not so much fail to render one-point perspective in the manner of a landscape painting as compose a kind of anti-ekphrasis, a moving perspective that cannot be rendered on a picture plane. Understood in this latter sense, the peculiar touching that Gilpin observes marks a transient end point turned on a rough tetrameter line: a winding and dropping that arrives at a misplaced presence, with trunks of ivy and the walls beneath them shifting into the foreground.[19]

Gilpin understands the recession along a surface and the covering of one surface by another as separate ways of seeing distance, whereas Dyer seems to think of recession and occlusion together, as a motion across and then coming close to an engaged world. The attempt in either case is to use the descriptive mode to see along a gradient, both over the ground and behind what is in front of you. James Thomson makes perhaps an even more interesting case because his poetry was once understood to be committed to abstract geometrical space, lines projected endwise, and distanced incurious viewing. This is the reading one associates most readily with John Barrell, who, writing in the heyday of the hermeneutics of suspicion (the 1970s), seemed unwilling to conceive of Thomson's landscape aesthetics as anything other than a ruse: "Thomson is able to see the landscape, not as something in which he is involved, and which is all round him, but as something detached from him, *over there*: his eye may wander over the view, but his own position is fixed, and from his viewpoint he can organize the landscape into the system of parallel bands and flat perspectives by which only he can comprehend what he sees."[20] Much of recent *Seasons* criticism has endeavoured to unsettle Barrell's powerful reading and to locate in the poem models of perception and action that bring the viewer and the viewed into closer proximity. Kevis Goodman, for example, has focused on moments in the poem in which Thomson's "microscopic eye" brings to the surface a teeming world of vegetable life otherwise unseen, while Heather Keenleyside has looked at Thomson's "use of personification to associate the instability of persons and things" with an ethics and ethos of patience that leaves "moving and being moved [as] impossible to parse."[21] Whereas Barrell understands Thomson to "create a space between the landscape and the viewer," Goodman and Keenleyside understand him to bring the two together.[22] In the language of so-called surface reading, we might say that this is the way we read Thomson now. We are more inclined to see Thomson involved in his world than to look for moments of detachment or ownership.[23] For my part, this inclination will be noticeable as a focus on Thomson's naiveté. This is Thomson's speaker lingering over items strewn between one place and another. This is distance perceived directly, Berkeley's empty space filled in.

And how does this happen? Thomson's eye moves along the surface of crowded space, so even air teams with bugs, dust, and droplets, each reflecting colour or shade along its wing or edge. Summer insects "people the blaze" on a kind of up and down, for example, swarming from winter's repose to land on moving streams or passing "through green-wood glade" to feed on fresh leaves.[24] The episode ends when the insects come up against a striking background, passing over and landing on a pail set at close distance:

> … Some to the house,
> The fold, and dairy, hungry, bend their flight;
> Sip round the pail, or taste the curdling cheese:
> Oft, inadvertent, from the milky stream
> They meet their fate; or, weltering in the bowl,
> With powerless wings around them wrapt, expire. (*Su.* 260–5)

With minimal visual cues, the lines etch the flying, landing, and dying of insects on liquid. The insects glide on a crooked thread to the bowl (and its lip) as milk streams nearby and cheese curdles at bottom. Like the flight they describe, the lines bend on a kind of metrical warp, lifting from the trochaic "oft" across the subordinated "weltering" and wrapping before getting to the delayed "expire." Thomson's writing out of perceptual presence so takes an overall shape. The bowl, speck, and milk come into view as one surface passes on top of another, as gauzy wings move over an opaque pail or a milky stream pours beneath a whirling speck.[25]

This simple example shows one method by which the poem attends to objects at a middle distance, not (again) as points on a grid but as features of an ecology that change with the position from which they are held. In this way, the perception of something solid – the filling in of distance – depends both on the layout of what is seen and the motion of who is seeing: the array in which a bowl placed just so will shear off when a glance from just here moves to just there. This is so, I think, even in the poem's more static-seeming still lifes, the "fruit empurpled deep" of autumn, for example, that

> Presents the downy peach, the shining plum
> With a fine bluish mist of animals
> Clouded, the ruddy nectarine, and dark
> Beneath his ample leaf the luscious fig. (*A.* 675–9)

Writing about the seventeenth-century Dutch still lifes that animate and lie behind these lines, Svetlana Alpers has described how they "encourage the mind to dwell on perceiving as a process [by featuring the] experience of an object as coming into its own, distinguishing itself from other things, taking shape."[26] Understood in this fashion, Thomson's still life makes the perceptual object less familiar, by describing how fruit takes shape from behind something one sees through or around. Apart from the merely "ruddy nectarine," each piece seems to stretch distance along an occluding surface or partial cover: a passing membrane of down or mist or leaf that brings the skin so close to ours. The fine blue of the animal shapes that cloud the skin of the plum, for example, brings the shine to a presence crowding out the quiet nectarine. The skin of the peach and the plum and the rind of the fig pop out because they form a curved background to a filmy covering, and the eye, like a finger, must pass from the one to land on the other.[27]

Seeing and Skill

In lines like these, Thomson seems to move from one middling sized object to another, dropping a line of sight along the gradient and so responding after a fashion to Berkeley's question about distance while providing an example of Addison's diffusive kind of touch. By the middle decades of the eighteenth century such ideas of perception as direct contact became more explicitly formulated in works of theory, often in stated contrast to ideas of perception as a relation between an internal image and an external entity. William Hogarth, for example, begins his aesthetics treatise, *The Analysis of Beauty* (1753), by declaring that he hopes to bring the "practical knowledge of the whole art of painting" to our understanding of the perception of beauty.[28] Hogarth distinguishes this practical knowledge – the skilled know-how of a working artist – from the abstract principles of such "connoisseurs" and theorists as the Third Earl of Shaftesbury and Francis Hutcheson. Apprenticed at age sixteen to the silver engraver Ellis Gamble, and for his life one who etched out lines on the surfaces of metal or canvas, Hogarth here draws on ideas of the artist's skill – techné in the Aristotelian language of craftwork – at creating what is at the end of one's fingers.[29] The practical knowledge of painting turns out to be the ability to decompose any object – a tree, a face, a table, what have you – into its constituent lines, including especially the "serpentine line" whose undulating wave marks the actual presence of beauty in the object itself (viii, passim). Beauty is in the world, not in our heads, Hogarth says, in contradistinction to Hutcheson and Hume and virtually every other aesthetics theorist of the period. To "learn to see objects truly" is to learn to identify the "nature of those lines … by which we are directed to call the forms of some bodies beautiful, others ugly" (1). In other words, it is to learn to put oneself in the position of the artist as she both makes and observes items in the world.

As Abigail Zitin has recently put it, this adjustment to the practitioner's stance "registers an incipient resistance to illusion, to being consumed by the representational content of an image."[30] That is, for Hogarth, aesthetic experience occurs in moments when the beholder identifies the lines that compose beautiful objects. The subjective impact of a finished artwork – the emotion or pleasure it raises in the viewer – is only of secondary importance. Of primary importance is the process of decomposing objects to their lines so they may be recomposed as beautiful works. Hogarth refers to this activity as a "manner of attending to forms" and for this reason Zitin has described his theory as a kind of "practitioner's formalism" (Hogarth, 26; Zitin, 555). Hogarth's theory is a formalism because it understands beauty to reside in objective shape; it is a practitioner's formalism because it understands that to view such a shape is to recreate, not to represent it. The, by then, standard commitment to the internal image in talk about beauty makes a full turn. According to Hogarth, the artist's skill is to see from within an object – by identifying its lines – and the artwork's end is to put the beholder in place to do the same. "Let every object under our consideration," he says, "be imagined to have its inward contents scooped out so nicely, as to have nothing of it left but a thin shell, exactly corresponding both in its inner and outer surface, to the shape of the object itself: and let us likewise suppose this thin shell to be made up of very fine threads, closely connected together, and equally perceptible, whether the eye is supposed to observe them from without, or within" (7). Once we do this, Hogarth continues, "we shall find that the ideas of the two surfaces of the shell will naturally coincide" and that to attend to individual threads is at once to observe and inhabit the entire object, to "enter into the vacant space within this shell, and there at once, as from a center, view the whole form within" (8). Hogarth's language in this passage seems to balance between a description of the techniques of visual perception used by practising artists and a lesson on how ordinary viewers can, like artists, turn objects to shells and shells to lines. ("I would desire the reader," he says, "to assist his imagination as much as possible, in considering every object, as if his eye were placed within it" [10].) In either case, the end towards which the practitioner's technique drives is to make contact with the object, in fact, to hollow out its insides and stand within its centre. At the same time, the contact presumed by Hogarth's theory is not only with a premade world, since, in keeping with the practitioner's stance, to pursue such objects is also to compose them. "We shall presume [a] principal ray moving along with the eye," he writes, "and tracing out the parts of every form we mean to examine in the most perfect manner: and when we would follow with exactness the course any body takes, that is in motion, this ray is always to be supposed to move with the body" (26). Hogarth intends to bring the practical knowledge of the painter to ordinary acts of perception, and for him that means bringing an ability to trace out the shape and motion of the world at hand. To experience the beauty of some object or body is both to draw its lines and to be led by them on a kind of chase.

Hogarth spells out his aesthetics of technique and know-how in argued contrast to moral sense theories of response, taste, and connoisseurship. An even more polemically engaged theory of direct perception, however, may be found in the roughly contemporary commonsense philosophy of Thomas Reid. For the duration of his long career, Reid's central preoccupation was to overturn the notion – common to empiricists from Locke to Hume – that "external things must be perceived by means of images of them in the mind."[31] These are his words from *An Inquiry into the Human Mind on the Principles of Common Sense* (1764) where he elaborates on them in lively and unabashed terms: "that we can have no conception of any thing, unless there is some impression or sense or idea in our minds which resembles it, is indeed an opinion in general very well received among philosophers but it is neither self-evident nor hath it been clearly proved: and therefore it [is] more reasonable to call in question this doctrine than to discard the material world, and by that means expose philosophy to the ridicule of all men, who will not offer up common sense as a sacrifice to metaphysics" (75). As Reid understands the representational theory of Locke and Hume, the notion that one perceives objects through a filter of ideas leads inevitably to a skepticism about whether these objects really exist. The goal then is to use the ordinary assumption that we access the world directly as a standard for thinking about perception and to assert that any challenge to this notion of access violates common sense. The means of achieving this goal is, in turn, in rejecting the language of mental imagery as a needlessly recondite picture of the everyday habits of viewing and acting. Whereas Locke and Hume found the need to come up with a separate panoply of mental states – impressions, ideas, senses, images, and the like – Reid admits only of our having "natural signs" that automatically and with no interference fasten experience to their objects. Unlike mental representations, natural signs bear no similarity to the world; they are simply part of it: "They pass through the mind instantaneously and serve only to introduce the notion and belief of external things, which by our constitution are connected with them" (63). So on Reid's view we are caught up in the world in the sense that there is only a slim distance between the sign we possess and the signified we inhabit. "Natural signs" go unnoticed in our experience as "the mind passes immediately to the thing signified without making the least reflection on the sign, or observing that there ever was such a thing" (63). In this respect, the theory of natural signs is not so far from Hogarth's hollowed out shells. Both draw perception out of the head so it may limn the surface of the world. According to Reid's dense and difficult account of what he calls "the geometry of the visibles," in fact, depth perception happens because vision projects on the surface of a sphere, not on a flat plain.[32] Sight tilts on a curve, Reid says, because it fastens to objects receding on a bent gradient. The formal theory of perceptual presence lagged behind its literary antecedents because it conceived of vision as a kind of touch and presented depth as curvature or occlusion among middle-sized objects.

What is common to Hogarth and Reid is the notion that if one is averse to a posture of detachment – in ordinary or aesthetic acts of perception – then one must also be averse to a theory of internal representations. The act of standing in relation to an image for both writers means that one is somehow not participating in what that image represents. Hogarth raises this objection in order to put the beholder of beautiful works of art or beautiful pieces of nature in a place to recreate them in time: it is not the image of the finished whole that concerns him but the various strands by which it is made. Reid asks his reader simply to trust her naive judgments about the encountered and lived world. The worry here (again) is that a representational theory leads to skepticism, and so, on his view, to disaster. We abide with the "sun, moon, stars and earth, [with] vegetable and animal bodies" themselves, not with their ideas or images (67). The world goes on without our having any account of it, Reid says, so we might just do our best to trust what we see and feel.

Where Hogarth directs his reader to attend to form, Reid directs his to attend to whole objects. The charge is perhaps most curious when it is made with respect to the prototypically mental property of colour, which Reid says is a property of bodies themselves: "By color, all men, who have not been tutored by modern philosophy, understand not a sensation of the mind, which can have no existence when it is not perceived, but a quality or modification of bodies, which continues to be the same, whether it is seen or not. The scarlet-rose, which is before me, is still a scarlet-rose when I shut my eyes, and was so at midnight when no eye saw it" (85). Reid was nearly alone among eighteenth-century theorists in holding that colour was a mind-independent and enduring feature of the bodies it colours.[33] As elsewhere, he would have us accept our relation to the sun, the moon, and stars, to vegetable and animal bodies, to red and to blue, rather than throw that relation into doubt. In this respect, Reid's direct realism is an important if unacknowledged antecedent to the speculative realism on offer by, for example, Graham Harman's headline-grabbing "object-oriented ontology," which also argues, contra "the widespread empiricist view that the supposed objects of experience are nothing but bundles of qualities," that colours "*are bonded to the thing to which they belong*," while advocating for a naive approach to the encountered world.[34] Reid might stand as a background to the current mood, in this manner, but he also might draw attention to the strange way that speculative realism understands objects to retreat from us and from each other.[35] In contrast to such retreat, Reid's valuation of the naive and the ordinary would shrink the distance between our perceptual acts and the "earth, which we inhabit," the "country, friends and relations, which we enjoy," and the "land, houses, and moveables, which we possess" (18). And it would do so by conceiving of perception as a kind of motor skill, secured by the well-designed "fabric of the human body" (113). Vision, for example, is "skillfully and regularly performed" by "a system of unconnected muscles conspiring

[as] wonderfully in their various actions" as "excellent musicians in a concert" or "a company of expert players in a theatrical performance" or "good dancers in a country dance" (113).[36]

Apostrophe and Dwelling

Perception is direct on this view because we are adept at using our bodies to bring the world – the earth, our friends, and dwelling – within reach. One word for this skill is the ability to achieve what Henry Home, Lord Kames, called "presence," both "ideal" and "real," in his 1762 *Elements of Criticism* – the "laying open [of] things existing and passing around us" – and much of the dissident line that I've been attempting to reconstruct aims to consider and realize something like presence in aesthetic and perceptual acts.[37] Consider one more loco-descriptive poet, William Cowper, whose task it is to sing of the sofa, "who long in thickets and in brakes/ Entangled, winds now this way and now that/ his devious course uncertain, seeking home."[38] Entanglement is a nice word for the tactile account of vision. The idea would be that to see the world is to reach out to something that is already there. Here again the perceptual theory matches up with the literary form. For while critics have long separated the apostrophe with which *The Task* begins from the meandering entanglements to which it proceeds – as if sofas were one thing and thickets another – there is an important sense in which Cowper writes of both within a common notion of a world up close. Apostrophe, writes Kames, aims "to bestow a momentary presence upon a sensible being who is absent" (2:554–5). When this figure joins with personification, he adds, it aims to bestow presence and sentience at once, so "things inanimate" may qualify "for listening to a passionate expostulation" (2:555). For my purposes, momentary presence describes the formal and figural way of bringing something to hand, the reaching out to things just past one's fingers so they may be brought into view. Momentary presence is by its nature fleeting and, as it is set out in the poem, requires one's skill and handiwork. If the apostrophic speaker is at home in the world, that is because he knows how to bring it in reach, and if he knows how to bring it in reach, that is because he is good at paying it attention, like his skilled gardener of cucumbers pinching the bud of each second stalk so to yield "summer fruits brought forth from wintry suns" (3:553). If he is good at paying attention, finally, that is because Cowper is good at the apostrophe and personification that "raise the prickly and green-coated gourd/So grateful to the palate," as if the form of the trope could trace the edge of each sofa and the skin of each cucumber (3:446–7).

What Is It Like to Be a Starling?

Like the pail of milk or the bunch of fruit, the cucumber is not over there, but right here, and it is right here because it is the subject of apostrophe's momentary presence, one that shows up for a creature with a certain kind of body and a certain kind of motility. The loco-descriptive poets understood this because they were working through the ecology of perception, on the ground, naively, as it were. I have argued that this naiveté extends to the idea that the world shows up as present, not as a mental representation, and that presence is something achieved through a kind of skill. Seeing is like touching is like gardening. I'll turn now in the final pages of this essay to some versions of presence in a few moments from Sterne. The first is from an early letter that Sterne wrote to Elizabeth Lumley before they were married, the rest from *Sentimental Journey*. Lumley was apparently about to leave her family's country house:

> Thou sayest thou wilt quit the place with regret – I think so too – Does not something uneasy mingle with the very reflection of leaving it? It is like parting with an old friend, whose temper and company one has long been acquainted with. – I think I see you looking twenty times a day at the house – almost counting every brick and pane of glass, and telling them at the same time with a sigh, you are going to leave them – Oh happy modification of matter! They will remain insensible of thy loss. – But how wilt thou be able to part with thy garden? – The recollection of so many pleasing walks must have endeared it to you. The trees, the shrubs, the flowers, which thou reared with thy own hands – will they not droop and fade away sooner upon thy departure – Who will be the successor to nurse them in thy absence. – Thou wilt leave thy name upon the myrtle-tree. – If trees, and shrubs, and flowers could compose an elegy, I should expect a very plaintive one upon this subject.[39]

The letter is one of only a few that Sterne kept from the period (the 1740s), and it is clear that he continued to think through its contents over the course of his career. For my current purposes, the letter is remarkable for its use of apostrophe and personification to entwine its recipient in the fold of a built and natural environment. Lumley is at home in the world, or rather the home – its walls and windows, walks and gardens – *is* her world made present to mind. Seen this way, the apostrophe and personification provide a kind of linguistic shape and poignancy to the familiar acquaintance she has with the house and the gardens. "The apostrophizing poet," writes Jonathan Culler (a twentieth-century Lord Kames of sorts), "identifies his universe as a world of sentient forces."[40] In this case, the brick and the glass and the flower, the shrubs and trees are present as available to Lumley, just as she is present as available to them (or at least to the shrubs and flowers; the brick and glass are insensible, after all). Each mourns the other. Each mourns the other in anticipation of the other's no longer being available. Each is present to the other as a living thing.

The kind of presence sketched by the trope, as Sterne writes about it, stems from the tactile know-how Lumley brings to gardening, as if to see the world beyond the end of one's fingers one must actually reach out to touch it. As with Hogarth and Reid, the acquaintance Lumley has with created and living things takes some work and some skill, even as it seems to extend, on Sterne's vision, to more naive and ordinary acts of perceiving. The latter point will become clearer years later when Sterne returns to and embellishes this understanding of presence in that most tactile of all eighteenth-century novels, *Sentimental Journey* – that novel of handholding and pulse taking. He returns in fact to the very myrtle tree upon which Lumley wrote her name and does the same. Arriving at Calais, Yorick contrasts his sense of worldly entanglement with the jaundiced and inward view of those unresponsive to travel. The world is all barren "only to him who will not cultivate the fruits that it offers," he says, and then declares while clapping his hands, "was I in a desart, I would find out wherewith in it to call forth my affections … I would fasten them upon some sweet myrtle, or seek some melancholy cypress to connect myself to – I would court their shade, and greet them kindly for their protection – I would cut my name upon them, and swear they were the loveliest trees throughout the desert: if their leaves wither'd, I would teach myself to mourn, and when they rejoiced, I would rejoice along with them."[41] Once again personification traces a line of contact between the ends of one's fingers and the places one inhabits, and in so inhabiting, perceives. The novel simply removes the letter's earlier and more explicit references to Lumley's skilled handiwork while retaining the feel of acquaintance and the work of the trope to bring the world within reach.

The episodes in which objects and persons and animals are found to be in reach in *Sentimental Journey* are of course many, and I'm not going to detail them here. No eighteenth-century novel (again) is more concerned with touch. I would turn instead to a passage that clarifies that this putting of touch into the foreground makes a point about vision in particular and perception at large. This is Yorick soon after he arrives in Paris:

> I own my first sensations, as soon as I was left solitary and alone in my own chamber in the hotel, were far from being so flattering as I had prefigured them. I walked up gravely to the window in my dusty black coat, and looking through the glass saw all the world in yellow, blue and green, running at the ring of pleasure ... Alas poor Yorick! cried I, what art thou doing here? On the very first onset of all this glittering clatter, thou art reduced to an atom – seek – seek some winding alley with a tourniquet at the end of it ... there thou mayest solace thy soul in concourse sweet with some kind grisset of a barber's wife, and get into such coteries! (47)

In her preface to the 1927 signet edition of *Sentimental Journey*, Virginia Woolf cited this passage (and this passage alone) as the quintessence of what she calls Sterne's "pure poetry."[42] It is easy to see why. We are asked to consider Yorick gazing out his window onto the busy street below and to follow or adopt the rushing scene of colour that saturates his visual field: a dusty black coaxes yellow and blue to combine into green. But we are asked also to consider the structural layout of the scene. Once the line of sight passes over the coat, it remains fixed at the window looking out at the street, while Yorick remains "solitary *and* alone" in the room. The hotel fills out Locke's metaphor of the camera obscura, in other words, as light from the street projects an image in a closed chamber, but it does so to some critical effect. In this respect, Sterne echoes no one more than Reid, who also took aim at just this metaphor. "Locke's doctrine of ideas," Reid writes, "alleges, without any manifest proof, that every man shut in, as it were, in a *camera obscura* perceives nothing outside but only the images or ideas of things depicted in his own *camera*."[43] For Sterne as for Reid, the account of vision as a screening of images in a dark room puts too much emphasis on detachment and pictorial representation. The world does not project to a point.

In drawing attention to the Reidian and realist elements of Sterne, I aim to provide a context different from the long-standing association of the novelist with the project of Adam Smith and David Hume and, indeed, even from the project of sympathy, as that has been modelled, for example, as an inter-subjective encounter in James Chandler's very recent and magisterial *Archaeology of Sympathy*.[44] Sterne's is a realism not limited to the emotions or to forming images of what is on someone else's mind. Rather, I want to say it is a realism of the surrounded world conceived as something drawn close. On this view, perception is a kind of ability and a kind of technique, not the sitting in a darkened room so much as a walking about a crowded city or a reaching out to plants and stones. Sterne shows this technique in scenes of making the world present by bringing it to hand or seeing it with one's fingers. He also elicits this technique in skill of his own, using his own craft to show how objects are made present to whoever beholds them. So, for example, when Yorick encounters his famous starling, the sentences bend to elicit the visual zigzag of a moving human body. "I had some occasion," Yorick writes, "to step in the court yard," and so "walk'd down the stairs," whereupon hearing a cry, "I look'd up and down," returned back, and "looking up again I saw it was a starling hung in a cage" (68–9). The visual zigzag mimics a kinetic unfolding: this is what Yorick sees as he walks this way with his head turned that way, as he brings the visual field within reach. With the attention to physical movement and shifting lines of sight, in other words, the sentences create the sense of an available world: a bird unseen from one vantage will come into view with a head moved liked this; a court yard will back onto a street when entered from a room. They create points that are both "movement dependent," in Noë's words, with the slightest motion of the body modulating the sensory relation to the object of perception, and "object dependent," with the slightest motion at the edges of the visual field grabbing our attention.[45] They turn finally to a kind of seeing that is not simply pictorial, as Yorick "takes both hands" to the cage and wrestles with the "twisted and double twisted wires" while the bird flies to the spot of his fingers and, "thrusting his head through the trellis" and pressing "his breast against it, as if impatient," repeats "I can't get out" (69). Personification – Sterne's know-how and handiwork – traces two bodies in close, moving proximity and shows Yorick caught up with what he touches and, in so touching, makes present.

The encounter begins with some doubt on Yorick's part about whether the starling is really asking to be set free or is merely a mechanical thing insensibly repeating words taught by a previous owner. It ends by discarding skepticism and accepting a common place in a shared world, one that unfolds in time and at the end of one's fingers. This turn from the skeptical to the naive might stand as the common thread among my disparate writers. As I've intimated from time to time, I also think it sheds some light on our current naiveté – our more accepting interest in objects and surfaces and forms. We really do see things directly, Reid said. The world outstrips what is in our head. Just look. But know too, and this might be the lesson from the eighteenth-century techniques of presence, how much skill there is in seeing what lies between here and there, as Berkeley said, or turning a beautiful object to its lines, as Hogarth said, or finally, for everyone reading, simply engaging works in the way that we do. There is a lot to see, and there is a lot to lose.

NOTES

A portion of this contribution appeared in *European Romantic Review* 26.4 (2015).

1 Thomas Hobbes, *Leviathan, or the Matter, Forme, & Power of a Common-Wealth Ecclesiasticall and Civill*, ed. Richard Tuck (Cambridge: Cambridge University Press, 1996), 14. Further references are to this edition and noted in parentheses.

2 By presence, I mean simply the property of being here rather than not here, close rather than far away, or as Hans Ulrich Gumbrecht puts it, "a spatial relation to the world and its objects … tangible to human hands." *Production of Presence: What Meaning Cannot Convey* (Stanford: Stanford University Press, 2004), xiii. The word presence has religious and semantic connotations that I do not mean to suggest, as in the presence of the lord in the host or of meaning in the signifier (the "metaphysics of presence," so called).

3 On the literary critical end, the texts here are well known: Stephen Best and Sharon Marcus's chart-topping "Surface Reading: An Introduction," *Representations* 108.1 (2009): 1–21, along with the essays on description and suspicion that have appeared largely in *NLH* (by Rita Felski and Heather Love, for example), and finally the turn to ontology in so-called speculative realism, especially Object-Oriented Ontology. On the philosophical and cognitive end, the terrain is perhaps less familiar to humanists, but covers the broadly enactive, embodied, and extended theories of mind of recent years. See, for example, Alva Noë, *Action in Perception* (Cambridge, MA: MIT Press, 2004) and Daniel D. Hutto and Erik Myin, *Radicalizing Enactivism: Basic Minds without Content* (Cambridge, MA: MIT Press, 2013). Different in topic and method, these features of the current academic scene share a certain revaluation of the naive and the direct. Although I don't see myself as adhering in any particular way to any one of them, I share the impatience.

4 David Hume, *A Treatise on Human Nature* (1739), ed. P.H. Nidditch and L.A. Selby-Bigge, 2nd ed. (Oxford: Oxford University Press, 1978), 2.1.6. Further references are to this edition and noted in parentheses. I take Hume at face value here, as repeating then received wisdom, not stating the skeptical conclusions he would draw from such wisdom. The representational stance may be necessary for Hume's skepticism (about, for example, what we may know about causal relations), but it is not sufficient for it. Reid will disagree.

5 David Hume, *An Enquiry Concerning Human Understanding* (1748), ed. Tom L. Beauchamp (Oxford: Oxford University Press, 1999), 2.12.9. Further references are to this edition and noted in parentheses.

6 The sort of physical picture I refer to here does not require materialism or monism. The official position of someone like Boyle (and the Royal Society) stuck to immaterial souls while maintaining that only the material world fell within the purview of science. I discuss some of the directions this position took in *Actions and Objects from Hobbes to Richardson* (Stanford: Stanford University Press, 2010). The classic analysis is John W. Yolton, *Thinking Matter: Materialism in Eighteenth-Century Britain* (Minneapolis: University of Minnesota Press, 1984).

7 I explore this connection at greater length in "Empiricism, Cognitive Science, and the Novel," *The Eighteenth Century: Theory and Interpretation* 47.3 (2007): 263–85. For an extended riff on this eighteenth-century background to contemporary cognitive science via a shared emphasis on representation see Jerry A. Fodor, *Hume Variations* (Oxford: Oxford University Press, 2005). For a discussion of the varied technical meanings of the word "representation" in cognitive science and the philosophy of perception see Gary Hatfield, *Perception and Cognition: Essays in the Philosophy of Psychology* (Oxford: Oxford University Press, 2009), 43–123. Among the differences between eighteenth-century empiricism and classical cognitive science would be that the former understands representation to be picture-like and the latter understands it to be symbol-like, with the further understanding that the pictures cannot be part of a syntax, whereas symbols can.

8 David Marr, *Vision: A Computational Investigation into the Human Representation and Processing of Visual Information* (San Francisco: Freeman and Co., 1982), 3.

9 James J. Gibson, "A Theory of Direct Visual Perception," in *The Psychology of Knowing*, ed. J.R. Royce and W.W. Rozeboom (New York: Gordon and Breach, 1972), 218.

10 See Gibson, *The Ecological Approach to Visual Perception* (New York: Psychology Press, 1986). The category of "dwelling" (of intermittent

importance to this essay) descends from Heidegger (*wohnen*), especially the "Building, Dwelling, Thinking" chapter from *Poetry, Language, Thought*. My use here is simply to provide a companion point to seeing the world as action potentials. One also perceives the world in terms of nested living.

11 Alva Noë, *Varieties of Presence* (Cambridge, MA: Harvard University Press, 2012), 5. Hereafter in parenthesis.

12 See the influential theory of affordances in Gibson (1986), 127–43. An affordance is a feature of the environment as it shows up for a certain body with a certain motility: a chair affords sitting if you have legs that bend in a specific way; a tree affords dwelling for a squirrel if has an opening of a particular depth, and so on. It is, as Gibson says, subjective and objective and yet neither.

13 George Berkeley, *An Essay Towards a New Theory of Vision* (London, 1709), 2. Hereafter in parenthesis.

14 Donald F. Bond, ed., *The Spectator*, 6 vols. (Oxford: Clarendon Press, 1965), 4:536. Further citation is to this edition and noted in parenthesis.

15 See, for example, Ronald Paulson, *The Beautiful, Novel, and Strange: Aesthetics and Heterodoxy* (Baltimore: Johns Hopkins University Press, 1995).

16 Whether there were perceptual features or properties special to each sense was a puzzle extending back to Aristotle, and for the eighteenth-century culminating in the Molyneux problem.

17 Mark Akenside, John Dyer, Robert Aris Willmott, and Myles Birket Foster, *The Poetical Works of Mark Akenside and John Dyer* (London: G. Routledge, 1855), lines 1; 59–60; 63–4; 69–74.

18 William Gilpin, *Observations on the River Wye; and Several Parts of South Wales &c., Relative Chiefly to Picturesque Beauty, Made in the Summer of the Year 1770* (London, 1782), 61.

19 On the one-point perspective in eighteenth-century painting and aesthetics, see Peter de Bolla, *The Education of the Eye: Painting, Landscape, and Architecture in Eighteenth-Century Britain* (Stanford: Stanford University Press, 2003). For a Renaissance background, see James Elkins, *The Poetics of Perspective* (Ithaca: Cornell University Press, 1994).

20 John Barrell, *The Idea of Landscape and the Sense of Place, 1730–1840: An Approach to the Poetry of John Clare* (Cambridge: Cambridge University Press 1972), 21.

21 Kevis Goodman, *Georgic Modernity and British Romanticism: Poetry and the Mediation of History* (Cambridge: Cambridge University Press, 2004), 38–56. Heather Keenleyside, "Personification for the People: On James Thomson's *The Seasons*," *ELH* 76.2 (2009): 449.

22 Barrell, *The Idea of Landscape*, 21.

23 Barrell and Keenleyside make a good study in contrasts in this respect, the former remaining wary of what he understands to be Thomson's (Whig aristocratic) ideology and the latter attracted to what she presents as an extension of personhood to non-human animals.

24 James Thomson, *Summer*, in *The Seasons*, ed. James Sambrook (Oxford: Clarendon Press, 1981), lines 253, 255. Further citation is to this edition (based on the 1746 edition), and noted in parenthesis, with the seasons abbreviated to *Su*, *A*, and so on.

25 For an account of such "kinetic occlusion" in the realist novel, see Elaine Scarry's beautiful and brilliant *Dreaming by the Book* (Princeton: Princeton University Press, 1999), 10–31. Scarry considers such occlusion to be "reproducing the deep structure of perception" itself and so, like Gibson and Noë, descends from the dissident line I'm locating in the eighteenth century (9).

26 Svetlana Alpers, *The Vexations of Art: Velázquez and Others* (New Haven: Yale University Press, 2005), 27.

27 For a discussion of *The Rape of the Lock* as a kind of still life, both an examination of set objects and a consideration of Belinda as a painter, see Jonathan Lamb's *The Things Things Say* (Princeton: Princeton University Press, 2011), 98–125.

28 William Hogarth, *The Analysis of Beauty: Written with a view of Fixing the Fluctuating Ideas of Taste* (London, 1753), iv. Hereafter in parenthesis.

29 For Hogarth's early experience in craft, see Jenny Uglow, *Hogarth: A Life and World* (New York: Farrar Strauss & Giroux, 1997), 21–42. For more on the aesthetics of craft as handiwork in contrast to the standard model of viewing, see Pamela H. Smith, *The Body of the Artisan: Art and Experience in the Scientific Revolution* (Chicago: University of Chicago Press, 2004) and Ronald Paulson, *Breaking and Remaking* (New Brunswick, NJ: Rutgers University Press, 1989). In thinking about Hogarth and the aesthetics of craft, I've benefited from sharing these pages with Ruth Mack and from reading her chapter in progress, "Practical Aesthetics: Hogarth and Everyday Form."

30 Abigail Zitin, "Thinking Like an Artist: Hogarth, Diderot, and the Aesthetics of Technique," *Eighteenth-Century Studies* 46.4 (2013): 555–6. Hereafter in parenthesis.

31 Thomas Reid, *An Inquiry into the Human Mind on the Principles of Common Sense* (1764), ed. Derek R. Brookes (State College, PA: Penn State University Press, 1997), 74. Further citation is to this edition and in parenthesis.

32 Ibid., 103–11. Reid has been understood by some to have here anticipated non-Euclidian geometry. See for example, Norman Daniels, *Thomas Reid's*

Inquiry: The Geometry of Visibles and the Case for Realism (Stanford: Stanford University Press, 1974), 1–24.

33 The empiricist theory of colour as a secondary quality moves from Boyle, to Newton, to Locke. Here is Addison summing up the conventional wisdom: "I have here supposed that my Reader is acquainted with that great Modern Discovery, which is at present universally acknowledged by all the Enquirers into Natural Philosophy: Namely, that Light and Colours, as apprehended by the Imagination, are only Ideas in the Mind, and not Qualities that have any Existence in Matter" (413: 552). Reid quotes and criticizes this sentence in particular. Intriguingly, at the end of the section on "the beautiful in feeling" in *A Philosophical Enquiry into the Origin of Our Ideas of the Sublime and Beautiful*, Burke considers the possibility that one might be able to touch colour.

34 Graham Harman, *The Quadruple Object* (Alresford, Hants: Zero Books, 2010), 11. This is Harman's version of the naive stance: "Objects are units that both display and conceal a multitude of traits. But whereas the naive standpoint of this book makes no initial claim as to which of these objects is real or unreal, the labor of the intellect is usually taken to be *critical* rather than naïve. Instead of accepting this inflated menagerie of entities, critical thinking debunks objects and denies their autonomy. They are dismissed as figments of the mind, or as mere aggregates built of smaller physical pieces. Yet the stance of this book is not critical, but sincere. I will not reduce some objects to the greater glory of others, but will describe instead how objects relate to their own visible and invisible qualities, to each other, and to our own minds – all in a single metaphysics" (7).

35 The risk is that for all the object orientation one falls into a dualist picture of the physical, with objects on the one hand, and (tacitly and with some embarrassment) experience on the other. In contrast, the point for both Locke and Reid (as well as, say, Thomas Nagel) is to recognize that phenomenology is no less a part of the objective structure of the universe than space dust or Coke cans.

36 The argument for direct perception here gets close to the enactive theorists of contemporary embodied cognition, except for where Reid would look to providence as to why this all works so well, the embodied theorists would look to natural selection.

37 Henry Home, Lord Kames, *Elements of Criticism* (1762), ed. Peter Jones, 2 vols. (Indianapolis: Liberty Fund, 2005) 1:66. Hereafter in parenthesis.

38 William Cowper, *The Task* (1785), in *The Task and Selected Other Poems*, ed. James Sambrook (London: Longman, 1994), 2: lines 1–3. Further references are to this edition and noted in parenthesis.

39 Melvyn New and Peter de Voogd, eds., *The Florida Edition of the Works of Laurence Sterne*, 8 vols. (Gainesville: University Press of Florida, 2009), 7:9.
40 Jonathan Culler, *The Pursuit of Signs: Semiotics, Literature, Deconstruction* (Ithaca: Cornell University Press, 1981), 139. Culler's further point that apostrophe is "a sign of a fiction that knows its own fictive nature" runs counter to the point I'm trying to make, however (146).
41 Laurence Sterne, *A Sentimental Journey through France and Italy by Mr. Yorick*, ed. Paul Goring (London: Penguin, 2001), 28. Hereafter in parenthesis.
42 Virginia Woolf, *The Second Common Reader* (New York: Mariner Books, 2003), 82.
43 Thomas Reid, *The Philosophical Orations of Thomas Reid*, ed. D.D. Todd (Carbondale: Southern Illinois University Press, 1989), 61.
44 James Chandler, *An Archaeology of Sympathy: The Sentimental Mode in Literature and Cinema* (Chicago: University of Chicago Press, 2013), 5–12 and passim.
45 Noë, *Action in Perception*, 130 and passim.

3 Reading Locke after Shaftesbury: Feeling Our Way Towards a Postsecular Genealogy of Religious Tolerance

DAVID ALVAREZ

Since the 1960s, John Locke's *A Letter Concerning Toleration* (1689) has been given a prominent position in histories of the development of liberal religious tolerance.[1] Liberal political theorists find in the empiricist Locke a forebear to Immanuel Kant, a rather violent yoking justified by understanding Lockean tolerance in terms of dispassionate judgment and the mutual recognition of religious freedom.[2] A Neo-Kantian framework, however, both distorts Locke and forecloses a fuller understanding of the formation of religious tolerance in the English Enlightenment. Focusing on Locke's definition of religion as private belief, his skepticism about theological truth, and the epistemological grounds for his separation of church and state, such accounts neglect how Locke reinterprets religious passions and sensations to establish the preconditions of his conceptual framework for tolerance.[3] As a result, these approaches also overlook the role his rhetoric plays in putting this implicit background in place. Accounts that enshrine Locke at the origin of liberal religious tolerance tend to reproduce his rhetorical framing of it as a dispassionate stance, in which religious zeal is opposed to reasonable tolerance. This not only disavows the pains and passions related to tolerance but also naturalizes the politics of the regimes of sensation and affect that support it.

If Locke's now-canonical *Letter* has been used to support an "intellectualist orientation" to religious tolerance, rereading it through the early affective turn of his pupil's *Characteristics of Men, Manners, Opinions, Times* (1711) opens up for analysis the implicit background of sensation and feeling that Locke's *Letter* transforms. The reverse has usually been the case: Locke distorts our reading of Shaftesbury and tolerance through an emphasis on epistemology and autonomy.

Shaftesbury's writings, however, are a powerfully illuminating example of how the transformations of religion that contribute to the Enlightenment formation of tolerance are not only conceptual but sensorial. Theorizing religious tolerance through what he argues is an alternative, empowering system of religious passions, Shaftesbury puts in place new "historical conditions of possibility for both the affective and evaluative response" to religious difference.[4] Moreover, his explicit, self-conscious practice of cultural politics foregrounds how his rhetoric appeals to and transforms the felt meanings of religious passions, pains, and concepts.[5] The rhetorical actions of Enlightenment texts – philosophical, literary, or otherwise – are key to seeing how discourses of nascent liberal tolerance manage anxieties caused by threats to religious identity. Such rhetorical moves also motivate the practice of tolerance by identifying and promoting the resources of resilience needed for endurance and self-restraint. To shift our understanding of the formation of religious tolerance from Locke to Shaftesbury, however, is neither to treat Shaftesbury as its origin nor to hold up his defence of tolerance as correct. Rather, Shaftesbury's attention to sensation and the passions offers a corrective to dominant approaches of understanding the formation of religious tolerance through conceptual analysis and historical contextualizations that elide the history of the emotions.

A Shaftesburian approach to tolerance shares some similarities to Lars Tønder's recent critique of the prevailing Neo-Kantian "intellectualist orientation" in contemporary political philosophy, which, Tønder argues, disavows "the affective intensities and perceptual shifts that underpin the endurance and resilience embedded in the practice of tolerance."[6] Because it ignores what tolerance always involves – pain – such an approach distorts our understanding of the meaning and political potential of practicing tolerance. The word "tolerance" itself is derived from the Latin *tolerāntia*, "endurance of pain," and, as Tønder observes, pain "resonates with the phenomenology of tolerance as well as with everyday uses of tolerance as a response to something or someone of which or whom one disapproves."[7] Arguing for a "sensorial orientation" to tolerance, Tønder suggests that analysing how "regimes of discourse and sensation" define and politicize the pains of tolerance can further democratic goals by expanding "the conditions of contestations and deliberation."[8] Moreover, a sensorial orientation is able to illuminate how the "pleasurable pains" of discourses of tolerance (e.g., satire and the sublime) enable a "resilient endurance" through a "feeling of pleasure" that augments one's power and moves one towards others.[9] Tønder also affirms the pains of tolerance for their liberating potential, their ability in some contexts to be "world-making rather than world-shattering" and to empower the creation of "new constellations of thought and action."[10] Although Shaftesbury's consideration of pain is less affirmative, he understands his own effort to promote tolerance as the resignification of a regime of sensation and passion, and he treats tolerance as a "pleasurable pain" by identifying sources of resilience and endurance. He offers an immanent Enlightenment critique of liberal theories of tolerance such as Locke's that disavow and relegate the passions to a tacit, unexamined background.

Attending to Shaftesbury's transformation of religious regimes of passion and sensation also enables the pursuit of a postsecular genealogy of tolerance. Shaftesbury's conceptualization of a tolerant public rationality not only requires repressing an earlier set of religious passions but redefining and promoting new felt meanings for religion. Tolerance is not separated from religious understandings and feelings but is formulated in relationship to them. This is not to reduce "the secular" to "the religious" or to claim that religion contaminates secular tolerance; instead, Shaftesbury's work provides ample evidence in support of revisionist scholarship in the wake of Talal Asad that understands these categories as "interdependent and necessarily linked in their mutual transformation and historical emergence."[11] And while much has been written about Locke's reliance on Christian theology in his arguments for religious tolerance, reading Locke with a Shaftesburian lens highlights how his text enables the endurance of religious difference by transforming and appealing to religious passions.[12] Focusing on the background of sensation and passion that these texts put into play suggests their continuing power to inform and animate political liberalism not only conceptually but in terms of the felt meanings they put in place.[13] Turning to Shaftesbury to open up a postsecular genealogy of tolerance can enable "the modern articulation of the secular … to *loosen and lighten up*" by offering an in-depth opportunity for "the secular to historicize and contextualize itself."[14] Such an approach also foregrounds the politics of tolerance. Shaftesbury's efforts to promote tolerance are deeply political in ways that "compromise the possibility of a deep, genuinely pluralistic democratic politics."[15] Overall, Shaftesbury's work invites an analysis of religious tolerance that focuses on the space between the secular and the religious, alert to its ambiguous political effects.

Shaftesbury and Religious Tolerance: Passions, Cognition, and Politics

Shaftesbury's argument for religious tolerance is usually considered in relation to his promotion of polite conversation in a rational public sphere self-regulated by the "test of ridicule."[16] Characterizing Shaftesbury's conception of sociability and conversation along Habermasian lines, Lawrence Klein influentially describes him as arguing "for broad religious and intellectual toleration in the context of a public sphere, a worldly domain of free and open discussion in which exchange and criticism advanced both truth and refinement."[17] As "epistemological practices," wit, raillery, and polite conversation liberate the mind from prejudice and self-deception, allowing religious tolerance to develop within a public sphere of open discussion.[18] Viewing Shaftesbury through a Habermasian lens, however, obscures the constitutive role played by the passions in his reformulation of public reason. "Good humour" is not a tool for freeing the mind from the influence of the passions but rather a political sensibility and practice that enables a particular kind of rationality. For example, as part of his critique of Hobbes's reduction of human motivation to "only one Master-Passion, Fear, which has, in effect devour'd all the rest," Shaftesbury not only contends against the regime of passion and sensation that supports Hobbesian and Anglican High Church politics and forms of reasoning but also seeks to put in place a new one with a different set of political and cognitive possibilities and limitations.[19] Analysing "good humour" as primarily an epistemological tool tends to emphasize its possibilities (e.g., the ability of wit to "put the mind at liberty"), while downplaying the disciplinary force of politeness and the rhetorical power of ridicule (159).[20] For Shaftesbury, however, good humour as an "epistemological practice" cannot be separated from its rhetorical ability to transform the passions: it is a political practice before it is an epistemological one.

Viewing Shaftesbury within the framework of Habermas's casually secular account of public reason in *The Structural Transformation of the Public Sphere* also shifts attention away from the theological elements that inform Shaftesbury's construction of public reason and religious tolerance.[21] Specifically, he does not oppose religious passion to reason but instead reinterprets and reforms a religious sensibility, which then conditions the practice and contours of public reason. Accounts like Sammy Basu's that see Shaftesbury's polite civility as "post-theological" risk rendering his defence of religious tolerance in terms of a "subtraction story," in which emancipation from the yoke of an oppressive religious sensibility permits truth and tolerance to naturally manifest themselves in a liberated modernity.[22] Charles Taylor criticizes such narratives on the grounds that they misrepresent "newly constructed self-understandings and related practices" for "perennial features of human life" that "were there all along, but had been impeded" by "certain earlier, confining horizons or illusions."[23] To the extent that Shaftesbury is construed along early Habermasian lines, we risk not only an "intellectualist orientation" to tolerance but also an ahistorical, presumptively secular one.[24]

Shaftesbury, however, understands religious passion as a historical, politicized regime of discourse and sensation. It is both the object of Shaftesbury's analysis of tolerance and the target of his transformative rhetoric. He contends that the felt meaning of a Hobbesian interpretation of religious passion as fear provided implicit, powerful background support to the justification of persecution, political absolutism, and the power of High Church Anglicans. To promote tolerance, he aims to transform this meaning of religious passion and subvert its politics. He argues in *A Letter Concerning Enthusiasm* (1709) that controlling religious violence requires recognizing and calming "men's natural fears":

> And thus is religion also panic when enthusiasm of any kind gets up as oft, on melancholy occasions, it will. For vapours naturally rise and, in bad times especially, when the spirits of men are low, as either in public calamities or during the unwholesomeness of air or diet, or when convulsions happen in nature, storms, earthquakes or other amazing prodigies – at this season the panic must needs run high, and the magistrate of necessity give way to it. For to apply a serious remedy and bring the sword or *fasces* as a cure must make the case more melancholy and increase the very cause of the distemper. To forbid men's natural fears and to endeavor the overpowering them by other fears, must needs be a most unnatural method. The magistrate, if he be any artist, should have a gentler hand and, instead of caustics, incisions and amputations, should be using the softest balms, and, with a kind of sympathy, entering into the public and taking, as it were, their passion upon him, should, when he has soothed and satisfied it, endeavor, by cheerful ways, to divert and heal it ... [In antiquity,] superstition and enthusiasm were mildly treated and, being let alone, they never raged to that degree as to occasion bloodshed, wars, persecutions, and devastations in the world.[25]

For Shaftesbury, when nature threatens death through disease, natural catastrophe, and "other amazing prodigies," humans feel fear and anxiety. While he insists that such melancholic religious fears are natural, he denies that they inevitably lead to violence: "when the spirits of men are low … the panic must needs run high." The task, therefore, is to raise men's spirits. A magistrate should use "the softest balms," "exercise sympathy," and share the passion of the people so that he might by "cheerful ways divert it." Instead of urging a dispassionate, rational stance that relegates the passions to an unacknowledged background, Shaftesbury presents religious tolerance as fundamentally about managing religious passions. They must be acknowledged and assuaged, vented and transformed, since "to forbid men's natural fears" is as dangerous as "to endeavor the overpowering them by other fears." Though they are irresistibly "natural," such passions require a controlled and transformed expression because of their political volatility: to respond to religious fears with "caustics, incisions, and amputations" – to use state violence ("the sword" or "fasces") – only amplifies the debilitating panic that Shaftesbury links to political oppression, irrationality, and sectarian violence. In contending against Hobbes's philosophical anthropology, which justified political order and religious uniformity by appealing to the fear of death, Shaftesbury offers a new economy of the passions to support a new politics.[26] This passage acknowledges religious pain and anxiety but also seeks to transform the political discourse through which the subject interprets its emotions and understands its experience. Instead of a politics based on religious fear, Shaftesbury offers and practises, in Albert Hirschman's terms, a theory of religious tolerance conceived in terms of countervailing passions.[27] The magistrate manages fear with cheer, panic with sympathy. For Shaftesbury, religious tolerance begins with mood management.

The rhetoric of the passage also supports this claim, since it positions religious anxiety in a larger, more reassuring frame. If religious fear is "natural," it is also an unnatural "distemper" that requires "healing." Structuring his argument around medical tropes, Shaftesbury figures the magistrate's intervention as the encouragement of a natural process, framing it less as a manipulative political intervention than a physician's healing hand. These figures also distinguish Shaftesbury from Hobbesian and High Church political absolutists and persecutors, who not only propose "incisions and amputations" but do so with the comically horrific and clumsy medical instruments of the sword and, especially, the fasces. Even in his diagnosis of religious melancholy,

Shaftesbury practises the rhetorical cure of good humour: the passage both advocates and practises the magistrate's role. As part of this effort, it also links religious fear to a limited time frame, to "seasons" of calamities and convulsions that will naturally pass. And it depicts the magistrate as sharing and sympathizing with the melancholy passions that can afflict the public. Indeed, in the face of such panic, "the magistrate of necessity [must] give way to it." Before he can "divert and heal," he must "soothe and satisfy." Shaftesbury insists on the force of the "natural passion of enthusiasm" with which religious tolerance must reckon.[28] He counters that force, however, not with rational-critical public debate but by acknowledging and transforming religious passion: this passage is an example of how Shaftesbury theorizes, urges, and practises that transformation.

The key term in this transformation is, of course, "enthusiasm," which, Shaftesbury claims, "is a matter of nice judgment and the hardest thing in the world to know fully and distinctly" (27). Its conceptual ambiguity, however, is less important for him than its affective indeterminacy. The equivocal nature of this feeling enables him to reinterpret and reframe its meaning in support of a new political regime of the passions. Shaftesbury makes a primitive existential predicament equivalent to a Hobbesian or Lockean state of nature. Instead of fearing a violent death at the hands of others or, worse still, the loss of our property, the original condition of humans is marked by ambiguous religious feelings of enthusiastic anxiety and wonder.[29] In his speculative history of the origin of religious violence, it is the difficulty of interpreting our confused religious emotions that opens the door to political oppression, economic exploitation, and violent sectarianism:

> We can admire nothing profoundly without a certain religious veneration. And because this borders so much on fear and raises a certain tremor or horror of like appearance, it is easy to give that turn to the affection and represent all enthusiasm and religious ecstasy as the product or mere effect of fear: *Fear first created gods in the world.* But the original passion, as appears plainly, is of another kind. (354)

Our experience of wonder, "to admire … profoundly," includes feeling "religious veneration," and yet the passion is confusing: it "borders … on fear" and the "tremor or horror" it produces has a "like appearance" to fear. For Shaftesbury, humanity's struggles to interpret this equivocal passion inaugurate religious history. From ancient Egypt to the Anglican Church, this hermeneutical problem, our "human weakness," has been exploited by priests to extort believers and to establish and maintain political power (360).[30] The manipulative practices and rhetoric of priestcraft interpret our confused religious feelings as fear, empowering religious authorities to gain "whatever extent of riches or possession could be acquired by practice and influence over the superstitious part of mankind" (358).[31] This political interpretation of religious passion continues in the rhetorical practices of the Anglican Church, "the writing Church Militant," whose "imposture" and "formalism" create an oppressive, exploitative "melancholy" that foments religious violence.[32] Against priestcraft, Shaftesbury seeks to return us to the "original passion," to interpret an ambiguous religious emotion not as an experience of the "astonishing and frightful" but of the "amiable and delightful." This latter passion – and not fear – "*first created gods in the world.*"

The foundations of any religion, according to Shaftesbury, find their "first beginnings ... in that natural complacency and good humour which inclines to trust and confidence in mankind ... The first scene of doctrine ... fails not to present us with agreeable views of joy, love, meekness, gentleness and moderation" (386–7). Good humour is less a feeling of happiness than a religious disposition to trust and engage with others and the world.[33] It is a sensibility of delight and wonder marked by an openness, an affirmation of life, and an enhancement of our natural social affections. More than a feeling, good humour is an expansive mode of cognition and experience.[34] Because Shaftesbury insists on the power of the passions to determine our perceptions, his interpretation of religious passion as good humour instead of fear becomes the basis for an alternate discourse of sensation, politics, and public reason.[35] His text poses a choice not between religious passion and secular reason, nor between religious and secular passions, but between religious sensibilities. Because he connects the emancipation of reason to a reinterpretation of religious passion, critique for Shaftesbury is something other than secular. So is religious tolerance.[36]

Priming the Passion for Religious Tolerance

In the last volume of *Characteristics*, the "Miscellaneous Reflections," Shaftesbury impersonates a commentator on his earlier essays, offering several illustrations of the magistrate's "moderating art" for overcoming religious violence.[37] These examples prioritize the political benefits of managing religious passions over any epistemological promise. They also highlight the mutual construction of religion and polite good humour. God, for instance, handles the "melancholy and forward temper" of the "pettish" Jonah by exhorting him to "good humour" with a "lusory [and] most tender manner" (388–90). Similarly, Shaftesbury suggests "a certain festivity, alacrity, and good humour" in the "sharp, humorous, and witty … repartees, reflections, fabulous narrations or parables, similes, comparisons and other methods of milder censure and reproof" of Jesus (390). Good humour is a Christian passion and practice in the strictest sense. God models it. Shaftesbury's claim that he borrows his style from the rhetorical practices of Jesus and his use of these divine examples to cast Christianity as "in the main a good humored and witty religion" reveal how religion and polite public reason are mutually transformative Enlightenment constructions (390).

Shaftesbury most fully illustrates "that magisterial science or policy which our author recommends" by recounting a passage from the book of Acts about a town clerk of Ephesus who calmed "a religious panic" upon the arrival of Paul (375, 374). When Paul began preaching Christianity, the Ephesians responded to "their established church [being] called into question" by crying out, "All with one voice, about the space of two hours … 'Great is Diana of the Ephesians'" (374). Urged on by the town's artisans, who profited from crafting idols of Diana, a "rage or epidemical frenzy" passed through the crowd, and "the new religionists [Christians]" were threatened with persecution. This catastrophe was avoided, however, because the clerk assured the people that "everyone acquiesced in their ancient worship of that goddess and in their tradition of the image which fell down from Jupiter," that "these facts were undeniable," and that "the new sect neither meant the pulling down of their church nor so much as offered to blaspheme or speak amiss of the goddess" (375). As Shaftesbury points out, the clerk "went pretty far," since "this, no doubt, was stretching the point sufficiently, as may be understood by the event in after time" (375). In after time, of course, the worship of Diana ceased. The town clerk's claims were a lie.

The "moderating art," therefore, seems relatively unconcerned with epistemological issues. Promoting the tolerant politics of "good humour" has no necessary connection to promoting truth. Equally significant is the passage's identification of anxieties about religious identity (not the fear of death) as the potential source of violence. The town clerk's particular lie matters, since he claims that the existing religious order is not threatened but will endure. The lie is a political response to the manipulation of the public's religious fears: it calms the Ephesians and robs the artisan "priests" of their power, enabling a peaceful religious transition (in this case from paganism to Christianity) that Shaftesbury considers natural were it not for the politics of fear. Since his examples often describe his own rhetorical practices, the town clerk's actions show Shaftesbury's concern not to refute religion with truth but rather to make it possible to hold onto religious identity more loosely by liberating believers from fear. Thus the direct implication of the town clerk's example for contemporary British politics would seem to be for the state/magistrate to sympathize with the public's anxiety over "the Church in danger" and then simply proclaim its safety. This might be "stretching the point sufficiently," but Shaftesbury thinks that it would undermine the political power of High Church Anglicans and defuse religious turmoil. Failing such a declaration, the cultural politics he pursues in *Characteristics* aims to transform religious feeling and render the public less vulnerable to the political exploitation of religious fear.

The subordination of truth to tolerance also appears in Shaftesbury's historical examples of political failures to manage religious passion with good humour. If, when Roman Catholic priests had faced the Reformation, they had not "as is usual, preferred the love of blood to all other passions, they might in a merrier way, perhaps, have evaded the greatest force of our reforming spirit" (16). Similarly, if the Jews had rejected the "sovereign argument" of "Crucify! Crucify!" and instead "taken the fancy to act ... puppet shows in [Jesus's] contempt" then they "might possibly have done our religion more harm than by all their other ways of severity" (16). Both of these provocative examples emphasize that sectarianism must be countered with good humour – not with violence, which produces more fear and therefore replicates absolutist politics, and not with reason, which ignores the meaning and politics of religious feeling. Basu also notes that these examples entail "either that ridicule could in fact defeat the truth, or that Christianity and Protestantism contained many untruths."[38] Or both.

Read in the light of his commentary on the magistrate, Shaftesbury's somewhat famous celebration of satirical puppetry in *A Letter Concerning Enthusiasm* further undercuts the claim that good humour is primarily an epistemological tool. Such puppet shows are a version of the magistrate's practice of soothing fears caused by "amazing prodigies" and threats to religious identity. The *Letter* thus objects to the persecution of some zealous French Huguenots who had recently arrived from

France on the grounds that it would only inflame religious zeal and violence.

> Their own mob [i.e., the Huguenot ministers] are willing to bestow kind blows upon them and fairly stone them now and then in the open street. … But how barbarous still and more than heathenishly cruel are we tolerating Englishmen! For, not contented to deny these prophesying enthusiasts the honour of a persecution, we have delivered them over to the cruelest contempt in the world. I am told, for certain, that they are at this very time the subject of a choice droll or puppet-show at Bartholomew Fair. There doubtless their strange voices and involuntary agitations are admirably well acted, by the motion of wires and inspiration of pipes. For the bodies of the prophets in their state of prophecy, being not in their own power but (as they say themselves), mere passive organs, actuated by an exterior force, have nothing natural or resembling real life in any of their sounds or motions, so that how awkwardly soever a puppet show may imitate other actions, it must needs represent this passion to the life. And while Bartholomew Fair is in possession of this privilege, I dare stand security to our national Church that no sect of enthusiasts, no new venders of prophecy or miracles, shall ever get the start or put her to the trouble of trying her strength with them, in any case.[39]

Shaftesbury's willingness to "stand security" to the established church might be as truthful as the town clerk's guarantees to the Ephesians, but the passage is usually read in earnest. While their fellow French Huguenots – shaped by an absolutist political regime – want to "stone [the enthusiasts] now and then," and while the Anglican Church is also interested in "trying her strength," the puppet show, Shaftesbury claims, enables the public to regulate itself. Self-regulation via puppetry is often linked to the ability of humour, wit, and satire to "correct abuses and excess" since "the exercise of raillery recalled adversaries to a more reasonable view."[40] Thus, raillery's power to puncture enthusiastic "imposture" enables autonomy and judgment. The passage, however, does not straightforwardly support either claim about a self-regulating public or the establishment of a "more reasonable view." Rather, Shaftesbury's appeal to and description of these entertainments demonstrates his trust in the coercive power of wit and raillery to affectively reposition readers and spectators in ways that – while manipulative – resist strengthening the absolutist politics of fear. Puppet satire regulates the public by producing a difference between fanatic Huguenots and tolerant British readers/spectators.[41]

The need to draw a boundary is motivated by the threat of contamination posed by a religious panic "raised in a multitude and conveyed by aspect, or, as it were by contact or sympathy ... The fury flies from face to face, and the disease is no sooner seen than caught."[42] To counter the force of this "social and communicative" passion, Shaftesbury links the prophets to mechanism, figuring their bodies as "mere passive organs ... hav[ing] nothing natural or resembling real life." Passive, unnatural, lifeless: the puppets' "involuntary" actions produced by "wires" and "pipes" imitate the enthusiasts' "passion to the life" (10). In Shaftesbury's representation of the puppet show, spectators dis-identify and distance themselves from the lifeless, mechanical behaviour of religious enthusiasts. Yet if satire is to prove more reliable than state authorized violence, these spectators – and Shaftesbury's readers – must also be mechanically moved. Insofar as satire urges us to reject a painful identification with the satiric object and to indulge the pleasure of identifying with the satirist, it works upon us prior to self-reflection. There is thus a tension between Shaftesbury's claims about humour's emancipatory power and the rhetorical action of satirical form, a tension between autonomy and Shaftesbury's paternal confidence in the power of satirical puppet shows to moderate religious passion. This suggests that such puppet shows are less "a potential opportunity for insight ... than simply an occasion for the mechanical application of values that we do not so much hold as are held by."[43] His description of puppetry depicts spectators at Bartholomew Fair as mistaking the action of satire for agency and the pleasure of satiric identification for judgment. Shaftesbury's satirical rhetoric in *Characteristics* invites readers to do the same. Good humour as satire, therefore, does not necessarily distance the subject from the "ardent solemnities of identity": wit and raillery can also plug us into the pleasurable, unreflective embrace of a new identity.[44] Since anxiety caused by the threat to religious identity can be exploited by the politics of fear (as the example of the Ephesians showed), Shaftesbury unsurprisingly turns to the rhetoric of satire to provide the consolations of a consolidated identity. Tolerance is made possible by alleviating this anxiety. The pleasure of derision also helps. This new identity, however, is not a secular separation from religion but rather a transformation of religious feeling: Shaftesbury's example of satirical puppet shows differentiates not between the religious and the secular but between melancholy enthusiastic Huguenots and good-humoured tolerant Anglicans.

In this case, Shaftesbury uses satire to transform a religious sensibility, undercutting a politics based on religious fear and jumpstarting a "natural" politics of tolerance based on religious good humour.[45] While his claims about the epistemological value of wit and raillery are prominently stated, he gives priority to good humour's political benefits.[46] First, he considers its political results as more certain and thus more valuable. He confidently predicts that good humour can promote religious tolerance, while acknowledging that it does not necessarily lead to truth. The examples he gives of polite conversations are marked both by "confusion" and "total uncertainty" as well as by an "improvement to the good humor of the company" that "set the appetite the keener to such conversations."[47] Shaftesbury clearly argues that good humour makes cognition more trustworthy, but the successes seem modest. While the transformation of religious fear into religious good humour has both epistemological and political benefits, epistemological progress cannot be the source of political progress. Both are independent possibilities of good humour, which underwrites a stable religio-political order for all and enables intellectual freedom for an open elite.[48] The management of religious passion is a political project prior to being an epistemological one, though part of Shaftesbury's politics is to emphasize the cognitive benefits of good humour.[49]

Second, Shaftesbury understands good humour as both a passion and a practice, as an enabling mood and as the cultivation of that disposition. To achieve the political and epistemological benefits of the passion of good humour requires the practice of good humour. This is one reason why Shaftesbury rejects "formal" modes of writing marked by "method" (e.g., sermons and academic treatises): whatever their content, they lack the rhetorical power to shift the passions away from the cultural politics of fear. Their form reproduces the discursive regime of the passions institutionalized by the court and the church and thus reinforces their power. Shaftesbury's *Characteristics,* therefore, works to rhetorically reconfigure the structure of religious passions in its audience, shifting moods away from the feeling and politics of "melancholy" and returning them to the "original passion" of religious good humour. It seeks to prime its readers to perceive and inhabit the world as more tolerant individuals. Because the passions politically condition perception and reasoning, they come first. Moreover, as a transformation of the background that orients virtuous practice, this priming act is itself also political.

Overall, Shaftesbury theorizes religious tolerance in terms of a dynamics of countervailing passions. He also explicitly links the political rationality of his tolerant public sphere to good humour, itself a transformation of religious passion. Religious tolerance for Shaftesbury, therefore, is not about separating religion from the state but about managing and shifting the meaning of religious feeling. His theorization of religious tolerance thus lays out not only the conceptual but also the affective contours within which the nascent practice of liberal tolerance makes sense: his conceptions of the public sphere and of "religion" are mutually reinforcing. Shaftesbury's analysis is especially useful, however, not for his particular model of religious tolerance – about which one might have many reservations – but for his general approach. His explicit attention to the passions distinguishes his defence of tolerance from dominant Neo-Kantian histories of its development and enables us to interrogate the taken-for-granted categorical schemes through which Enlightenment arguments about religious tolerance are usually disseminated.

Reading Locke after Shaftesbury makes it easier to apprehend the implicit background roles played by transformed regimes of sensation and passions in *A Letter Concerning Toleration*, both as preconditions for Locke's arguments and as motivations for tolerance, despite a rhetorical frame in the *Letter* that disavows them. Locke transforms Christianity into a tolerant "religion," not only by rendering it as "belief" – as is widely known – but also by rhetorically transforming the felt meaning of religion in support of religion as belief.[50] And while Locke attempts to anchor religious tolerance in such binaries as belief/practice, mind/body, and church/state, because Shaftesbury thinks between the terms of these binaries through the passion of good humour, his approach enables us to illuminate the discursive construction of the binaries themselves. As a passion, good humour both unsettles the distinction between belief and practice and belongs neither to mind nor body (nor strictly to the individual). Finally, Shaftesbury's focus on religious fear as a cognitively and politically debilitating pain that must be acknowledged, balanced, and transformed raises questions not only about how Locke handles anxiety in relation to religious identity but also how he promotes the resilience and endurance needed to counter the resentments of tolerating and being tolerated. Since tolerance for Shaftesbury is the effect of a "natural" religious passion of good humour, he seeks to strengthen and enable that passion. His approach to tolerance in terms of countervailing passions opens up questions about the relationship between pain and tolerance in terms of compensatory pleasures: "What compensations do tolerators get for self-restraint? What pleasures check their resentment?" or "To what extent do discourses of tolerance acknowledge and manage the humiliation of the tolerated?" One might also consider, as Tønder does, the vitalizing, world-making pleasures of pain itself. Locke's *Letter*, however, obscures these kinds of questions. His disavowal of religious pain has become central to our self-understanding in relation to the formation and meaning of religious tolerance, which tends to downplay or ignore the pain endured by tolerators and tolerated alike.[51] Yet if a tolerant society must somehow address the desire for the security of religious certainty and identity, then, as Shaftesbury recognizes through his investment in good humour, part of the rhetorical work of discourses of religious tolerance must be to make tolerance appealing.

Locke and Religious Tolerance: Sensing Proper Pains and Fears

If intellectualist theories of religious tolerance as a detached, dispassionate stance appeal to Locke's *A Letter Concerning Toleration*, his text is nonetheless a passionate performance. The first aim of its frequently visceral language is to turn readers against clerical authority. Locke condemns hypocritical "Fiery zealots," those with "a burning Zeal … burning, I say, literally with Fire and Faggot," who "persecute, torment, destroy, and kill other Men upon pretence of Religion."[52] He often stokes fears of men "striving for Power and Empire over one another" in the name of religion (25, 23). By framing tolerance not as a problem of religious difference but of hypocritical clergy driven by "irregular passions," the text directs readers' resentments and fears towards the menace of those who seek "to deprive them of their estates, maim them with corporal punishments, starve and torment them in noisome Prisons, and in the end even take away their lives" (25, 24).[53] The pretenses of the zealous promise worldly pain. The clergy should be feared not for their religious authority, which Locke in any case denies, but because they threaten human bodies and property. This effort to separate laity and clergy based on fears of worldly suffering is part of the *Letter's* larger rhetorical strategy to support the binaries of state/church, mind/body, and reason/passion by managing readers' fears, a project that depends both on defining what counts as pain and how those pains can be resolved. Its rhetoric aims to inculcate a sensibility for whom such binaries and religious tolerance would feel naturally reasonable.

This effort requires, however, appealing to and transforming both sides of these binaries. As Matthew Scherer notes, the *Letter's* argument for the separation of church and state "is buttressed at every turn by arguments that acknowledge and even intensify the interconnection of religion and politics."[54] For example, Locke's Christian rebuke of clerical rapaciousness redefines how religion should manifest itself publicly. Situating his text in the long history of Church reform, he builds upon late seventeenth-century reconceptualizations of Christianity that equate religion with morality: "The Business of True Religion … [is] the regulating of Mens Lives according to the Rules of Vertue and Piety."[55] He includes tolerance as part of this ethical code – "Toleration is the chief Characteristical Mark of the True Church" – and decries how prone the clergy are to violate it (23). Intolerant because irreligious, they not only threaten civil interests but also betray true Christianity. A "burning zeal" should "make War upon [one's] own Lusts and Vices," and not "bend all its Nerves … to the introducing of Ceremonies, or to the establishment of Opinions" (24). Locke's version of Christianity reduces articles of faith to mere opinion, and its emphasis on ethical practice has no place for public religious experience or communal ritual. As Elizabeth Pritchard emphasizes, "At the time of Locke's writing, religion's ability to affiliate bodies across vast spaces or to segregate them despite close quarters was unrivaled."[56] She argues that Locke responds to this power not by privatizing and excluding religion from the public sphere but by transforming its public forms. Religion is not the other of liberalism. Nor is liberalism a religion. Rather, religion and liberal politics are constructed in relation to one another. While scholarship has called for more attention to the affective dimensions of this transformation, the focus of analysis has remained mostly on concepts.[57] Approaching the formation of religious tolerance through Shaftesbury, however, suggests the importance of analysing the regime of sensation – the *Letter's* interpretation and invocation of pain and fear – that Locke rhetorically constructs as part of these conceptual transformations. This not only provides a fuller understanding of how Locke creates a new political rationality but also provides a sense of its limits, both in terms of its relevance to non-Western cultures and the extent to which Locke's rhetorical construction and appeal to sensation and the passions is both pre-reflective and political.

My argument builds on and qualifies Kirstie McClure's claim that Locke is enabled to "distinguish exactly the Business of Civil Government from that of Religion, and to settle the just Bounds that lie between the one and the other" by limiting suffering to our "Civil Interests," namely "Life, Liberty, Health, and Indolency of Body; and the possession of outward things such as Money, Lands, Houses, Furniture, and the like."[58] For McClure, drawing this boundary depends on an empiricist conceptualization of pain: "the *Letter* consistently inscribes factual considerations of worldly harm or benefit as the defining feature and boundary of a civil discourse that at once articulates and circumscribes the proper exercise of political power."[59] Worldly pain is "factual" because it is "represented as empirically knowable in a manner specifically denied with respect to the 'truth' of religious claims" (380).[60] An empiricist approach to pain thus provides the state with "a civil language of facticity" that is "neutral with regard to the 'truth,' of particular religious practices and to the theological idioms through which they are articulated."[61] Contrasting Locke's approach to pain with our current understandings of "the historically and culturally unstable signification of 'harm,'" McClure argues that the political logic of Locke's formulation of religious tolerance should not be extended to "incommensurable secular and social visions of the good life."[62] This is because "any exercise of civil power will necessarily privilege one or another politically invested interpretation of social harm."[63] Because she focuses on the inapplicability of Locke's theory of religious tolerance to today's struggles over difference, McClure does not pursue the possibility of reading Locke in terms of "the historically and culturally unstable signification of 'harm'" that her argument opens up. His text, however, redistributes and rearranges suffering. It conceptualizes and seeks to inculcate a new regime of sensation that is the condition for the legal justification and practice of religious tolerance.[64] He moves away from understanding religious difference in terms of conflicting truth claims not by appealing to the truth of a neutral space where real, empirical, secular pain exists but by shifting the ground from determining the truth content of religion to interpreting and transforming the felt meaning of pain. The text is structured by the fearful representation of bodily and religious pains and the promise of their relief.

In tandem with its attack on the clergy as a threat to bodies and property, the *Letter* represents the experience of religious difference as painless. Tolerant subjects fear for their "Civil Interests" but not for their religious identity: religious difference is met with emotional indifference. As McClure argues, state empiricism interprets intersubjective religious pain as "literally immaterial in both civil and epistemological terms," and this determination of what counts as pain is partly how the text draws the boundary between church and state.[65] In terms of their religion, other people are not Hell but adiaphora:

> If Christians are to be admonished that they abstain from all manner of Revenge, even after repeated Provocations and multiplied Injuries, how much more ought they who suffer nothing, who have had no harm done to them, forbear Violence and abstain from all manner of ill usage towards those from whom they have received none.[66]

Although Locke links religious identity to painful provocation and violent conflict in the *Two Tracts on Government*, the *Letter* argues that religious difference causes no harm or suffering.[67] Granted, in this passage Locke defines tolerance as abstaining from "Revenge," implying that he expects readers to experience religious difference as a provocation. But the *Letter's* explicit account of the experience of religious difference buries any acknowledgment that "to become tolerant is not only to endure the pain of something or someone of which or whom we disapprove; it is also to endure the anxieties and hardship that arise from resisting the desire to eliminate the tolerated's presence in a situation of difference and disagreement."[68] Such endurance seems particularly significant in relation to religious difference, since one's sense of the ultimate meaning and value of life, communal ties, and perhaps even one's salvation are called into question. Instead of considering tolerance as the endurance of any kind of pain associated with others' religion, Locke calls attention to the "pains and industry" required for "the comfortable support of our Lives."[69] Claims to suffering based on religious identity are reduced to hypocritical attempts to cover self-interest: while some may claim to be injured by "the Contagion of Idolatry, Superstition, and Heresie," they "bear [it] most patiently" unless "strengthened by the Civil Power" (33). Religious intolerance masks worldly desire; its political dangers are linked not to religious anxieties but to fears about self-preservation and the violation of private property. Locke's *Letter* explicitly argues against intersubjective religious pains.

The *Letter* renders religious difference innocuous partly by building upon Protestant definitions of Christianity as intellectual assent to creeds:

> If a *Roman Catholick* believe that to be the body of Christ, which another man calls Bread, he does no injury thereby to his Neighbor. If a Jew do not believe the New Testament to be the Word of God, he does not thereby alter anything in men's Civil Rights. (46)

As the repetition of "believe" in this passage emphasizes, pain-free religious difference is propositional. Beliefs cannot cause bodily pain or property damage. Distinguishing between mind and body to support his demarcation of church and state, Locke argues that the beliefs of others can have no effect on the body and, more famously, the reverse: "such is the nature of the Understanding, that it cannot be compell'd to the belief of any thing by outward force" (27). Defining religion as belief justifies the claim that religious difference cannot cause bodily pain and that bodily pain cannot cause people to change their religion. Locke's separation of church and state transforms and appeals to a regime of sensation. As Tønder argues in relation to Thomas M. Scanlon's invocation of the principle of autonomy as the foundation for tolerance, Locke's binaries entail "a framing of the experience of pain that citizens must internalize" before they can be invoked.[70] The body has nothing to do with religion as belief, and yet this conception of religion entails and is supported by claims about what bodies and minds feel.

A Relish for Tolerance: The Pleasurable Pain of Privatizing Religion

Enabling a dispassionate stance towards religious others, Locke's disavowal of intersubjective religious pain makes his text amenable to Neo-Kantian approaches to religious tolerance. But if the *Letter* downplays suffering related to religious identity, its rhetoric heightens individuals' fears for salvation:

> the *principal Consideration*, and which absolutely determines this Controversie [the power of the magistrate to enforce religious belief], is this. Although the Magistrate's Opinion in religion be sound ... yet if I be not thoroughly persuaded thereof in my own mind, there will be no safety for me in following it.[71]

The curious word here is "safety." The passage focuses on individuals' feelings about their "opinion" – whether or not it makes them feel safe. Even if the magistrate's religious opinions are true, this makes no difference to an individual's religious anxiety. Locke appeals to the religious fears of his readers, not their capacity for judgment. Feeling safe is more important than possessing the truth.

Locke declares that "the highest obligation" and "our utmost Care, Application, and Diligence" should be to ensure our "Eternal Happiness" (38, 47). But if the text emphasizes individuals' private religious fears, it also places the resolution of those fears completely within the individual's power:

> every man [has] the care of his own eternal happiness, the attainment whereof can neither be facilitated by another man's industry, nor can the loss of it turn to another man's prejudice, nor the hope of it be forced from him by any external violence. (47)

One's salvation cannot be assisted by others, the failure to obtain it does not harm others, and it can be achieved despite the violence of others. It is a private matter, indifferent to others' religious concerns: "the care of each man's salvation belongs only to himself" (47). Locke isolates religious pain as individual and incapable of spreading, but not hopeless. If one cannot will what to believe, and if one cannot be forced to believe, one can nonetheless sense with certainty how one feels about one's belief. For Locke, religious reasoning is a form of reflective judgment. We cannot know the truth of our religious beliefs, but we can know with certainty the truth of our feelings about them. And this is the truth, Locke claims, that matters most to God. Locke appears to have great confidence that individuals will manage their religious feelings in ways that will assuage their fears for salvation. After all, "everyone is orthodox to himself" (23). Everyone will believe in ways that will lessen their private pains and fears. And if they do not, the fault and responsibility is entirely theirs. Both the fear and its resolution are private. Locke's reform of religion draws upon and deepens Protestant subjectivism, both conceptually and affectively. As in Shaftesbury, the goal is to manage religious fear, although Locke does not oppose fear to good humour but instead heightens fear and harnesses its theological resolution for political ends. He offers no Shaftesburian raptures: the overwhelming urgency and ultimate uncertainty of religious truth will always goad the religious with uneasiness. For Locke, the right kind and amount of fear (subjective religious uneasiness combined with fears for the safety of one's body and property) produces not violence but tolerance.

The emotional satisfaction provided by authentic belief permeates the *Letter's* analysis of the relationship between salvation and truth:

> Whatever profession we make, to whatever outward worship we conform, if we are not fully satisfied in our own mind that the one is true and the other well pleasing unto God, such profession and such practice, far from being any furtherance, are indeed great obstacles to our salvation. (26)

Again, Locke's theology is not concerned with the objective truth of one's "profession" but with being "fully satisfied in our own mind."

The phrase is suitably ambiguous, suggesting both satisfactory judgment and emotional satisfaction. Overall, Locke's secular separation of church and state is premised on a religiosity so passionate that it overrides cognitive concerns. The definition of religion as private belief does not mean emotional distance from one's religious practice but rather emotional intensification, both in terms of the urgent need to attend closely to one's feelings about one's beliefs and in terms of the intense respect religion deserves from others. Christianity is privatized as religion in the *Letter* by tamping down intersubjective religious passion in the public sphere while intensifying it as private experience.

But how can religious indifference towards others ground a public respect for religion? Locke justifies "the supreme and absolute authority of judging for oneself" in religious matters "because nobody else is concerned in it, nor can receive any prejudice from his conduct therein" (47). He argues for autonomy not by urging respect for the dignity of others based on their ability to reason autonomously about their salvation but by making religious judgments intersubjectively irrelevant – and thus politically risk-free. The practice of tolerance as indifference towards the salvation of others is grounded in Locke's disavowal of intersubjective religious pain: the text's definition and invocation of pain justifies and motivates individual sovereignty over their religion. Likewise, autonomy matters for the individual not because it enables the apprehension of truth but because only autonomy can offer the promise of addressing religious fear. It is a politico-theological balm. The *Letter* offers religious freedom not in response to our dignity but in response to our fears: its definition of pain motivates both subjectivized religion as belief and intersubjective tolerance as indifference.

Locke's text, therefore, cannot be invoked as a forerunner to a Neo-Kantian paradigm of mutual perspective taking oriented towards understanding. The insularity of the passions in Locke's conception of religion does not orient tolerant subjects towards intersubjective understanding or even reason-giving in the context of the acknowledgment of the "finitude of reason."[72] If Locke's text cultivates respect for others, it is not based on a "basic right to justification" that persons "owe to each other" because others are "reasonable and worthy of being given adequate reasons."[73] Instead, tolerance is an intersubjectively indifferent, politically harmless practice of feeling one's way towards eternal happiness, of privately working out one's salvation in fear and trembling. Locke grounds tolerance not on communicative rationality but on the individually shared religious fear that conditions that rationality.

Tolerant subjects are one not in their beliefs or values but in their passions: individually feeling together in fear and relief, they are distanced but not dispassionate.

Locke's text not only teaches us what and whom to fear, it also invokes that fear and then resolves it in ways that support his conceptualization of religious tolerance. James Tully has tracked in Locke's work a shift from theorizing assent as governed by evidence to its determination by "custom, education, and fashion."[74] Neither "a natural disposition ... to the true or the good" nor "the weight of the evidence" govern belief. Instead, it is "governed by acquired dispositions."[75] Background dispositions can be transformed because "the relish of the mind is malleable like that of the body."[76] Tully defines "relish" as "the mechanism that brings absent goods within one's view of happiness, renders them desirable, and thus disposes the agent to them."[77] Another name for such a mechanism is rhetoric. Locke's repeated invocation of fears for salvation gains added significance in the light of Tully's observation that "even the infinite pleasures and pain of heaven and hell can be contemplated without desire or aversion until a person has cultivated an uneasiness for heaven and made it part of his or her happiness."[78] Locke's text seeks to rhetorically provide a "relish" – "the acquired mental habit in virtue of which specific ways of thinking and acting are pleasant to the agent" – for religious tolerance.[79] The *Letter* is an effort to rhetorically jumpstart those habits by positioning readers within its framework for self-understanding and the felt meaning of pain. Building on Tully's analysis of Locke's educational theory, Pritchard contends that Locke's pedagogy "is designed to yield religious subjectivities who are not susceptible to injury or offense, who are not brittle and unyielding but open-minded, who can tolerate and even enjoy exposure to the global circulation of religions as ideas, fashions, or commodities."[80] This description of Locke's interest in education also captures the *Letter's* rhetorical work.

Both Shaftesbury's and Locke's arguments for religious tolerance involve a shift from questions of truth to questions of feeling, a shift that makes practices of reason politically valuable for their affective and not their epistemological function. For Locke, what matters religiously (i.e., the efficacy of belief) and thus politically (i.e., preventing violence and preserving property) is not the truth of what one believes but what one feels about what one believes. And just as the shifting of affects, of mood management, was a political act in Shaftesbury – but one that occurred outside of and prior to public reason – so in

Locke: the privatization of religious judgment and the propositionalization of religion as the rational site of agonistic dispute rely on and reproduce a prior political shift in affect. Thus the political separation of church and state is established on the pre-reflective but political rhetorical definition and invocation of the passions. While the text places the agonistic frame of democracy at the level of autonomy, this hides the already politicized regime of sensation and passion that enables autonomy. In both Locke and Shaftesbury, politics appears to operate within a rational space of dialogue and criticism, but such forms of communicative rationality are already politically determined. For both, the pre-reflective felt meaning of religious passion that these texts inculcate enables the formation of religious tolerance. Because these background conditions motivate and structure communication and judgment, they also limit the ability to take up the perspectives of others. In Locke's *Letter*, insofar as fear directs attention and motivates reasoning, his text links being reasonable to inhabiting a disposition of fear that orients our assessment of ourselves and others. As Shaftesbury contends, such a fearful disposition might come with limitations. Indeed, Locke's *Letter* teaches us the difficulty of practising tolerance as mutual recognition, since the regime of sensation and the framework of the passions that his text promotes already put in place a particular understanding of religion and communicative rationality. To extend the democratic potential of religious tolerance, therefore, requires expanding "the conditions of contestations and deliberation" to include the politics of the pre-reflective regimes of sensation and passion within which discourses of tolerance make sense.[81]

The shift to feeling also engineers the resilience necessary for tolerance by providing the individual with certainty. Tolerators endure others because their religious security does not depend on others. In Locke's *Letter*, the religious identity of the tolerant self cannot be fundamentally threatened, but the text nonetheless addresses such threats by locating the resources of resilience needed to endure difference in the subjective certainty of sentiments about salvation. For both Locke and Shaftesbury, the risks related to tolerance are managed independently of encounters with religious others. As Nancy Yousef has argued in relation to Shaftesbury's theory of moral sentiment, the "feeling for others he names 'natural affection' appears troublingly dissociated from the perception of others."[82] Affective certainty substitutes for the risks of intersubjectivity. Likewise, the priority Shaftesbury gives to "good humour" renders tolerance less an intersubjective enterprise than an "autonomy [that] seems to arise, or be wrested from, epistemological premises [the certainty of feeling] which surrender the aspiration to intersubjective understanding."[83] Locke's account of religious tolerance is similarly structured. Insofar as his text acknowledges that one might feel threatened by religious difference, it anchors the subject in a religious identity confirmed by the certainty of sentiment. What enables tolerance is not a respect for the other's autonomy but one's sense of security in how certain one feels about one's beliefs. Locke's text does not orient the tolerant self towards a dependency on others since this would involve politically dangerous intersubjective risks. And yet although Locke seeks to make intersubjectivity less volatile, his position cannot be characterized as intellectualist or dispassionate. Tolerance in Locke is a pleasurable pain oriented to a particular politics but not to other people.[84] As in Shaftesbury, Locke trusts in the certainty of subjective religious sentiment to engineer a tolerant society.

Religious Reason in Public

Yet if religion cannot harm or be harmed by others – if it lacks any motive for intersubjectivity – why communicate about it? Locke separates religious feeling from truth claims so thoroughly that it is unclear what would motivate an individual to engage with another's religious difference. He makes it clear that civil society has no religious interest: "the temporal good and outward prosperity of the society … is the sole reason of men's entering into society, and the only thing they seek and aim at in it."[85] Religious society is a contradiction in terms, and Locke denies that it offers any social benefits that might be lost:

> every one joins himself voluntarily to that Society in which he believes he has found that Profession and Worship which is truly acceptable to God. The hopes of Salvation, as it is the only cause of his entrance into that Communion, so it can be the only reason of his stay there. (28)

These hopes are fundamentally private: church members are linked by a contingent agreement on creeds and practice, but there is no emotional connection between them. The flip side of no intersubjective religious pain is that there is no intersubjective religious pleasure. Even excommunication has no traumatic consequences, since it merely entails losing "the participation of some certain things which the society communicated to its members" (31). The diction of "certain things" discounts the significance of those things. Indeed, Locke even denies "Civil Injury" to an excommunicant's loss of bread and wine, since it "was not bought with his, but other men's Money" (31).

Pritchard explains Locke's commitment to religion publicly "circulating as argument, sign, and fashion" as part of an effort to achieve "just enough distance from vulnerable bodies to allow those bodies a wider range of social, economic, and political intercourse."[86] Treating religion as a set of concepts enables emotional distance, reducing "the occasion of injury, profanation, and pollution."[87] Pritchard's insight paradoxically links the public manifestation of religion in Locke to limiting pains and fears related to threatened religious identities: a problem that the text explicitly denies is a problem. Although the *Letter* does not explicitly address the political danger posed by threats to religious identity that Locke raises in the *Two Tracts* and elsewhere, it implicitly addresses such threats by transforming public religion into discourse and thus weakening passionate attachments to religious identities.[88] Locke also limits those risks by making religious debate in the public sphere a Christian virtue:

> I would not have this understood, as if I mean thereby to condemn all charitable Admonitions, and affectionate Endeavors to reduce Men from Errors; which are indeed the greatest Duty of a Christian. Any one may employ as many Exhortations and Arguments as he pleases towards the promoting of another man's Salvation.[89]

Anyone "may" but no one must. Locke's tolerance opens up the possibility of intersubjective reasoning but does not require it. Only Christian charity, for Locke, can motivate public reasoning about religion. Just as good humour in Shaftesbury was a theological imperative that structured the rationality of the public sphere, Locke's practice of public reasoning about religion is understood as an exemplary Christian practice. Locke's text reforms Christianity publicly and privately in ways that advance both the aims of theology and governance. It does not downplay the religious in favour of the worldly but moves forward on two interrelated fronts: "A Good Life, in which consists not the least part of Religion and true Piety, concerns also the Civil Government: and in it lies the safety both of Mens Souls, and of the Commonwealth" (46).[90] Promoted by an appeal to Christian duty, public religious discourse is not about subordinating religion to the secular but about managing anxieties related to religious identity.

Fears for safety relating both to "Mens Souls, and of the Commonwealth" unify the divided concerns for "Eternal Happiness" and "the Defence of ... Temporal Goods." Ingrid Creppell argues that Locke's *Letter* transforms a Christian identity to a "plural or multiple self."[91] She sees the separations between mind/body, public/private, state/church as productive of a "psychological plurality," a subjectivity more amenable to religious difference because its own identity is fractured.[92] Such divisions, however, are premised on a philosophical anthropology in which the unity of individuals and of society is founded on the passions. Behind the conceptual binaries that structure Locke's arguments for religious tolerance lies the unifying sensation of fear.

Towards a More Tolerant Tolerance

A Shaftesburian framework for analysing the formation of Enlightenment religious tolerance not only wrests Locke free from teleological readings that place him on the ineluctable road to Kant, it also reminds us that religious autonomy is just one form and legacy of Enlightenment tolerance. *Characteristics* challenges us to tolerate a more pluralist history of Enlightenment tolerance. Shaftesbury's focus on the transformation of religious sensibilities, moreover, suggests the importance of analysing how conceptions of tolerance are organized by background regimes of sensation and passion not only in Locke but elsewhere. His work thus contributes to "expos[ing] the intellectualist orientation to politics to the plurality embedded in its own history."[93] Yet because it is reassuring to hold onto tolerance as a sign of political – if not epistemological – progress and as a move away from the violent barbarism of the past, examining the conditions of its justification and its moral and political ambiguities can be annoying. Moreover, its moral desirability can also make religious tolerance easier to celebrate than interrogate. Shaftesbury's work is useful partly because its foregrounding of the interpretation of the passions teaches us how to read religious tolerance. It also invites a subtler questioning, a reflection on how we continue to inhabit a felt meaning of religion that preserves the contours of the secular and tolerance with which we identify.

Overall, reorienting our approach to the formation of religious tolerance from Locke to Shaftesbury provides a wedge for a more sensorial approach to the formation of Enlightenment religious tolerance, an approach that is alert to the politics of the pre-reflective. A Shaftesburian focus on mood management also invites analysis of how discourses of tolerance address the pains related to religious difference and the resentments related to tolerating and being tolerated. Significantly, both Locke and Shaftesbury locate the resources of resilience and endurance outside of intersubjectivity. Finally, because tolerance requires defining and managing pains and passions, a conceptual analysis of religious tolerance must always be incomplete, as must historical contextualizations that neglect to engage with the rhetorically productive powers of texts.

Shaftesbury's broadly hermeneutical approach to the pains, pleasures, and rationality of religious tolerance also implies that the Enlightenment may not offer a definitive, one size fits all solution to global religious violence. For we have not arrived through this Shaftesburian criticism of an "intellectualist" Locke to some universal calculus of pleasure and pain that applies to all times and places. As the contingent religious premises and passions of these two thinkers demonstrate, the meanings of pleasure and pain are not known in advance. In both Locke and Shaftesbury, moreover, calculations designed to promote tolerance are as rife for the necessity of politics as they are for the potential of peace. Alternative formations of religious passions and sensibilities, such as might be found outside of Christianity and "religion," could form the basis for equally reasonable, alternative forms of religious tolerance. While discourses of tolerance constructed in relation to "religion" may make deep sense for us, they may not for others.[94] An awareness of how deeply regimes of sensation and feeling structure and limit communication appears necessary for a more self-reflective secularism and the possibility of Neo-Kantian mutual perspective taking. Most optimistically, a postsecular genealogy of religious tolerance might open the possibility of thinking past the categories of religion and the secular, or at least of being open to their continued transformation. Such an openness would require the examination of these categories from within the Western tradition and from without. All recent writing about religious tolerance usually ends up quoting a passage from Jacques Derrida, and I will not resist a reiteration: "Let us suppose it agreed upon, among ourselves, that all of us here are for 'tolerance,' even if we have not been assigned the mission of promoting it, practising it, or founding it. We would be here to try to think what 'tolerance' could henceforth be."[95] Reading Locke – and Enlightenment discourses of tolerance more generally – after Shaftesbury not only expands our ability to rethink what tolerance could be but also suggests the importance of reflecting on how we feel our way to such a future tolerance.

NOTES

1 On the recent reception of Locke's *Letter*, see Lars Tønder, "Toleration Without Tolerance: Enlightenment and the Image of Reason," in *Political Theologies: Public Religions in a Post-Secular World*, ed. Hent de Vries and Lawrence E. Sullivan (New York: Fordham University Press, 2006), 330.
2 See, for example, Jürgen Habermas, "Religious Tolerance – The Pacemaker for Cultural Rights," *Philosophy* 79.1 (2004): 6. Core scholarship on the historical formation of religious tolerance includes W.K. Jordan, *The Development of Religious Toleration in England*, 4 vols. (Cambridge: Harvard University Press, 1932–40); Ingrid Creppell, *Toleration and Identity: Foundations in Early Modern Thought* (New York: Routledge, 2003); Perez Zagorin, *How the Idea of Religious Toleration Came to the West* (Princeton: Princeton University Press, 2003); Ole Peter Grell, Jonathan I. Israel, and Nicholas Tyacke, eds., *From Persecution to Toleration: The Glorious Revolution and Religion in England* (Oxford: Clarendon Press, 1991). Key philosophical approaches include John Rawls, *Political Liberalism* (New York: Columbia University Press, 1993); Susan Mendus, ed., *Justifying Toleration: Conceptual and Historical Perspectives* (Cambridge: Cambridge University Press, 1988); David Heyd, ed., *Toleration: An Elusive Virtue* (Princeton: Princeton University Press, 1996); Michael Walzer, *On Toleration* (New Haven: Yale University Press, 1999); and Rainer Forst, "Toleration, Justice and Reason," in *The Culture of Toleration in Diverse Societies: Reasonable Tolerance*, ed. Catriona McKinnon and Dario Castiglione (Manchester: Manchester University Press, 2003), 71–85.
3 James Tully lays out this epistemological framework, though he sees it as supplemented by new habitual conduct, in "Governing Conduct," in *An Approach to Political Philosophy: Locke in Contexts*, ed. James Tully (Cambridge: Cambridge University Press, 1993), 192–6.
4 Judith Butler, "The Sensibility of Critique: Response to Asad and Mahmood," in *Is Critique Secular? Blasphemy, Injury, and Free Speech* (Berkeley: University of California Press, 2009), 115.
5 I restrict the term "feeling" to private sensation prior to its determinative judgment. "Emotion" refers to a determinate feeling. I use the term "affect," to include the communicative force of a feeling. Since so much of Shaftesbury's cultural politics turns on the interpretation of feeling and affect, I use the word "passion" to designate an emotion that has been interpreted and placed in an overarching taxonomy.
6 Lars Tønder, *Tolerance: A Sensorial Orientation to Politics* (Oxford: Oxford University Press, 2013), 13. I hope the extent of my reliance on this groundbreaking work is obvious.

7 Ibid., 6.
8 Ibid., 46, 118.
9 Ibid., 95.
10 Ibid., 76, 93. Tønder's analysis of pain and tolerance seems to hover between a model of compensation, in which "pleasurable pains" and "the range of opportunities and relationships presenting themselves as a consequence of acting tolerantly" provide motives for tolerance and resources of resilience, and a model that affirms pain insofar as it "embodies *both* a transition from a state of more power to a state of less power … *and* a creative, perhaps even affirmative power defined in its own right" (82, 10). Tønder seems most invested in the latter, since he wants the resources for engaging with difference and for enduring resentments caused either by self-constraint or the slights of being tolerated to be located in the experience of tolerance itself. He argues for tolerance as an outward turn towards intersubjectivity, an "empowerment [that] stages relationships between tolerator and tolerated" (11). Both Locke and Shaftesbury, however, locate resources of resilience and endurance outside of the encounter with the other.
11 Saba Mahmood, "Religious Reason and Secular Affect: An Incommensurable Divide?," *Critical Inquiry* 35.4 (2009): 64. Cf. Talal Asad, *Formations of the Secular: Christianity, Islam, Modernity* (Stanford: Stanford University Press, 2003), 1–2, 14, 25; "Thinking about Religion, Belief, and Politics," *The Cambridge Companion to Religious Studies*, ed. Robert A. Orsi (Cambridge: Cambridge University Press, 2012), 38–9.
12 For both thinkers, the meanings of sensation and feeling stand in a liminal relation to mind and body and are less rigid than concepts. As such, these sites are more flexible and powerful locations of transformation, providing an anterior matrix to the rhetorical conceptualization of religion and arguments for tolerance. On the religious elements of Locke's argument for toleration, see John Dunn, *The Political Thought of John Locke: An Historical Account of the Argument of the "Two Treatises of Government"* (Cambridge: Cambridge University Press, 1969), Jeremy Waldron, *God, Locke, and Equality: Christian Foundations of Locke's Political Thought* (Cambridge: Cambridge University Press, 2002), and Micah Schwartzman, "The Relevance Of Locke's Religious Arguments For Toleration," *Political Theory*, 33.5 (2005): 678–705. For the ultimate historical contextualization of Locke's letters on toleration, see John Marshall, *John Locke, Toleration, and Early Enlightenment Culture* (Cambridge: Cambridge University Press, 2010).
13 Approaching the formation of the secular through the trope of conversion, Matthew Scherer's *Beyond Church and State: Democracy, Secularism, and*

Conversion (Cambridge: Cambridge University Press, 2013) examines how the trope works to retroactively construct an absolute break "between a Christian past and a secular present" that can turn us away from an awareness of deep transformation: "figuring secularism as conversion shows how the image of separation constitutes the authorized surface of a deeper, crystalline process of transformation" (74, 3). My analysis of the rhetorical transformation of the formative background of sensation and passion in Locke seeks to build on Scherer's examination of how conversion enables what we might call the inertia of the religious within the secular, since the affective frameworks these texts put in place may continue to animate the practice of religious tolerance even in the absence of their conceptual analogues. I am also obviously indebted to Scherer's emphasis on secular "comportment" and his focus on how "the *Letter's* rhetorical construction reflects its participation within the ongoing processes of conversion that were reshaping religious and political sensibilities in its time" (78).

14 Hent de Vries, "Global Religion and the Postsecular Challenge," in *Habermas and Religion*, ed. Craig Calhoun, Eduardo Mendieta, and Jonathan VanAntwerpen (Malden, MA: Polity Press, 2013), 204. Cf. Habermas's call for a genealogy of postsecular reason that would urge "secular thought to engage in a reflection on its own origins" and thus "break with the self-immunizing mindset that closes itself against any historical reflection on the context out of which it developed." *Essay on Faith and Knowledge*, forthcoming. Qtd. in Amy Allen, "Having One's Cake and Eating It Too: Habermas's Genealogy of Postsecular Reason," in ibid., 136.

15 Scherer, *Beyond Church and State*, 4.

16 Anthony Ashley Cooper, Third Earl of Shaftesbury, *Characteristics of Men, Manners, Opinions, Times*, ed. Lawrence E. Klein (Cambridge: Cambridge University Press, 1999), 7–9, 29–38. For useful historical contextualizations of Shaftesbury's claims about wit and truth, see Patrick Müller, "Ridentem dicere verum quid vetat: Shaftesbury, Horatian Satire, and the Cultural (Ab)Uses of Laughter," *RSÉAA XVII–XVIII* 70 (2013): 47–72; and Roger D. Lund, *Ridicule, Religion and the Politics of Wit in Augustan England* (Surrey: Ashgate Publishing, 2013), 127–54. On wit's relation to tolerance, see Sammy Basu, "'Woe unto you that laugh now!': Humor and Toleration in Overton and Shaftesbury," in *Religious Toleration: "The Variety of Rites" from Cyrus to Defoe*, ed. John Christian Laursen (New York: St Martin's Press, 1999), 147–72.

17 Lawrence E. Klein, "Introduction," *Characteristics of Men, Manners, Opinions, Times*, xviii. See also Klein's seminal study, *Shaftesbury and the Culture of*

Politeness: Moral Discourse and Cultural Politics in Early Eighteenth-Century England (Cambridge: Cambridge University Press, 1994), which describes Shaftesbury's conception of conversation in Habermasian terms as "an ideal speech situation." *Culture of Politeness*, 98. Cf., 12–14, 96–9, 195–8.

18 Basu, "Humor and Toleration," 159. While he notes that humour also provides a "dispositional finesse" insofar as it "defuses" and "gives vent" to enthusiasm, Basu focuses on the power of humour to distance us from epistemologically disruptive passions and to enable sympathy: "humor facilitates the dialogic relationships vital to tolerant liberal politics" and "inclines one toward sympathy" (159–60, 165, 160).

19 Shaftesbury, Preface to *Select Sermons of Benjamin Whichcot*, in *Complete Works, Selected Letters and Posthumous Writings: in English with Parallel German Translation* [Sämtliche Werke, ausgewählte Briefe und nachgelassene Schriften in englischer Sprache mit paralleler deutscher Übersetzung], ed. Gerd Hemmerich and Wolfram Benda (Stuttgart-Bad Cannstatt: Frommann-Holzboog, 1981–), vol. 2, pt. 4, 50.

20 Basu, "Humor and Toleration," 159. Mary Astell criticizes the limits of Shaftesbury's conception of dialogic relationships and public reason in *Bart'lemy Fair: or, an Enquiry after Wit* (London, 1709). On the rhetorical force of satire, see Fredric V. Bogel's *The Difference Satire Makes: Rhetoric and Reading from Jonson to Byron* (Ithaca: Cornell University Press, 2001).

21 Jürgen Habermas, *The Structural Transformation of the Public Sphere: An Inquiry into a Category of Bourgeois Society*, trans. Thomas Burger and Frederick Lawrence (Cambridge, MA: MIT Press, 1989). Cf. David Zaret, "Religion, Science, and Printing in the Public Spheres in Seventeenth-Century England," in *Habermas and the Public Sphere*, ed. Craig Calhoun (Cambridge, MA: MIT Press, 1992), 212–35. In response to the continued presence of religion in modernity, Habermas has taken a postsecular turn that not only pursues a more reflexive understanding of Enlightenment rationality through a genealogy of postsecular reason but also calls for the translation of the normative content of religious language into secular terms as part of an effort to reinvigorate democratic struggles. See most recently his "Reply to My Critics," trans. Ciarin Cronin, in *Habermas and Religion*, ed. Craig Calhoun, Eduardo Mendieta, and Jonathan VanAntwerpen (Malden, MA: Polity Press, 2013), 347–90.

22 Basu, "Humor and Toleration," 161.

23 Charles Taylor, *A Secular Age* (Cambridge, MA: Belknap Press of Harvard University Press, 2007), 22. Talal Asad argues similarly in *Formations of the Secular* (Stanford: Stanford University Press, 2003): "'the secular'

should not be thought of as the space in which real human life gradually emancipates itself from the controlling power of 'religion' and thus achieves the latter's relocation. It is this assumption that allows us to think of religion as 'infecting' the secular domain or as replicating within it the structure of theological concepts … Secularism doesn't simply insist that religious practice and belief be confined to a space where they cannot threaten political stability or the liberties of 'free-thinking' citizens. Secularism builds on a particular conception of the world" (191).

24 Perhaps in response to J.C.D. Clark's revisionist historiography, Klein resists a secular approach: Shaftesbury's cultural era was "neither secular nor secularized but within a regime in which religion has been subjected to new political and intellectual disciplines" (*Culture of Politeness*, 9).

25 Shaftesbury, *Characteristics*, 10–11.

26 Shaftesbury first criticizes Hobbes in his Preface to *Select Sermons of Benjamin Whichcot* (1698), which also links Hobbes's philosophical anthropology to the Anglican Church: "It must be confess'd, that it has been the Reproach of some Sects of Christians amongst us; that their Religion appear'd to be, in a manner, opposite to Good-nature; and founded in Moroseness, Selfishness, and Ill-will to Mankind" (52). His fullest criticism of Hobbes appears in *Characteristics*, 42–5. For this effort, see Alfred Owen Aldridge, "Shaftesbury and the Deist Manifesto," *Transactions of the American Philosophical Society* 41.2 (1951): 311.

27 Albert O. Hirschman, *The Passions and the Interests: Political Arguments for Capitalism before Its Triumph* (Princeton, Princeton University Press, 1997), 20–31.

28 Shaftesbury, *Characteristics*, 11.

29 Shaftesbury considered religious enthusiasm "natural" and noted "a wondrous disposition in mankind towards supernatural objects" (24).

30 Cf. Shaftesbury's discussion of Francis Bacon seeing religious fear as deriving "from an imperfection in the creation, make or natural constitution of man" (368).

31 For a reading that links this allegory of priestly accumulation (see *Characteristics*, 356–79) as registering the accumulation of capital, see Jordana Rosenberg's *Critical Enthusiasm: Capital Accumulation and the Transformation of Religious Passion* (Oxford: Oxford University Press, 2011): "In pathologizing theocratic accumulation as symbolic of a distant past … Shaftesbury periodized the contemporary English state. That this periodization unfurls around the allegorical figure of theocratic

accumulation reflects England's grapplings with regulating vast accumulations of capital, both at home and in the colonies" (58).

32 Shaftesbury, *Characteristics*, 342. The passage is both a speculative history and an allegory of the practices of the Roman Catholic Church and the Anglican Church, figured by Egypt and Israel. See Klein, *Culture of Politeness*, 169–74.

33 Müller links Shaftesbury's "good humour" to Whichcote's "good nature": "The *first* thing in Religion," says Whichcote, "is, to refine a Man's Temper: And the *second*, to govern his Practice" (*Select Sermons*, 290). Properly understood, "*Religion* produceth a sweet and gracious Temper of Mind; *calm* in its self, and *loving to Men*. It causeth a *Universal Benevolence* and *Kindness* to Mankind." Having listed the several virtues included in his notion of "*GOOD-NATURE*," Whichcote concludes that religion proper "causeth the greatest Serenity and Chearfulness to the Mind; and prevents groundless Fears, foolish Imaginations, needless Suspicions, and dastardly Thoughts" (*Select Sermons*, 294). ("Ridentem dicere," 52).

34 The priority given to "good humour" and the need for an appropriate conception of the universe to justify it also appears in Tønder's claim, for example, that the world's richness depends on "an attitude of critical engagement and presumptive generosity" (*Sensorial Orientation*, 122).

35 On the influence of the passions on perception, see *Characteristics*, 228–9, 422–3.

36 I resist designating Shaftesbury's approach to religious tolerance as "secular" or "religious" because I am not trying to unmask the secular as religious. Rather, by trying to keep the master terms of "secular" and "religious" in abeyance and resisting the need to classify Shaftesbury as one or the other, it seems possible to take a step towards a postsecular engagement with the Enlightenment. I am inspired here by Saba Mahmood's resistance to "simply posing a 'yes' or 'no' answer" to the query "Is Critique Secular?" at the close of her essay "Religious Reason and Secular Affect: An Incommensurable Divide?" in *Is Critique Secular? Blasphemy, Injury, and Free Speech* (Berkeley: University of California Press, 2009), 91–2. Cf. Asad, "The Trouble of Thinking: An Interview with Talal Asad" in *Powers of the Secular Modern: Talal Asad and His Interlocutors*, ed. David Scott and Charles Hirschkind (Stanford: Stanford University Press, 2006), 284–5; and Amy Allen's discussion of postsecular genealogy as a "problematizing" effort that "aims not at a normative evaluation but in Colin Koopman's words seeks 'to clarify and intensify the difficulties that enable and disable' the practices it studies." "Having One's Cake," 134. For an opposed though historically informed approach, see Howard

D. Weinbrot, *Literature, Religion, and the Evolution of Culture, 1660–1780* (Baltimore: Johns Hopkins University Press, 2013).

37 Shaftesbury, *Characteristics*, 375.

38 Basu, "Humor and Toleration," 171. Cf. Shaftesbury's claim that "Were two travelers agreed to tell their story separate in public, the one being a man of sincerity but positive and dogmatical, the other less sincere but easy and good-humoured, though it happened that the accounts of this latter gentlemen were of the more miraculous sort, they would yet sooner gain belief and be more favourably received by mankind, than the strongly asserted relations and vehement narratives of the other fierce defender of truth" (*Characteristics*, 384).

39 Shaftesbury, *Characteristics*, 15–16.

40 Daniel Carey, "Two Strategies on Toleration: Locke, Shaftesbury, and Diversity" in *Studies on Voltaire and the Eighteenth Century* (Oxford: Voltaire Foundation, 2009), 66. For Carey, Shaftesbury "could allow for dispute and disunity in religion precisely because he had located an area of stability and consensus in morals and taste" via Stoic thought ("Two Strategies," 61). I am arguing that this stability is located in religious sentiment.

41 The subsequent reading draws heavily on Bogel's analysis of satiric form in *The Difference Satire Makes*, 1–83.

42 Shaftesbury, *Characteristics*, 10.

43 Bogel, *The Difference Satire Makes*, 81.

44 Basu, "Humor and Toleration," 161. Basu finds that humour in Shaftesbury "breaks the connection between the cognition of another as unlike oneself, and the dispositional and political stance that the other is unlikeable," but the puppet show example shows that humour can but does not necessarily make it possible to "recognize humanity in the other … to acknowledge the other as another" (ibid.). To take a recent example, the Dutch cartoon controversy was not especially humanizing in this way. As Bogel explains in relation to satiric form, "By aligning our reading selves … with a satirist whose ambiguity we refuse to acknowledge and whom we take to be normative or ideal … we cast out our own ambiguity of identity and our ambiguous relation to both satirist and satiric object" (*The Difference Satire Makes*, 66). This is not to say that satire necessarily works to consolidate identity. The form can call attention to its own operation, asking us to confront our confusion about whether to stand with the satirist or the satiric object, forcing us "to invent our intelligence" (ibid., 66).

45 Shaftesbury's appeal to aesthetic force in the service of virtue is another example of this kind of jumpstarting: "He seems to assert that there are certain moral species or appearances so striking and of such force over

our natures that, when they present themselves, they bear down all contrary opinion or conceit, all opposite passion, sensation, or mere bodily affection" (*Characteristics*, 353). It is the force and not the truth of such images that most interests Shaftesbury.

46 With some reservations, the "Miscellaneous Reflections" also offer a successful and unexpected example of the orchestration of countervailing religious passions to achieve political stability, an example that makes no claim to intellectual emancipation. The Roman Catholic Church "cannot but appear in some respect august and venerable," Shaftesbury contends, because its leaders can control religious passions so effectively: "all these seeming contrarieties of human passion they knew how to comprehend in their political model" (*Characteristics*, 378, 377). The church appeals to the superstitious through "external proportions, magnificence of structures, ceremonies, processions, choirs, and those other harmonies that captivate the mind and ear," while those "of another character and complexion … were allowed to proceed … by the inward way of contemplation and divine love" (*Characteristics*, 377, 378). But when enthusiasm goes so far as "either expressly or seemingly to dissuade the practice of the vulgar and established ceremonial duties," then "to ingenious writers they afford the liberty, on the other side, in a civil manner, to call in question these spiritual feats" (*Characteristics*, 378). Shaftesbury seems to approve of how the church balances each religious passion with the other. The passage underlines the irrelevance of epistemological concerns to Shaftesbury's promotion of religious tolerance, firmly places his understanding of it in the context of religious passions, and emphasizes his understanding of the need to regulate the public's self-regulation. For a less enthusiastic reading of this passage, see Klein's *Culture of Politeness*, 172–3.

47 Shaftesbury, *Characteristics*, 33.

48 Shaftesbury states that wit and raillery should be limited to the "liberty of the club," a claim difficult to square with his publication of *Characteristics* (36). He seems, however, to also hold out good humour as a path for the individual from a vulgar, general public to an enlightened elite. Good humour is thus a political repositioning of the public through a redefinition of religious passion, a mood conducive to epistemological success, and a gateway passion to the elite (for this last claim, see 271). Müller helpfully contextualizes the politics of Shaftesbury's theory of laughter.

49 Efforts to consider liberal religious tolerance as something other than an unqualified achievement of Western modernity have recently accelerated, following a line of thought opened up by Herbert Marcuse's essay

"Repressive Tolerance," in *A Critique of Pure Tolerance*, ed. Robert Paul Wolff (Boston: Beacon Press, 1969), 95–137. See Wendy Brown, *Regulating Aversion: Tolerance in the Age of Identity and Empire* (Princeton: Princeton University Press, 2006); Stanley Fish, "Mission Impossible: Settling the Just Bounds between Church and State," *Columbia Law Review* 97.8 (Dec. 1997): 2255–333; Slavoj Žižek, "Tolerance as an Ideological Category," *Critical Inquiry* 34.4 (Summer 2008): 660–82. Hans Erich Bödeker, Clorinda Donato, and Peter Hanns Reill, eds., *Discourses of Tolerance and Intolerance in the European Enlightenment* (Toronto: University of Toronto Press, 2009) shows the influence of this revisionist scholarship on Enlightenment studies.

50 Conceptual analyses of Locke's arguments still tend to focus on the universality of claims about the nature of belief without fully considering the limitations implied by Locke's definition of religion as belief.

51 See, for example, Tønder's discussion of UNESCO's Declaration of Principles on Tolerance in *Sensorial Orientation*, 34.

52 John Locke, *A Letter Concerning Toleration*, ed. James Tully (Indianapolis: Hackett, 1982), 24, 23.

53 On Locke's anticlericalism, see Richard Ashcraft, "Locke and the Problem of Toleration" in *Discourses of Tolerance and Intolerance in the European Enlightenment*, ed. Hans Erich Bödeker, Clorinda Donato, and Peter Hanns Reill (Toronto: University of Toronto Press, 2009), 60–72; and Scherer's analysis of Locke's tropes of pretense and zealotry, *Beyond Church and State*, 88–92.

54 Scherer, *Beyond Church and State*, 82. As Michael Warner notes, Locke's reliance on religious concepts to argue for tolerance has become a commonplace in scholarship, as has the observation "that in order to manage religious freedom, secular government first regulates what counts as religion" (613). "Is Liberalism a Religion?" in *Religion: Beyond a Concept*, ed. Hent de Vries (New York: Fordham University Press, 2008), 610–17.

55 Locke, *Letter*, 23. On reform and the secular, see Charles Taylor, *A Secular Age*, 61–88.

56 Elizabeth A. Pritchard, *Religion in Public: Locke's Political Theology* (Stanford: Stanford University Press, 2013), 3.

57 Tønder's *Sensorial Orientation* is the groundbreaking exception. An early inspiration for this essay comes from Saba Mahmood's suggestion in an online posting at *The Immanent Frame*: "I think the 'feeling good' part of the secular story cannot be belittled. It should in fact be studied in all seriousness so as to apprehend the visceral force secular discourses and practices command in our world today. While it is common to ascribe passion to religion, it would behoove us to pay attention to

the thick texture of affinities, prejudices, and attachments that tie us (cosmopolitan intellectuals and critics) to what is loosely described as a secular worldview ... How does secular culture feel?" Saba Mahmood, "Is Critique Secular?," *The Immanent Frame* (blog), 30 March 2008, http://blogs.ssrc.org/tif/2008/03/30/is-critique-secular-2/.

58 Locke, *Letter*, 26.

59 Kirstie M. McClure, "Difference, Diversity, and the Limits of Toleration," *Political Theory* 18.3 (1990): 380.

60 Ibid.

61 Ibid.

62 Ibid., 382, 381. McClure claims that this is because of "a double transformation of Lockean categories over the last three centuries," in which "mental cruelty and distress" became legal categories and "'facts' are no longer represented as generally isolated occurrences independent of one another but as knit together in a complex web of cause and effect" (383). For an argument that links religious tolerance to cultural rights, see Habermas, "The Pacemaker."

63 Ibid., 387.

64 Veena Das suggestively sums up Asad on this point: "secularism is not simply an intellectual argument offered in response to a question of enduring social peace and toleration – it is also a way of distributing and rearranging forms of suffering so that it becomes legitimate to acknowledge some forms of suffering and to practice indifference (or worse) towards others." "Secularism and the Argument from Nature," in *Powers of the Secular Modern: Talal Asad and His Interlocutors*, 93.

65 McClure, "Difference," 378.

66 Locke, *Letter*, 34.

67 McClure, "Difference," 370–2.

68 Tønder, *Sensorial Approach*, 7.

69 Locke, *Letter*, 47.

70 Tønder, *Sensorial Approach*, 115.

71 Locke, *Letter*, 38.

72 Rainer Forst, "Toleration, Justice and Reason," in *The Culture of Toleration in Diverse Societies: Reasonable Tolerance*, 80.

73 Ibid., 81.

74 Tully, "Governing Conduct," 189. Cf. 212.

75 Ibid., 183.

76 Ibid., 222.

77 Ibid., 221–2.

78 Ibid., 218.

79 Ibid., 222.
80 Pritchard, *Religion in Public*, 132.
81 Tønder, *Sensorial Approach*, 118.
82 Nancy Yousef, "Feeling for Philosophy: Shaftesbury and the Limits of Sentimental Certainty," *ELH* 78 (2011): 628.
83 Ibid.
84 For Tønder's account of Lockean resilience in terms of indifference and active forgetting, see *Sensorial Orientation*, 66–71.
85 Locke, *Letter*, 48.
86 Pritchard, *Religion in Public*, 36.
87 Ibid., 58.
88 In addition to McClure, "Difference," 370–2, see Ingrid Creppell's discussion of Locke's understanding of the political dangers posed by religious identity in *Toleration and Identity: Foundations in Early Modern Thought* (New York: Routledge, 2003), 104–7.
89 Locke, *Letter*, 47.
90 Tully places Locke only in relation to "the preservation of life." "Governing Conduct," 182.
91 Creppell, *Toleration*, 122.
92 Ibid., 122–3.
93 Tønder, *Sensorial Approach*, 55.
94 See Talal Asad's discussion of Locke's conception of religion as belief in relation to Islamic formulations in "Free Speech, Blasphemy, and Secular Criticism," in *Is Critique Secular? Blasphemy, Injury, and Free Speech*, 20–63.
95 Jacques Derrida, "Faith and Knowledge: The Two Sources of 'Religion' at the Limits of Reason Alone," trans. Samuel Weber, in *Acts of Religion*, ed. Gil Anidjar (New York: Routledge, 2002), 59.

4 Rethinking Superstition: Pagan Ritual in Lafitau's *Moeurs des sauvages*

MARY HELEN MCMURRAN

In the eighteenth century, several major works on the world's religious ceremonies were published. These encyclopedic projects catalogue, describe, and provide visual illustrations of the diversity of worship around the globe, including the increasingly baggy category of paganism. The source material for what they called "idolatry" or "pagan superstitions" was recycled, for the most part, from travellers' and missionaries' accounts.[1] In this same period, many French, Dutch, and British writers inquired into paganism's origins, essence, and the history of its forms, and they too combed this corpus of travel and missionary accounts for information.[2] Comparison was the dominant method in both encyclopedias and treatises: the polytheists of the Americas, Africa, and Asia were compared to one another, and to the pagan cults of antiquity.[3] This early foray into comparative religious customs has been seen as a watershed in the understanding of religion. Guy Stroumsa has argued that eighteenth-century works about rituals contributed to a "genuine revolution in knowledge and attitudes" about religion.[4] Lynn Hunt, Margaret Jacob, and Wijnand Mijnhardt have made a similar point about the *Cérémonies et coûtumes religieuses de tous les peuples du monde* – a monumental work compiled by Jean-Frédéric Bernard and illustrated by Bernard Picart – claiming that it fostered secularist toleration in part by "consistently shin[ing] the most favorable light possible on idolatrous customs and practices."[5]

Most historians agree that a broader transformation from blinkered Christian dogmatism to secular relativism regarding the world's religions took place in the seventeenth and eighteenth centuries. They attribute this paradigm shift to several factors including this dissemination of "factual information" about the "vast and murky area" of indigenous polytheistic religions, as well as to the emergence of scholarly methods of scrutinizing classical, biblical, and doctrinal authorities, and the rise of criticism of religious institutions.[6] One potential problem with these arguments as they pertain to paganism is their proleptic differentiation of the European's observational mode from pagans' participatory experience. If pagan ritual is seen as a case of the viewer versus the viewed, it presumes a certain objectifying distance already associated with rational and scientific inquiry. Yet how does a pagan rite become observable in the first place? Pagan ceremonies, which are necessarily fleeting and yet eminently repeatable performances of subjective and communal spirituality, may have visible and audible aspects, but something remains unobservable in such acts. Before submitting the early eighteenth-century's view of pagan ceremonies to a familiar narrative in which rituals become yet another province of modern knowledge production, we might look more carefully at the period's suppositions about how pagan ceremonies did – and did not – become objects of knowledge.

As Jean-Frédéric Bernard explains in *Cérémonies et coûtumes religieuses de tous les peuples du monde*, rituals were not entirely a function of the empirical gaze. His prefatory dissertation on religious cult begins: "La plus grande partie des hommes ignoreroit qu'il y a un dieu, si le culte qu'on doit lui rendre n'étoit accompagné de quelques marques extérieures. Moins on a connu l'Être suprême et plus ces marques ont été bizarres et extravagantes." (Most of mankind would have no knowledge of a God, were not that worship that is due him accompanied by some external signs. The less the supreme being has been known, the more these signs have been whimsical and extravagant.)[7] Bernard treats religious rituals as visible and audible expressions of our knowledge of the supreme being, though he states it negatively: without such external signs, the supreme being would not be known. According to this view, which Bernard shared with many of his contemporaries, the human mind is innately endowed with the capacity to know the deity, and worship is the privileged medium of inherent human religiosity. Nonetheless, Bernard derogates the immodesty of pagan ceremonies, listing rites such as human sacrifice – "barbare et cruelle" – among other obtrusions of rational worship, and asserting that "peu de gens ont été capables de s'élever jusqu'à la Divinité" (few have been able to raise their minds up to the divinity).[8] This statement seems to challenge the view that Bernard, a Protestant, is a tolerant secularist. Yet the relation between the trappings of ritual and the natural knowledge of "the divinity" is significant precisely because he neither judges pagans based on Christian beliefs alone, nor does he secularize ritual. Protestants and Catholics alike deprecated the excesses of pagan rites on the assumption that all people tend to become dependent on outward signs of worship, but Bernard does not equate ceremonial whimsy with a denial of divinity in pagan cults. Fetishes and idols, which also attract an abundance of attention in this period, appeared to Westerners as false embodiments of the deity and were often condemned in theory. In practice, material objects deemed to be fetishes or idols were sometimes destroyed to carry out the condemnation, but were also seen as curiosities and taken from their original sites by traders and collectors, thus undergoing a complex process of desacralization.[9] Pagan ceremonies, however, were not dismissed as counterfeits of (the monotheist) God, and for many, they were the natural embodiments of the unseen divinity.

Thus, rites of all kinds were necessarily available to empirical observation and ethnographic description as externalized acts, and yet, as Bernard reveals, rituals also conveyed imperceptible being. The concept of natural religion, which deemed all humanity capable of knowledge of the supreme deity, appeared to reconcile monotheism with paganism, at least for a time, but my emphasis here is not on Europeans' mediations of religious difference. Rather, the question relates to ritual's suturing of imperceptible being to observable acts, and how this bears on knowledge production in the early Enlightenment. To pursue this question, I turn to a single-authored work that deals extensively with pagan religious customs from a comparative perspective, published just one year after Bernard and Picart's grand project began to appear in print. Joseph-François Lafitau's *Moeurs des sauvages amériquains, comparées aux moeurs des premiers temps* (*Customs of the American Indians Compared with the Customs of Primitive Times*) deals with several aspects of native culture, but the book's predominant concern is with pagan rites in the Americas and in antiquity. The 350-page chapter on religion occupies most of the first of its two volumes, whereas a more conventional ethnographic chapter on the physical and mental qualities of native peoples – "caractère des sauvages" – is only a few pages long. Lafitau continually returns to religious rituals in subsequent chapters on native customs, including government, medicine, as well as death, burial, and mourning. In the introduction he writes: "La Religion influait en tout" (Religion played a part in everything), and then again at the conclusion of the chapter on religion, he states: "La

Religion influait autrefois dans tout ce que faisaient les hommes" (Formerly, the influence of religion was important in everything men did).[10]

Lafitau was a French Jesuit missionary who spent five years at a mission in New France and has long been seen as a forerunner of modern anthropology. His firsthand contact with indigenous groups recorded in the *Moeurs* appears to be among the first scientifically based, observational works of ethnography.[11] In his early history of French anthropology, Arnold Van Gennep, author of the classic *Rites of Passage*, places Lafitau in the company of Enlightenment writers such as Montesquieu, Voltaire, Rousseau, and d'Alembert, but signals Lafitau's "connaissance étendue et précise" (extensive and precise knowledge) of Native Americans.[12] Ethnography has become the standard framework in which to read the *Moeurs*. Yet, as Mary Baine Campbell has written, Lafitau also seems to yearn for a "less disenchanted world."[13] Campbell does not account for this conjunction, nor does Michel de Certeau, whose persuasive exegesis of the *Moeurs'* frontispiece supposes a division of labour between the powerful, emergent discourse of ethnography and Lafitau's "mysterious vision."[14] Other scholars have explored Lafitau's Jesuit background in its historical context, but a more developed discussion of what William Fenton calls "the troublesome morass of 'Religion'" in the *Moeurs* is lacking.[15] In part, the difficulty is that Lafitau's comparative project challenges clear distinctions between the two domains of empirical ethnography and religiosity. The *Moeurs* contains descriptions of pagan rites, but the empirical or scientific value of the descriptions is undermined by Lafitau's unrelenting analogies between pagans of antiquity and North American indigenous peoples. These comparisons between different religious cultures, which are oriented entirely to resemblance, were called "conformities" in the early modern era, and can be distinguished from the modern comparison in that the latter draws out both similarity *and* difference. I argue that the conformity has a rhetorical and explanatory function, but in the *Moeurs* it is also a model for apprehending the unobservable nature of pagan ritual.

The conformity's emphasis on resemblances deters ethnographic fact-making and its secularizing effects. It is not, however, merely a misperception or concealment of differences, attributable to the lens of Western, Christian ideology, or as a step towards the Enlightenment's theory of primitive mentality. To demonstrate that the conformity is an alternative view of pagan ritual, I contextualize it in early modern comparativism, and then analyse the most developed of the *Moeurs'* conformities: that the ancient rites of Bacchus stand for all pagan cult – in antiquity and among all indigenous peoples. The Bacchic rites, which are recuperated by Lafitau from their associations with malignant enthusiasm, are obscure, formless rituals. At their core is the "frenzy," which is not a set of ritual regulations to perform, but a sensory and meta-sensory experience that mingles human and nonhuman being. The conformity apprehends ritual by approximating this ontological perplexity. Its significance in the early eighteenth century is that rather than constitute paganism as a culture or religion, the conformity elicits a kind of counter-productive knowing.

Comparing Comparisons

Jacques Revel has argued recently that the comparison had multiple purposes rather than a single, stable use in the early eighteenth century.[16] He notes that despite the scientific aims of projects like Bernard and Picart's, comparisons were often allegorical, or used for argumentative purposes. Revel usefully establishes and contextualizes certain aspects of comparison, but his brief study is limited to three examples. A survey of the larger spectrum of comparisons in the period reveals a correlation between the purpose of comparing and the relative investment of the comparatist in similarity or difference. Thus, the "conformity," which lies at one end of this comparison spectrum, focused exclusively on resemblances and often served a specific argumentative purpose. It is found in the works of several French Protestants, including Jonas Porée and Pierre Mussard, as well as British Protestants like Conyers Middleton, who contended that the ostensible similarities between ancient heathen rites and those of the Roman Catholic Church were proof of the impurity of the Church's historical foundations.[17] Noël Alexandre's *Conformité des cérémonies chinoises avec l'idolâtrie grecque et romaine* (*Conformity of Chinese ceremonies with Greek and Roman Idolatry*) uses the conformity in an East–West comparison, and the goal here is also to defend a position in a theological controversy. In this case, Alexandre uses conformities to critique Jesuit missionary practices in China. La Créquinière's *Conformité des coûtumes des Indian orientaux, avec celles des Juifs et autres peuples de l'antiquité* (*The Agreement of the Customs of the East Indians with those of the Jews and Other Ancient People*), which catalogues conformities between Hindu and Jewish customs, represents a shift in the aims of the device.[18] His stated purpose is not polemical, but a kind of reverse illumination of ethnography for antiquarianism: "La connaissance des Coûtumes Indiennes prises en elles-mêmes n'étoit d'aucune utilité; que je ne croyois devoir m'en servir que pour justifier ce que l'on nous rapporte des Anciens, & pour l'éclaircir lorsque l'occasion s'en présenteroit; qu'en un mot, l'Antiquité était mon unique but" (The knowledge of the customs of the Indians is no ways useful in itself, that I thought myself obliged to make use of it, only to justify what is told us of the ancients and to explain it whenever an occasion offers, and in a word that antiquity was my only aim).[19] The conformity, which was elastic enough to be deployed for theological debates, antiquarianism, and ethnography, also had a place in natural science, where displays of "objects of the most disparate provenances ... [were] arranged to maximize resemblance rather than diversity."[20] Lorraine Daston has traced a shift from this resemblance orientation in seventeenth-century displays to early eighteenth-century scientific practices, which "arrange or show the plenitude of nature as a continuous series," underwritten by a new commitment to the universalization of nature.[21] The conformity was still a predominant method of comparison around 1700, and despite the variety of agendas it served, it consistently focused on resemblances and continuities rather than differences. More important, the conformities are presumed by their authors to be indubitable and immediately evident rather than a labour of judgment.

The early eighteenth-century comparison was transformed, however, by Linnaeus's use of "collation" in plant morphology, which represents, for the purposes of situating the *Moeurs'* comparisons, the empirical end of the spectrum of comparisons. The collation designates a comparison that assesses both similarity and difference, which made it possible to identify the general attributes of individuals that inform the species, and those of the species that inform the genera.[22] Some historians of science have remarked that Linnaeus's use of the type specimen, which combines features of particular plants rather than representing a unique individual specimen, reveals an idealizing tendency in his otherwise scientific pursuit.[23] The type specimen was used, however, for purposes of illustration, not categorization. In terms of comparisons, the salient point is that the collation was a process of induction from observed traits of particulars. In this way, the collation is the closest relative of the modern scientific comparison, and it is worth noting that the modern anthropological study of religious rituals follows the collation in large part. The anthropologist often acts as a participant-observer of a rite or receives reports given by participants. Detailed descriptions of the rite then help classify it according to its function in the culture's symbolic system and as one of its structural mechanisms. Or, the classification proceeds by generating a typology of rites across cultures.[24]

It has been difficult to characterize Lafitau's comparative project and to unpack his conformities because he explicitly subscribes to several agendas at once. He states in the introduction that his work is based on observations he and his missionary colleagues gathered in the field, which suggests proto-scientific aims.[25] Lafitau also seems to follow La Créquinière's use of the conformity, explaining that information on Native peoples was used to verify ancient sources: "J'avoue que si les Auteurs anciens m'ont donné des lumières pour appuyer quelques conjectures heureuses touchant les Sauvages, les Coûtumes des Sauvages m'ont donné des lumières pour entendre plus facilement, et pour expliquer plusieurs choses qui sont dans les Auteurs anciens" (I confess that, if the ancient authors have given me information on which to base happy conjectures about the Indians, the customs of the Indians have given me information on the basis of which I can understand more easily and explain more readily many things in the ancient authors).[26] More than two hundred sources are cited in the *Moeurs*, and Lafitau often includes a commentary on their documentary value, suggesting a rationalist approach. Lafitau also emphasizes that his goal is not only to compare indigenous groups and the ancients, but to rediscover a distant prehistory. Here, he engages in pure speculation: "J'ai cherché dans ces pratiques et dans ces coûtumes des vestiges de l'antiquité la plus reculée" (I have sought in these practices and customs vestiges of the most remote antiquity) – the *premiers temps* of his title.[27] Lafitau conjectured that "America was peopled a short time after the flood" by early Greeks, and this genealogy is visible in the conformities of their customs.[28] His adherence to historical diffusionism is obliquely related to another conjecture about prehistory – that pagan cults retain traces of an originary belief in a supreme being – and again relies on conformities to make this point.[29] The *Moeurs* appears to vacillate, then, between ethnography, antiquarian pursuits, and conjectural history as well as between scientific, rationalist, and speculative methods.[30]

A careful reading of Lafitau's work reveals an inordinate amount of convoluted syntax, which would seem to merely manifest the confusion of the book's aims as a whole. A closer look at certain rhetorical patterns, including the use of perplexing locutions, however, exhibits a turn away from the argumentative conformity, as well as from the scientific comparison. For example, in one of Lafitau's earliest claims about pagan ceremony, he asserts that the Americans have a religion that has

> des rapports d'une si grande conformité avec celle des premiers temps, avec ce qu'on appelloit dans l'Antiquité les Orgyes de Bacchus et de la Mère des Dieux, les mystères d'Isis et d'Osiris, qu'on sent d'abord à cette resemblance que ce sont partout et les mêmes principes et le même fonds
>
> [such great conformity with that of the first times in its manifestations and with what were called, in antiquity, the bacchanalian orgies and those of the Mother of the Gods and the mysteries of Isis and Osiris that one thinks at once by this resemblance that there are everywhere both the same principles and the same basic belief].[31]

The reference to prehistorical "first times" turns the comparative dyad of native and ancient into a triangulated affair. Yet Lafitau's use of the conjunction "and" is unclear: indigenous religions manifest a "great conformity with religion of the first times *and* with what were called in antiquity, the bacchanalian orgies." Are there two sets of vestigial religious practices, the dead (ancients) and the living (indigenous), which both emanated from prehistory? Or is native paganism a manifestation of one ancient model? It is also unclear whether the religion of the first times signifies a philosophical fiction like the state of nature, or a historical practice that streams into recorded antiquity, or whether the first times may be a historical vanishing point, which can be retraced through indigenous practices, if only asymptotically.

As William Fenton and Elizabeth Moore explain, Lafitau's *premiers temps* is probably taken from the French historian Bossuet, for whom the term designated the three millennia before Moses and the Flood, but Lafitau uses the notion in ways that are less clear and consistent.[32] The comparison here between actual religious customs and an imaginary prehistorical religion is significant nonetheless because it implies that resemblances are the focal point, but that such similarities are not of observable particulars alone. This abdication of a purely evidentiary rationale is reinforced by Lafitau's reference to orgies and mysteries – a particular group of ancient cultic practices in which the initiates were sworn to secrecy, and few records of their actual features exist. I will return to the bacchanalian orgies in greater detail below, but in the context of Lafitau's rhetoric, the point here is that the interposition of prehistory as a *tertium comparationis* refers to some realm outside of historical record and observed fact. The final convolution of the passage is its illogical segue from the comparison to the conclusion that religious principles and beliefs are "everywhere the same." The work of the conformity consists, then, in both presenting comparable particulars, but then withdrawing from particularity to obscurity and from thence to absolute indistinction where all religious principles are "the same."

In a further abandonment of an evidentiary rationale, the conformities are presumed to be self-evident. The very statement of a similitude is, for Lafitau, a sufficient demonstration of it. For example, he writes that the Carib ritual of offerings of cassava and *ouicou*, placed "sur une espèce d'autel au fonds de leurs cabanes, où qu'il's mettent devant certains pieux qu'ils enfoncent en terre, sont les présents de Bacchus et Cérès, leur vin et leur pain qui sont la matière de leurs sacrifices" (on a kind of altar in the back of their huts or place[d] before appointed posts driven into the earth, are the presents of Bacchus and Ceres, their wine and bread which are the substance of their sacrifice).[33] The Carib gifts of *ouicou*, a beer made of potato, cassava, and banana, and cassava, a root, simply "are" the gifts of Bacchus (wine), and Ceres (bread/grain). This conformity elides differences since the appositive "Bacchus and Ceres, their wine and bread," seems to indicate that the gods' names are not metaphors here: the similitude is not attended with the recognition of any material difference of wine from *ouicou*, and bread/grain from cassava. Other discursive symptoms of the conformity include the recurrence of such phrasing as "in the same way," "in the same manner," or "is the same as," and the rhetorical question "shouldn't we also say?"[34] Like his predecessors, Lafitau assumed the self-evident status of conformities, and he even occasionally abandons his own role in drawing comparisons altogether. At the conclusion of a section on musical instruments and dance in ancient rites, he obviates the anticipated comparison with the Huron and Iroquois: "Il me semble avoir déjà si bien dépeint nos Sauvages dans ce que je viens de décrire des Sacrifices et des solemnités des Anciens, que je ne croirais pas avoir besoin d'ajoûter rien davantage" (It seems to me that, in the foregoing descriptions of the sacrifices and ceremonies of the ancients, I have already described so well [those of] the Indians that I believe that there is no need to add anything by an additional description).[35] Descriptions and comparisons are not driven by sectarian conviction, nor do they obey the logic of scientific comparison, not least because Lafitau ignores the differences that generate categories. Even though he uses concepts like "worship" "offering," "sacrifice," and "initiation," he does not systematically derive their general features to construct ritual types.[36]

Although Lafitau was reintroduced in the twentieth century as the rootstock of the social-scientific method, the *Moeurs* elicited caustic criticism in the decades following its publication.[37] Commenting on Lafitau's theses about the diffusion of cultures and the origins of Native peoples of the Americas, Voltaire was characteristically sarcastic:

> Enfin Lafitau fait venir les Américains des anciens Grecs; et voici ses raisons. Les Grecs avaient des fables, quelques Américains en ont aussi. Les premiers Grecs allaient à la chasse, les Américains y vont. Les premiers Grecs avaient des oracles, les Américains ont des sorciers. On dansait dans les fêtes de la Grèce, on danse en Amérique. Il faut avouer que ces raisons sont convaincantes.

> [He would derive the Americans from the ancient Greeks and these are his reasons: the Greeks have myths, some Americans have them too. The first Greeks went hunting, the Americans go too. The first Greeks had oracles, the Americans have sorcerers. They danced at the festivals in Greece, they dance in America too. It must be avowed these reasons are convincing.][38]

By mimicking Lafitau's conformities in condensed and simplified form, Voltaire exposes their fallacy. Any coincidences of material life like hunting or those of religious life such as oracles, sorcerers, and ritual dances do not originate in historical contact, as Lafitau assumed, but can be explained instead by our shared humanity. Corneille de Pauw also found Lafitau's conformities wanting. Unlike Voltaire, he recognized that "les superstitions religieuses des peuples de l'Amérique ont eu un rapport sensible avec celles qu'ont pratiqué les nations de l'ancien continent" (the religious superstitions of the peoples of America had a perceptible relation with those that the nations of the ancient continent practised), but he quickly takes a similar stance of rational resistance to the ostensible resemblance and proposes, like Voltaire, that similarities can be explained by the human condition: "malgré la diversité des climates, l'imbecilité de l'esprit humain a été constante et immuable" (despite the diversity of climates, the imbecility of the human mind has been constant and unwavering).[39] In his *History of America*, William Robertson echoes others' objections to Lafitau's claim that Native Americans originated in the old world, and argues that any similitude comes from "situation" and "state of society." Robertson goes on to critique the conformities of religious rites in particular as "destitute of solid foundation," explaining that "we may ascribe this uniformity, which in many instances seems very amazing, to the natural operation of superstitions and enthusiasm upon the weakness of the human mind."[40] Again, the admission of "amazing" resemblances of customs is followed by an insistence on a simpler explanation: "the natural operation of superstitions." Any conformities can be replaced by the assertion of a single, overarching cause: mental weakness. These criticisms are posited as correctives to the analogical method and its misguided historical speculation.

The idea that mental weakness enables pagan superstition has deep roots in Western philosophy and Christian theology. If Pauw's and Robertson's explanation of similarities between polytheistic cults is not entirely novel, they nonetheless replace its conventional terms with a universalist premise that allowed Enlightenment writers to hold up the mirror to our mental frailties. Although their ridicule is biting and their accounts apparently more persuasive than Lafitau's immoderate comparisons, they do not definitively refute his analogical approach. Having acknowledged that the resemblances between pagan superstitions are indeed perceptible, they sidestep them by imposing, in their place, a form of psychological profiling, which separates those who possess ratiocinative powers from the unenlightened who remain naturally superstitious. Enlightenment primitivism has long been critiqued for its covert denial of human equality and for unethical blindness to the cultural integrity of non-Western cultures. The cultural politics of comparison notwithstanding, I would argue that the stakes of a pagan mentality may lie elsewhere. Voltaire, Pauw, and Robertson pretend that similarities between religious customs of different groups are irrelevant by conjuring the explanatory power of universal mental weakness. This anthropocentric theory also sets aside the relation in customary worship to any being that may not be perceived empirically. That is, if all pagan superstitions arise from a mental predisposition to fear or awe, ritual's mediation of the human and nonhuman is nullified. Seen from this angle, the conformity – even with its desultory arguments and convoluted rhetoric – recasts the high Enlightenment's confidence in the human sciences as incapable of theorizing such mediations.

Bacchic Rites

As we have seen, Lafitau proposes the conformity of indigenous religious customs "with that of the first times in its manifestations and with what were called, in antiquity, the bacchanalian orgies."[41] This hypothesis, which is largely overlooked by scholars of Lafitau, is central to the project. It is found in the book's introduction, and is restated early in the chapter on religion: "Tout le fonds de la Religion ancienne des Sauvages de l'Amérique est le même que celui des Barbares, qui occupèrent en premier lieu la Grèce, et qui se répandirent dans l'Asie, le même que celui des Peuples qui suivirent Bacchus dans ses expeditions militaires, le même enfin qui servit ensuite de fondement à toute la Mythologie payenne, et aux fables des Grecs." (The entire basis of the former religion of the American Indian as well as that of the barbarians who first occupied Greece, spreading later into Asia, is the same as the followers of Bacchus in his military expeditions, and as that which served afterward as the basis of all pagan mythology and of the Greek myths.)[42] In a footnote to this section, he adds that "according to Servius, people called orgies all rites that had the name of sacrifice in Greece and that of ceremony in Rome."[43] Lafitau's several statements of the conformity of the Bacchic rites to pagan religious cult as a whole, he boldly subsumes all paganism into one reputedly licentiousness, violent, and irrational cult that gripped a huge portion of the ancient world. It is the cult of the god who, according to Euripedes's *Bacchae,* travelled through Asia and attracted crowds of followers, returning to Thebes only to have his rites banned by his cousin, King Pentheus. Bacchus then takes his vengeance on the city as his followers, the Bacchae, wreak havoc, ripping a herd of cows to pieces with their bare hands before performing omophagy on Pentheus.

Bacchus, or as the god is known in Greek, Dionysus, has been described by contemporary classicists as "the most complex and multifaceted of all the Greek gods."[44] In post-Nietzschean interpretations of Dionysus, this complexity stems from the god's polarities and contradictions: life/death, suffering/ecstasy, mortal/immortal. Dionysus's complexity is symbolic, but it also derives from a complicated and little-known history of the cult's cosmopolitan transmission. In the myths, Dionysus was a foreign god, the "étrange étranger," which suggests that the cult was taken by the Greeks from elsewhere before spreading widely by late antiquity.[45] Henk Versnel argues that the Dionysian myths of cultic transit may be the first reflection in antiquity on the mobility of religion.[46] Seventeenth- and early eighteenth-century antiquarians and mythologists were not unaware of the complex nature of the god and his cult; they note that Bacchus was called Biformis for his appearances as both a youth and elder, Bimater for having two mothers (born from the womb of Semele and from the thigh of Zeus), or Dithyrambus for being twice born, and also Liber pater because he frees his followers from constraint. François Pomey's popular *Pantheon* includes a lengthy entry on Bacchus with separate sections on his birth, names, actions, sacrifices, and historical interpretation of the cult. Pomey concludes with a moral allegorization of the god of wine – "the cradle of life, but yet the grave of reason."[47] While Bacchus continued to represent the passion that deranges one's reason or the social threat of enthusiasm, there was increasing interest in gathering a more complete inventory of the god's depictions and supplementing the written sources with archaeological descriptions of medals and sculptures.[48] And, euhemerist interpretations of the god multiplied: Dionysus was assumed to have been a real personage who was later deified. The turn to euhemerism from allegorism put additional pressure on the question of Bacchus' actual origins, which were possibly Greek, Egyptian, or Judaic, as well as putting pressure on the question of the cult's history. There may have been more than one Bacchus, seventeenth- and eighteenth-century scholars surmised, or only one god whose cult spread across occidental–oriental realms. In attempting to answer these difficult questions, several eighteenth-century mythologists and antiquarians rationalize the stories by explaining the multiple and inconsistent histories, like much of ancient religion generally, as intentional chicanery. Thus Antoine Banier, the early eighteenth-century Catholic author of the influential compendium, *La mythologie et les fables expliqueés par l'histoire* (1738–40), dealt with the various stories of Bacchus's origins this way: "Il semble que les anciens aient répandu à dessein … l'obscurité mystérieuse" (It would seem that the Ancients had formed a design to throw a veil of obscurity over the true history).[49] In *The New Pantheon* (1753), Samuel Boyse dismisses the possibility of a historical Bacchus and sees the god as little more than a gross mystification: "no real Bacchus ever existed … he was only a masque or figure of some concealed truth."[50]

Lafitau admits the inconsistencies in Bacchus' mythology, but rather than treating them as obstacles to the production of rational knowledge, he deploys them for other purposes. Lafitau concurs that Bacchus is the same god as the Egyptian Osiris, and equates him with other pagan deities: "la divinité, le soleil, nôtre premier père, et les types du libérateur" (the divinity, the sun, our first father and the types of liberator).[51] Moreover, Lafitau sees a resemblance between the accrual of the names and attributes of pagan deities as seen here with Osiris/Bacchus/first father/liberator, etc. and that of the Christian God. Lafitau writes that God is known as the Redeemer and as Christ. As Christ he has human and divine natures: as human, God is identified under the name Adam, the first father and sinner, and as divine, known by symbolic names, "Soleil de Justice, la lumière du Monde, le Pain Céleste" (the Sun of Justice, the Light of the World, Celestial Bread).[52] This conformity between Christ and Bacchus works on more than one level: both are father figures, both are liberator figures, and both have multiple names and attributes, but are not a multiplicity of separate deities. Both are (the) one. For Lafitau, theistic multiplicity is not a veil, and therefore he does not rationalize Bacchus's cult by attempting to unmask discrepancies as a conspiracy of obfuscation. Resemblances, once again, lead to identity, and in the special logic of the conformity, the one cult of Bacchus subsumes all pagan rituals.

The true stakes of Lafitau's conformity of "all former religion" with the "followers of Bacchus" lies, however, in those who performed the rites more than in the god who leads them. There are two groups of Bacchus's followers according to the mythological traditions: the mixed-gender participants in the bacchanal or *orgia*, a public ritual, and second, the bacchantes, a group of female initiates in the mystery cult of Bacchus, which is a private and secret rite. Lafitau correlates both groups to indigenous Americans, "L'image en est toute naturelle dans ce nouveau Monde" (The image [of these followers of Bacchus] is quite familiar in the New World).[53] The key feature of public rite of *orgia* and the mystery cult of Bacchus is that the participants are variously described as being out of their minds, often termed "frenzy" in eighteenth-century texts. In the *Moeurs*, Lafitau includes an image of a bacchante in frenzy, taken from Jacob Spon's work on antiquities, which helped revive a visual tradition of the bacchante that had largely disappeared from Renaissance mythologies due to its prurience[54] (Figure 4.1). It closely resembles images of the bacchante in other antiquarian catalogues such as that of La Chausse's *Le grand cabinet romain ou receuil d'antiquitez romaines* and Bernard de Montfaucon's frequently cited *L'Antiquité expliquée* (Figure 4.2). Antoine Banier describes bacchantes as running "toutes échevelées avec des grimaces et des contorsions affreuses, branlant la tête d'une manière effrayante, et ressemblant en tout à des sorcenées" (loose and dishevelled in grimaces and contorsions, tossing their heads in a frightful manner, and in every thing resembling mad women).[55] This image of Bacchic frenzy reinforced its reputation as drunken and salacious degeneracy, but Lafitau aims to

Figure 4.1. Lafitau, *Moeurs des sauvages*, Vol. 1, Plate 17, Figure 9. Taken from Jacob Spon in Jan Gruter, *Miscellaneae Eruditae Antiquitatis*, 2 vols. (Lyon, 1685), used to illustrate the "Isiac cross." This item is reproduced by permission of The Huntington Library, San Marino, California.

prove that these rites were corrupted only in later antiquity, that is, by the time the Romans famously proscribed them.[56] In his section on the bacchanals of antiquity, Lafitau inserts a passage from the ancient Greek geographer, Strabo, which addresses the mystery cult of Bacchus and the public bacchanals. Strabo explains that all these rites in which frenzy enters are, in fact, in accord with "nature and reason." He explains why:

> in the first place, the relaxation draws the mind away from human occupations and turns the real mind towards that which is divine; and, secondly, the religious frenzy seems to afford a kind of divine inspiration and to be

Figure 4.2. Bernard de Montfaucon, *Antiquity Explained* (London, 1722), vol. I, plate 18. The bacchantes are re-engraved from works of Paolo Maffei, Michel Ange de La Chausse, and Jacob Spon. This item is reproduced by permission of the Huntington Library, San Marino, California.

very like that of the soothsayer; and, thirdly, the secrecy with which the sacred rites are concealed induces reverence for the divine, which is to avoid being perceived by our human senses; and, fourthly, music, which includes dancing as well as rhythm and melody, at the same time, by the delight it affords and by its artistic beauty, brings us in touch with the divine.[57]

Where Lafitau's contemporaries had consigned the bacchante to indecipherable madness, this passage from Strabo makes sense of the image of the bacchante – her kinetic, skyward-bent pose and her solitary religiosity – which is the antithesis of the period's typical depictions of pagans, who appear in the illustrations to works like Lafitau's or Bernard and Picart's as prostrate worshippers gravely subjugating themselves to their idols, or whose bodies, if animated by dance, remain in the circular formation of communal regulation.[58] Lafitau adds that he takes Strabo's explanation of Bacchic frenzy "comme un principe" (as a principle), suggesting that the quotation is not merely a defence of the piety of ancient bacchanals, but the conformity that defines all ancient and indigenous pagan cult.

First, the passage reinforces that Bacchic rites and by extension, pagan cult, do not consist in formal acts alone, but in something that the participant undergoes. In the mystery cults, as Sarah Iles Johnston explains: "initiates into mysteries not only *did* and *said* things, as part of their initiation, but *experienced* things ... those in the cult of Dionysus are said to be *bebaccheumenoi* (they have been 'bacchiated')."[59] Second, Strabo states that the initiate reaches the divinity through the "real mind," which is drawn away from its human occupations, and further, that the rite is properly done in secret to avoid being perceived. These parts of the passage evoke a dualism of the senses and mind, the former leading away from divinity and the latter towards it. Yet, Strabo's last point appears to contradict such dualism. The passage ends with melody and rhythm inducing the sense-experience of "delight," which brings the bacchante "in touch with the divine." This pleasure is further connected to the aesthetic or "artistic beauty" of dance and music, reinforcing the godliness of sensory experience. Perhaps the passage is not at odds with itself, however. Frenzy moves into or "enters" the initiate by means of several corollary motions of relaxing, receiving, inducing, and "being in touch with" in a dialectical move from the senses into the mind and then back to the senses. Elsewhere in the religion chapter, Lafitau addresses ancient and Native American theurgy, or communication with the gods, and returns to "des Initiations des Orgies."[60] Specifically, he notes that in all cases, the soul is cleansed of the "contagion of the senses" as a preliminary step. Despite this apparent dualism of the contemplative mind and the earthly senses, he quotes cryptic passages from Pausanius, Dio Chrysostom, Apuleius, and Plato to explain that the purification of the senses subsequently brings initiates back to their senses in a heightened state of perception and knowledge. Lafitau paraphrases Dio Chrysostom, a Greek orator and philosopher who lived during the Roman imperial era: "un homme initié dans cet état de vision mystérieuse, aux oreilles de qui plusieurs voix se sont entendre, sous les yeux duquel se présentent en spectacle plusieurs scènes différentes" (a man initiated into this state of mystic vision to whose ears many voices make themselves heard, under whose eyes many different scenes present themselves).[61] In his dissertation on religious practices quoted above, Jean-Frédéric Bernard explains that the rationality of proper worship consists in expressionless mental contemplation, and that pagan rituals are fraught with excesses that distract them from pure meditation. Lafitau reconsiders this supposedly inferior mentality of pagans and its dependence on sensory allure. Pagan cult does not mire the participant in sense-perception as a diversion from the supreme being, but rather, according to the ancients, disrupts the senses and mind to restore them.

Let us return, then, to the significance of this conformity between the bacchanalia and all pagan cult. The conformity, first of all, does not proceed by using descriptors of observed pagan practices for the purposes of outlining a formal category, for Bacchic rites are not a particular entity, but a historical and translocal adaptation. Lafitau suggests that pagan cult is also a transport of the mind from the senses and back into the senses, and an ineffable event of "being in touch with" the deity. To define Bacchic rites as the essence of pagan cult is, in fact, to upset the idea that ritual is reducible to a set of observable external signs or prescriptions for action. Thus, ethnographic descriptions of pagan rites did not necessarily change European attitudes about religion from close-minded belief to tolerant secularization. Rather, such descriptions, reinforcing the link between externalized sensory experience and meta-sensory being, appear to preserve the nonrationality in which the mind, the senses, and divinity remain conjugated, as consequent to empirical observation.

It would oversimplify the *Moeurs* to assume that if it is not scientific ethnography with secularist effects, then its engagement with religious practices is itself religiously motivated. Lafitau's apparent defence of pagan ritual may be allied with natural religion, but to argue that it also serves a Counter-Reformation ideology in the wake of Protestant anti-ritualism, or as a justification of Catholic missions, which were widely known for their emphasis on ritual, is insufficient.[62] Pagan ceremonies, elaborated in the *Moeurs* through the conformities between ancient and native pagans, grapple with a relation to (the one) being as distinct from the monotheists' god – further evinced in the consistent use of terms "divinity" or "supreme being." Is the divine immanent in the human mind and then expressed in signs of human worship? Or is ritual frenzy the agent by which a return of the mind to the senses newly accommodates the divine each time it is carried out? The *Moeurs* stops short of providing an answer, but its particular dedication to the conformity effectively resists the regime of collecting, accumulating, and ordering knowledge.

In *The Order of Things*, Michel Foucault put analogical thinking and its hermeneutic circularity to rest at the end of the Renaissance. He explains that the uniform layer of interwoven signs and things breaks down, and similitude comes to be seen as deceptive and quixotic.[63] Since the publication of Foucault's work, the dominant model for interpreting many aspects of European thought, and perhaps particularly ideas about non-Europeans, has been to analyse representations as constructions of a knowledge regime that was made possible by the liberation from premodern analogy. A more complete account of pagan superstition reveals that it absorbed analogical thinking, exemplified here by the conformity.[64] If Lafitau's bewildering analogies are reconsidered, they may provide a re-entry to the conjunctions of embodied practices, mentalities, and spirit-worlds.

NOTES

1 On religion as a category in early modern travel narrative see Joan-Pau Rubiés, "Instructions for Travellers: Teaching the Eye to See," *History and Anthropology* 9.2–3 (1996): 139–90. On paganism in taxonomies of world religion see Tomoko Masuzawa, *The Invention of World Religions, Or, How European Universalism Was Preserved in the Language of Pluralism* (Chicago: University of Chicago Press, 2005), ch. 1.

2 Pierre Bayle, Balthasar Bekker, Bernard de Fontenelle, Voltaire, Gerhard Vossius, and numerous English Deists wrote on these questions in the late seventeenth and early eighteenth centuries.

3 Analogies were also made between indigenous religions, ancient paganism and the survivals of pagan-like traditions of European Christendom, as well as Roman Catholic rituals or "pagano-papism" often for more polemical purposes.

4 Guy G. Stroumsa, *A New Science: The Discovery of Religion in the Age of Reason* (Cambridge, MA: Harvard University Press, 2010), 2.

5 Lynn Hunt, Margaret Jacob, and Wijnand Mijnhardt, *The Book That Changed Europe: Picart and Bernard's* Religious Ceremonies of the World (Cambridge, MA: Harvard University Press, 2010), 221. Jean-Frédéric Bernard and Bernard Picart, *Cérémonies et coûtumes religieuses de tous les peuples du monde* (Amsterdam, 1723–43), http://digital2.library.ucla.edu/picart/index.html. Asia, the Americas, and Africa occupy two volumes. With over 130 folio-page engravings, borrowed or re-engraved from existing works, the pagan volumes are the most extensively illustrated portion of the work.

6 Eric J. Sharpe, *Comparative Religion: A History* (London: Duckworth, 1975), 18. See Julie Boch, *Les dieux désenchantés: La fable dans la pensée française, de Huet à Voltaire 1680–1760* (Paris: Champion, 2002); Justin Champion, *Republican Learning: John Toland and the Crisis of Christian Culture, 1696–1722* (New York: Manchester University Press, 2003); Peter Harrison, *"Religion" and the Religions in the English Enlightenment* (New York: Cambridge University Press, 1990); Peter N. Miller, "Taking Paganism Seriously: Anthropology and Antiquarianism in Early Seventeenth-Century Histories of Religion," *Archiv für Religionsgeschichte* 3 (2001): 183–209; J. Samuel Preus, *Explaining Religion: Criticism and Theory from Bodin to Freud* (New Haven: Yale University Press, 1987); Francis Schmidt, "Des inepties tolérables: La raison des rites de John Spencer (1685) à W. Robertson Smith (1889)," *Archives de Sciences Sociales des Religions* 85 (1994): 121–36, http://www.jstor.org/stable/30128906. Much of this scholarship overlooks the fact that European views of polytheistic practices were marred by misapprehensions and biases. Studies of travelogues, however, frequently reveal errors in reporting, the use of hearsay in place of observation, and the ideological suppositions of the travel writers.

7 Jean-Frédéric Bernard and Bernard Picart, "Dissertation sur le culte religieux," *Cérémonies et coûtumes religieuses de tous les peoples du monde* (Amsterdam, 1723), 1: iii, http://digital2.library.ucla.edu/picart/index.html.

8 Ibid.

9 See Jonathan Sheehan, ed., "Thinking About Idols in Early Modern Europe," special issue, *Journal of the History of Ideas* 67.4 (2006), http://www.jstor.org/stable/30141045; William Pietz, "The Problem of the Fetish I," *Res* 9 (1985): 5–17; "The Problem of the Fetish II: The Origin of the Fetish," *Res* 13 (1987): 23–45; "The Problem of the Fetish IIIa: Bosman's Guinea and the Enlightenment Theory of Fetishism," *Res* 16 (1988): 105–24; "Bosman's Guinea: The Intercultural Roots of an Enlightenment Discourse," *Comparative Civilizations Review* 9 (Fall 1982): 1–22.

10 Joseph-François Lafitau, *Moeurs des sauvages amériquains, comparées aux moeurs des premiers temps* (Paris, 1724), 1:17, 1:453. Hereafter, *Moeurs*. *Customs of the American Indians Compared with the Customs of Primitive Times*, trans. William Fenton and Elizabeth Moore (Toronto: The Champlain Society, 1974), 1:36, 1:281.

11 The reputation is based on Lafitau's supposed fieldwork as well as that of his colleague Julien Garnier. See Christian Feest, "Father Lafitau as Ethnographer of the Iroquois," *Native American Studies* 15.2 (2001): 19–25; Alfred Métraux, "Les Précurseurs de l'ethnologie en France du xvie au xviiie siècle," *Cahiers d'histoire mondiale* 7 (1962): 721–38; William Fenton, "J.-F. Lafitau (1681–1746), Precursor of Scientific Anthropology," *Southwestern Journal of Anthropology* 25.2 (1969): 173–87; Andreas Motsch, *Lafitau et l'émergence du discours ethnographique* (Sillery, Quebec: Septentrion, 2001); Anthony Pagden, *The Fall of Natural Man: The American Indian and the Origins of Comparative Ethnology*, rev. ed. (New York: Cambridge University Press, 1986), chapter 8; Sol Tax, "From Lafitau to Radcliffe-Brown: A Short History of the Study of Social Organization," *Social Anthropology of North American Tribes*, ed. Fred Eggan, 2nd ed. (Chicago: University of Chicago Press, 1955). Gilles Thérien criticizes the overemphasis on ethnography in "Les 'Amériquians' de Joseph-François Lafitau," in *Apprendre à porter sa vue au loin: Hommage à Michèle Duchet*, ed. Sylviane Albertan-Coppola (Lyon: ENS Éditions, 2009), 193–202.

12 Arnold van Gennep, "Contributions à l'histoire de la méthode ethnographique," *Revue de l'histoire des religions* 67 (1913), 325.

13 Mary Baine Campbell, *Wonder and Science: Imagining Worlds in Early Modern Europe* (Ithaca: Cornell University Press, 2004), 294.

14 Michel de Certeau, "Writing vs. Time: History and Anthropology in the Works of Lafitau," *Yale French Studies* 59 (1980): 43.

15 William Fenton, "Lafitau, Joseph-François," in *Dictionary of Canadian Biography* (University of Toronto/Université Laval, 2003), http://www.biographi.ca/en/bio/lafitau_joseph_francois_3E.html. See Andreas Motsch, "De l'aperçu au système Lafitau et l'anthropologie de la contre-réforme," and Jean-Michel Racault, "La Preuve par l'autre, ou du bon usage du paganism: Théologie de la révélation primitive et comparatisme religieux chez Lafitau," in *Transhumances divines: Récits de voyage et religion*, ed. Sophie Linon-Chipon and Jean-François Guennoc (Paris: Presses de l'université Paris-Sorbonne, 2005), 123–65.

16 Jacques Revel, "The Uses of Comparison: Religions in the Early Eighteenth Century," in *Bernard Picart and the First Global Vision of Religion*, ed. Lynn Hunt, Margaret Jacob and Wijnand Mijnhardt (Los Angeles: Getty

Research Institute, 2010), 331. Also see Marcel Detienne, *Comparing the Incomparable*, trans. Janet Lloyd (Stanford: Stanford University Press, 2008), and Barbara Maria Stafford, *Visual Analogy: Consciousness as the Art of Connecting* (Cambridge, MA: MIT Press, 1999), both of whom defend the experimentalist comparison.

17 Pierre Mussard, *Les conformités des cérémonies modernes avec les anciennes* (Leiden, 1667), translated into English as *Roma Antiqua Recens* (London, 1732); Jonas Porée, *Histoire des cérémonies et des superstitions, qui se sont introduites dans l'Église* (Amsterdam, 1717); Conyers Middleton, *A Letter From Rome*, 2nd ed. (London, 1729).

18 La Créquinière's work, published in Brussels, 1704, was reprinted in Bernard and Picart's *Cérémonies et coûtumes religieuses*, and translated by the deist writer John Toland into English in 1705.

19 M. de La Créquinière, *Conformité des coûtumes des Indiens orientaux, avec celles des Juifs et des autres peuples de l'antiquité*, in Bernard and Picart, *Cérémonies et coûtumes*, 3:7 (vol. 3, pt. 2, following p. 215), http://digital2.library.ucla.edu/picart/tableContents.html. Trans. *The Agreement of the Customs of the East-Indians with those of the Jews and Other Ancient People* (London, 1705), viii. On Alexandre see Frank Manuel, *The Eighteenth Century Confronts the Gods* (Cambridge, MA: Harvard University Press, 1959), 18. Also see Peter N. Miller, "History of Religion Becomes Ethnology: Some Evidence from Peiresc's Africa," in Sheehan, ed., "Thinking about Idols," 675–96, http://www.jstor.org/stable/30141052; and *Peiresc's Orient: Antiquarianism as Cultural History in the Seventeenth Century* (Burlington, VT: Ashgate, 2012).

20 Lorraine Daston, "Description by Omission: Nature Enlightened and Obscured," in *Regimes of Description: In the Archive of the Eighteenth Century*, ed. John Bender and Michael Marrinan (Stanford: Stanford University Press, 2005), 22–3.

21 Ibid.

22 Staffan Müller-Wille, "Collection and Collation: Theory and Practice of Linnaean Botany," *Studies in the History and Philosophy of Biological & Biomedical Sciences* 38 (2007): 541–62, doi:10.1016/j.shpsc.2007.06.010.

23 Lorraine Daston and Peter Galison, *Objectivity* (New York: Zone Books, 2010), 58–63; Daniela Bleichmar, *Visible Empire: Botanical Expeditions and Visual Culture in the Hispanic Enlightenment* (Chicago: University of Chicago Press, 2012), chapter 2.

24 See Catherine Bell, *Ritual: Perspectives and Dimensions*, rev. ed. (New York: Oxford University Press, 2009).

25 Lafitau, *Moeurs*, 1:2–3, 25, trans., 1:26–7, 41.

26 Ibid., 1:3–4, trans., 1:27.
27 Ibid.
28 Lafitau, *Moeurs*, 1:40, 89, trans., 1:49, 79–80. See Anthony Pagden, "Eighteenth-Century Anthropology and the 'history of mankind,'" in *History and the Disciplines: The Reclassification of Knowledge in Early Modern Europe*, ed. Donald Kelley (Rochester, NY: University of Rochester Press, 1997), 222–35; Michèle Duchet, "Discours ethnologique et discours historique: le texte de Lafitau," *Studies on Voltaire and the Eighteenth Century* 152 (1976): 607–23 (Oxford: Voltaire Foundation, 1976).
29 See Peter Byrne, *Natural Religion and the Nature of Religion: The Legacy of Deism* (New York: Routledge, 1989). In the context of Lafitau and others, the theory is often referred to as "primitive monotheism," but this is an anachronism. Henryk Zimon, "Wilhelm Schmidt's Theory of Primitive Monotheism and Its Critique within the Vienna School of Ethnology," *Anthropos* 81 (1986): 243–60.
30 See, for example, Lafitau, *Moeurs*, 1:129, trans., 1:172 and 1:453, trans., 1:280.
31 Lafitau, *Moeurs*, 1:7, trans., 1:30.
32 William Fenton and Elizabeth Moore, "Introduction," in Joseph François Lafitau, *Customs of the American Indians Compared with the Customs of Primitive Times* (Toronto: The Champlain Society, 1974), lxxiii.
33 Lafitau, *Moeurs*, 1:179, trans., 1:133.
34 Ibid., 1:244, trans., 1:168, and 1:336, trans., 1:217. The tendency is especially prevalent in 1:236–48, trans., 1:164–170.
35 Ibid., 1:205, trans., 1:148. See also 1:241, trans., 1:171.
36 One reason for the elisions of cultural differences is a practical one: he was probably unable to produce a detailed ethnographic account of Native American religious customs because many rites were no longer practised, and even if they were, missionaries would probably not have been privy to most of them, as opposed to other kinds of Native customs. Lafitau thus writes that he had limited knowledge of the initiation rites of the Huron, Iroquois, and Algonquian, and even less of the Virginians, though he is certain they are alike. "Ils eussent déjà perdu beacuoup de leurs coûtumes, lorsque les Europeans ont commencé à les fréquenter" (they have lost many of their first customs and since contact with Europeans altered them even more). Lafitau, *Moeurs*, 1:336, trans., 1:217. See also 1:282, trans., 1:189.
37 Also see the review of Lafitau's *Moeurs* in *Bibliothèque françoise: ou Histoire littéraire de la France* 4 (1724): 109–20 and 5 (1725): 330–41. Lafitau was praised by the Jesuits' own *Journal de Trévoux* 22 (1722): 2189–92; 24 (1724):

1565–1609; and 25 (1725): 197–239. Thanks to Andreas Motsch for these and other documents regarding Lafitau.

38 François Marie Arouet de Voltaire, *Essai sur les moeurs et l'esprit des nations*, ed. René Pomeau (Paris: Garnier frères, 1963), 1:30.

39 Corneille de Pauw, *Recherches philosophiques sur les Américains, ou mémoires intéressants pour servir à l'histoire de l'espèce humaine* (London, 1770), 1:xvii. *Eighteenth Century Collections Online*. The work was first published in Berlin, 1768–1769.

40 William Robertson, *The History of America* (London, 1777), 1:4, 268, 269, 270. See Neil Hargraves, "Beyond the Savage Character: Mexicans, Peruvians and the 'Imperfectly Civilized' in William Robertson's *History of America*," in *The Anthropology of the Enlightenment*, ed. Larry Wolff and Marco Cipolloni (Stanford: Stanford University Press, 2007), 103–18. Also see Matthew Binney, "Joseph-François Lafitau's *Customs of American Indians* and Edmund Burke: Historical Process and Cultural Difference," *Clio* 41.3 (2012): 311–37.

41 See above n. 33.

42 Lafitau, *Moeurs*, 1:113, trans., 1:95. Lafitau's claim is not consistently developed. See 1:281–2, trans., 1:189.

43 Ibid., 1:114n, trans., 1:95n.

44 Thomas H. Carpenter and Christopher Faraone, eds., *Masks of Dionysus* (Ithaca: Cornell University Press, 1993), 1. See G.W. Bowersock, *Hellenism in Late Antiquity* (Ann Arbor: University of Michigan Press, 1996); Albert Henrichs, "Loss of Self, Suffering, Violence: The Modern View of Dionysus from Nietzsche to Girard," *Harvard Studies in Classical Philology* 88 (1984): 205–40, http://www.jstor.org/stable/311453?seq=1#page_scan_tab_contents.

45 Marcel Detienne, *Dionysos at Large*, trans. Arthur Goldhammer (Cambridge, MA: Harvard University Press, 1989), 10.

46 See Henk Versnel, "*Heis Dionysos*! – One Dionysos? A Polytheistic Perspective," in *A Different God? Dionysos and Ancient Polytheism*, ed. Renate Schlesier (Boston: De Gruyter, 2011), 23–46.

47 François Pomey, *The Pantheon, Representing the Fabulous Histories of the Heathen Gods*, trans. Andrew Tooke, 10th ed. (London, 1726), 77. Originally published in Latin (1675), it went through multiple English and French editions. See Jan Assmann, *Moses the Egyptian: The Memory of Egypt in Western Monotheism* (Cambridge, MA: Harvard University Press, 1997).

48 See Martin Muslow, "Antiquarianism and Idolatry: The *Historia* of Religions in the Seventeenth Century," in *Historia: Empiricism and*

Erudition In Early Modern Europe, ed. Gianna Pomata and Nancy G. Siraisi (Cambridge, MA: MIT Press, 2005), 181–209.

49 Antoine Banier, *La mythologie et les fables expliquées par l'histoire* (Paris, 1738–40), 2:257; *The Mythology and Fables of the Ancients, Explain'd from History* (London, 1739–40), 2:437. Banier also published an altered version of Bernard and Picart's *Cérémonies et coûtumes* (Paris, 1741).

50 Samuel Boyse, *The New Pantheon or, Fabulous History of the Heathen Gods, Goddesses, Heroes, etc.*, 4th ed. (Salisbury, 1761), 127. On early eighteenth-century mythologies see Burton Feldman and Robert D. Richardson, *The Rise of Modern Mythology, 1680-1860* (Bloomington: University of Indiana Press, 1972).

51 Lafitau, *Moeurs*, 1:254, trans., 1:174. See also 1:129–30, trans., 1:104.

52 Ibid., 1:254, trans., 1:174.

53 Ibid., 1:220, trans., 1:156.

54 See Malcolm Bull, *The Mirror of the Gods* (New York: Oxford University Press, 2005), ch. 6. Representations of mixed-gender bacchanals continued to be part of the visual tradition.

55 Antoine Banier, *La mythologie*, 2:272, trans., 2:256. Also see Bernard de Montfaucon, *Antiquity Explained and Represented in Sculptures*, trans. David Humphreys (London, 1722, reprint, New York: Garland Publishing, 1976), 1:164. Bacchantes are said to be either the nymphs who educated Bacchus, or female followers of Dionysus' expeditions to the East, or his priestesses. Also see Cornelia Isler-Kerenyi, "New Contributions of Dionysiac Iconography to the History of Religions in Greece and Italy," in *Mystic Cults in Magna Graecia*, ed. Giovanni Casadio and Patricia A. Johnston (Austin: University of Texas Press, 2009), 61–72; Albert Henrichs, "Greek Maenadism From Olympias to Messalina," *Harvard Studies in Classical Philology* 82 (1978): 121–60; Caroline Houser, *Dionysos and his Circle: Ancient through Modern* (Cambridge, MA: Fogg Art Museum, Harvard University Press, 1979).

56 Lafitau, *Moeurs*, 1:185, trans., 1:137.

57 Strabo, *The Geography 5*, trans. Horace L. Jones, Loeb Classical Library (Cambridge, MA: Harvard University Press, 1928), 93–5 (Book x, chapter 3, section 9). Lafitau, *Moeurs*, 1:186, trans., 1:137.

58 See Lafitau, *Moeurs*, vol. 1, plate 7, figure 1, which is a re-engraving from Theodor de Bry's *America* (1590) from a lost watercolour by Jacques Le Moyne de Morgues of the Timucua Indians of northeast Florida circa 1562–5. Bernard and Picart reused de Bry's illustrations of American rituals for *Cérémonies et coûtumes*. See also Lafitau, *Moeurs*, vol. 1, plate 18, figure 1 for which no existing visual source has been identified; and vol. 2,

plate 6, figure 1, also re-engraved from Theodor de Bry's *America* which is altered from John White's watercolour of religious dance of Virginians. See Kim Sloan, *A New World: England's First View of America* (Chapel Hill: University of North Carolina Press, 2007), 110–11, 116–17.

59 Sarah Iles Johnston, "Mysteries," in *Religions of the Ancient World: A Guide*, ed. Sarah Iles Johnston (Cambridge, MA: The Belknap Press of Harvard University Press, 2004), 105. See also Stella Georgoudi, "Sacrificing to Dionysos: Regular and Particular Rituals," in Schlesier, *A Different God?*, 47–60, and Edgar Wind, *Pagan Mysteries in the Renaissance*, rev. ed. (London: Faber and Faber, 1968).

60 Lafitau, *Moeurs*, 1:342, trans., 1:219.

61 Ibid., 1:342, trans., 1:220.

62 See Édith Flamarion, ed., *La chair et le verbe: Les jésuites de France au xviiie siècle et l'image* (Paris: Presses Sorbonne nouvelle, 2008).

63 Michel Foucault, *The Order of Things: An Archaeology of the Human Sciences* (New York: Vintage Books, [1966] 1994), 43, 47.

64 One example is Ann Thomson, *Bodies of Thought: Science, Religion and the Soul in the Early Enlightenment* (New York: Oxford University Press, 2008).

PART TWO

Materialisms

5 Defoe on Spiritual Communication, Action at a Distance, and the Mind in Motion

SARA LANDRETH

It is much the same thing whether a Man's Head be full of Vapours or Proclamations: Wind in the Brain makes Men giddy.

– John Goodman, *A Winter-Evening Conference between Neighbours* (1705)[1]

In Daniel Defoe's 1705 lunar voyage narrative, *The Consolidator,* the narrator discovers a number of fanciful instruments on the moon. No device is more astounding than the "Cogitator" or "thinking engine."[2] This "mechanick Chair" has the power to make men's thoughts "obedient to mechanick Operation" and, most crucially, to put the wild agitations of "the Memory, the Understanding, the Will, and the thinking Faculty … into regular Motions."[3] As I show below, the *Consolidator's* lunar instrumentation functions as a complex satire of both materialist models of the mind/soul and representations of mental activity in print.[4] We should not, however, mistake Defoe's satire for a wholesale dismissal of the possibility that the motions of thoughts and feelings might resemble the movements of material substances. To do so would be to ignore Defoe's persistent tendency to depict the mind/soul as a rarefied kinetic substance, a quasi-material vapour or ether that simultaneously obeys and defies the laws of physics. For Defoe, the mind/soul belongs to both the material world and the "angelick" world; it is neither wholly physical nor wholly metaphysical, but somewhere vexingly in-between. As Jayne Elizabeth Lewis has recently shown, during the eighteenth century "spirits themselves were a notional hybrid blending immaterial and material accounts of reality in response to the later seventeenth-century demand for discursive compromise."[5]

Defoe's fraught terminology expresses the philosophical and representational difficulties posed by this "hybrid blending" of psyche and soma; his narrators self-consciously adopt phrases that are reminiscent of John Locke's "body without body": "non-entity," "a middle class of spirit," and "things that are not."[6] Many of his publications approach thought as a species of motion itself, a "commotion" or "agitation." Defoe has etymology on his side here; our English word *cogitate* comes from the Latin *agitare,* meaning to "to turn" or "to agitate."[7] It is easy for us in the twenty-first century to forget that the phrase, "I'll have to turn that over in my mind," has its origins in a time when this "turning" was a literal description of mental activity.

This chapter is not a complete history of the many depictions of the mind/soul as a quasi-material substance in the Restoration and eighteenth century. Rather, I focus on how Defoe represents the mind/soul as an airy substance that is not only moved by stimuli, but also moves through various spaces: the upper atmosphere, the printed page, and other minds.[8] I follow Helen Thompson and Natania Meeker in their use of the word "substance" rather than "matter," because "in the eighteenth century substance could claim the qualifiers material and immaterial."[9] I have chosen Defoe's works in part because his contemporaries associated him with the twinned topics of visions and vapours (one literary adversary accused Defoe of suffering from "volatile effluvia of [the] brain"), but primarily because Defoe both compiled and produced a mammoth body of work on apparitions, spiritual communication, and the nature of what he called "vapourous matter."[10] I read the blustery minds in *The Consolidator* and *Vision of the Angelick World* (1720) not merely as meditations on the fine line between ecstatic visions and madness, but also as demonstrations of the difficulties of integrating a scholastic subject like pneumatology – which for much of the sixteenth and seventeenth centuries consisted of the study of angels, demons, spirits, and the nature of the soul – into newer empirical Enlightenment classifications of knowledge.[11] Defoe was not, of course, alone in grappling with these difficulties. Like the Latitudinarian Cambridge Platonists who developed theories about the soul's "airy vehicle," Defoe's narrators are keenly interested in what happens when pneumatics and pneumatology collide. Henry More, Joseph Glanvill, Defoe, and many others take for granted that the mind/soul moves and perhaps can travel as an entity separate from its body. This view raises a number of questions: how can we understand motion and its laws when the thing that is moving is not a *thing,* per se? How can we represent the motion of an entity that, although it has extension and therefore tallies with the traditional Cartesian definition of material substance, is nevertheless invisible or so rarefied as to be almost immaterial?

My focus on vapours, winds, ethers, and other quasi-material substances is significant for both philosophy and literature, because writing about the airy qualities of the mind/soul allowed Defoe to reflect on the way that the act of reading begets its own mists and *ignes fatui*, its apparitions and evanescent beings. Printed texts, like minds and winds, are neither wholly tangible nor intangible. Particularly significant are illustrated editions of Defoe's works, which test theories about how the reader's mind is moved by a text, and how a mind might move out and act on the external world. I turn to Jay David Bolter's and Richard Grusin's "double logic" of immediacy and hypermediacy to more fully explain how Defoe understood the experience of reading as an intermingling of multiple representations, both mental and physical.[12] Media theory provides a framework for thinking through the ways that Defoe places both mind/souls and printed works on a continuum of quasi-material substances that act as mediums out in the world. Defoe was also concerned with how figurative language might address the problem of "vapourous" substance. I argue that Defoe challenges the modern privileging of "plain" language and suggests that allegory and emblems might be better suited to the representation of the mind/soul. Furthermore, Defoe takes on the instrumentation of the new philosophy in his insistence that the most accurate optical device would be one that reflexively revealed the cloudy and contradictory motions of the human perceptive faculties.

I. Mind as "Vapourous Matter"

Recent scholarship has tended to divide *The Storm* (1704) and *The Consolidator* along modern disciplinary and generic boundaries, separating Defoe's satirical science fiction from his natural-philosophical journalism.[13] By reading *The Storm* and *The Consolidator* as two halves of the same narrative experiment, we can better understand how Defoe approached the challenges of representing the invisible motions of the mind/soul. Both texts borrow an experiment that was published in Francis Bacon's 1622 *Experimentall History of Winds* and reprinted in Richard Bohun's 1671 *Discourse Concerning the Origine and Properties of Wind*, a text that Defoe's critics accused him of plagiarizing.[14] Bacon's three "feather trials" observed the motions of "a Crosse of Feathers" when it was suspended first over a fire, second over a boiling kettle, and finally over both a fire and boiling kettle simultaneously.[15] During the third trial, "the agitation of the Crosse of Feathers was very vehement" and it "whirle[d] up and downe, as if it had been a petty Whirlwinde."[16] From this, Bacon infers that one likely cause of strong winds is the sun heating water vapour. In *The Storm,* Defoe's narrator doubts whether this is "a sufficient Demonstration" that "all the Causes of Wind are from the Influence of the Sun upon vaporous Matter" and surmises that this is "at best ... a probable Conjecture."[17] What is at stake for Defoe's narrator is, in part, a question of first and second causes. If one assumes that the cause of the wind is indeed superheated "vaporous matter," this weakens Defoe's providential account of the Great Storm of November, 1703, in which God has expressed his wrath directly – as a Prime Mover and first cause – through the tempest. After all, if one wants to strike terror into the hearts of sinners, it certainly lessens the blow if one cannot say, "the wind *is* God's wrath," but only, "the wind is a by-product of a natural system of rarefaction and condensation set in place by God four or five millennia ago." Bacon's "vaporous matter" also reduces the mysterious nature of wind – its intangible quasi-materiality and its apparently self-moving force – to an amalgamation of inert particles. Even if Bacon's hypothesis does not preclude Defoe's argument, that the wind is a medium through which God punishes humankind, it thickens and befogs that medium by adding a series of second causes (sunlight heating water, water becoming vapour, vaporous particles moving ever faster in a chain reaction) between the Prime Mover and the motions of the material world. Divine action at a distance becomes ever more distant.

Bacon's feather trials were more useful for Defoe as a metaphor for the human mind/soul. *The Consolidator,* which was published only ten months after *The Storm,* features a feathered spaceship that both satirizes pneumatic models of the mind/soul and lampoons volatile members of the House of Commons: "The Head of every Feather is ... full of a vigorous Substance, which gives Spirit ... some are so full of Wind, and puft up with the Vapour of the Climate, that there's not Humid enough to Condence the Stream; and these are so ... continually fluttering and troublesome, that they greatly serve to disturb and keep the Motion unsteddy ... The fluttering hot-headed Feathers are the most dangerous."[18] Defoe has shifted the "vapourous matter" of Bacon's trials from the realm of pneumatics (the outer air) to pneumatology (the motions of the mind/soul). The imagery in this passage playfully samples from humoural medicine, classical descriptions of the soul as *pneuma* or breath, and iatromechanical models in which animal spirits and nervous fluids in the brain might behave like the vapours in Bacon's laboratory.[19] This is also, in another sense, a metaphor made literal, in that *The Consolidator* imagines what actual "hot-headed[ness]" might look like. It is this very tendency in English common usage – to refer to mental phenomena as airy substances – that Hobbes scorns in *Leviathan* (1651). While "the common language of men" equates "idols of the … distempered brain" with "wind, or breath," Hobbes insists that such freaks of fancy are "nothing but tumult, proceeding … from the disorderly agitation of the organs of our sense."[20] In his *Consolidator* and elsewhere, Defoe implicitly rejects a Hobbesian position in which "substance and body signify the same thing; and therefore *substance incorporeal* are words, which when they are joined together, destroy one another."[21] Instead, Defoe explores the notion that the mind/soul might exist on a continuum somewhere in between materiality and immateriality.

For many eighteenth-century readers, images of an airy mind/soul would have alluded directly to Latitudinarian Cambridge Platonists such as Henry More, who argued that the immaterial soul was united to the material body through an "aerial vehicle," and that "the place of [the disembodied soul's] abode [was] the Air."[22] James Chandler describes More's vehicular hypothesis as a direct challenge to "the mechanistic theses of Descartes, the materialist-mechanist theses of Hobbes, and the materialist theses of Spinoza."[23] More and his followers Ralph Cudworth and Joseph Glanvill insisted that the soul was indeed immaterial, but for it to be united with a material human body, it followed that it must be encased in a quasi-material substance. This gave rise to the central quandary of the vehicular hypothesis: how can one imagine an adequate intermediary between matter and spirit? Like the air, the soul's vehicle is *like* matter but not wholly material, and also *like* spirit but not purely spiritual. This conundrum continued to spur debate throughout the century. As late as 1777, Joseph Priestley's *Disquisitions Relating to Matter and Spirit* derided "modern metaphysicians" who, upon "finding some difficulty in uniting together things so discrepant … as a pure immaterial substance and such gross matter … have imagined that this connection may be better cemented by means of some intermediate material substance."[24] Priestley's concretizing verb, "cemented," expresses the impossibility of fully articulating an "intermediate … substance" that is incorporeal and yet capable of joining, with the subtlest of bonds, incompatible substances.[25]

For More, the soul's vehicle resembled the air itself in that it both took up space and moved through space but was not, strictly speaking, *matter*.[26] This is nowhere more evident than in More's discussion of the "dangers" that a soul in its vehicle might face when buffeted by "tempests" in the upper atmosphere: "And yet Rain, Hail, Snow, and Thunder, will incommodate her still less. For they pass as they do through other parts of Air, which close again immediately, and leave neither wound nor scar behind him. Wherefore all these Meteors … may be a pleasure to her and [a] refreshment."[27] Here, the soul in its vehicle has qualities of both *psyche* and *soma*: on the one hand, even the most inclement British weather cannot physically damage it – no more than hail can "wound" the air – but, on the other hand, it is moved by physical objects in that it experiences "pleasure" and "refreshment" as a result of coming in contact with raindrops and snowflakes.

Defoe's *Consolidator* explores what happens when analogies between the mind/soul and the motions of vapours or gasses are taken to an illogical extreme. The lunar civilization boasts "another sort of Machine" called an "Elevator," which allows one to experience "Revelation" "in a Mechanick way" "helped by Fire" in which "the more vigorous Particles of the Soul" in "the Head" are "by the heat of strong Ideas … fermented to a strange height … beyond it self."[28] Here, the mind/soul has "Particles" that resemble a rarefied substance like the vapours of Bacon's feather experiment. The "Elevator" engine causes the imaginative faculty of the mind/soul to be in a state of *ex-stasis* that allows it to exit the body and act on the external world. Here, the lunar traveller makes an abrupt shift in tone and quotes a line from Defoe's own popular poem, *The True-Born Englishman* (1701): "for Spirits without the helps of Voice converse."[29] Defoe added this line to later editions of the poem; it appears immediately after the speaker's command, "Satire, be silent!," and insists, in a newly sincere manner, that it is possible for humans to communicate with "distant worlds of spirits."[30] Defoe's Elevator makes a jibe at those who would puff up the capacity of philosophical instrumentation. Although the mind/soul might indeed resemble an airy substance, it is absurd and hubristic to imagine that human agency could achieve a divine vision through pneumatic experiments or mechanical engines. True visions are not subject to, nor caused by, philosophical demonstration. Hence, man-made instruments will never enable "the Intelligent Soul to have a clear Prospect into the World of Spirits, and converse with Visions, Guardian-Angels, [and] Spirits."[31] Even if the mind/soul is quasi-material, it will never be subject to the virtuoso's air pump.

As I show below, the notion that the mind/soul might actually resemble an airy, rarefied substance is crucial not only to Defoe's cosmology, but also to his generic choices. It is, after all, the mind's "vigorous" or "hot-headed" tendencies that enable one of Defoe's favourite narrative forms: the *visio* or dream-vision, in which the narrator's mind ecstatically "travels" or "soars." Defoe's narrators often describe visions in terms of gasses, vapours, and particulate matter. In describing his *Vision of the Angelick World*, Crusoe borrows one of the most iconic images in Defoe's *The Storm*: "When the soul is more than ordinarily agitated ... I can liken it to nothing so well as the Wheels of a Wind-mill ... which if the Wind blow a Storm, run round so fast they will set all on Fire."[32] Yet again, cogitation and agitation are one and the same, and thus Crusoe can best represent the motions of his mind/soul by forming analogies with the movements of pneumatic substances. Similarly, in Defoe's *Continuation of Letters Written by a Turkish Spy at Paris* (1718), Mahmut describes an ecstatic vision-state as "a Ferment" that thrusts "the Soul ... forcibly out of the Body ... as dilated Air bursts even the fiercest Mountains, on the fortuitous Meeting of the sulphurous and nitrous Particles in which it is imprisoned."[33] Mahmut admits, however, that although the analogy holds when one considers "dilated Air" and diaphanous "Particles," it ceases to function when the quasi-material is replaced with a vehicle that resembles gross matter. Hence, if we imagine the soul as a physical mass, the distance it must travel "is so great, that a Velocity of Motion, swift as a Ball from a Cannon, could not perform the Labour in a Million of Ages."[34] Crusoe and Mahmut agree that, rather than attempt to understand the mind/soul as a body that moves *through* what Isaac Newton called the "aetherial medium" or "ambient medium," it is more apt to envision the mind/soul *as* the in-between medium itself. This corresponds in interesting ways to Kevis Goodman's work on changing seventeenth-century conceptualizations of mediums and media. Goodman shows that whereas in the older, Aristotelian tradition, "the human faculty ... [is] stimulated *by* the in-between" or "conducting bodies" of the intervening medium, for Bacon the new, man-made "Organe" of writing "*is* the in-between" medium.[35] In one sense, we can view this as a shift from an understanding of a medium as something that impacts upon or happens to human beings, to an understanding of a medium as something that humans send out into the world. Defoe's works, as I show below, certainly follow this shift to a conceptualization of the print medium as a human faculty that moves out beyond and in between individual minds. For

Crusoe and Mahmut, it is both the mind/soul in its vision-state and the writings produced as a result of such visions that become "the in-between" that is "both an activity and a substance."[36]

It is perhaps no surprise, then, that pictorial representations of Defoe's vision-narratives tend to depict various mediums: ether, vortices, celestial fluids, angelic spirits. Printed illustrations of Crusoe's visions bear a striking resemblance to seventeenth- and eighteenth-century diagrams of the atmosphere, which often employed concentric rings to make different kinds of "vapourous matter" visible (see Figures 5.1 and 5.2).[37] Figure 5.1 depicts a series of nesting circles filled with an engraved stippling effect, which indicates a celestial fluid or ether rather than a void. This substance fills the space between the orbits of the seven known planets, each identified by their astrological symbol. The 1722 engraving also depicts Jupiter's four "Galilean moons" and the more recently discovered fourth and fifth moons of Saturn.[38] This level of accuracy urges the reader to associate this illustration with the familiar form of the natural philosophical diagram, which in turn lends credibility to Defoe's cosmology. Similarly, in Figure 5.2, the unnamed engraver uses concentric bands to illustrate the changing density of the air, with cumulonimbus clouds hugging the Earth in "son athmosphere" [*sic*] to the gradually expanding particles in "son tourbillon d'air" (the ether or upper atmosphere), and finally to the outermost "matiere celeste de notre grand tourbillon," Cartesian or Leibnizian vortices, an extended and quasi-material body of perpetually moving celestial fluid that carries the planets in their orbits.[39] The illustrations of Crusoe's visions conform to readers' expectations that such diagrams represented what could not be seen with the naked eye or even through a telescope.

Both engravings also make visible Defoe's insistence that the mind/soul and empyrean substance moved in analogous ways. Eighteenth-century discourse on spiritual communication was one crucial area of overlap between the old pneumatology of angels and the soul and a renewed late seventeenth-century focus on the quasi-material properties of the mind.[42] As John Durham Peters explains, "If floor space is in fact scarce" when angels dance on the head of a pin, then "clearly angelic bodies occupy space, however infinitesimal" and hence, "things intellectual do indeed have a corporeal correlate – thoughts might have weight and extension."[43] This notion that the mind/soul might take up space raises crucial questions about its motions, because a substance with extension also requires time to move though that space, and could potentially be hindered in its motions by contact with other substances.[44]

Figure 5.1. *Vision du Monde Angélique,* 1721, printed engraving, 16 cm. Image courtesy of the Rare Books Collection, Raynor Memorial Libraries, Marquette University. From: *Reflexions Serieuses et Importantes de Robinson Crusoe … avec Sa Vision Du Monde Angelique.* Amsterdam: L'Honore et Chatelain, 1721. Frontispiece to Volume 3.[40]

Figure 5.2. *Vision du Monde Angélique,* 1761, printed engraving, 30 cm. Image courtesy of the Lyon Public Library. From: "Vision du Monde Angélique" in *La vie et les Aventures Surprenantes de Robinson Crusoe,* Vol. 3. Paris: Cailleau Dufour Cuissart, 1761. Frontispiece to Part 5.[41]

How, then, did souls or thoughts travel? Was physical proximity or immediate contact necessary for a mind/soul to "converse" with angels, apparitions, or other embodied minds? In his *History and Reality of Apparitions* (1727), Defoe's narrator relies on intermediary spirits to explain direct communication between the heavens and humans.[45] He insists that only an arrogant fool would presume that the Prime Mover or even the Devil himself might stoop to whisper warnings to the individual minds of mere mortals. Instead, we must assume that there is a "middle Class of Spirit" that has "the Power of conversing among us ... and can by Dreams, Impulses, and strong Aversions, move our Thoughts."[46] To explain how a human mind comes to be moved by a spiritous being, Defoe's narrator must place them both (the mind and spirits) on a continuum of corporeal and incorporeal substances. These go-between beings are neither "Angelick-heavenly [n]or Anglick-Infernal" but rather bodies without body that inhabit the "Abyss of Space" in countless numbers.[47]

Hence, the illustration in Figure 5.1 depicts a region that is neither an "abyss" nor empty "space." Instead, the solar system is densely populated with winged, shadowy spirits. The image of Crusoe's body is a placeholder for his "agitated" soul; he, too, in this context of this vision, is a body without body. Like Mahmut's letters, this engraving prompts the reader to understand a vision as an instance of the soul thrust "forcibly out of the body" as if it were in More's aerial "vehicle." It is also important to note the significance of linear perspective in the image. Crusoe's soul-body appears as the largest object in space, presumably because he is closest – as a first-person narrator – to the reader's imagined point of view. The Earth, as Crusoe's point of departure, is the next-largest body in the solar system. The "middle-class" spirits are, in many instances, larger on the page than the planets, and must be read as closer to the reader's field of vision. Hence, the perspective of the illustration suggests that souls and angels both have extension and move, albeit very swiftly, within the bounds of time and space.

In Figure 5.2, Crusoe's body is surrounded by a field of diaphanous spheres that seem to cling to his outstretched arms and legs, almost as if he were enveloped by his own personal atmosphere: a spiritual spacesuit. But of course, Crusoe's narrative does not imply that his body is actually swimming through a sea of celestial fluids, rather that his "Intelligent Soul is made to converse with its own Species, whether embody'd or not."[48] Hence, because the illustration has already established itself as a representation of substances that cannot be seen by human eyes (vortices, orbital paths, mediating spirits, souls), we might read the atmosphere that surrounds Crusoe's body as something akin to a thought-bubble or thought-balloon, that graphic externalizer of cogitation found in graphic novels and cartoons.[49] The reader sees Crusoe's internal thoughts – what he envisions in his mind's eye during his vision – as beads or particles of an extended substance. For Defoe, the genre of the vision narrative requires that thoughts take up space. That visions necessitate states of in-between-ness – between mind and body, spirit and substance, heaven and earth – also reflects Defoe's theories about a reader's ideal state of mind. In the preface to *Apparitions,* Defoe's narrator warns his reader that to comprehend the world of spirits, one's mind must assume "a right Temper between th[e] Extreams" of "Imagination and solid Foundation."[50] The reader must accustom herself to dwelling in the uncertain realm between fiction and fact, metaphysics and physics, pneumatology and pneumatics. This "in-between" state of mind is a necessary precondition for contemplating both the "in-between" genre in which he is writing – the apparition narrative – and the "in-between," quasi-material nature of the "invisible world" itself, which he describes as existing "between *Some-where* and *No-where* … none of us know *where,* and yet we are sure must have Locality … very near us."[51]

Defoe's quasi-material models of spiritual communication, whether satirical, in *The Consolidator*, or sincere, in Crusoe's *Vision* or Mahmut's *Letters,* demonstrate two of the definitions of *communication* in Johnson's *Dictionary* (1755): first, as a "conversation" or "interchange of knowledge," and second, as a "passage or means … from one place … to another" that enables physical motion through space.[52] In light of this double meaning of communication – both as an interchange of knowledge and as the movement of things or people – Defoe's account of moving, vaporous visions resembles nothing so much as printed texts, objects that have both a circulating, physical component (words on paper) and an imaginative one (what the reader sees in her mind's eye).[53] Indeed, Defoe playfully suggests that *The Consolidator* is both a text *and* a vision. The Baconian feathers function as an allegory for a Parliamentarian critique of the Crown (the lunar analogue of Charles I is said to have "guided the [Consolidator] with so unsteddy a Hand … that the Feathers could not move") and also stand in for the unreliable narrator's own "unsteddy" and potentially "dangerous" flights of fancy.[54] It is a figurative device that makes a critique (as a symbol for dysfunctional government) and, at the same time, pre-emptively defuses that critique (because, in doing double-duty as a symbol for the iatromechanical mind, it draws attention to the fact that this feathered spaceship could be nothing more than a delusion caused by the narrator's own overheated animal spirits). Defoe wrote *The Consolidator* just months after the fallout from the publication of *The Shortest Way with the Dissenters* (1702) landed him in prison. It is not surprising, then, that he chose to deliver much of *The Consolidator's* political critique from behind the mask of a contradictory narrator who is at best "hot-headed" and at worst stark raving mad. Defoe's narrator admits that it is "no uncommon thing for [a] Person to be intirely [sic] deceived by himself, not knowing the brat of his own Begetting, nor be able to distinguish between Reality and Representation."[55] Hence, the subject and object of the narrator's vision is the mind/soul reflexively trying to glimpse its own operations. Here, the joke is on the reader: Defoe's text and the feathered spaceship share the same name; both the piece of writing and the gaseous engine have the power to drive one, as it were, out of one's mind.

II. Mind as Apparition

For Defoe, the mind/soul – especially a reader's mind, which has the ability to jump between perspectives and to assume various points of view – is a thing that moves. One of the most widely reprinted vignettes from Defoe's *Apparitions* speaks to the unique ability of print to represent the mind/soul as a medium that might extend out into the external world. The story centres on "a certain Man who was brought to the Bar of Justice on Suspicion of Murder" and who is subsequently overcome by the "agitations" of his guilty conscience.[56] Defoe's narrator describes the murderer's actions as he imagines that he sees his dead victim enter the courtroom:

> the Man ... gave a Start at the Bar, as if he was frighted; but recovering his Courage a little, he stretches out his Arm towards the Place where the Witnesses usually stood to give Evidence upon Tryals, and pointing with his Hand, My Lord, says he, (aloud) that is not fair, 'tis not according to Law, he's not a legal Witness. The Court is surpris'd, and could not understand what the Man meant; but the Judge, a Man of more Penetration, took the Hint, and checking some of the Court that offer'd to speak, and which would have perhaps brought the Man back again to himself; Hold, says the Judge, the Man sees something more than we do, I begin to understand him.[57]

The narrator switches back and forth between tenses, using the present tense for most actions and speech ("stretches," "pointing," "says") and the past tense for mental processes ("could not understand," "took the hint," "brought … back again to himself"). This emphasizes the difference between those activities that are observable and those that must be inferred from external signs. Hence, from the outset of the tale, the narrator grants the reader a privileged but limited view on events. The sequence in which the narrator divulges tantalizing details to the reader is also typical of Defoe's *Apparitions*. Although the narrator prefaces this story with a discussion of the "Force" of "Conscience" that "makes a Man view things that are not, as if they were" – and hence, presumably, the reader can guess the cause of the man's "frigh[t]" – the narrator withholds crucial information to let the events unfold in chronological "real-time" as if from a third-person limited perspective.[58] This perspective places the reader in a curious position; she is not, like other observers in the courtroom, "surpris'd" and unable to "understand what the Man meant," but is rather, like the Judge, granted "more penetration" through "Hint[s]." And yet, the dialogue that follows this passage makes clear that the narrative is focalized neither through the perspective of the judge nor through that of the guilty man. Rather, like a theatregoer in a playhouse, the reader "hears" the Judge's "aside" – his furtive "Hold … " – when the guilty man and other courtroom observers do not. The narrator's use of the passive voice (the guilty man "was observed to be in a great Consternation") seems to suggest that most of the people in the courtroom practice an unthinking – or at least less actively "penetrat[ing]" – species of observation. They, unlike the judge and the reader, are unable to determine the cause of the man's apparent distress. Defoe's text does not allow the reader direct or consistent access to the thoughts of either the judge or the murderer, but rather urges her to read external signs (gestures and words) and to infer the internal, mental causes thereof.

After the judge exhorts the murderer to confess, the narrator interjects and reveals that the man at the bar had seen "the murder'd Person standing upon the Step as a Witness … ready to shew his Throat which was cut … and who … stood staring full upon him with a frightful Countenance."[59] Defoe's narrator makes clear that "no body saw any thing but the Man at the Bar."[60] This last claim is of double significance: first, it insists that the observers in the courtroom saw nothing but the guilty man standing before them; and second, it suggests that the man at the bar was the only person who "saw any *thing*" of note (emphasis mine). This is because, as the narrator announces in his conclusion to the anecdote,

> there was no real Apparition, no Spectre, no Ghost or Appearance, it was all figur'd out to him by the Power of his own Guilt, and the Agitations of his Soul ... the Soul of the Murderer is like the Ocean in a tempest, he is in continual Motion, restless and raging, and the Guilt of the Fact, like the Winds to the Sea, lies on his Mind like a constant Pressure, and ... 'tis hurry'd about by its own Weight, rolling to and again, Motion increasing Motion, 'till it becomes a mere Mass of Horror and Confusion.[61]

As with the Baconian feather-minds in *The Consolidator*, Defoe turns to a pneumatic analogy to explain mental activity. The narrator does not clearly distinguish between "Soul" and "Mind"; both experience "Agitations," "Motion," and "Pressure" that approximate the movements of liquids or airs with "Weight" and "Mass." And yet this is another example of mental motion without a *thing* that moves. Jayne Elizabeth Lewis has argued that Defoe approaches apparitions as "pure media: pneumatic impersonations of the absent that both validate and objectify the very faculties that perceive them."[62] In this anecdote, what the guilty man sees – or thinks he sees – is not only an "impersonation of the absent," but also an externalization of the internal.[63] The "thing" that the man at the bar sees is his own mental agitation, which, like the wind itself, is an invisible causal force that only becomes visible in its effects. In short, the mind *is* the Baconian, in-between medium.

Defoe's wind-in-the-mind metaphor is complicated by the illustration that accompanies the story of the man at the bar (see Figure 5.3).[64] The image depicts the accused murderer, with his ankles shackled, starting back from a cloud of vapour that seems to envelop the head and neck of the victim. But who sees what is pictured in this engraving? Certainly not the observers in the courtroom, who – even in the case of the more "penetrat[ing]" judge – see only the accused man and his "Consternation." Indeed, not even the guilty man himself sees what is pictured here. There is no mention in his confession of a cloud of vapour – reminiscent of the damning "Flaming-Sword ... coming out of a Cloud" that H.F. dismisses in *A Journal of the Plague Year* (1722) – nor of a floating, disembodied head.[65] On the contrary, the man at the bar views the victim as a decidedly flesh-and-blood personage who can "stan[d] on the step as a witness" and "shew his throat." We cannot, then, interpret this cloud as a thought bubble. So what, precisely, does this engraving represent? It is important to note that the illustration of the man at the bar is the only "cut" in eighteenth-century editions of *Apparitions* that represents a rarefied vapour or airy substance. The other five engravings represent spirits "case[d]" in "Flesh and Blood" that on the page appear to be no different than their corporeal counterparts.[66] This is especially significant when we consider that the picture of the man at the bar is the only one that portrays an apparition that is, as Defoe's narrator insists, "no real Apparition" at all. The other illustrations show actual mediating spirits who exist outside the confines of the percipient's mind. Hence, Defoe and the engraver, J. Van Der Gucht, were tasked with differentiating between illustrations that represented actual spirits, and one that represented the "tempest[uous]" "agitations" of a man's mind/soul.

What the reader sees in this engraving, then, is a reification of the narrator's analogy between a guilty conscience and the "constant pressure" and pneumatic force of the wind "in a tempest." The cloud of vapour in the picture suggests the quasi-material nature of the mind/soul: those "pressures" that – like the wind – might also have "Weight" and "Mass." Hence, the disembodied head suspended in cloud functions not as a spectre of the murdered victim, but rather as a mirror image of the guilty man's mind/soul and its motions. We see an illustration not of a ghost, but rather of the agitated animal spirits of a murderer's mind made manifest in the world. This of course does not happen in the narrative; Defoe's text does not suggest that there is a cloud of spirits billowing out of the murderer's brain. Rather, this externalization is a visual approximation of causality: it allows the viewer to see, simultaneously, both the visible effects (the man's "Consternation") and the invisible causes thereof (the agitated "tempest" of spirits in his brain). Most strikingly, this engraving represents in pictorial form what it is like to be a reader of Defoe's *Apparitions*. It is a picture not of the events in the courtroom, but rather what happens when the narrative is mediated through the reader's mind's eye. The illustration approximates what the reader visualizes as she reads the words on the page: here, a third-person perspective on the courtroom; there, a first-person glance through the murderer's eyes; and finally, an omniscient glimpse of what the guilty man's mind/soul might look like were its agitations projected out into the world. It captures Defoe's treatment of the story as both an immediate experience, complete with dramatic dialogue and descriptions of gestures, and a hypermediated one in which an intrusive narrator not only draws attention to the fictionalized status

Figure 5.3. J. Van Der Gucht, *The Man at the Bar*, 1727, printed engraving, 21 cm. Image courtesy of the Boston Public Library. From: Defoe, *An Essay on the History and Reality of Apparitions*. London: J. Roberts, 1727.[67]

of his story ("I have heard a story which I believe to be true") but also insists on its veracity as a particular example of a general truth ("Conscience ... shows us many an Apparition that no other Eyes can see").[68]

Defoe's man at the bar is an example of what Bolter and Grusin call the "double logic of immediacy and hypermediacy": when a medium promises us a "more immediate or authentic experience," it inevitably also leads us to become aware of that medium as a medium.[69] An audience thus experiences, simultaneously, a "transparent presentation of the real and ... the opacity of media themselves."[70] This double logic is pertinent not only in the context of remediation and new digital media, but also, in past centuries, to an illustrated book's "integration of text and image."[71] Hence, the engraving of the man at the bar both presents the reader with a window onto the real events in the courtroom and reminds that reader that this exhibition is, in fact, not real, but rather a printed representation. On the one hand, if we read the disembodied head as the victim as seen by the murderer, the illustration shows us the "real Apparition" that the guilty man believes that he sees before him (immediacy). On the other hand, if we read the disembodied head as a representation of the guilty man's mental "Agitations," the vaporous cloud reminds us that the man only *imagines* that he sees the victim, and in fact sees a mental representation thereof (hypermediacy). This double logic also extends to the reader's experience. The engraving gives the reader a sense of immediacy (in that we can glimpse the man's invisible thoughts) and yet also reminds us that we are viewing a representation (an engraving) of another representation (the narrator's written account) of yet another representation (the oral story that the narrator "heard") of what is, finally, a mental representation (the apparition that exists only in the guilty man's mind's eye). Bolter and Grusin explain that hypermediacy "acknowledges multiple acts of representation and makes them visible" "particularly when the illusion of realistic representation is somehow stretched or altogether ruptured."[72] Here, one such "rupture" occurs when – although the narrator insists that the apparition exists only in the murderer's thoughts – the illustration suggests quite the contrary: that the agitations of the guilty man's mind are not, in fact, limited to the confines of his brain, but have a causal force that extends not only out into the courtroom, but also to the minds of readers in distant locales. The hypermediacy of the printed page allows Defoe to explore the ways in which mind/souls – especially when engaged in the practices of imagining or reading – are mobile substances. Print can both represent the fact that mind/souls act as mediums outside the confines of the skull and also cause the mind/soul to move.

This model of the mind/soul as a moving body without body recalls Bacon's theories about spiritual communication in *Sylva Sylvarum* (1627), what he calls the "operation of the spirits of the mind of man upon other spirits."[73] Bacon insists that imagination is the most mobile faculty in this regard, because it "hath most force upon things that have the lightest and easiest motions. And therefore above all, upon the spirits of men."[74] Here, the dynamics of spiritual communication obey physical laws. Joseph Glanvill's *Vanity of Dogmatizing* (1661) – one of Defoe's many sources of inspiration for *Apparitions* – followed Bacon's lead with its famous anecdote of the Scholar-Gypsy, who is able to both penetrate and move his friends' minds with the power of thought alone: "what he did was by the power of Imagination, his Phancy binding theirs; and that himself had dictated to them the discourse they held together" while he was physically removed in another room.[75] Glanvill explains that the movement of thoughts is analogous to those of physical bodies:

> I see not why the phancy of one man may not determine the cogitation of another rightly qualified, as easily as his bodily motion. This influence seems to be no more unreasonable, then that of one string of a Lute upon another; when a stroak on it causeth a proportionable motion in the sympathizing consort, which is distant from it and not sensibly touched ... so then, the agitated parts of Brain begetting a motion in the proxime Aether; it is propagated through the liquid medium, as we see the motion is which is caus'd by a stone thrown into the water ... And thus the motion being convey'd from the Brain of one man to the Phancy of another, it is there receiv'd from the instrument of conveyance, the subtil matter ... [76]

The "agitat[ion]" of the "Brain" "beget[s] a motion in the ... Aether," which transmits this motion to the "distant" and yet "sympathizing" "Phancy of another." Here, unlike More and his airy vehicle, Glanvill's chain of causality seems to take for granted that the mind/soul might immediately act upon and move a quasi-material "medium" or "subtil matter." While Defoe very clearly laid out his argument for how angels might move the minds of men, his writings are equivocal on the subject of how minds might move other minds. Rather than weigh in definitively on the existence of an airy vehicle or vibrating ether, Defoe's *Apparitions* suggests that the most effective medium for the transmission of the agitations of the mind/soul is print. Specifically, one requires a particular combination of representations – an illustration that depicts invisible substance and a narrative that is both limited and partially omniscient – if one hopes to "causeth," in Glanvill's words, "a proportionable motion" in the "Phancy" of the reader.

III. Mind as Emblem

I have been arguing that there is a connection between Defoe's tendency to depict the mind/soul as an airy substance and his interest in what we in the twenty-first century might call the hypermediacy of the printed page. I want now to return to *The Consolidator* to examine how Defoe's treatment of the mind/soul as a moving substance not only tests the efficacy of different methods of representation but also functions as a critique of the movement towards "plainness" in philosophical writing in the late seventeenth century.[77] As I show below, Defoe challenges the argument put forth by Thomas Sprat, Robert Hooke, and others that plain, non-metaphorical language was the best way to represent reality. If we take for granted that the mind/soul is like an airy substance that – with the aid of printed text and illustrations – moves outward, what we *see* with our eyes is not reality, but rather a projection of our mind out in the world. This is not to suggest that Defoe is embracing a form of Berkeleian idealism in which external objects are entirely mind-dependent. Rather, his satire points to how any writer hoping to represent the nature of human sensory experience needs allegories and emblems, which can capture the ways in which the agitated mind/soul tends to see or jump between multiple things at once.

The Consolidator is another of Defoe's texts that imagines ways in which the mind/soul is not only moved by sensory stimuli, but also moves out into and even acts upon the external realm. The narrator finds fantastical optical instruments in the lunar realm, including "a strange sort of Glass that did not so much bring to the Eye, as by I know not what wonderful Operation carried out the Eye to the Object."[78] It is not, however, the viewer's physical eye that travels outward, but rather his mind's eye. These glasses allow Defoe's narrator to view, externally and out in the world, the mental images that, ordinarily, only his imagination would "see" in the act of reading. What is most germane to my discussion here is how the glasses show "allegorical" and "Emblematic Representation[s] of the Soul," in which "the Analogy is remarkable, even in the very Simily; for … they represent … the Soul … as a Great

Eye, embracing the Man, enveloping, operating, and informing every Part."[79] Although one might argue that this symbolism serves primarily to mock the universal language schemes of Restoration writers like Bishop Wilkins or John Webster (whose tongue-tripping "Hieroglyphical, Emblematical, Symbolical" Defoe's narrator here parrots), Defoe's optical emblems also function as a serious exploration of the advantages of allegory over modern empirical methods. These glasses do the work of Defoe's satire as a whole; when the narrator peers through them, he sees not bare reality, but rather a figurative version of reality that is more *real* than that available to the senses.[80] This is because, whenever we look at the world, whether through instruments or with our naked eye, what we see is in large part an image or projection of the agitation of our mind/soul. For Defoe, allegorical or emblematical representations – which often present a concrete image that prompts the reader's mind to move onward or outward to other, more abstract ideas – can, unlike other forms grounded in empirical description, begin to explain the nature of "body without body" and airy substance. Hence, when the narrator of *The Consolidator* looks at a politician through the glasses, he sees "a great Eye with Six or Seven pair of Spectacles on ... [as] they happen to have occasion ... to ... understand so many contrary ways upon one and the same thing."[81] Here, a static emblem of an eye wearing "Six or Seven pair of Spectacles" captures the perpetually moving nature of the human/mind soul in its tendency towards contradiction and changeability.

It is no coincidence that the lunar glasses' emblematical representation of the mind/soul is also wearing glasses. Unlike Hooke's *Micrographia* (1665), which claimed that optical instrumentation would help humankind avoid mistaking "similitudes for definitions" and see instead "the true nature of the things themselves," Defoe's satire suggests that a more accurate optical instrument would reflexively illustrate the contradictory and "contrary" motions of the human mind and its perceptions.[82] Here, Defoe's narrator joins the Bear-Men of Margaret Cavendish's *Blazing-World* (1666), who insist that although their telescopes are indeed "false Informers," they "take more delight in Artificial delusions, than in Natural truths."[83] Mistaking what Hooke calls "similitudes" for "the things themselves" is the most pleasurable – and indeed, most human – way of seeing the world. What Defoe's lunar glasses show the narrator is, primarily, a reflection of his own mind/soul – with all its "unsteddy" and yet pleasing "agitations" – projected outward into his field of vision.

We can also read the lunar glasses as a defence of allegory in the wake of late seventeenth-century attacks on figurative language. Sprat's *History of the Royal Society* (1667) had famously set the "discourse" of the New Science above other kinds of writing by claiming that it avoided "specious tropes and figures."[84] The "trick of metaphors," although formerly used to clarify abstractions in that it "represent[ed] truth, clothed with bodies," has in modern times, according to Sprat, become a "vicious abundance" that "give[s] the mind a motion too changeable."[85] To counteract the mind/soul's tendency towards erratic movement, Sprat prescribed "a return back to the primitive purity ... when men delivered so many things, almost in an equal number of words."[86] Such a "shortness" and plainness that demands proportionality between *verba* and *res* naturally precludes the "seeming Mysteries" of allegory, where one says a great number of things but means quite another.[87] Allegory's reputation for changeability and "obscurity" persisted into the eighteenth century.[88] Johnson's *Dictionary* uses as its first example of *allegory* a line from Ben Jonson's *Discoveries* (1641) that emphasizes the negative connotation of the term: "Neither must we draw out our allegory too long, lest either we make ourselves obscure, or fall into affectation, which is childish."[89] In *The Dyet of Poland* (1705), which was published in the same year as *The Consolidator,* Defoe defends the use of extended allegorical narrative: "But suppose there are not places call'd directly by those Names; if there are places apply'd to the same uses, what has any Body to question the Allegories? A poor Author must never Write at all, if he is not at Liberty to chuse his Metaphors, and all the rest of the necessary Figures of Speech to help out his Expression."[90] Defoe's lunar glasses emphasize that although all representation is imperfect, one needs these "Figures" – emblems, similes, allegories – to understand the nature of in-between substances that are neither wholly material nor purely spiritual. More specifically, if one wants to represent the perpetual motions of the human mind/soul, one can only do so by acknowledging that *all* acts of perception, whether sensory or imaginary, are in some sense a reflexive act of seeing our own agitated minds projected outward.

Thompson and Meeker have argued that "the problem of substance is ... one that must be posed in literary, figural, or formal terms because substance can only be apprehended as figure."[91] We can apply this notion – that airy substances can only be represented through metaphorical language – to *The Consolidator's* multiple representational strategies for *seeing* the mind/soul in motion. In this regard, *The Consolidator's* naive narrator serves as a cautionary figure. He forgets that although allegory is an effective mode for exploring "Immaterial Substance," it does not function in the same way as literal representation. Hence, most of the narrator's "emblematical" depictions do not fulfill their promise. Rather than teaching the viewer the vital secrets of matter and motion, analogies (e.g., "the memory is like a bee-hive"), when taken too literally, tend merely to convert immaterial substances into material things. The Lunarians' most prized artefacts include "anatomical dissections of Thought," including "a Fancy preserv'd a la Mummy," a calcified sample of poetic inspiration, and the "Part of the Head" containing the "Memory" "turn'd in-side outward" to reveal a "Glass Bee-Hive" full of forgotten thoughts.[92] Here, the dynamic faculties of the mind have become mere matter. Defoe echoes Locke's admonition that the phrase, "Faculties of the mind," might "breed … confusion in Mens Thoughts, by being supposed … to stand for some real Beings in the Soul."[93] The lunar concretions of fancy, poetic inspiration, and memory satirize those writers who would take a material model of the mind too far. Those vibrancies of the human mind/soul become nothing but lifeless husks: mummified flesh, calcium salts, and an abandoned apiary. Hence, the "consolidation" to which the eponymous engine refers is not only the fraught, political "combination into … one body" required of the House of Commons, but also that petrifaction implied by its Latin roots: *con + solidāre*: "to make firm or solid, to form into a … solid mass, to solidify."[94] Strict analogies between immaterial thought and material things fail in part because the human mind would seem to possess, as a necessary condition, the inability to turn the glasses inward and observe the causes of its own motions. The mental faculties, in their very potencies and capacities, rely in some unfathomable way on their being unfathomable to the mind/soul itself.

Defoe's lunar glasses underscore the immediacy of the experience of reading: that instant when the reader stops seeing the black marks on a white page and instead looks *through* the page, as it were, at a series of mental images in her mind's eye. And yet, the forms of representation produced by the glasses – allegory, emblem, analogy, and simile – all emphasize, like the engraving of the man at the bar in *Apparitions*, that immediacy paradoxically entails hypermediacy. This is especially true when the lunar traveller uses the glasses to flirt with blasphemy and to skirt the boundary between human discovery and divine revelation. At these doubtful moments, the lunar glasses stop showing allegories and emblems – with their proliferation of moving images and abstract ideas – and start reproducing printed letters. When Defoe's narrator, much to the horror of his lunar hosts, attempts to look through the glasses to foresee his own death, he sees two lines of verse hovering "as it were on the edge of the Horizon": *"The Verge of Life and Death is here. / 'Tis best to know where 'tis, but not how far."*[95] Notably, Defoe's narrator insists that he "plainly saw ... these Words" and did not hear them, as one might expect in a vision narrative, in the spoken form of an angelic voice. When he turns the "Glasses Up ... towards the Zenith" in order to "pr[y] into the Mysteries of the Great Eye of the World" he sees "these Words in the Air, REVELATION, in large Capital Letters."[96] Here, the emphasis on "*these* Words ... in large Capital Letters" suggests that the narrator sees not handwriting, but rather printed characters [emphasis mine]. At the outer edges of human understanding, print, with its reproducibility and predictable sameness, can both halt the infinite regress of abstraction and remind us that such regress is, indeed, infinite. The act of looking, when mediated through an instrument such as these "second-sight glasses," produces neither ordinary sense data nor airy visions, but rather the printed word, which requires the reader to do the work of interpretation. As with the illustration of the man at the bar, Defoe calls attention to the hypermediated nature of experience. Rather than observing an emblem that represents abstractions such as Life, Death, or Revelation, the narrator sees printed words that denote these concepts. One cannot escape that what seems like a representation of reality is in fact a representation of a representation. Defoe urges his readers to laugh at his lunar traveller who, in a caricature of Sprat's directive, conflates *verba* and *res*. The narrator claims that the lunar glasses grant him the power "to know the separate meaning of *Body, Soul, Spirit, Life, Motion ...* "[97] Of course, knowing the "separate meaning" of terms is not the same as understanding how body and soul coexist, or how spirit is imbued with motion. Sprat's "purity" and "shortness" of language ultimately fail where more elaborate metaphors – whether allegorical hot-headed feathers or similes that liken the mind/soul's agitations to stormy seas – succeed in demonstrating the reflexive and hypermediated nature of perception.

NOTES

1 John Goodman, *A Winter-Evening Conference between Neighbours* (London: W.B. Dan Brown, 1705), 111.

2 Defoe, *The Consolidator: or, Memoirs of Sundry Transactions from the World in the Moon* (London: B. Bragg, 1705), 99.

3 Ibid., 98–9.

4 For the purposes of this essay, I will use the term "mind/soul," because Defoe and his contemporaries used the two words interchangeably.

5 Jayne Elizabeth Lewis, *Air's Appearance: Literary Atmosphere in British Fiction: 1660–1794* (Chicago: Chicago University Press, 2012), 32. Lewis is referring to Steven Shapin, *The Scientific Revolution* (Chicago: University of Chicago Press, 1996), 56.

6 See Locke's *Essay*, 2.13.23. Locke, *An Essay Concerning Human Understanding* (London: J. Churchill, 1706), 106. See Defoe, *Consolidator*, 86; Defoe, *An Essay on the History and Reality of Apparitions* (London: J. Roberts, 1727), 44; and Defoe, *The Storm*, ed. Richard Hamblyn (New York: Penguin, 2003), 31. For more on the term "non-entity" in seventeenth-century poetry and scientific discourse, see Anthony R. Archdeacon, "'Things Which are Not': Poetic and Scientific Attitudes in Non-Entities in the Seventeenth Century," in *The Arts of 17th-Century Science: Representations of the Natural World in European and North American Culture*, ed. Claire Jowitt and Diane Watt (Burlington, VT: Ashgate, 2002), 25–42.

7 *Oxford English Dictionary Online*, s.v. "cogitate," http://www.oed.com.proxy.bib.uottawa.ca/view/Entry/35859?redirectedFrom=cogitate#eid.

8 For more on Defoe and philosophies of mind see Geoffrey Sill, "Defoe and the Natural History of the Passions," in *The Cure of the Passions and the Origins of the English Novel* (Cambridge: Cambridge University Press, 2006), 69–85. Sill discusses *The Consolidator* but does not address pneumatic models of the mind.

9 See Natania Meeker and Helen Thompson, "Empiricism, Substance, Narrative: An Introduction," *The Eighteenth Century: Theory and Interpretation* 48.3 (2007): 184. For more on the material status of spiritual substances, see Ann Thomson, *Bodies of Thought: Science, Religion, and the Soul in the Early Enlightenment* (Oxford: Oxford University Press, 2008), 65–134.

10 Joseph Browne, *The Moon-Calf: Or, Accurate Reflections on the Consolidator*, ed. Maximillian Novak (New York: AMS Press, 1996), 28. See also Novak's "Introduction" (especially page vii) to this volume for Defoe and Browne's debates about the nature of the soul. For Defoe's phrase "vapourous matter," see note 17.

11 For more on the status of pneumatology in the eighteenth century, see Sara Landreth, "Breaking the Laws of Motion: Pneumatology and Belles Lettres in Eighteenth-Century Britain," *New Literary History* 43.2 (2012): 281–308.

12 Jay David Bolter and Richard Grusin, *Remediation: Understanding New Media* (Cambridge, MA: MIT Press, 1999), xiii–11.

13 Ilse Vickers, *Defoe and the New Sciences* (Cambridge: Cambridge University Press, 1996), 1–8.

14 *The Rebublican Bullies; Or, a Sham Battel between Two of a Side, in a Dialogue between Mr. Review and the Observator* (London: J. Nutt, 1705), 2. Quoted in Richard Hamblyn, "Introduction," in Defoe, *The Storm* (New York: Penguin, 2003), xxxiii.

15 Francis Bacon, *The Naturall and Experimentall History of Winds* (London: R.G. Gent., 1653), 111. Defoe's source for this experiment is very likely Bohun's *A Discourse Concerning the Origine and Properties of Wind. With an Historical Account of Hurricanes, and other Tempestuous Winds*, from which *The Storm* makes verbatim excerpts.

16 Bacon, *Naturall*, 112.

17 Defoe, *Storm*, 16.

18 Defoe, *Consolidator*, 47–8.

19 For more on the longevity of Galenic and humoural theories about the effects of digestive vapours in the brain, see John Rogers, *The Matter of Revolution: Science, Poetry, and Politics in the Age of Milton* (Ithaca, NY: Cornell University Press, 1998), 156; and also Denise Gigante, *Taste: A Literary History* (New Haven: Yale University Press, 2008), 30–56.

20 Thomas Hobbes, *Leviathan*, ed. Edwin Curley (Indianapolis: Hackett, 1994), 262.

21 Ibid.

22 Henry More, "The Immortality of the Soul," in *A Collection of Several Philosophical Writings of Dr. Henry More* (London: J. Downing, 1712), 169. Originally published in More's *Immortality of the Soul* in 1659. For more on the vehicular hypothesis in the eighteenth century, see James Chandler, *An Archaeology of Sympathy: The Sentimental Mode in Literature and Cinema* (Chicago: Chicago University Press, 2013), 176–94; and Sara Landreth, "The Vehicle of the Soul: Motion and Emotion in Vehicular It-Narratives," *Eighteenth-Century Fiction* 26:1 (2013): 93–120; and Philip C. Almond, *Heaven and Hell in Enlightenment England* (Cambridge: Cambridge University Press, 1994), 29–32.

23 Chandler, *Archaeology*, 189.

24 Joseph Priestley, *Disquisitions Relating to Matter and Spirit* (London: J. Johnson, 1777), 74.

25 Also cited in Landreth, "Vehicle," 117.

26 More, *Collection*, 173. More argues that the soul's vehicle is "of the very nature of the Air."

27 Ibid., 173.

28 Defoe, *Consolidator*, 110–11.

29 Defoe, *The True-Born Englishman* (London: J. Wilford, 1731), 34.

30 Ibid.

31 Defoe, *Consolidator*, 110–11.
32 Defoe, "Vision of the Angelick World," in *Serious Reflections During the Life and Surprising Adventures of Robinson Crusoe* (London: W. Taylor, 1720), 25. Defoe uses a very similar analogy in *The Compleat English Tradesman* (London: C. Rivington, 1727), 103.
33 Defoe, *A Continuation of Letters Written by A Turkish Spy at Paris* (London: W. Taylor, 1718), 109.
34 Ibid., 112.
35 Kevis Goodman, *Georgic Modernity and British Romanticism: Poetry and the Mediation of History* (Cambridge: Cambridge University Press, 2004), 17–20.
36 Ibid., 17.
37 For more on spatially oriented drawings and pictorial representations of atmosphere, see Lewis, *Air's Appearance*, 212–14.
38 Eighteenth-century sources usually credited Cassini with the discovery of these moons in 1684 and 1686, respectively.
39 This was, of course, one of the main debates between Newton and Leibniz regarding action at a distance: Newton argued that "gravity without a miracle could keep the planets in," whereas Leibniz insisted that this formulation reduced gravity to an "occult cause" of action at a distance, and hence maintained that the planets were carried by fluid vortices. In Query 21 of his second edition of the *Opticks*, Newton hypothesized that a "much rarer" "Medium" or ether might allow planets to act on each other at a distance, but elsewhere he maintained that no such substance was necessary. See Newton, *Opticks* (London: W. & J. Innys, 1718), 325.
40 In Defoe, *Reflexions Serieuses et Importantes de Robinson Crusoe, Faites pendant les Avantures surprenantes de sa Vie avec Sa Vision du Monde Angelique* (Amsterdam: L'Honore et Chatelain, 1721), vol. 3. I would like to thank the Raynor Memorial Libraries at Marquette University for permission to use this image.
41 In Defoe, *La vie et les avantures surprenantes de Robinson Crusoe… Réflexions sérieuses et importantes de Robinson Crusoe … avec sa Vision du Monde Angélique*, trans. Thémiseuil de Saint-Hyacinthe and J. Van Effen (Paris: Cailleau Dufour Cuissart, 1761), 3.198, http://books.google.ca/books?id=2tBPz_ggSUgC&dq=La%20vie%20et%20les%20Aventures%20Surprenantes%20de%20Robinson%20Crusoe&pg=PA198#v=onepage&q=La%20vie%20et%20les%20Aventures%20Surprenantes%20de%20Robinson%20Crusoe&f=false.
42 For more on Enlightenment angelology, see both Nick Wilding, "Galileian Angels" (67–89) and Simon Schaffer, "Newtonian Angels" (90–124), both in *Conversations with Angels: Essays Towards a History of Spiritual*

Communication, 1100–1700, ed. Joad Raymond (New York: Palgrave, 2011). See also Joad Raymond, *Milton's Angels: The Early-Modern Imagination* (Oxford: Oxford University Press, 2010), 48–161.

43 John Durham Peters, *Speaking into the Air: A History of the Idea of Communication* (Chicago: University of Chicago Press, 1999), 75.

44 Bishop Wilkins famously argued that, "amongst all created substances, there are not any of so swift a motion as Angels or Spirits. Because there is not … without them in the medium, any such impediment as may, in the least manner retarde their courses." John Wilkins, *Mercury, or the Secret and Swift Messenger* (London: J. Norton, 1641), 118–22. See also Guillory, "Genesis of the Media Concept," 335–8.

45 Rodney Baine has argued that this is one of the most unique arguments in Defoe's angelology. See Baine, *Defoe and the Supernatural* (Athens, GA: University of Georgia Press, 1968), 16–18.

46 Defoe, *Apparitions*, 35. See also page 56: "Nor are these Notions of them at all absurd or inconceivable, tho' the Manner how they act may not be understood by us: 'Tis but Soul conversing with Soul, Spirit communicating with Spirit, one intellectual Being to another, and by secret Conveyances, such as Souls converse by."

47 Ibid., 44, 28.

48 Defoe, *Consolidator*, 109.

49 For more on the history of thought-bubbles see Scott McCloud, *Understanding Comics: The Invisible Art* (New York: William Morrow, 1994); and Steven Connor, "Thinking Things" (plenary lecture given at the 9th annual conference of the European Society for the Study of English [ESSE], Aarhus, Denmark, 25 August 2008 and as the Textual Practice lecture, University of Sussex, 14 October 2009).

50 Defoe, *Apparitions*, ii.

51 Ibid., 4.

52 Samuel Johnson, *The Dictionary of the English Language: in which Words are Deduced from their Originals* (London: W. Strahan, 1755), 1.437.

53 Lewis draws similar conclusions when she argues that "the rise of air as an object … meaningfully coincides with that of the ubiquitous print medium and with new ways of seeing indirectly." See Lewis, *Air's Appearance*, 25.

54 Defoe, *Consolidator*, 50.

55 Ibid., 111.

56 Baine suggests that Defoe borrowed the courtroom setting from the Salem witch trials as described by Cotton Mather and Deodat Lawson. See Baine, *Defoe*, 79.

57 Defoe, *Apparitions*, 101–2.

58 Ibid., 101.
59 Ibid., 103.
60 Ibid.
61 Ibid., 103–4.
62 Lewis, *Air's Appearance*, 122.
63 Terry Castle has also examined apparitions as the externalization of thought in her discussion of how the magic lantern was, in later decades, "the obvious mechanical analogue of the human brain, in that it 'made' illusionary forms and projected them outward." See Castle, "Phantasmagoria: Spectral Technology and the Metaphorics of Modern Reverie" *Critical Inquiry* 15 (Autumn, 1988): 26–61.
64 This engraving appears in eight of the nine eighteenth-century editions of *Apparitions* (1727–70) available on the *ECCO* Gale Cengage database (only the 1752 London edition does not include it among its "suitable cuts"). For more on illustrations of Defoe, see David Blewett, "The Illustration of Robinson Crusoe: 1719–1840," in *Imagination on a Long Rein: English Literature Illustrated*, ed. Joachim Möller (Marburg: Jonas, 1988), 66–81. There has been surprisingly little written about the illustration of the man at the bar, perhaps because narratives about ghosts who return to condemn their killers are so common in the seventeenth and eighteenth centuries. See Sasha Handley, *Visions of an Unseen World* (London: Pickering and Chatto, 2007), 34, 56–63, and 136. Ronald C. Finucane describes the illustration simply as "a murderer sees the ghost of his victim, though no one else sees it" in "Historical Introduction: The Example of Early Modern and Nineteenth-Century England," in *Hauntings and Poltergeists: Multidisciplinary Perspectives*, ed. James Houran and Rense Langue (Jefferson, NC: McFarland, 2001), 12.
65 "And no Wonder, if they, who were poreing continually at the Clouds, saw Shapes and Figures, Representations and Appearances, which had nothing in them, but Air and Vapour. Here they told us, they saw a Flaming-Sword held in a Hand, coming out of a Cloud, with a Point hanging directly over the City. There they saw Herses, and Coffins in the Air … I could see nothing, but a white Cloud …" See Defoe, *A Journal of the Plague Year* (London: E. Nutt, 1722), 27–8.
66 "Why should it be thought so strange a thing, that those Spirits should be able to take upon them an Out-side or Case? Why should they not be able, on Occasion, or when they think fit, to dress themselves up as we do *a la Masquerade,* in a Habit disguis'd like Flesh and Blood, to deceive human Sight, so as to make themselves visible to us?" Defoe, *Apparitions*, 4–5. The other illustrations in *Apparitions* represent clouds as part of the

natural atmospherics of the British landscape, but these are of the ordinary meteorological variety and seem unrelated to the appearance of the apparitions pictured.

67 Defoe, *An Essay on the History and Reality of Apparitions* (London: J. Roberts, 1727), 101, https://archive.org/stream/essayonhistoryre00defo#page/n121/mode/2up.

68 Defoe, *Apparitions*, 100–1.

69 Bolter and Grusin, *Remediation*, 19. John Guillory argues that although seventeenth- and eighteenth-century writers did not use the term "medium" in this way, the "premodern arts are also, in the fully modern sense, media ..." See Guillory, "Genesis of the Media Concept," *Critical Inquiry* 36 (Winter 2010), 322.

70 Ibid., 21.

71 Ibid., 11–14.

72 Ibid., 34.

73 See Bacon, "Sylva Sylvarum," in *The Works of Francis Bacon, Baron of Verulam* (London: A. Millar, 1765), 1.327.

74 Ibid., 336.

75 Joseph Glanvill, *The Vanity of Dogmatizing: The Three Versions*, ed. Stephen Medcalf (Sussex: Harvester Press, 1970), 198.

76 Ibid., 199–200.

77 For more on Defoe's satire of contemporary science, see Vickers, *Defoe*, 55–80; and Mark Jordan, "'A Lexicon Technicum for this Present Age': Scientific Satire in Defoe's *Consolidator*" (MA diss., McMaster University, 1991).

78 Defoe, *Consolidator*, 72.

79 Ibid., 85, 91–2.

80 Defoe parodies John Webster's description of his universal language scheme in *Academiarum Examen Or the Examination of Academies* (London: Giles Calvert, 1654), 24.

81 Defoe, *Consolidator*, 92.

82 Robert Hooke, *Micrographia: or some Physiological Descriptions of Minute Bodies made by Magnifying Glasses* (London: Martin & Allestry, 1665), ii.

83 Margaret Cavendish, "The Blazing-World," in *Paper Bodies: A Margaret Cavendish Reader* (Peterborough: Broadview Press, 2000), 170.

84 Thomas Sprat, *The History of the Royal Society of London, Second Edition* (London: R. Scot, 1702), 112.

85 Ibid.

86 Ibid., 113.

87 Ibid., 112.

88 For more on eighteenth-century allegory – particularly its visual forms in Enlightenment Britain – see Kevin L. Cope, "Directions to Signify: Exploring the Emblems of Enlightenment Allegory," in *Enlightening Allegory: Theory, Practice, and Contexts of Allegory in the Late Seventeenth and Eighteenth Centuries*, ed. Cope (New York: AMS Press, 1993), 171–211.

89 Johnson, 1.118.

90 Defoe, *The Dyet of Poland: A Satyr* (London: B. Bragg, 1705), 3.

91 Meeker and Thompson, "Empiricism," 185.

92 Defoe, *Consolidator*, 18.

93 Locke, ed. Phemister, *Essay*, 143.

94 *Oxford English Dictionary Online*, s.v. "consolidate," accessed 7 May 2014. http://www.oed.com.proxy.bib.uottawa.ca/view/Entry/39689?rskey=3quxMv&result=2&isAdvanced=false#eid.

95 Defoe, *Consolidator*, 89.

96 Ibid., 90.

97 Ibid., 86.

6 The Persistence of *Clarissa*

SARAH ELLENZWEIG

—Let it run, therefore; for it will run—

(Letter 37: Miss Howe to Miss Clarissa Harlowe, 173)

At 1,500 pages, Samuel Richardson's *Clarissa*, still the longest novel written in English, does nothing if not persist. His novel's persistence is a subject that, notoriously, caused Richardson anxiety. Ever "diffident in relation to this article of *length*," Richardson, in the final paragraph of the novel's postscript, defends himself on this count, insisting that "length ... must add proportionably to the pleasure that every person of taste receives from a well-drawn picture of nature."[1] The novel's textual history – multiple revisions, four editions in Richardson's lifetime, companion texts to supplement prior versions, and yet another rewrite in the works upon the author's death – underscores its extraordinary tendency to perpetuate itself.[2] Through Richardson's ongoing editorial exploits, curtailed only by death, the formidable life of *Clarissa* endures.

The plot of *Clarissa* hinges on problems of persistence – problems that enable and stretch the novel's extended length. In brief, Clarissa's family persists in their insistence upon her marriage to Solmes; Solmes persists in his suit for her affections; Clarissa persists in her opposition to both; Lovelace persists in his attempt at Clarissa's seduction; Clarissa persists in her resistance to it. True, a rape intervenes, yet it barely interrupts the pattern. Although Lovelace claims at this juncture that he "can go no further" (883), his persistence returns apace: "Have I gone so far, and am I afraid to go farther?" he asks Belford (943). Clarissa's resistance likewise persists: consider Lovelace's suggestively cryptic comment after the rape that she "lives" (883). Clarissa's "living" post-rape develops into a persistent waiting for death (almost 500 pages of it), yet the point to understand here is, we might say, that persistence persists.[3]

Richardson also peppers his novel with the term "persistence" and its close associate, "perseverance." On the subject of her family's dogged determination to push Solmes as a lover, Clarissa remarks on "Such a strange perseverance in a measure so unreasonable!" (206). Adding that "if they will still persevere; if that strange persister against an antipathy so strongly avowed, will still persist, say, what can I do?" (231). Her solution is to "take example by their perseverance! – Indeed I will!" (191). Solmes declares repeatedly that he is "determined to persevere" (266). "I must persist," he avows, "and happy shall I be, if by patience and perseverance, … I may at last overcome the difficulty laid in my way … Pardon me, dear miss, but I must persevere" (160). Lovelace, needless to say, is the novel's persister par excellence. As Anna Howe tells Clarissa early on, "in anything he sets his heart upon, or undertakes, he is the most industrious and persevering mortal under the sun. He rests, it seems, not above six hours in the 24" (74). Lovelace frequently brags about his skills in persistence. He self-describes as "an intrepid persevering enterpriser" (428), telling Belford that "Importunity and opportunity no woman is proof against, especially from a persevering lover, who knows how to suit temptations to inclination" (426). When his efforts to seduce Clarissa become so protracted that they arouse skeptical ribbing from the women in Sinclair's brothel, Lovelace returns, "Why then should I be reflected upon … for my patience and perseverance in the most noble of all chases?" (558). "What but difficulty," he explains to Belford, "engages me to so much perseverance here?" (810). All this persistence, needless to say, consumes many pages, deferring resolution and suspending closure. Surely Richardson smiles at his readers when, 1,400 pages in, upon Clarissa's long anticipated death, Anna Howe bewails, "And is this all! – is it all of my Clarissa's story! … This cannot, surely, be all of my Clarissa's story!" (1402, 1403). Richardson would appear to have inaugurated the new novel form with the insight memorably articulated by Henry James a century later: "really, universally, relations stop nowhere."[4]

In this essay, I will ponder the manifold ways in which the problem of persistence informs *Clarissa*. In particular, I will examine how the novel's fascination with persistence tracks back to early modern materialist philosophy, especially the revival of Epicurean materialism and its legacy in Hobbes.[5] We're not inclined to consider Richardson, humbly educated and of the eighteenth-century commercial class, to be a philosophical writer and thinker, but I will put this assumption to the test.[6] While readers have long noted that Lovelace is a materialist who takes his cue from Hobbes, critics have ignored the larger implications of Richardson's evident familiarity with materialist thinking and its significance for the "close, hot, day-dreamy continuity" of his novel more generally.[7]

In his essay, "'Alien Spirits': The Unity of Lovelace and Clarissa," John Allen Stevenson points us in a useful direction, proposing that we have been too quick to assume that Lovelace and Clarissa represent opposite attitudes towards the world, nature, the body, and sex. Clarissa's early readers, he suggests, were thus doing more than just voicing a sentimental whim when they "begged Richardson to end his novel happily."[8] Readers' desire for the main protagonists' ultimate union, on this view, reflected their uncomfortable awareness of Lovelace and Clarissa's "shared subversiveness," particularly their "strange" refusal to affirm marriage, a refusal that undermines the Christian ethics that Richardson claimed to defend.[9] Yet while Stevenson roots the novel's transgression in what he sees to be Lovelace's and Clarissa's Gnostic repudiation of matter and the flesh, I will argue that our intuition of Lovelace's and Clarissa's radical strangeness in fact reflects Richardson's deep, if troubled, exploration of materialist theories of life and the inclinations that move us.

With *Clarissa* as my example, I will suggest that the development of narrative form in the early novel was driven by the insight, as Hobbes puts it, that "Life it selfe is but Motion," a view that calls for the capacious formal register characteristic of the novel for its fullest expression.[10] Although it is true that Hobbes's wisdom made its mark in poetic forms as well as in drama, I contend that the novel becomes the form of choice for contemporaries seeking to explore imaginatively the ways that life moves and develops dynamically through time and space. (It was Hobbes himself, incidentally, who suggested in his *Answer to Davenant* that "the ways and motions" of narrative "are so uncertain and undistinguished, like the way and motion of a ship in the sea.")[11] In his essay "Why the Novel Matters," D.H. Lawrence described the novel as "the one bright book of life." We learn from the novel, he argues, because in it, "the characters can do nothing but *live*."[12] Himself inspired by Lawrence as well as by such naturalist philosophers as Nietzsche and Spinoza, Gilles Deleuze argues similarly in his literary criticism for the novel's deep-seated investment in life's creativity and variability. I'd like to suggest that the novel's primordial concern with what Lawrence calls "man alive," an embodied being of "flow and change" that continues through an ongoing defiance of inertia, was integral to the novel form from its earliest expressions in texts like *Clarissa*.[13]

The fundamentally open-ended nature of the novel so important to Lukács's and Bakhtin's foundational theories of the novel lends itself to a restless persistence that seeks future possibility. In the novel, Lukács argues, our goals and our way to them are no longer "directly given." And as Bakhtin puts it, "The novel took shape precisely at the point when … the object of artistic representation was being degraded to the level of a contemporary reality that was inconclusive and fluid."[14] The implication here may be prosaic, but it's worth making all the same: when our subject is a present-day reality whose meaning is understood to be uncertain from the start, our writing about it might struggle to come to an end. In addition to emphasizing the novel's open-endedness, much of the best work on narrative theory since the 1980s has underscored the *dynamic* quality of narrative, the desires and forces that propel narrative forward and that find themselves, in Peter Brooks's words, butting up against "man's time-boundedness, his consciousness of existence within the limits of mortality." (This idea takes up Bakhtin's assertion that "the novel, from the very beginning, developed as a genre that had at its core a new way of conceptualizing time.")[15]

For Brooks and his student, D.A. Miller, psychoanalysis provides an especially productive framework for understanding narrative movement. The key concept for their paradigm is desire, which on their view is "always there at the start of a narrative, often in a state of initial arousal, often having reached a state of intensity such that movement must be created, action undertaken, change begun." Because desire, on Freud's account, is a perpetual want, "never wholly satisfied or indeed satisfiable," it continues to generate the longing to tell.[16] This model helps us to grasp how desire comes to drive the logic of narration and how narrative desire keeps us striving towards narrative ends. Yet to the extent that desire, ever insatiable, cannot achieve rest, even upon its arrival at these narrative ends, for Miller "the narratable inherently lacks finality." If truth be told, "it can never be properly brought to term. The tendency of a narrative," Miller provocatively concludes, "would therefore be *to keep going*."[17]

I will argue below that a long-standing materialist heritage (from Lucretian naturalism to its revival in Hobbes) emphasized the problem of desire's persistence long before Freud theorized the drives.

Materialism has been a neglected source in our understanding of narrative dynamics. What's more, although both Brooks and Miller mention the eighteenth-century novel in passing, their examples draw from the nineteenth-century narrative tradition as the decisive moment, as Brooks puts it, "when one no longer can look to a sacred masterplot that organized and explains the world."[18] If, on Brooks's view, secularization informs the novel's narrative dynamics, all the more reason to begin a study of narrative motion in the literature of the Enlightenment when the new form first imagined an account of human experience that was not providentially informed.[19] My interest here, then, is to show that the link between narrative and problems of persistence gives rise to the novel at its moment of origin in the eighteenth century. The novel's affinity with materialism is crucial to this story.

Before turning to persistence and to its relationship to materialism in *Clarissa*, I'd like to return to Hobbes's famous dictum that "Life it selfe is but Motion" as an entryway into the larger problem of persistence for materialist philosophy. Part of my interest in this essay will be to argue that Hobbes's philosophy of motion, traditionally seen to be unambiguously mechanistic, had a more vital, Lucretian tendency than has been appreciated.[20] Moving off from Galileo, Hobbes's materialism grew out of the fundamental insight from physics that motion, once started, will continue indefinitely until or unless an external force intervenes to stop it. In the history of philosophy, Hobbes's physics is seen to follow from Descartes's similar formulation of what he calls the laws of motion. Yet, given Hobbes's rejection of God's role in the workings of the universe, Lucretius, for whom motion's persistence played a key role in the rejection of Aristotle and his view that all motion seeks rest in the centre of the universe, was a far more likely intellectual influence. "No rest is given," Lucretius explains, to the bodies moving through the void. "Always the business of the universe is going on with incessant motion in every part."[21] Life itself, in other words, is but motion.

Unlike Descartes but like Lucretius, Hobbes emphasizes the magnitude of the break from the scholastic emphasis on rest, allowing that while we can understand that a thing at rest will remain in rest unless something comes to "stirre it," the flip side of the proposition, "that when a thing is in motion, it will eternally be in motion, unless somewhat els stay it, … is not so easily assented to."[22] What Hobbes implies but does not say is that the principle of persistence is perhaps met with resistance because it calls to mind the nagging problem of the origin of motion. Here again, Hobbes departs from Descartes's and mechanism's emphasis on God's role in beginning motion, suggesting instead that in his search back "from cause to cause," man "will not be able to proceed eternally, but wearied will at last give over," never quite able to arrive at "some first eternal movement." One senses here Hobbes's covert reliance on the radically naturalist view from Lucretius that "nature is ... free ... of proud masters, herself doing all by herself of her own accord, without the help of the gods."[23]

Yet what does the physics of motion tell us about the behaviour of human beings? "After *physics*," Hobbes writes in *De Corpore*, "we must come to *moral philosophy*; in which we are to consider ... *appetite*, *aversion*, *love*, *benevolence*, *hope*, *fear*, *anger*, *emulation*, *envy*, *&c*; what causes they have, and of what they be causes."[24] Here, too, we find that Hobbes's "moral philosophy," the study of the motions of the mind, fits uneasily within a mechanistic conception of material life. Once again, Hobbesian psychology follows logically from Lucretius's teachings on the restlessness of matter. For Lucretius, just as bodies can never stand still in the void, so too is man's mind and its search for pleasures ever moving and seeking: "one unchanging thirst of life fills us and our mouths are for ever agape." While Epicurean philosophy commits itself to providing a therapy against this unquenchable and thus often destructive lust for life, Hobbes takes a darker view.[25] Like it or not, for him our minds' processes are inexorably marked by this appetitive tendency – what Hobbes often calls *conatus* or endeavour. Though purportedly absent in nonliving things, these appetites follow the same principles of motion as all matter.[26] That is so because the appetites in Hobbes's system *are themselves* instances of motion. It's just that they begin internally and thus invisibly: "although unstudied men, doe not conceive any motion at all to be there, where the thing moved is invisible; or the space it is moved in, is (for the shortnesse of it) insensible; yet that doth not hinder, but that such Motions are." Even when we cannot see it, appetitive motion is the driving force, the *sine qua non* in any explanatory paradigm. The "appetite to go, or move" is definitive of organic life, a view that takes Hobbes beyond mere physicalism in its identification of an origin of motion that is internal to bodies.[27]

Once we allow that the appetites are invisible life motions that follow the physical rules of motion and its persistence, we begin to understand from Hobbes that our appetites are endlessly ongoing, and, strictly speaking, insatiable.[28] The upshot is that our appetites (as well as our aversions, as the case may be) are what help keep us alive; they impel us as we strive, like all things in nature, to persevere.[29] When Hobbes argues that "Life it selfe is but Motion," he adds for clarification that it "can never be without Desire."[30] And when we consider the whole system, we understand why. Desire is constitutive of and co-terminus with life. Desire determines our activity.[31] Emphasizing man's tendency to crave *ad infinitum* – when we attain what we think we want, we then crave something else – Hobbes is explicit about the fact that desire is itself a motion that follows nature's principle of persistence: "for while we live, we have desires," he writes in *Human Nature*, "and desire presupposeth a further end ... Seeing all delight is appetite, and presupposeth a further end, there can be no contentment but in proceeding." *Leviathan* argues similarly that "the object of mans desire, is not to enjoy once onely, and for one instant of time; but to assure for ever, the way of his future desire." The important thing to know about appetite and desire, then, is that, like all forms of motion, they have a tendency to continue.[32]

Writing Desire's Persistence

How do materialism's teachings on the appetites help us understand *Clarissa*? To put it simply, *Clarissa* is symptomatically long precisely because it buys into Hobbes's and Lucretius's linking of life with desire and its motive persistence.[33] Diderot, himself a vital materialist, suggests as much in his *Éloge de Richardson*, defending *Clarissa* against accusations of excessive length: "the smallest enterprise" in Richardson, Diderot insists, "display[s] [the] passions," recalling us to the truth of "what go[es] on daily right under your eyes that you never see." At the broadest level, as Diderot esteemed, bringing out the passions requires the spontaneous activity and persistent present-ness of writing itself, which in Richardson's able hands, "shows me the nature of things that surround me."[34] To the extent that life is something that goes on, so does writing. As Clarissa tells Anna Howe of her "passion for scribbling," "I know not how to forebear writing ... And I must write on, although I were not to send it to anybody" (483, see also 757). Lovelace understands the process as similarly endless: "Write ... I can do; and as well without a subject, as with one" (142). "I must write on," he tells Belford, "and cannot help it" (721, also 846).

In his preface, Richardson links the "Length" of *Clarissa* to the formal conceit in novels of letters that he termed writing "to the moment" (721, see also 882, 1178). Richardson's signature technique, in which "the hearts of the writers must be supposed to be wholly engaged in their subjects" (35), strives above all to close the gap between writing and life. And as the bulk of *Clarissa* bears testament, such a mandate requires infinite textual generativity, productivity, and proliferation, an attempt that, as Terry Eagleton observes, leads paradoxically to a break from representational realism: how could any group of people actually write this many letters?[35] For Richardson, however, what might be called the hyperrealism of writing-to-the-moment gives the reader something more important than strict plausibility: its deepest ambition is to offer up the epistolary novel as nothing less than the continuous pulse of life in its processes of embodied unfolding, for writing-to-the-moment necessarily assumes writing to the *live* moment. That is the point.[36]

In the epistolary world of *Clarissa*, for better and for worse, the boundlessness of writing makes it a libertine activity, one that necessarily frustrates the established moral order.[37] We learn of Lovelace simultaneously that he is "notoriously … a man of pleasure" as well as "a great plotter, and a greater writer" (50), who "rests … not above six hours in the twenty-four," and "has always, when he retires, a pen in his fingers" (74).[38] Early in the novel, as Anna Howe is musing on Lovelace's reputation as a writer and particularly on the fact that "all his vacant nightly hours are employed in writing," she wonders, "what can be his subjects?" (74). Anna does not have to answer her own rhetorical question for us to understand that, however latent, the subject of the letter in *Clarissa* always returns to the unfathomably complex motions of desire. Anna contrasts the "twenty innocent subjects" that she and Clarissa "scribble upon" (75) to the "secret" and "treasonable" content of Lovelace's "great correspondence by letters" (74). Yet here, too, the reader recognizes that Richardsonian letters, leaving traces of ink on fingers in their striving to capture life alive, are never, strictly speaking, innocent (75, 345).[39] Mrs Harlowe likens writing to insubordination and to the "stiffen[ing]" of "will," preferring her daughter to read, an activity seen to teach "duty" (328).

In a letter preceding her escape with Lovelace, Clarissa admits her struggle to "govern" (333) her pen and her self-designation as a "scribbler" suggests that a libertine tendency towards lawlessness and license underlies her letters as well: "My talent is scribbling," she reflects to Anna, "and I the readier fell into this freedom, as I found delight in writing" (408). Delight in writing bespeaks an illicit freedom as well as a flux of feeling, an emotional dynamism, and a volatility of desire and intention, all of which Clarissa struggles to regulate. Lovelace relishes the complex set of moving interrelations set off by writing, in particular what he sees to be the erotic implications of Clarissa's contradictory behaviour, of "every changeable motion of your pen" (392).[40] Despite herself, Lovelace insinuates, Clarissa's erratic variability, her unpredictability, shows that "a sweet girl" is also "a rogue" (400). For this reason, Clarissa obsessively blames her personal downfall on her consent to correspond clandestinely with Lovelace, a correspondence that, as she admits, was not in her "power to discontinue" (408, also 381). Once it begins, the libertine motion of writing in this novel appears to endure. "Never was there such a pair of scribbling lovers as we," remarks Lovelace to Belford after successfully abducting Clarissa from her imprisonment at Harlowe Place (416). Glorying in Clarissa's "blameworthy" correspondence with him, Lovelace recognizes that a correspondence begun is one that will go on: "Has she been *capable* of error? – Of persisting in that error?" (427).

Libertinism's Persistent Aspirations

Lovelace ties his assurance of eventual success with Clarissa to his conviction of desire's persistently seeking quality. It is because desire seeks that love, in his view, "is an encroacher. Love never goes backwards. Love is always aspiring. Always must aspire" (704).[41] Lovelace's imperative here is theatrical and its sexual politics suspect. Yet let's pursue for a moment its Hobbesian philosophical underpinnings, which are rigorous in their own right. When Lovelace claims that love aspires, he wants to conjure up something bigger about human experience than his libertine attitudes towards women might otherwise suggest. Insofar as life is motion, and cannot be without desire, the good life is to be found in the accentuation of that motion, its forward trajectory, its futurity. According to this logic, if Clarissa appears on the outside to be a "frost-piece," this is merely a culturally imposed artifice that cannot belie the appetitive force that we know to be constitutive of living things.[42]

We also see Lovelace's assurance of the truth of Clarissa's appetite through his tendency to emphasize her bodiliness (and thus her inscription in the natural order of things and its tendency to strive). With a "constant glow upon her lovely features; eyes so sparkling; … health so florid; youth so blooming: air so animated … How then can she be so impenetrable?" he asks (145). At the moment of the abduction,

Lovelace is particularly fired with this materialist conviction about the covert desire animating Clarissa's resistance, waxing ecstatically to Belford:

> this lady is all alive, all glowing, all charming flesh and blood, yet so clear, that every meandering vein is to be seen in all the lovely parts of her which custom permits to be visible ... And I saw, all the way we rode, the bounding heart; by its throbbing motions I saw it! Dancing beneath the charming umbrage. (399–400, also 431, 575, 633)

After the rape, when Lovelace is forced to admit that in fact he has "nothing to boast of as to her will," he meditates again with some confusion on those secret life signs that purportedly cannot lie: "such a glowing, such a blooming charmer" (886). "How had I known that a but blossoming beauty, who could carry on a private correspondence and run such risks with a notorious wild fellow, was not prompted by inclination?" (912).

Lovelace's way out of this seeming contradiction is to assume that "had she been sensible, she must have been sensible, so they say" (943). His belief in Clarissa's post-rape pregnancy forwards the same kind of case for her inclination. Just as Clarissa's glow, the coursing of her blood, and the bounding of her heart would appear to reveal an incontrovertible bodily truth about inclination, so does conception, in the views of the period, assume a prior consent to, and thus appetite for, sex.[43] Clarissa's pregnancy would "prove," Lovelace says, "in this charming frost-piece, the triumph of nature over principle" (1147, also 916). Once again, Lovelace stresses the body's latent (and always infinite) desire. He here reflects Hobbes's insistence that appetite is precisely that inclination towards an object whose persistent motion is unseen (and unseeable) because it is psychological, occurring first in the imagination and from there transferring its motive endeavour outward to the body's actions.[44] The women in Sinclair's brothel give a salacious spin to this particular insight, assuring Lovelace, as he tells Belford, that because appetite begins internally, one cannot know the status of a woman's desire: "and that yet, and yet, and yet, I had not tried enough" (971–2). While the reader is positioned against Lovelace at these key moments of libertine vaunting, it is, as I will argue, Richardson's great accomplishment to show that Lovelace's faith in the force of appetite, of inclination, is confirmed, though not in the way he imagines.

The Endeavour of Aversion

And yet Lovelace must still account for the difficulty of aversion, that other striving endeavour that propels us forward and that drives *Clarissa*'s plot. As Hobbes explains, our general impulse towards continued self-preservation consists of two forms of motion: 1) endeavours towards what assists our persistence, or what Hobbes calls appetite, and 2) endeavours away from what we feel impedes it, or what he calls aversion.[45] The point here is that *both* appetite and aversion are expressions of endeavour, the broader striving for life's and thus desire's persistence. Aversion, in other words, is a local means to the furthest reaches of desire. This is a fundamental tenet of materialism, originating with Epicurus's dictum that "pleasure" is "our first innate good, and ... our starting point for every choice and avoidance."[46]

Lovelace is more than ready to sexualize the materialist heritage, to read Clarissa's extreme aversion to Solmes as a sign of her secret appetitive propensity. Yet in a key and unanticipated extension of materialism beyond Lovelace, it is the Harlowes, and even Anna Howe, who become the most committed followers of this logic.[47] James Harlowe consistently construes Clarissa's aversion for Solmes as a mask for her rabid concupiscence, as a confirmation, in his terms, that "Virgil's *amor omnibus idem* [love is the same for all] ... is verified in you [Clarissa], as well as in the rest of the animal creation" (218). As Mrs Harlowe puts it, "Such extraordinary antipathies to a particular person must be owing to extraordinary prepossession in another's favour" (98). Anna Howe reiterates the point: "Nor must you have Solmes, that's certain: not only because of his unworthiness in every respect, but because of the aversion you have so openly avowed to him; which everybody knows and talks of; as they do of your approbation of the other" (330). "On inquiry," Anna teases Clarissa, "it will come out to be love" (71). Sounding much like Lovelace, Anna seeks to access Clarissa's "one secret" (71), that "unowned inclination" (356) that despite prudence makes Clarissa's face "glow," her "heart" "go throb, throb, throb, as you read just here" (71). Mrs Howe sums up everyone's shared conviction of Clarissa's desire thus: "Is it such a mighty matter for a young lady to give up her own inclinations to oblige her friends? ... Either ... the lady must be thought to have very violent inclinations (and what nice young creature would have that supposed?) which she could not give up; or a very stubborn will, which she would not" (245). A good Hobbesian critic herself, Mrs Howe makes clear here that in the final analysis, "inclination" and "will" circle back to the same appetitive place, particularly in matters involving deliberation. "*Will*," explains Hobbes in a demystifying gesture, "therefore *is the last Appetite in Deliberating*."[48]

Let me pause for a moment. It is no surprise that Lovelace understands life through an appetitive Hobbesian lens. It is perhaps more surprising that the Harlowes and the Howes do as well. Yet the real question that Richardson prompts is whether this lens illuminates anything apposite to Clarissa and her status as a living body. Is Clarissa pressed by inclination? And if so, what does this mean outside the concupiscent readings of others? As we have seen, Clarissa's various interlocutors, via Hobbes, want to insist that aversion signals desire and that desire enlivens the body despite itself. Life for them is thus assumed to be animate and striving and driven by appetite. Yet on Clarissa's own account, by contrast, aversion is not animate, and life would seem to persist as a kind of motive inertia more than as an appetitive inclination in any particular direction. As Jonathan Kramnick has shown, we know Clarissa best by her "posture of inaction," her "stillness," her tendency to "stand … apart from life."[49] The novel begins as Anna Howe introduces us to Clarissa's preference for inertia, as Anna commiserates with her friend on the familial tumult sparked by Lovelace's suit: "So steady, so uniform in your conduct; so desirous, as you always said, of sliding through life to the end of it unnoted" (39–40). Clarissa knows that like all bodies, she moves through time and space, yet she wants to maintain, via mechanism's teachings, that her motion has no internal dynamism; if she is set going and goes, it is only because of the impact (usually unwanted) of other bodies.[50]

From Inertia to the Swerve

Clarissa is bewildered to find herself drawn from mechanism's inertia to materialism's activity, however unwanted, and she struggles to understand her passage from one state to the other. "I know not how it comes about, but I am, in my own opinion, a poor lost creature," she writes to Anna, "and yet cannot charge myself with one criminal or faulty inclination. Do you know, my dear, how this can be?" (565, also 1261). Despite herself, Clarissa's question confronts a crucially important lesson from materialism about the progress of living things and their appetites and aversions through time. Although Descartes's and Newton's law of inertia considered matter to be constitutionally inert, sluggish, and incapable of self-animation, an unintended outcome of the discovery of persistent motion was the repudiation of this supposed passivity, the recognition that somewhere along the path of seemingly passive motion, the habits of inertia ever so slightly diverge.[51]

At its most dangerous logical endpoint, persistent motion in its materialist formulations takes us back before Hobbes to the unpredictable, capricious inclinations of Lucretian bodies, inclinations that, like Clarissa's, break out of inertia below the threshold of exact measurement. As Lucretius teaches, all bodies "bring with them a nature secret and unseen." This nature is on the one hand "unchangeable," a stable force that explains why a bird remains constant as a bird; a tree always a tree, and so forth. On the other hand, however, the "distinct power" in things also explains their liveliness, their capacity to evolve, to explore novelty, even while preserving, at the same time, their existing form: "but who is there who can perceive that [bodies] never swerve ever so little from the straight undeviating course?"[52] In Lucretius's famous account, the declination of the atoms is what makes life possible in the first place, for in declination from motive equilibrium, the atoms connect and form the complex structures that comprise live bodies. In swerving to life, Lovelace hopes that Clarissa will prove his variety of sexual materialism right, and, with him, make more life: as he asks Belford, "But why shouldst thou imagine that such a mind as hers, meeting with such a one as mine; and, to dwell upon the word, meeting an inclination in hers to meet, should not propagate minds like her own?" (558).

Lovelace thus hinges his hopes of success with Clarissa on her having already "swerved," as he concedes, "in lesser points" (430). "A Clarissa (herself her judge) has failed," so "may she not further fail? Fail in the greatest point, to which all the other points in which she has failed, have but a natural tendency?" (429). Clarissa's "swerve," her "deviation," her "false step," thus invokes this essential element of the materialist tradition, the almost undetectable declination of Epicurus's atoms as they fall downward through the void.[53] It is difficult to imagine that Richardson had no inkling of this tradition (and its libertine implications) when he imagined Clarissa's "error" as a departure or step away from the straight path, from the inertial status quo: "One devious step at setting out! – That must be it: ... for, although but one pace awry at first, it has led me hundreds and hundreds of miles out of my path" (565–6, also 643, 1036).[54]

Related to Clarissa's acknowledgment of the necessary animacy of her position vis-à-vis Lovelace is the painful recognition that she has, indeed, put something in motion that she can no longer stop: "My faults began early," she bemoans to Anna, "for I ought not to have corresponded with him. I thought I could stop or proceed as I pleased" (381). "One evil draws another after it; and how knows she, or anybody, where it may stop?" (480). The point becomes a consistent refrain in the novel. Colonel Morden takes it up in his resonant summary letter ending volume three: "And how do you know," he asks Clarissa on the subject of marrying a rake, "if you once give way, where you shall be suffered, where you shall be able to stop?" (563).[55] How do we understand the pressure of this refrain? The answer, I want to suggest, points us to the novel's vital materialism and to Richardson's commitment to rendering the continual progress of dynamic passions that make up any life's impulsion to keep going. No living body, strictly speaking, *can* start or stop as it pleases, for as Clarissa learns too well, we never proceed as self-contained, isolated actors; there is no individual agency, no passive course through life apart from relational entanglement with others. All appetites and aversions unfold in reciprocal, multifaceted relation with other agents and the result, as Hobbes explains in *De Corpore*, is both "a certain continual progress" and "a continual mutation in the ... agents."[56]

Clarissa attempts to determine a single origin point for the causal chain she finds herself perpetually moving along – the "one devious step at setting out!" – yet this attempt once again assumes that causation involves singular actors and a sequence of distinct events. The protracted length of *Clarissa* is itself enough to give the lie to Clarissa's causal emphasis on her "first fatal step" (1016), bearing testament instead to the unfathomable difficulty of causation, to the impossibility of identifying a single act as the "sole" cause because no one occasion can be plucked from its embeddedness in an always active antecedent world. We see Clarissa's implicit awareness of this truth when, after she escapes to the Widow Moore's in Hampstead, she repeatedly answers the ladies' queries about her relations with Lovelace with the wearied assertion that her story is "too long" (791, 799). Clarissa's failure to master the intricacies of her own story betrays her struggle to capture the complexity of material experience, an experience that resists being reduced to her clandestine correspondence with Lovelace or to any other preliminaries. This irreducible complexity anchors Richardson's theory of the novel, one in which epistolary form saturates us with competing interpretive accounts that no final authority ever adjudicates.[57]

Thus, while Lovelace's and the Harlowes' libertine reading of Clarissa's animacy is biased at best, even Clarissa knows that they are not wrong to claim that indifference and motive inertia in live things is a fallacy. And in a certain sense, she has understood this truth all along. Were she truly indifferent, she would not feel such aversion for Solmes.[58] In an especially revealing letter to Anna a quarter of the way through the novel, Clarissa reflects on her recognition that this aversion, "an aversion so *very* sincere!" (506), is indeed based precisely on an active sensitivity, on what she calls "the finer sensibilities," on the impossibility of her "*indifference*" to sex (507). Had she been capable of the indifference to which she aspired ("I wish I had been able in some very nice cases to have known what *indifference* was"), she admits, "my *duty* should have been the conqueror of my *inclination*" (506). As a living being, then, Clarissa is an animate, desiring body, and no living thing, even a Clarissa Harlowe, *can* persist in the real world in a purely inertial and static state. Clarissa unwittingly suggests as much in a letter to Anna about her family's steadfast support of Solmes: "Astonishing persistence! ... I was quite tired with so many attempts, all to the same purpose. I am amazed that they are not! So little variation! And no concession on either side" (344). As Lovelace later comments, adding materialism's crucial layer of complexity to the principle of persistence, "'*Tis human to err, but not to persevere* – I hope my charmer cannot be inhuman!" (731, emphasis in text). The essence of Clarissa's misfortune is captured in this offhand remark, for, as novelist, Richardson wants us to understand that as they persist and persevere, all living things necessarily deviate from the straight path. The tragedy of Clarissa, as Christine Roulston suggests, is that her inclination would appear to have no play outside "the terms on which Lovelace offers it."[59]

Materialism and the Death of Clarissa

In the end, despite having swerved, Clarissa manifestly fails to act as things in nature do (on Lovelace's reckoning, at least).[60] Indeed, after the rape, Clarissa appears to behave most *un*naturally: far from seeking the perseverance of life and desire, she welcomes death and does so with legendary persistence, as suggested by Johnson's oft-cited grumbling of her "unconscionable time a-dying." Yet it is precisely this persistence that alerts us to this novel's gravest embrace of materialism. Such a claim admittedly seems perverse at first glance, for Richardson is explicit that *Clarissa* is formed on a "religious plan" (1495) and a "Christian system" (1498) that requires the death of his heroine: "And who that are in earnest in their profession of Christianity but will rather envy than regret the triumphant death of Clarissa, ... whose Christian humility; whose forgiving spirit; whose meekness, whose resignation, HEAVEN *only* could reward?" (1498).[61] Yet it is crucial to remember that this defence of the unity of art and orthodoxy follows from accusations by Richardson's early readers that Clarissa's death in fact smacked of heterodoxy. For Colley Cibber, her death implied Richardson's questioning of Providence despite the author's protestations to the contrary.[62]

Modern critics have perhaps been too quick to dismiss Cibber's skeptical reading of the "end" of Clarissa. Richardson claims that his design in *Clarissa* was "to inculcate upon the human mind, under the guise of an amusement, the great lessons of Christianity" (1495), yet as Cibber's comment suggests, on another level, the "guise" of Christianity also provided cover for the author to explore philosophical thinking about death that had little truck with religious consolations. For all of Lovelace's libertine aplomb, in fact he voices the conventional view on this matter much as Richardson's readers do. There is something about Clarissa's attitude towards death, Lovelace insinuates, that's not quite fit or proper. "Tell the dear creature," he writes to Belford, "she must not be wicked in her piety. There is a *too much*, as well as a *too little*, even in righteousness. Perhaps she does not think of that" (1308). Clarissa may invoke "Honest Job" as a safeguard, yet no actual Christian, Lovelace contends, looks at death without fear.

To be sure, as critics have long shown, Clarissa approaches death like a Christian: she trusts in the release of her immortal soul from her suffering body.[63] Yet at the same time, she also looks at life and death with a stark frankness worthy of the best of the Epicureans: "What," she asks Anna, "is even the long life which in high health we wish for?" (1318). And later she reflects skeptically, "We flutter about here and there, with all our vanities about us, like painted butterflies, for a gay but a very short season, till at last we lay ourselves down in a quiescent state, and turn into vile worms: and who knows in what form, or to what condition, we shall rise again?" (1318, 1337). Indeed, in devoting more than a quarter of his novel to the excruciatingly protracted death of his heroine, Richardson seems to challenge his readers to face up to Lucretius's enduring challenge: "And will you hesitate, will you be indignant to die?"[64]

Through the death of Clarissa, Richardson thus unexpectedly invokes Lucretius's most haunting question: "What is this great and evil lust of life that drives us to be so greatly agitated amidst doubt and peril?"[65] Hobbes argued that our innate impulsion to keep going is, in its most fundamental form, the impulsion to avoid death, yet Lucretius emphasized that our lust for life is in a certain sense always based on an illusion of our perpetual persistence, at least in this life. Death, he explains, merely returns us to the earth from which we came, where our bodies disperse and form new combinations, only "in a moment of time [to] yield it up again." To the materially unmystified, then, death is not to be feared and perhaps not necessarily to be avoided.[66]

As we know, Freud later took up the centrality of death to the moment in time that is life, arguing in his theory of the death drive for a sort of libidinal force in death that is "instinct with life, the very source of life and life's strivings."[67] Yet, beginning with Lucretius, materialism had its own prior version of this story, one in which, in the eternal cycles of matter, the tireless progress of matter's perpetual striving takes us beyond our individual death by transcending any *particular* life's activity.[68] The Epicureans faced death with equanimity for this very reason: not only is there no desiring self who continues after death to seek pleasure (rewards) and avoid pain (punishment), but matter also endures, and, across its endless formations, never stops striving.[69] The truest materialist, then, is one who is *not* afraid to die.

Poor Lovelace thus recognizes with horror that it is in fact through "woo[ing]" (1098) and "mak[ing] court" (1097) to death that Clarissa best shows herself, paradoxically, to be a desiring, aspiring participant in the natural world, embedded in its order of things, at last the "forward … girl" (1098), the "blooming, glowing charmer" he thought he wanted her to be, one who, following Lucretius, swerved to life and therein started on a course bound inexorably towards decline yet also towards infinite futures beyond his grasp. "Strange and perverse," Lovelace complains, relishing the illicit pun despite himself, "that she should refuse and sooner choose to die – oh obscene word!" (1107).[70] In eroticizing Clarissa's choice to die, Lovelace – and the reader with him – intuit Clarissa's "strange subversiveness," her "outlaw" attempt to seek the futurity of matter beyond the individual as, in Diderot's words, a space of "growth still to come."[71] Richardson turns the screw on us again with Lovelace's mock-prudish reaction to Clarissa's "encouragement" of death as a lover (1096), for we see here what we have long suspected: Lovelace is more vulnerable to idealist illusions than Clarissa is.[72]

As the truest materialist, Clarissa, bound for death, emerges at the end of the novel in the full paradoxical light of her libertinism. The "fancy" of "gadding after a rake" here finds its logical endpoint in the equally subversive refusal to "get sons and daughters" (970), to "keep her own secret" (1149, also 1084), or to "recover" the "overwhelmed path for the sake of future passengers" (1044). If Clarissa, as Stevenson argues, indeed finds "her true identity" in death, what looks to be a flight from the body, from desire, in fact asserts her inclination – her endeavour – with a vengeance, in a body's most inevitable natural act.[73] *Clarissa* is as long as it is in large part because Lovelace [and Richardson] notoriously resists fruition – preferring "preparation and expectation" – though both know that "nature will not be satisfied without it" (163, also 616).[74] While Clarissa's death might be said to mark the satisfaction of nature in a way that rape cannot, it actually calls our attention to the ghostly persistence of a desire about which we still know almost nothing, even after 1,500 pages. To drive home the point, Richardson leaves us to brood over the mysterious and suggestive devices on Clarissa's infamous coffin, devices that, showing "more fancy than would perhaps be thought suitable," demand explanation yet keep interpretation at once open-ended and indeterminate (1306).[75] As Terry Castle has shown, everyone strives to decipher the coffin's message, but no one really understands what it means. Its provocative ambiguity entices us to puzzle over it again and again. Clarissa's coffin thus brings us back, in microcosm, to the novel's vital persistence, to the lesson that the story is never finished, the meaning of a life and death unlimited.[76]

This essay has made the case that materialism permeates the world of Richardson's novel more fully than scholarship has tended to grant. Clearly Richardson was immersed in materialism's problems and tensions and was fascinated by its implications for narrative form, where persistence would appear to be an informing principle. Critics have not fully appreciated the significance of Diderot's powerful esteem for *Clarissa*, and particularly for the novel's treatment of its heroine's death. Is it a coincidence that Diderot's letters speak to his mistress, Sophie Volland, of the profound poignancy of "Clarissa's will and funeral" and of his materialist belief that "whatever lives has always lived and will live for ever"? "Re-read him, my friends," Diderot urges in his *Éloge de Richardson*, "read Richardson; read him without ceasing."[77] It is here that we discover Richardson's voice behind Lovelace's roguish query: "What is the enjoyment of the finest woman in the world to the bustle of a well-laid plot?" (92).[78] Patricia Meyer Spacks argues that Lovelace "conceives of plotting as capable of forestalling even death, as a way of fulfilling the desire of the self," and there is a way in which Spacks's insight captures a truth about Richardson's novel at its most primal level.[79] In directing our attention to this narrative that persists through motions that are decidedly aesthetic, we find Richardson offering the new novel form as an imaginative answer to the ongoing problems of life.

NOTES

1 Samuel Richardson, *Clarissa, or, The History of a Young Lady*, ed. Angus Ross (New York: Penguin Books, 1985), 35, 1499. Future page references to *Clarissa* will be cited parenthetically in the body of the essay.

2 As Tom Keymer observes, each revision of *Clarissa* "casts its predecessor as provisional or transitional only." See "Assorted Versions of Assaulted Virgins; or, Textual Instability and Teaching," in *Approaches to Teaching the Novels of Samuel Richardson*, ed. Lisa Zunshine and Jocelyn Harris (New York: The Modern Language Association of America, 2006), 24. On Richardson's multiple revisions of *Clarissa*, see also Terry Eagleton, *The Rape of Clarissa: Writing, Sexuality and Class Struggle in Samuel Richardson* (Minneapolis: University of Minnesota Press, 1982), 20–3. Eagleton aptly observes that "the Richardsonian text, like the Brechtian theatre script, can never be definitive" (*Rape of Clarissa*, 12).

3 See Corrinne Harol's assertion that "though a short summary of the plot [of *Clarissa*] might revolve around seduction and tragically early death, the real action of the narrative revolves around anxiety about time and delay." *Enlightened Virginity in Eighteenth-Century Literature* (New York: Palgrave, 2006), 169.

4 James Edwin Miller, Jr, ed. *Theory of Fiction: Henry James* (Lincoln: University of Nebraska Press, 1972), 172.

5 For an early example of the significance of Hobbes for the eighteenth-century English novel, see Carol Kay, *Political Constructions: Defoe, Richardson, & Sterne in Relation to Hobbes, Hume, & Burke* (Ithaca: Cornell University Press, 1988), esp. 25–33, 159–93.

6 Jocelyn Harris argues persuasively that Richardson was far better and far more widely read than critics have assumed; see "Richardson: Original or Learned Genius?," in *Samuel Richardson: Tercentenary Essays*, ed. Margaret Anne Doody and Peter Sabor (Cambridge: Cambridge University Press, 1989), 188–202. On Richardson and Hobbes, see James Grantham Turner, "Lovelace and the Paradoxes of Libertinism," in *Samuel Richardson*, ed. Doody and Sabor, 70–88; Jocelyn Harris, "Protean Lovelace," *Eighteenth-Century Fiction* 2.4 (1990): 327–46; Jayne Elizabeth Lewis, "*Clarissa*'s

Cruelty: Modern Fables of Moral Authority in *The History of a Young Lady,*" in *Clarissa and Her Readers: New Essays for The Clarissa Project*, ed. Carol Houlihan Flynn and Edward Copeland (New York: AMS Press, 1999), 45–67; R.F. Brissenden, *Virtue in Distress: Studies in the Novel of Sentiment from Richardson to Sade* (London: Macmillan, 1974), 172–3; Margaret Anne Doody, *A Natural Passion: A Study of the Novels of Samuel Richardson* (Oxford: Clarendon Press, 119, 123–4, 342, 344; Tony Tanner, *Adultery in the Novel: Contract and Transgression* (Baltimore: The Johns Hopkins University Press, 1979), 104–5; Leopold Damrosch, Jr, *God's Plot & Man's Stories: Studies in the Fictional Imagination from Milton to Fielding* (Chicago: University of Chicago Press, 1985), 246–9; Christine Roulston, *Virtue, Gender, and the Authentic Self in Eighteenth-Century Fiction: Richardson, Rousseau, and Laclos* (Gainesville: University Press of Florida, 1998), 35–6.

7 Samuel Taylor Coleridge, "Notes on *Tom Jones*," in *Coleridge's Essays & Lectures on Shakespeare & Some Other Old Poets & Dramatists* (New York: E.P. Dutton, 1909), 363.

8 John Allen Stevenson, "'Alien Spirits': The Unity of Lovelace and Clarissa," in *New Essays on Samuel Richardson*, ed. Albert J. Rivero (New York: St Martin's Press, 1996), 95.

9 Ibid. On the subversiveness of Clarissa's resistance to marriage, see also Harol, *Enlightened Virginity*, 170, 174.

10 Thomas Hobbes, *Leviathan*, ed. C.B. Macpherson (London: Penguin, 1968), 130.

11 Hobbes, *The Answer of Mr. Hobbes to Sir William Davenant's Preface Before Gondibert*, in *The Collected Works of Thomas Hobbes*, ed. William Molesworth, 12 vols. (London: Thoemmes Press, 1994), 4:446.

12 D.H. Lawrence, "Why the Novel Matters," in *Selected Literary Criticism*, ed. Anthony Beal (New York: Viking Press, 1969), 105, 106–7.

13 See Gilles Deleuze, "On the Superiority of Anglo-American Literature," in *Dialogues: Gilles Deleuze and Claire Parnet*, trans. Hugh Tomlinson and Barbara Habberjam (New York: Columbia University Press, 1987), 36–76; Deleuze, "Literature and Life," in *Gilles Deleuze: Essays Critical and Clinical*, trans. Daniel W. Smith and Michael A. Greco (Minneapolis: University of Minnesota Press, 1997), 1–6; Lawrence, "Why the Novel Matters," 107, 106. Sandra Macpherson suggests that the problem of inertia is "an important and underexamined feature" of the plot of *Clarissa*. *Harm's Way: Tragic Responsibility and the Novel Form* (Baltimore: The Johns Hopkins University Press, 2010), 61.

14 Georg Lukács, *The Theory of the Novel*, trans. Anna Bostock (Cambridge, MA: MIT Press, 1971), 60; Mikhail Bakhtin, *The Dialogic Imagination: Four*

Essays, ed. Michael Holquist, trans. Caryl Emerson and Michael Holquist (Austin: University of Texas Press, 1981), 39. For the classic treatement of fiction's complex relationship to narrative ends, see Frank Kermode, *The Sense of An Ending: Studies in the Theory of Fiction* (Oxford: Oxford University Press, 200), esp. 3–24, 166–7, 174–80. On the novel's formal open-endedness, see also J. Hillis Miller, "Narrative and History," *ELH* 41 (1974): 460–12. Most recently, as Michael Schmidt affirms in his new "biography" of the novel form, for most readers, novels "possess an enchanting presence," a tendency to resist conclusion at book's end. *The Novel: A Biography* (Cambridge, MA: Belknap Press at Harvard University Press, 2014), 4. Schmidt's decision to call his study of the novel a biography reflects this present-ness, this peculiar and unique tendency for novels to feel like people, like living things. For the view that the novel is "less mediated" than other literary genres, see Michael Holquist and Walter Reed, "Six Theses on the Novel, and Some Metaphors," *New Literary History* 11 (1980): 419.

15 Peter Brooks, *Reading for the Plot: Design and Intention in Narrative* (New York: A.A. Knopf, 1984), xi; Bakhtin, *The Dialogic Imagination*, 38.

16 Brooks, *Reading for the Plot*, 38, 55, 54. See also D.A. Miller, *Narrative and Its Discontents: Problems of Closure in the Traditional Novel* (Princeton: Princeton University Press, 1981), xi. For the view that "the archetype of all fiction is the sexual act," see Robert Scholes, *Fabulation and Metafiction* (Urbana: University of Illinois Press, 1979), 26; also Judith Roof, *Come As You Are: Sexuality & Narrative* (New York: Columbia University Press, 1996).

17 Miller, *Narrative and its Discontents*, xi. Scholes associates the novel's latent tendency to want to keep going with its link to sex: "In the sophisticated forms of fiction, as in the sophisticated practice of sex, much of the art consists of delaying climax within the framework of desire in order to prolong the pleasurable act itself" (*Fabulation*, 26).

18 Brooks, *Reading for the Plot*, 6.

19 See Lukács's well-known assertion that "the novel is the epic of a world that has been abandoned by God" (*Theory of the Novel*, 88). For him, this sense of abandonment predates the Enlightenment, let alone the nineteenth century. The first great novel of world literature is *Don Quixote* (1605, 1615), which "stands at the beginning of the time when the Christian God began to forsake the world; when man became lonely … ; when the world … was abandoned to its immanent meaninglessness" (*Theory of the Novel*, 103).

20 For a brilliant discussion of non-mechanistic readings of Hobbes's materialism by his contemporaries, see J.G.A. Pocock, "Thomas Hobbes:

Atheist or Enthusiast? His Place in a Restoration Debate," *History of Political Thought* 11 (1990): 737–49. Pocock's essay is an important counterpoint to the standard source on the reception of Hobbes: Samuel I. Mintz, *The Hunting of Leviathan: Seventeenth-Century Reactions to the Materialism and Moral Philosophy of Thomas Hobbes* (Cambridge: Cambridge University Press, 1970), esp. 30–1, 63–79. For other challenges to the predominant view that Hobbes was a stark mechanist, see William Sacksteder, "Speaking About Mind: *Endeavor* in Hobbes," *The Philosophical Forum* 11 (1979): 65–78; Samantha Frost, *Lessons from a Materialist Thinker: Hobbesian Reflections on Ethics and Politics* (Stanford: Stanford University Press, 2008), esp. 1–14; Gary B. Herbert, *Thomas Hobbes: The Unity of Scientific and Moral Wisdom* (Vancouver: University of British Columbia Press, 1989), esp. 113–14. For a recent revisionist study in history of philosophy that also complicates Hobbes's mechanist legacy, particularly his distinction from Spinoza, see Daniel Garber, "God, Laws, and the Order of Nature: Descartes and Leibniz, Hobbes and Spinoza," in *The Divine Order, the Human Order, and the Order of Nature: Historical Perspectives*, ed. Eric Watkins (Oxford: Oxford University Press, 2013), 45–66.

21 Lucretius, *De rerum natura*, trans. Ronald Melville (Oxford: Oxford University Press, 1997), 1.992–3; 1.995–6.

22 Hobbes, *Leviathan*, 87.

23 Hobbes, *Collected Works*, 1:412; Lucretius, *De rerum natura*, 2.1091–3. On Hobbes's exclusion of "the doctrine of God" in his philosophy, see also *Collected Works*, 1:10–11. On the role of God in Descartes's laws of motion, see René Descartes, *Principles of Philosophy*, in *The Philosophical Writings of Descartes*, trans. John Cottingham, Robert Stoothoff, and Dugald Murdoch, 2 vols. (Cambridge: Cambridge University Press, 1985), 1:2.36 (240). Hobbes refutes the possibility of man's self-motion in *De Corpore* (see *Collected Works*, 1:510), yet as C.B. Macpherson suggests, while "the apparatus was not, strictly speaking, self-moving, … in a looser sense it *was* self-moving, because it had, built into it, a desire or endeavour to maintain its motion. This same impulsion to keep going could be said to determine the whole activity of the individual system" ("Introduction," *Leviathan*, 28).

24 Hobbes, *Elements of Philosophy. The First Section, Concerning Body*, in *Collected Works*, 1:72. The connection between the behaviour of inorganic and human/animal bodies became canonical for materialist philosophy. See, for example, Frederick Engels, *Dialectics of Nature*, ed. and trans. Clemens Dutt (New York: International Publishers, 1973), 35. As Alfred

North Whitehead puts it, "the energetic activity considered in physics is the emotional intensity entertained in life." *Modes of Thought* (New York: The Free Press, 1968), 168.

25 Lucretius, *De rerum natura*, 3.1084–5. As James I. Porter explains, "Epicurus's view is that the best artists of life ... will give up on their longing for life while loving life in the mere practice of living: they stand impartially, as it were, toward the desirability of living per se and reap what there is to enjoy in life." "Love of Life: Lucretius to Freud," in *Erotikon: Essays on Eros, Ancient and Modern*, ed. Shadi Bartsch and Thomas Bartscherer (Chicago: University of Chicago Press, 2005), 123. For a brilliant examination of Epicureanism's contradictory attitudes towards love of life, see Martha C. Nussbaum, *The Therapy of Desire: Theory and Practice in Hellenistic Ethics* (Princeton: Princeton University Press, 1994), 192–238.

26 See Hobbes's *De Corpore* for the argument that "inanimate bodies have no appetite at all." *Collected Works*, 1:510. For Hobbes's theory of endeavour, see *Leviathan*, 118–19; *Collected Works*, 1:206–7, 1:216–17, 1:406–8. Hobbes is inconsistent about the difference between animate and inanimate bodies. In his account, while inanimate bodies do not have appetite, they do endeavour, and to the extent that Hobbes makes appetite co-extensive with endeavour, the distinction between animate and inanimate bodies begins to break down. For a useful discussion of these tensions, see Susan James, *Passion and Action: The Emotions in Seventeenth-Century Philosophy* (Oxford: Oxford University Press, 1997), 76–8.

27 Hobbes, *Leviathan*, 118–19, 119. On Hobbes's concept of endeavour as suggestive of an active force inside bodies, see Sacksteder, "Speaking About Mind," 70, 74, 76–7.

28 As James explains the process, "since the internal motions that constitute endeavour persist as long as the body continues to function in the manner that qualifies it as existing, we can never be without a susceptibility to passion. When the internal motions that are our appetites and aversions cease, we die, and become corpses rather than human beings. But as long as they continue, we are subject to passion, to short-term satisfaction allied to lifelong insatiability." *Passion and Action*, 131.

29 Hobbes makes the point famously in *De Cive* when he declares that man shuns death "by a certain impulsion of nature, no less than that whereby a stone moves downward." *Collected Works*, 2:8. What follows is "the first foundation of natural right," namely that "every man as much as in him lies endeavours to protect his life and members." *Collected Works*, 2:9; see also *Leviathan*, 189. This conviction in nature's innate impulsion to

keep going is definitive for materialism. Lucretius's foundational first principle – the certainty that nothing comes from nothing – grows logically out of the prior confidence that things in the natural world exhibit a fundamental drive to remain what they are, to defend and continue to express their "distinct power" (1.172), their "character" (1.190), their "fixed material" (1.204), their "nature secret and unseen" (1.779).

30 Hobbes, *Leviathan*, 130.

31 For a useful account of the centrality of desire in Hobbes's materialism, see Herbert, *Thomas Hobbes*, esp. 85–116.

32 Hobbes, *Human Nature*, in *Collected Works*, 4:33; Hobbes, *Leviathan*, 160. See also the starker version of this position in *De Corpore*: "All endeavour, whether strong or weak, is propagated to infinite distance; for it is motion." *Collected Works*, 1:216.

33 My reading of Richardson's use of Hobbes differs from the tendency in eighteenth-century literary studies to assume that contemporaries read Hobbes as a mechanist. See, for example, Damrosch's references to Lovelace's "grossly mechanistic theory of behavior" and his assumption that "Hobbesian psychology is both reductive and predictive." *God's Plot & Man's Stories*, 247–8. In linking the novel's engagement with life to what I have called "materialism," my argument draws from recent debates in seventeenth- and eighteenth-century studies on mechanistic vs. more vital understandings of matter. Broadly speaking, most historians now agree that by the 1740s, contemporaries concerned with understanding the nature of life grew dissatisfied with Descartes's passive conception of matter, a conception seen as insufficient to explain organic processes. By the middle of the century, living matter was increasingly understood to function less like a machine and more like an interlocking system of vital, active forces, animated from within rather than from without. This is not to suggest that more vital forms of materialism were absent before the 1740s but rather to gesture towards a general trend. On the transition from mechanism to vital materialism in the eighteenth century, see, for example, Stephen Gaukroger, *The Collapse of Mechanism and the Rise of Sensibility: Science and the Shaping of Modernity, 1680–1760* (Oxford: Clarendon Press, 2010), 328–64; Minsoo Kang, "From the Man-Machine to the Automaton-Man: The Enlightenment Origins of the Mechanistic Imagery of Humanity," in *Vital Matters: Eighteenth-Century Views of Conception, Life, and Death*, ed. Helen Deutsch and Mary Terrall (Toronto: University of Toronto Press, 2012), 148–73; Theodore M. Brown, "From Mechanism to Vitalism in Eighteenth-Century English Physiology," *Journal of the History of Biology* 7 (1974): 179–216; Robert E. Schofield, *Mechanism and Materialism: British*

Natural Philosophy in An Age of Reason (Princeton: Princeton University Press, 1970), esp. 191–232; Peter Hanns Reill, *Vitalizing Nature in the Enlightenment* (Berkeley: University of California Press, 2005), 1–16, 42–7; Thomas L. Hankins, *Science and the Enlightenment* (Cambridge: Cambridge University Press, 1985), 113–45.

34 Diderot, *Éloge de Richardson*, in *Clarissa: The Eighteenth-Century Response, 1747–1804*, ed. Lois E. Bueler, 2 vols. (New York: AMS Press, 2010), 1:395, 393. Diderot seems to have understood Richardson's aim with notable discrimination, writing in his *Éloge* that "the passions he paints are those I detect in myself; they are moved by the same objects and have the very energy that I know them to have; the characters' setbacks and afflictions are such as ceaselessly menace me" (1:393).

35 Eagleton, *The Rape of Clarissa*, 92.

36 In "Literature and Life," Deleuze describes the significance of writing to life in a way that Richardson would have embraced: "Writing is a question of becoming, always incomplete, always in the midst of being formed, and goes beyond the matter of any livable or lived experience. It is a process, that is, a passage of Life that traverses both the livable and the lived ... The shame of being a man – is there any better reason to write?" *Essays Critical and Clinical*, 1.

37 On libertinism as a style of writing as well as a sexual or philosophical stance, see Turner, "Lovelace and the Paradoxes of Libertinism," in *Samuel Richardson*, ed. Doody and Sabor, 75–8. On Clarissa's anxious references to her writing as the act of a "roving pen," see *Clarissa*, 65, 82, 112.

38 As Eagleton argues of Lovelace, "Linguistic lawlessness is the other face of his sexual libertinism: a writing which brooks no closure is a desire which knows no mercy." *The Rape of Clarissa*, 83.

39 It is for this reason that early in the novel, Anna's lively teasing about Clarissa's barely conscious "prepossession in [Lovelace's] favour" (49) leads Clarissa to worry about "what turn my mind had taken to dictate so oddly to my pen" (72).

40 As Roulston argues, on Lovelace's account to Belford, "the authentic narrative of Clarissa's escape collapses into a story of seduction desired by her, thereby proving the ambivalent nature of female virtue." *Virtue, Gender, and the Authentic Self*, 35.

41 Lovelace never abandons hope for Clarissa's submission: "What once a lady hopes, in love matters, she always hopes while there is room for hope" (1108).

42 See Lovelace's famous question to Belford, "This must be all from education too – must it not, Belford? Can education have stronger force in a woman's heart than nature? – Sure it cannot" (695).

43 As Hobbes argues in ch. 6 of *Leviathan*, entitled, "Of the Interiour Beginnings of Voluntary Motions; commonly called the Passions," "The best signes of Passions present, are either in the countenance, motions of the body, actions, and ends, or aimes, which we otherwise know the man to have" (129). On the period's view of pregnancy as a subsequent expression of desire in the prior act of conception, see Frances Ferguson, "Rape and the Rise of the Novel," *Representations* 20 (1987): 103–4.

44 See Hobbes, *Leviathan*, 118–19.

45 On appetite and aversion, see *Leviathan*, 119–21; *Collected Works*, 1:406–8.

46 Epicurus, "Letter to Menoeceus," in *The Epicurus Reader: Selected Writings and Testimonia*, ed. and trans. Brad Inwood and L.P. Gerson (Indianapolis: Hackett, 1994), 30.

47 See Clarissa's complaint to Anna: "You would imagine, by what he writes, that I have given him reason to think that my aversion to Mr Solmes is all owing to my favour for him!" (345). On the Harlowes as Hobbists "at [their] core," see Doody, *A Natural Passion*, 123.

48 *Leviathan*, 128; see also *Collected Works*, 1:408–9.

49 Jonathan Kramnick, *Actions and Objects from Hobbes to Richardson* (Stanford: Stanford University Press, 2010), 204, 225. On Clarissa's inaction, see also Tony Tanner, *Adultery in the Novel: Contract and Transgression* (Baltimore: Johns Hopkins University Press, 1979), 107. Clarissa's preference for an inertial model of human psychology and action is perhaps best represented through her aspiration for "the *single state*" (281) or what she elsewhere refers to as living "sole" (78, also 358). The fantasy of living "sole" bespeaks Clarissa's wish to be a self-contained, self-sufficient entity, one whose passive course never intersects with another body. We see this preferred logic of self-containment in play most powerfully when Clarissa anxiously relinquishes possession of her letter to Lovelace agreeing to leave Harlowe Place under his protection. Upon depositing the letter in the brick wall, Clarissa understands with horror that she has rendered both the letter and herself "out of my power" (352). Her subsequent letter of retraction, expressing her wish "to suspend, for the present, my intention of leaving my father's house" (362–3) (which Lovelace crucially never receives), displays Clarissa's attempt to freeze time and motion at the instant of her suspended intention, clinging hereby in vain to a worldview in which "sole" actors exert themselves across discrete and disconnected moments. In a desperate attempt to hold on to this logic of autonomous self-containment at the moment of the abduction, Clarissa refuses the fact that the first letter has already contributed to creating a fuller, more multi-faceted reality than the fixity of her revised intentions – marking a

particular stopped instant in time – wants to grant: "Oh Mr Lovelace, … I cannot go with you! – *Indeed* I cannot – I wrote you word so! – Let go my hand and you shall see my letter. It has lain there from yesterday morning till within this half-hour" (374).

50 See Keith Hutchison for the view that mechanism's passive conception of matter served as a safeguard for a Christian, law-bound, world view. "Supernaturalism and the Mechanical Philosophy," *History of Science* 21 (1983): 297–333.

51 The trajectory from Descartes's inert conception of matter to Spinoza's vital one is a crucial instance in the history of materialism's thinking about motion. In Spinoza's legendary 1676 letter to Tschirnhaus, he confronts the viability of matter's supposed passivity, assumed by Descartes's version of the law of inertia, head-on: "from Extension as conceived by Descartes, to wit, an inert mass, it is not only difficult, as you say, but quite impossible to demonstrate the existence of bodies. For matter at rest, as far as in it lies, will continue to be at rest, and will not be set in motion except by a more powerful external cause. "Spinoza to Tschirnhaus, 5 May 1676," in *Spinoza: Complete Works*, ed. Michael L. Morgan, trans. Samuel Shirley (Indianapolis: Hackett, 2002), esp. 81, 956. Susan James cites inertia among the phenomena that tended to push back against mechanism's wholly passive view of bodies, as Spinoza's letter to Tschirnhaus demonstrates. *Passion and Action*, 76–81. When Newton later asserts that by the principle of inertia alone – the passive principle by which bodies persist in their motion or rest – there never could have been any motion in the world, his assertion betrays the anxiety of its opposite claim: matter's immanent motion. See Betty Jo Teeter Dobbs and Margaret C. Jacob, *Newton and the Culture of Newtonianism* (Atlantic Highlands, NJ: Humanities Press, 1995), 98; also Jacob, "John Toland and the Newtonian Ideology," *Journal of the Warburg and Courtauld Institutes* 32 (1969): 321.

52 Lucretius, *De rerum natura*, 1.779; 1.790. On things remaining constant, see also 1.167–207; 1.174; 2.249–50. On the secret, hidden nature of the vital force in bodies, see also 3.273–81.

53 Clarissa uses the term herself when imagining the chance to speak to her father in her distress: "Oh my dear papa, … had you known how I have been punished, ever since my swerving feet led me out of your garden doors to meet this man!" (650). James Harlowe observes that Clarissa is "The most admirable young creature that ever swerved!" (1380). Anna urges Clarissa to consider herself as "a prudent person" who "endeavours to mend her error, and … to recover the path she has been rather driven

out of than chosen to swerve from" (578). Lovelace also refers to Clarissa's "sliding" step (431) or "fall" (440, 450).

54 See Natania Meeker for the view that "the Epicurean *clinamen* ... becomes the emblem of a libertine freedom that inheres not only within human bodies but as part of the structure of the material world itself. "Libertine Lucretius," *Rivista di storia della filosofia* 2 (2012): 227.

55 "Take care," Clarissa warns Anna on the subject of their forbidden letters, "how you fall into my error; for that began with carrying on a prohibited correspondence; which I thought it in my power to discontinue at pleasure" (408). The pedantic clergyman, Mr Brand, writes to Clarissa's Uncle "that *one false step* generally brings on *another*; and peradventure *a worse*, and *a still worse* ...." (1292). Brand's sentiments are relayed to the women in the Milliner's shop across from Clarissa's final lodging with Mrs Smith, who confirm to Belford that "it was but too natural to think that where a lady had given way to a delusion, and taken so wrong a step, she would not stop there" (1296).

56 Hobbes, *Collected Works*, 1:123; see also Herbert, *Thomas Hobbes*, 59. On causation as a process of "intra-action" between mutually embroiled agents, see also Karen Barad, *Meeting the Universe Halfway: Quantum Physics and the Entanglement of Matter and Meaning* (Durham: Duke University Press, 2007), 132–88.

57 See Kramnick, *Actions and Objects*, 229; Tom Keymer, *Richardson's Clarissa and the Eighteenth-Century Reader* (Cambridge: Cambridge University Press, 1992), 218–44. Alluding in particular to the complexities of desire, Anna Howe speaks to epistolarity and the intricacy of experience thus: "for I may venture to affirm, that anyone who should read your letters, and would say you were right, would not on reading mine, condemn me for being quite wrong" (276).

58 Significantly, it is upon Clarissa's mistaken claim to indifference that her fatal correspondence with Lovelace is first grounded (47). No one around her buys it: "With what ap-*pa*-rent indifference," James Harlowe teases (58).

59 Roulston, *Virtue, Gender, and the Authentic Self*, 37.

60 See Lovelace's gloomy lament that "my charmer has no passions; that is to say, none of the passions that I want her to have" (897).

61 Criticism has been largely unanimous in taking Richardson at his word here, particularly in relation to the death of Clarissa. See, for example, Allan Wendt, "Clarissa's Coffin," *Philological Quarterly* 39 (1960): 481–95; Peggy Thompson, "Abuse and Atonement: The Passion of Clarissa Harlowe," in *Passion and Virtue: Essays on the Novels of Samuel Richardson*,

ed. David Blewett (Toronto: University of Toronto Press, 2001), 152–69; James Bryant Reeves, "Posthumous Presence in Richardson's *Clarissa*," *SEL* 53 (2013): 601–21; Chad Loewen-Schmidt, "Pity, or the Providence of the Body in Richardson's *Clarissa*," *Eighteenth-Century Fiction* 22 (2009): 1–28; E. Derek Taylor, "The End of *Clarissa*," in *Reason and Religion in Clarissa: Samuel Richardson and "the Famous Mr. Norris of Bemerton"* (Farnham: Ashgate, 2009), 1–32; Alex Eric Hernandez, "Tragedy and the Economics of Providence in Richardson's *Clarissa*, *Eighteenth-Century Fiction* 22 (2010): 599–630. For notable exceptions to this trend that seek to explore the physical, organic nature of Clarissa's death, see Raymond Stephanson, "Richardson's 'Nerves': The Physiology of Sensibility in *Clarissa*," *Journal of the History of Ideas* 49 (1988): 267–85; Clark Lawlor, "'Long *Grief*, dark *Melancholy, hopeless natural Love*': *Clarissa*, Cheyne and Narratives of Body and Soul," *Gesnerus* 63 (2006): 103–12. Both Stephanson's and Lawlor's discussions of Richardson's friendship with the eighteenth-century physician and physiologist George Cheyne (1671–1743) suggest the influence of a non-mechanistic vital materialism on Richardson, an influence worthy of further scholarly investigation. On Cheyne and eighteenth-century vital materialism, see Schofield, *Mechanism and Materialism*, 57–62; Shirley A. Roe, "The Life Sciences," in *The Cambridge History of Science: Eighteenth-Century Science*, ed. Roy Porter (Cambridge: Cambridge University Press, 2001), vol. 4, 401–2.

62 See Anna Laetitia Barbauld, ed., *The Correspondence of Samuel Richardson*, 6 vols. (London: Richard Phillips, 1804), 2:128. For a discussion of early readers' outrage at the death of Clarissa, see Keymer, *Richardson's Clarissa*, 199–244; Adam Budd, "Why Clarissa Must Die: Richardson's Tragedy and Editorial Heroism," *Eighteenth-Century Life* 31 (2007): 1–28.

63 Richardson tells Aaron Hill that his decision to make Clarissa die fearlessly grew from his ambition to flout "vulgar" prejudice and "attempt what I have the Vanity to think was never yet attempted." *Selected Letters of Samuel Richardson*, ed. John Carroll (Oxford: Clarendon Press, 1964), 87. Yet even putting materialism aside, strictly speaking, the attempt to make his contemporaries think better of death was not as new as Richardson claims it to be. By 1747, much of Richardson's bold embrace of death had been well rehearsed in Charles Drelincourt's wildly popular *The Christian's Defence against the Fears of Death*, which appeared in its sixteenth edition at the time of Richardson's publication of *Clarissa*. Here Drelincourt proclaims that good Christians who rely on God "look [death] in the face … with an undaunted countenance." *The Christian's Defence* (London: Davies & Eldridge, 1800), 58. To fear death, Drelincourt suggests, is thus to

show one's infidelity: namely one's distrust in the providence of God and "the felicities which God hath promised to all those that shall come into his presence." Ibid., 71, 74.

64 Lucretius, *De rerum natura*, 3.1045.

65 Ibid., 3.1076–7.

66 Hobbes, *Collected Works*, 2:8, 4:82–3; Lucretius, *De rerum natura*, 2.1006. See also La Mettrie's Epicurean meditation on death: "Do we know any more of our end than of our beginning? Let us submit ourselves, therefore, to an invincible ignorance on which our happiness depends. Whoever thinks in this way will be wise, just, and tranquil about his fate, and consequently happy. He will await death neither fearing nor desiring it." *Man A Machine*, trans. Richard A. Watson and Maya Rybalka (Indianapolis: Hackett, 1994), 75. As Kramnick demonstrates, this is precisely Clarissa's attitude at the end of the novel. *Actions and Objects*, 219–29.

67 Porter, "Love of Life: Lucretius to Freud," 129.

68 For the canonical (and later) expression of this view, see in particular Diderot's *D'Alembert's Dream*, in which the figure of D'Alembert asserts the ongoing participation of each being in all other beings through the eternity of matter, asking, "Does this mean that I shall never die? ... Well, of course, in that sense I shall never die, neither I nor anything else for that matter ... Being born, living, dying – these are only changes of form ... And what difference is there between one form and another?" Jacques Barzum and Ralph H. Bowen, trans. *Rameau's Nephew and Other Works* (Indianapolis: Hackett, 2001), 124–5.

69 On Deleuze's reading of Lucretius, the illusion of infinite pleasure and the illusion of infinite rewards or punishments are two linked "false infinites" that materialism seeks to dismantle. See "Lucretius and the Simulacrum," in *The Logic of Sense*, ed. Constantin V. Boundas, trans. Mark Lester, with Charles Stivale (New York: Columbia University Press, 1990), esp. 272–8.

70 In his own perverse way, Lovelace registers materialism's version of the eternity of matter in his desire to embalm Clarissa's body and preserve her heart "in spirits" (1383–4). Richardson may have been influenced by vitalism's theory of death as a process and progress in which the boundary between life and death is inexact and variable, the heart seen to endure the longest. See Reill, *Vitalizing Nature*, 171–6.

71 Diderot, *Thoughts on the Interpretation of Nature and Other Philosophical Works*, trans. David Adams (Manchester: Clinamen Press, 1999), 75. See also La Mettrie, *Man A Machine*, 75; Stevenson, "Alien Spirits," 95. For a Marxist materialist reading of Clarissa's death as a political condemnation of "patriarchal and class society," see Eagleton, *The Rape of Clarissa*, 73–7.

Clarissa's "refusal" as an alternative, and for Lovelace, deeply threatening, version of an open futurity here stands as her "line of flight" from the oppressive stagnation of Lovelace's fantasy future, one in which a pregnant Clarissa will assure the rapist's identity and repetition: "a Twin Lovelace at each charming breast" (706). The fact that Lovelace imagines his progeny as doubled versions of himself epitomizes his desire to close off the future at its supposed moment of opening out. What looks to be a futural life orientation, in other words, is merely an inertial perpetuation of the same. Looking to death, Clarissa once again breaks out from inertia, though this time more on her own terms, following a drive that persists beyond the biological rhythms of generation and corruption.

72 See Lovelace's (only partially ironic) opening letter to Belford in which he blames the poets, "with their celestially-terrene descriptions," for "fir[ing] my imagination and set[ting] me upon a desire to become a goddess-maker" (142).

73 Stevenson, "Alien Spirits," 91. I here adopt Deleuze's concept of the "line of flight" to indicate his Epicurean interest in a *clinamen*-like trajectory or course of movement that seeks new and alternative pathways for desire. See "Literature and Life," in Smith and Greco, *Essays Critical and Clinical*, 1–6; "On the Superiority of Anglo-American Literature," in Tomlinson and Habberjam, *Dialogues: Gilles Deleuze and Claire Parnet*, 36–76.

74 In book four of *De rerum natura*, Lucretius argues powerfully against the joys of fruition, maintaining instead that "in the very time of possession, lovers' ardour is storm-tossed, uncertain in its course" (4.1077–8). Nature, Lucretius urges, denies us satisfaction, taunting us with "the hope that the fire may be extinguished from the same body that was the origin of the burning" (4.1086–88). For the view that "pleasure ... interrupts[s] the immanent process of desire," see also Deleuze, "Desire and Pleasure," in *Foucault and His Interlocutors*, ed. Arnold I. Davidson (Chicago: University of Chicago Press, 1997), 189.

75 See Mrs Smith's comment to Belford on the devices and inscriptions on Clarissa's coffin: "Lord bless me! Is a coffin a proper subject to display fancy upon!" (1305). Ian Watt argues for an erotic impulse in Clarissa's preparations for death as well as in the principle device on the coffin, the crowned serpent with its tail in its mouth. *The Rise of the Novel: Studies in Defoe, Richardson and Fielding* (Berkeley: University of California Press, 1957), 234. On the animacy suggested in Clarissa's will to die, see also Tanner, *Adultery in the Novel*, 107–8.

76 Terry Castle, "The Death of the Author: Clarissa's Coffin," in *Clarissa's Ciphers: Meaning & Disruption in Richardson's "Clarissa"* (Ithaca: Cornell University Press, 1982), 136–46.

77 Peter France, ed. and trans., *Diderot's Letters to Sophie Volland* (London: Oxford University Press, 1972), 93, 37; Diderot, *Éloge de Richardson*, in *Clarissa: The Eighteenth-Century Response*, 1:394, 395. On Diderot and Richardson, see Rita Goldberg, *Sex and Enlightenment: Women in Richardson and Diderot* (Cambridge: Cambridge University Press, 1984), 128–45; June S. Siegel, "Diderot and Richardson: Manuscripts, Missives, and Mysteries," *Diderot Studies* 18 (1975): 145–67. See also Arthur M. Wilson's speculation that Diderot likely appreciated the "suspenseful sort of prurience and eroticism" of *Clarissa*: "Perhaps Diderot recognized this for what it was, though he does not say so; perhaps he was taken in by it." *Diderot* (New York: Oxford University Press, 1972), 428.

78 Lovelace elsewhere asserts similarly: "And so able is fancy or imagination ... to outdo fact" (1334–5).

79 Patricia Meyer Spacks, *Desire and Truth: Functions of Plot in Eighteenth-Century English Novels* (Chicago: University of Chicago Press, 1990), 75.

7 The Early Modern Embodied Mind and the Entomological Imaginary[1]

KATE E. TUNSTALL

This essay takes a novel approach to the early modern debates about "the thinking matter hypothesis,"[2] or what we would today call "the embodied mind thesis," the question of whether or not the soul is material, whether bodies are sufficient for cognition or whether some spiritual substance is required instead, and where the soul or mind might be located in the body. Of course, such debates have a long history, dating back to the Ancients,[3] but they were conducted with particular intensity in early modern Europe, notably in France and England, following the remarkably successful institutionalization of Cartesian metaphysics in the second half of the seventeenth century,[4] with its mechanist body, animal spirits, and pineal gland, as well as its reinvigoration of the argument that man could have access to truth by means of his reason and by abandoning the dubious evidence of the senses. The aim here is not, however, to offer an intellectual history of the debates.[5] Instead, the approach on offer is literary, and it is so not simply on the understanding that any history of ideas is the history of material, often textual forms, and thus of genres, discourses, metaphors, and images, but also, and more important, because the texts that engage with or mobilize the claim that the body is sufficient for cognitive activity are particularly dense in imagery.[6] To be sure, intellectual historians have not completely overlooked that imagery,[7] but a literary approach enables us properly to read it, to work out how it illuminates and obfuscates, produces satirical and disqualifying effects as well as heuristic and enabling ones, and how such imagery may elicit consent or dissent in the reader by virtue of its being either particularly striking or perfectly banal and predictable, or somewhere in between.

One particular set of images, which appears in discussions of the embodied mind, forms the focus of this essay. The set is, loosely speaking, entomological ("loosely speaking," that is, for the modern reader because, in line with early modern taxonomy, the set includes some tiny animals that modern entomology would exclude from the category of insect).[8] There is, of course, a long-standing literary tradition in which human behaviours are figured metaphorically as insect activities – we might think of the industrious and communitarian bee, the thieving and plagiarizing ant, or the proud and self-sufficient spider.[9] However, while some of the texts in English and French that I will consider here draw on those classical tropes, they also mobilize their insects and other little creepy-crawlies for rather different ends. In the texts under consideration here, images of bees, spiders, worms, mites, and maggots make regular appearances as key elements in accounts of the human body and its cognitive and creative capacities (and incapacities).

The boundary between the human and the non-human, as well as the ethical and political implications of any such boundary, has recently been a focus of attention in the humanities and the social sciences, and as a result there is a growing body of work not only on animals, but also on bees and worms.[10] The question of such a boundary was also of interest to early modern writers, especially following Descartes's claim that animals, unlike humans, who possessed immaterial souls, were merely machines. The debate sparked by that claim, known as that over "l'âme des bêtes" [the souls of beasts], is bound up with the debate over embodied mind insofar as many of those who opposed the Cartesian view of animals argued, often by way of Epicurus and Lucretius's *De Rerum Natura* [On the Nature of the Universe] but also by means of Descartes's own *L'Homme* [Man] (1662), that the body, that which humans share with animals, is sufficient for all cognitive activity.[11] Such is, broadly speaking, the philosophical context – mechanist and anti-mechanist, materialist and anti-materialist – in which early modern writers mobilized classical literary insect tropes and invented novel ones to figure the body and its thoughts, ideas, desires, and imaginings as so many swarms and stings, bites, hops, and jumps of various kinds of bug. The aim now is to read these figures.

The texts in main (though not exclusive) focus here are two novels from the middle of the eighteenth century, Sterne's *Tristram Shandy* (1759–67) and Diderot's *Le Rêve de d'Alembert* [D'Alembert's Dream] (1769). They are, of course, very different, not least formally – one is a first-person narrative, the other a triptych of dialogues or conversations between two or more characters. However, each accords significant attention to the human body, and, most important for our purposes here, each has recourse to some striking insect imagery to figure and figure out psycho-physiological events or states.

In the case of the insect imagery accompanying Sterne's presentation of the embodied mind, scholarship has produced a paradox: that imagery has been at once frequently quoted and consistently overlooked. Among scholars of early modern representations of the mind and its relationship to the body, it is practically a commonplace to quote from Sterne's novel to show that thinkers and writers located the mind inside the body, to demonstrate that early modern writers conceived of the mind as internal, of mental life as inward.[12] In the passage routinely quoted, Sterne has his eponymous hero fantasize about being able to see inside other people's minds, but the focus on Tristram's fantasy of transparency has led critics to overlook what it is, precisely, that Sterne has Tristram imagine he could see.[13] And yet what he envisions is conveyed in a strikingly entomological image that is itself, so this essay contends, very far from transparent.

It is not, of course, sufficient merely to notice the details of Sterne's image of the embodied mind, however difficult a task noticing those details seems to have been. We also need to make sense of the image, which this essay argues is best done by setting it in relation to other instances of cognate imagery in other early modern works, notably those concerned with the brain. This essay will therefore also devote some space to such texts and particularly to Swift's mock-treatise, *A Discourse upon the Mechanical Operations of the Spirit* (1704),[14] which offers not only a satirical image of modern science, but also an image of the brain crawling with insects. Swift's *Discourse* does not only satirize one of the key images to which Diderot will later have recourse in *Le Rêve de d'Alembert*, however; it also makes a link between cerebral bugs and writing, a link further developed by a particular group of writers who promoted literary novelty and were associated with Grub Street.[15] This essay, then, intervenes in the debates about the nature of Sterne's inter-textual relations,[16] and, more important, it suggests that Sterne's insects figure the conceptions of the embodied mind or, rather, that they deliberately and self-satirizingly figure them as the misconceptions of the writer's creative imagination.

While Sterne's entomological imagery has gone unnoticed by scholars, Diderot's philosophico-comical dialogue is well-known to be buzzing with various kinds of insect.[17] This essay concentrates on one of those images, the swarm of bees, which is also present in a number of ancient texts,[18] and is used to propose a neo-Lucretian conception of the mind as the effect of a particular kind of material organization or an "emergent" property of matter, a conception that has recently been undergoing something of a revival in some branches of the philosophy of mind.[19] Two aspects of Diderot's novel use of the image in *Le Rêve de d'Alembert* will be identified and explored here. First, the essay will show that the image is used not only to demonstrate that a body made up of different material parts can think, but also to locate that embodied thinking throughout the body and in the relationships between bodies, thereby figuring thinking as a collective endeavour rather than, as it is in Sterne, an activity performed by an individual, private, interior mind, material or otherwise. (Or, to speak in the terms of some contemporary cognitivist scientists, Diderot uses the image of the swarm of bees to figure the mind as "extended" as well as "embodied.")[20] Second, the essay will argue that while the insect imagery to which Diderot has recourse in *Le Rêve* is not original to him and is, in fact, commonplace, particularly in medical texts of the period,[21] it has been chosen with the deliberate aim of underscoring the communal, collective dimension of thinking – and, crucially, of writing – as it is staged in and by the text.

Comparisons will occasionally be drawn between Sterne and Diderot in the course of this essay, but its arguments are not primarily comparatist.[22] Its aim is, instead, to reveal a hitherto neglected aspect of what might be called the early modern "materialist imaginary," to demonstrate that that imaginary did not only contain the Cartesian machines, clocks, springs, cogs, and pumps, which have been the subject of so much scholarly attention,[23] but that it also contained – indeed that it was positively buzzing and crawling with – all sorts of tiny beasts and bugs. The early modern materialist's imaginary was also, then, so this essay will argue, entomological.

Tristram Shandy: Mind, Matter, and Maggots

In chapter 23 of book 1, Sterne's eponymous narrator laments that "our minds shine not through the body, but are wrapt up here in a dark covering of un-crystallized flesh and blood,"[24] and imagines what it would be like were bodies to be in some way crystalline. Drawing on Lucian's fantastical story in which Momus suggests to Vulcan that he should insert a pane of glass into the human body so as to be able to see inside,[25] Tristram speaks as follows:

> Had the said glass been there set up, nothing more would have been wanting, in order to have taken a man's character, but to have taken a chair and gone softly, as you would to a dioptrical bee-hive, and look'd in, – view'd the soul stark naked; — observ'd all her motions, — her machinations; — traced all her maggots from their first engendering to their crawling forth; — watched her loose in her frisks, her gambols, her capricios; and after some notice of her more solemn deportment, consequent upon such frisks, &c. —— then taken your pen and ink and set down nothing but what you had seen, and could have sworn to.[26]

This is the passage that has frequently been mobilized to support the claim that the early modern mind was conceived of as something inward and internal, and that the new genre of the novel sought to offer its readers imaginary access to that inner space. It is also the passage the specific details of which, namely a bunch of frisky maggots gamboling about inside a dioptrical beehive, have been, quite simply, overlooked.[27] It is time to restore them to view.

Part of what is remarkable about Tristram's imagined vision is simply the fact that it presents character, the soul, the mind – the terminology is shifting – as an object available for empirical inspection,[28] but Sterne intensifies the strangeness by having Tristram suggest that if the soul is, in normal circumstances, invisible, it is not only because the body has been masking it from view; it is also because the soul is very tiny, invisible to the naked eye, and could in any case only be seen with the aid of a "dioptrical" lens or microscope. More remarkably still, Sterne suggests that the soul is itself rather unwilling to be seen – the adverb "softly" suggests that were it to see or hear us approach, it would hide (perhaps because if it saw us through the other end of the microscope, we would appear gigantic and scary). Playing, no doubt, on the terms "anima" and "animus," Sterne has Tristram envisage the soul as some kind of animal.

Quite what kind of animal the soul might be is later shown by the image of the newly revamped body as a "beehive," which further hints that if our approach should be made softly, it is not so much because, if disturbed, it might hide as because it might sting. Yet the animals inside that hive-body do not turn out to be quite what the metaphor had been leading us to expect: when Tristram comes to name the object of his imaginary microscopical gaze, it is not of bees that he speaks, but of a "soul stark naked." This takes us away from entomology and back to anthropology and, with it, to philosophy and physiology, since the presence of a "stark naked" soul inside the body suggests not only that the soul is itself another body, producing a comic *mise-en-abîme* (will this body inside the body also have a window in it?), but also that the body with the window in it might be female and, moreover, be pregnant. Of course, *Tristram Shandy* has much to say about sex and obstetrics, to which we shall return in due course, but for the moment, there is a more urgent set of questions: is there really any evidence that this is an image of what critics have suggested, namely the mind? And, in any case, what are we to make of the appearance of maggots? If this is a womb that Tristram is imagining himself looking into, it could, perhaps, account for why he imagines seeing not bees in the beehive, but maggots, that is to say baby bees or larvæ. But that is not all the maggots are doing there.

Inasmuch as the most obvious connotations of maggots are decay and putrefaction, their presence in Tristram's imagined vision might, of course, simply be understood as a satire on human vanity. Momus is, after all, the god of mockery, and his optical technology thus exposes that man is rotten to the core. Yet in the early modern period, the merest mention of the new-fangled dioptrical technology was often enough to trigger an automatic reference to maggots, for, following the success of Hooke's *Micrographia* (1665), modern science was strongly associated with maggots (and other minute animals). One name given to the Royal Society in the early eighteenth century was "Maggot-Mongers' Hall."[29] Moreover, the human body, when seen down the lens, did indeed appear to be teeming with maggots or worms, the choice of term depending on whether the author took their presence to be a rebuke to man's pride, a reminder of human sin and mortality, or a sign of the amazing spectacle of nature as created by God; and sometimes both are used in the same work.[30] Sterne's object of satire might therefore also be Momus himself; if his dioptrical lens is imagined to show the soul crawling with maggots, it is because maggots are the only things a microscopist ever sees.[31]

Yet decay and degeneration are not the maggot's only associations; indeed, in this period, they were almost synonymous with the opposite process, that is, with generation, and, in particular, with the theory of "equivocal" or "spontaneous" generation.[32] Such a theory, which held that insects – flies, lice, maggots – came into being out of rotting matter, was to be found in the Ancients, notably in Lucretius,[33] but it was much revisited in early modern science. If historians have sometimes observed that microscopy ought really to have put an end to the theory, this is to ignore the compelling political ends to which it was put.[34] It was a key element of Jesuit science, in which the existence in God's creation of what Aristotle had called "imperfect" beings was accounted for by spontaneous generation; and if it was indeed dismissed by anti-Jesuits and by Protestant physico-theologians, for whom the amazing "spectacle of nature" revealed God's hand in even the tiniest and lowliest part of nature, the theory was taken up by atheist, materialist thinkers, such as Diderot, who promoted it as a way of countering the theory of final causes, the teleological argument for the existence of God. Atheist materialists and Jesuits thus became strange bedfellows; indeed, Voltaire, no fan of either, dubbed the pro-spontaneous-generation scientist, John Turberville Needham, an atheist Jesuit, an accusation that seems to have stuck.[35] And, of course, microscopes also enabled the exploration of human generation, which was revealed, following Leeuwenhoek's observation of semen in 1677, also to involve tiny animals, akin to worms, which was indeed Hartsoeker's term for them.[36] If, then, we read Tristram's imaginary vision to be a view inside a womb, perhaps the maggots are to be understood as wriggling spermatozoa, and, moreover, perhaps Sterne is suggesting that there is something "equivocal" about human generation, that man, like the insects produced by spontaneous generation, is an "imperfect" animal.

The more closely we examine the passage, then, the more the connotations of its imagery seem to multiply, and though this is no doubt a deliberate textual staging of the vertiginous effects of microscopy, we seem to be losing sight of the possibility that it stages an embodied mind. However, if we turn to other texts of the period and explore the meanings and activities of maggots in other works of late seventeenth- and eighteenth-century writing, the possibility that this is, after all, an image of the embodied mind and, in particular, of the brain, comes back into view.

Bugs and the Brain: Thinking, Biting, and Writing

The term "maggot" was widely used in early modern English writing to refer to an idea conceived in the brain or the imagination. The *Oxford English Dictionary* defines it as a "whimsical, eccentric, strange, or perverse notion or idea," a meaning that the *OED* dates to the first quarter of the seventeenth century, and which Johnson's *Dictionary* (1755) confirms was still current in the eighteenth century: "Maggot: whimsy, caprice, odd fancy."[37] Usage, as given in the *OED*, makes it clear that the mind that spawns such ideas is embodied – we find, for instance, "Are not you mad my friend? ... Have not you Maggots in your braines?," and "Ther's a strange Maggot hath got into their braines";[38] and it is the material nature of such a mind, subject to decay and degeneration, that accounts for its spawning odd ideas. In the mid-eighteenth century, Samuel Butler adapts the image, drawing on contemporary interest in the theory of spontaneous generation, and saying of the character of "A Quibbler" (1759) that "all his conceptions are produced by equivocal generation, which makes them justly esteemed but Maggots."[39]

Such imagery may also be drawing on anatomical descriptions of the brain, such as that by Thomas Willis, who refers to its "vermiform or worm-shaped processes,"[40] a metaphor that may have enabled an updating of an existing comic association between odd ideas, maggots, and the brain, giving it a new "scientific" resonance, if it was perhaps not what made the association possible in the first place. And other aspects of early modern conceptions of the brain seem to have enabled writers and, notably, polemicists to make use of animal and insect imagery in their writing on the nature of the mind. We find, for instance, in a refutation of the embodied mind thesis entitled *Vindiciæ Mentis: An Essay of the Being and Nature of Mind* (1702), the assertion that the "Little Mass of Stuff within the Cranium ... can't be so infinitely Figured, or have its little Maggots friggle, at such an Infinite rate, as to cause or produce such innumerable variations as are made in Thoughts."[41] The author,[42] probably Thomas Emes, is clearly seeking to emphasize the materiality of the brain and therefore to disqualify any claim that it might be responsible for thought, but are we also to read the maggots as a metaphor for some aspect of early modern brain anatomy?

It is impossible, as well as undesirable, to pin it down, but it should be noted that, in addition to the "vermiform processes" observed by Willis, there are two other features of early modern brain science that may have enabled Emes's imagery. The first is the association between the brain and the animal spirits that were key to the Cartesian account of the mechanics of the body. Flowing in the blood, according to patterns determined by the pineal gland in the brain, animal spirits were thought to be the means by which physical movement and thinking or, rather, perceiving, imagining, and remembering, occurred. While Emes is seeking to debunk this conception of thinking by means of the maggot-image, it is clear that Sterne's image functions rather differently. That he may also associate maggots and animal spirits can be established by relating the passage back to the opening of the novel, where another association is made, namely that between animal spirits and spermatozoa.[43] When Tristram begins his life story at the very beginning, at the moment of his conception, he tells (in terms that echo Locke's *Essay Concerning Human Understanding*)[44] of how the animal spirits in his mother's brain had come to associate sex and clock-winding, of how that had led her to ask his father at a highly inopportune moment whether he had wound up the clock, and how that, in turn, led his father's "animal spirits" to be accidentally dispersed, resulting in his own (mis)conception.[45] Read in this context, the beehive-body, with a stark naked soul in it, and maggots, presents an image not only of a womb, as suggested earlier, but also of a brain, and perhaps even Tristram's own with its "strong propensity to begin ... very nonsensically."[46] In contrast, then, to Emes's imagery, Sterne's is lacking in polemical charge; instead, the novelist re-imagines the animal spirits as spritely animals and thereby suggests that the human mind, embodied as it is, is prone to quirky conceptions and capricious movements.

It is not only mechanist models of the body and of the brain that are subject to being imagined or re-imagined in entomological terms, however. Non-mechanist, materialist accounts of the brain also enable entomological images or, rather, they themselves explicitly use insect imagery to figure the brain, and it is these that are quoted and satirized, along with much else, in Swift's *Discourse*. We consider Swift's satire here because it lays the ground for Diderot's more serious staging of the same image in *Le Rêve*, and because when the satirist also uses the image to figure ideas in a particular kind of mind, that of a writer, it enables us to grasp a further dimension of the passage in Sterne.

The *Discourse* is a mock-treatise, satirizing materialism, mechanism, and any other modern scientific theories that would "reduce" man to the physical,[47] as well as the writers whose brains have spawned such theories. It contains a description of the brain, which draws not only on Willis's work (though probably only second-hand via William Wotton) with its Cartesian mechanism, Galenic humours, and Hippocratic spirits,[48] but also on Lucretius, combining his theory of equivocal generation, which microscopy had recently reinvigorated, with his atomism, according to which all bodies are made up of tiny particles of different shapes that hook onto each other, creating material assemblages, some of which can feel and think.[49] Swift has his narrator report favourably "the Opinion of choice *Virtuosi*," according to which the brain, like the rest of the body, is "only a Crowd of little Animals, but with Teeth and Claws extremely sharp, and therefore cling together in the Contexture we behold, like the Picture of Hobbes's *Leviathan*, or like Bees in a perpendicular swarm upon a Tree, or like Carrion corrupted into Vermin, still preserving the Shape and Figure of the Mother Animal."[50] Here, if it is the frontispiece to Hobbes's *Leviathan* that is referred to explicitly, there can be no doubt that Lucretius's *De Rerum natura* or, at least, imagery very strongly associated with it, is also being alluded to: the theory of spontaneous generation is present by means of the image of the rotting carcass crawling with maggots, and swarms of bees are a staple of both Epicurean and anti-Epicurean works as a means of figuring the assemblages of atoms. Richard Bentley, for instance, uses it to argue that it was impossible, *pace* the atheist materialists he was seeking to confute in *A Confutation of Atheism from the Faculties of the Soul* (1692), for a great number of atoms to "compose one greater individual animal, with one mind and understanding ... any more than a swarm of bees ... can be conceived to make up one particular living creature."[51] And if the "Teeth and Claws extremely sharp" mentioned by Swift are comical versions of the hooks that enable Lucretius's atoms to assemble and form a contexture, they are also that which enables the brain to conceive ideas.

An idea is conceived in the brain, as figured by the materialists satirized by Swift, when its little constituent animals use their teeth to bite. Swift's image of little biting animals may also draw on an early modern English expression that was sufficiently common to appear in an early eighteenth-century bilingual English-French dictionary, namely "I shall do it, when the maggot bites."[52] And biting, according to Swift's narrator, is what the brain bugs do when they get hot. He reports that "all Invention is formed by the Morsure of two or more of these animals upon certain capillary nerves, which proceed [from the brain]. ... Nothing less than a violent Heat can disentangle these Creatures from their hamated Station of Life, or give them Vigor and Humor to imprint the Marks of their little Teeth,"[53] and he encourages the wearing of "quilted caps" to overheat the brain and provoke the most intense bites. The effect of such a bite is to cause a person to take up a particular activity, namely writing: "if the Morsure be Hexagonal, it produced Poetry; the Circular gives Eloquence; if the Bite hath been conical, the person, whose nerve is so effected, shall be disposed to write upon the politics; and so of the rest."[54] If it is not surprising to discover at the end of the work that the narrator has himself been bitten, Swift may also be targeting the self-declared maggot-bite-induced writing of the late seventeenth century and early decades of the eighteenth. And though Sterne's maggots do not bite, they do make jerky, quirky movements, "frisks" and "capriccios," and by mid-century, maggots have come to be associated with the embodied (and thus unsound) brain of the writer.[55]

The association between maggots and the writer's brain is particularly common in the work of the circle of writers, journalists, booksellers, and literary entrepreneurs known as *The Athenian Society*, founded in 1691. One of them, Samuel Wesley, had published a collection of poems entitled *Maggots: Or, Poems on Several Subjects, Never Before Handled* (1685), which opens: "The Maggot Bites, I must begin:/ Muse! Pray be civil! Enter in!/ Ransack my addled pate with Care/ And muster all the Maggots there!"[56] And another, John Dunton, later expanded on the image as a figure for literary novelty in his autobiographical novel, *The Life and Errors of John Dunton, Late Citizen of London, Written by Himself in Solitude* (1705), which readers later in the century would compare to *Tristram Shandy*.[57] Dunton presents the work as follows:

> As this Idea of a New Life, is an ORIGINAL PROJECT; perhaps some will call it one of Dunton's Maggots: For having printed thirty of W[esley]'s writing, it wou'd be strange if I shou'd not by Imitation become one my self. But how little I deserve to be so accounted, is sufficiently shewn in the following Sheets. ... Now this Subject is New and Surprising, but is far from being Magotty; for if a Man must be call'd a Magot for starting Thoughts that are WHOLLY NEW, than Farewel Invention. In this sense the Understanding Lock, and the Metaphysical Noris are greater MAGOTS than John Dunton (as they publish Thoughts that are Newer and Better) but sure none are so stupid as to call these Gentlemen Magots, for obliging the World with their Ideal Discoveries; ... But (If after all I can say) my IDEAL LIFE must pass for a Magot, I must own it my own pure Magot; the Natural Issue of my Brain Pan, bred and born there, and only there.[58]

Here Dunton at once defends himself against the charge of being "maggoty" and asserts that his maggots are *sui generis*, and, moreover, aligning his work with that of Locke, as well as that of Locke's opponent, Norris, he registers the relative novelty in English in the early years of the eighteenth century of both the term "idea" and of first-person writing.[59]

The literary connotations of the term "maggot," as well as its appearance in satirical writing on modern philosophy and medicine, make it clear, then, that its appearance in Sterne's novel is significant. When Tristram peers inside the "beehive"-body in search of the mind and sees the "soul, stark naked," its "machinations" and its "maggots," Sterne is not only drawing on an association between maggots and ideas that is registered in dictionaries of the period and given a new currency by both anti-Cartesian images of the animal spirits, which Sterne locates in the womb as well as the brain, and anti-materialist uses of the materialist image of the brain as a swarm of bees or maggots; he is also suggesting that what the embodied mind engenders is the material of the modern novel. We understand, then, that what Tristram observes through Momus's glass is a womb spawning a new life and a brain spawning not only novel ideas, but also the ideas for a novel, that of his life. And so, by means of the maggots, Sterne does not only offer a comic image of the mind as embodied; he also ironically locates his own novel within the "maggotty" tradition.

~

We turn now to *Le Rêve de d'Alembert*, not to compare it with Sterne's novel, though we know Diderot had read *Tristram Shandy* in 1762,[60] but to explore another instance of the entomological imaginary in early modern materialist writing. We find in *Le Rêve* references to imaginary microscopes and what might be seen down them, and numerous images designed to explore and give support to the embodied mind thesis,[61] including harpsichords that play themselves,[62] a spider in its web,[63] and a swarm of bees. This essay concentrates on the latter image and shows not only how and why the materialist image of the swarm of bees, which we have seen satirized by Swift and used by Bentley to refute materialism, is presented in the text as a solution to the philosophical problem of the unity of the material body, but also how the image is itself embodied in the very material form of Diderot's text.

Le Rêve de d'Alembert: Swarm, Form, and Esprit de Corps

Diderot's text of 1769 is in three parts, the second of which, entitled "Le Rêve de d'Alembert," has given its name to the work as a whole. In the first part, entitled, "Suite d'un entretien entre Diderot et d'Alembert" [Continuation of a conversation between Diderot and d'Alembert], a title that suggests that there was more preceding it that has been omitted, a point to which we shall return, the two characters are engaged in a conversation about some of the major philosophical questions of the day, notably whether or not an immaterial soul exists, and, if not, where in the body a material soul might be located – the brain, the hand, or distributed throughout the body; and how, in the absence of an immaterial soul and given that the body is made up of many parts that undergo change over time, a continuous sense of self can exist.[64] D'Alembert is skeptical about Diderot's proposal to abandon the soul, conceptually problematic though it might be, and he wonders whether it might not leave us with even greater conceptual problems – wouldn't it mean, for example, that a stone has feeling?[65] Eventually, tiring rather of Diderot's conversation, d'Alembert makes his excuses and goes home to bed, where he has a dream, in which he further continues the conversation with Diderot. It is here that the most important image of the text, the swarm of bees, appears.

Before exploring it, a little more must be said about the text and, notably, about its form. D'Alembert had his dream during the night, most of which elapses between parts 1 and 2, but if we read of it in part 2, it is not because an awake d'Alembert offers a first-person account of his nocturnal experience. The reporting of d'Alembert's dream is given to another character, a woman named Mlle de Lespinasse, who has had access to his dream, not because she is able, Momus-like, to see into his mind, but because the conversation, of which the dream consisted, was conducted by d'Alembert out loud in his sleep. She sat by his bedside, noting it all down as he sleep-talked both in his own voice and in that of his interlocutor, Diderot. In the second part of the text, then, with d'Alembert now sleeping silently in the background, she reads out her notes to the doctor, Bordeu, whom she had called during the night. This extraordinary set-up, in which a dream, the most private and inward of experiences, is accessible to other people, and which involves a written text in which voices do voices doing other voices, has important implications for the way we understand the image of the swarm of bees.

The notes that Mlle de Lespinasse reads out to Bordeu make clear that the sleep-talker had mentioned the image of the swarm of bees in response to the question of how a body, possessing no immaterial soul and consisting of many parts, could act as a unified whole. In his sleep, d'Alembert replied as follows:

> Avez-vous quelquefois vu un essaim d'abeilles s'échapper de leur ruche? [...] Le monde, ou la masse générale de la matière est la grande ruche [...] Les avez-vous vues s'en aller former à l'extrémité de la branche d'un arbre, une longue grappe de petits animaux ailés, tous accrochés les

uns aux autres par les pattes? … Cette grappe est un être, un individu, un animal quelconque […] … [C]elui qui n'aurait jamais vu une pareille grappe s'arranger, serait tenté de la prendre pour un animal à cinq ou six cents têtes et à mille ou douze cents ailes ….

Have you ever seen a swarm of bees leaving their hive? … The world, or the general mass of matter, is the great hive […]. Have you seen them fly away and form a long cluster of little winged animals, hanging off the end of the branch of a tree, all clinging on to each other by their feet? […] This cluster is a being, an individual, some sort of animal […]. … [S]omeone who'd never seen the formation of a cluster like that would be tempted to think it was a single animal with five or six hundred heads and a thousand or twelve hundred wings […].[66]

So, a material body, made up of parts, has no more difficulty, according to the dreaming d'Alembert, in acting as a unified whole than the composite body that is the swarm or "cluster" of bees does. And he explained the motion of the swarm as a whole in a manner that recalls the little animals biting in Swift; d'Alembert's swarm moves in response to one of bees pinching another:

Si l'une de ces abeilles s'avise de pincer d'une façon quelconque, l'abeille à laquelle elle s'est accrochée, que croyez-vous qu'il en arrive? … Celle-ci pincera la suivante; … il s'excitera dans toute la grappe autant de sensations qu'il y a de petits animaux; … le tout s'agitera, se remuera, changera de situation et de forme.

If one of these bees decides to pinch somehow the bee it is clinging onto, do you know what will happen? … this one will pinch the next one; … as many pinching sensations will arise throughout the cluster as there are little animals in it; … the whole cluster will stir, move and change position and shape.[67]

Of course, Bentley contended, as we have seen, that even if the swarm of bees might appear from the outside to be a single being, it is not so, because there is no single consciousness inside it; it has no mind. However, Diderot's aim in putting these words in the mouth of a sleep-talking man is, precisely, to unsettle any attachment to the idea of consciousness, and to point out that, in fact, we regularly give it up, that is to say, every night when we sleep.[68]

Yet it is not only an attachment to the idea of consciousness that the text seeks to unsettle, it is also an attachment to inwardness and to first-personhood. The text's peculiar set-up means that d'Alembert's private dream happens in public; not only does he have the dream-conversation out loud and, in addition, describe the things he dreams he can see, notably down a microscope, but his ideas and perceptions are made visible by his body as he gestures, ejaculates, blushes, and sighs.[69] Furthermore, d'Alembert's dream has an effect on other characters' bodies and voices, which join the dream. The mind in *Le Rêve* is not only embodied, it is also extended, and not simply in the sense that it is distributed throughout the body rather than located in one place, such as the brain, but also in the sense, akin to that proposed by some branches of modern cognitive science, that it shapes and is itself shaped by the surrounding material environment.[70] In *Le Rêve*, that environment consists of other bodies and other voices, for there is something strangely contagious about embodied-mind theory in Diderot's text: it is as though anyone who hears it performs it.[71] Diderot spoke it to d'Alembert, who then spoke it in his sleep to Mlle de Lespinasse, who then speaks it to Bordeu; indeed, she declares, "Je n'écoute que pour le plaisir de redire" [I only listen for the pleasure of repeating what I hear].[72] And Bordeu then speaks it in his turn; indeed, he is able to predict what Mlle de Lespinasse's notes say without having seen them.[73] And as the characters repeat, predict, or ventriloquize, they lose track of who is who: "Bordeu. – Est-ce vous qui parlez? Mademoiselle de Lespinasse. – Non. C'est le rêveur. Bordeu. – Continuez. Mademoiselle de Lespinasse. – Je continue [...] Il a ajouté, en s'apostrophant lui-même. Mon ami, d'Alembert, prenez-y garde ..." [Bordeu. – Is it you talking? Mademoiselle de Lespinasse. – No, it's the dreamer. Bordeu. – Continue. Mademoiselle de Lespinasse. – I am continuing ... He added, addressing himself. D'Alembert, my friend, take a closer look ...].[74] Voices merge, and identities fuse and become continuous with each other to create a verbally performed swarm, in which each swarm-member is part of a greater conversational whole.

But what is the status of that performance? Many scholars have argued that *Le Rêve* is Diderot's most clearly materialist work, one in which he offers a philosophical and literary demonstration for embodied-mind thesis, a demonstration that he backs up with scientific evidence by means of the interventions of the medical doctor, Bordeu.[75] Yet the text also explores the nature of scientific truth, and indeed the swarm-form enables the suggestion that if the characters all speak embodied-mind theory, it is not so much because it is true as because it is the discursive practice of the group to which they belong; it is an esprit de corps. Mlle de Lespinasse makes use of this phrase when she glosses Bordeu's explanation of how it is, in the absence of an immaterial soul, that a body, which undergoes many changes over time, has a continuous identity. Bordeu explains to d'Alembert, who has now woken up, that had he gone suddenly from being a young man to an old, not only would people not recognize him, but he would have no idea who other people were, since: "Vous n'auriez plus été vous ni pour les autres ni pour vous, pour les autres qui n'auraient point été eux pour vous. Tous les rapports auraient été anéantis. Toute l'histoire de votre vie pour moi, toute l'histoire de la mienne pour vous, brouillée" [You would no longer have been you either to other people or to yourself, and they would not have been them to you. All relations would have been destroyed. Your entire life history as I know it, and my entire life history as you know it, scrambled].[76] This is the claim that Mlle de Lespinasse glosses by referring back to the swarm and observing: "Dans la grappe d'abeilles, il n'y en aurait pas une qui eût le temps de prendre l'esprit du corps" [In the cluster of bees, there wouldn't be a single one that had been there long enough to adopt the esprit de corps].[77] It is a good joke: in French "l'esprit du corps" literally means "the mind of the body," and the esprit de corps of the conversational swarm of which she is a member, is, precisely, the belief that the mind is embodied. Yet the pun also allows for the suggestion that materialism is not so much a scientific truth as a corporate ethos; and indeed Mlle de Lespinasse's subsequent comparison of the swarm of bees and a monastery underlines this: "Je dis que l'esprit monastique se conserve, parce que le monastère se refait peu à peu, et quand il entre un moine nouveau, il en trouve une centaine de vieux qui l'entraînent à penser et à sentir comme eux" [the spirit of the monastery is preserved over time because the monastery only renews itself gradually, and that when a new monk arrives, he is met by a hundred old hands who lead him to think and feel like them].[78] Of course, the idea of an atheist, materialist monastery is another good joke, but it also strengthens the suggestion that if embodied-mind theory is to be understood as a scientific truth, it can only be so on the condition that scientific truth is itself understood to be the shared discourses and practices, the *habitus*, of a particular community.[79]

That community would seem, at first glance, to have a kind of founding member insofar as the character, Diderot, appears to be at the origin of all the conversations: Mlle de Lespinasse reads out d'Alembert's dream, which continued an earlier conversation he had had with Diderot, who appeared to have initiated it, for, though the first words of the text are spoken by d'Alembert, they are clearly in reply to something Diderot had just said. Presenting Diderot as the prime mover would also seem to be a way for Diderot, the author, to assert himself as such.[80] And yet, on further inspection, a point of origin is hard to find. Not only is the first part of the text entitled, we recall, "Suite," suggesting the possibility that Diderot may be repeating to d'Alembert what someone else had earlier said to him,[81] but the work's imagery as a whole is very far from being original to Diderot, the author; indeed the imagery has been thought disappointingly banal.[82] It might, of course, be argued that it is precisely such banality that lends the images their legitimacy and persuasive force,[83] but another interpretation is also possible. If the images are commonplace, it is also because Diderot's concept of authorship is not invested in originality and is, instead, more concerned with participating in a communal literary imaginary.[84] Of course, within that very imaginary, literary activities are themselves often figured in entomological terms: where the spider is a figure for the writer who will acknowledge no predecessors, and the ant a figure for the literary thief or plagiarist, the bee is, by contrast, the writer who acknowledges the work of his forebears and reworks what he finds in them.[85] And it is this latter approach that best figures Diderot's in *Le Rêve*, and it might in this sense also be read as Lucretian for, when it comes to poetry, as it is with atoms, so it is with letters: there is only combination and recombination, and no such thing as creation *ex nihilo*.[86]

With *Le Rêve*, then, Diderot recombines existing entomological images, and assembles novel forms and new swarms. The swarm of bees does not only figure the body and the embodied mind; it also enables the figuring out of the way in which body parts cooperate and perform actions without the need for an immaterial soul. Moreover, the figuring-out activity is one in which bodies not only think but also think with other bodies, speak in cooperation with each other. What the image offers, then, is not so much a claim that the whole is greater than the sum of its parts, as a performance in which the soul is the hum of its parts.[87]

"La Cironalité Universelle"?

This essay contends, then, that the early modern materialist imaginary is not only stocked with clocks and machines, but also teeming with bugs. Indeed, the two sets of images, mechanist and organic, sometimes go hand in hand – in Sterne's novel, "maggots" appear just after "motions" and "machinations," and a similar collocation can be found in another novel not considered here, namely *Fanny Hill* (1748).[88] Indeed, we might go so far as to apply to early modern literature the memorable phrase coined by Cyrano de Bergerac to describe the universe, namely "la cironalité universelle" [universal little-critterdom].[89]

Moreover, it is significant that writers do not only employ entomological images to figure the embodied mind; they also use them to figure the books and texts in which the images appear: Sterne's brain-child is maggoty, and Diderot's dream-text a bee-swarm. If nothing else, such close attention to matters literary on the part of early modern embodied-mind theorists (and their critics) means that modern intellectual historians working on the history of materialism and the idea of "thinking matter" must also attend to its particular literary embodiments.

NOTES

1 I should like to acknowledge here the extent to which this essay has been informed by conversations, electronic and/or face-to-face, with Caroline Warman, Isabelle Moreau, Natalie Philips, Jonathan Kramnick, Joseph Drury, Brad Pasanek, Sylvie Kleiman, and Joanna Stalnaker, as well as the participants in the "Early Modern Dreams and Delusions" workshop, organized by Ita MacCarthy as part of Terence Cave's Balzan project "Literature as an Object of Knowledge."

2 See John W. Yolton, *Thinking Matter: Materialism in Eighteenth-Century Britain* (Oxford: Basil Blackwell, 1984); *Locke and French Materialism* (Oxford: Clarendon Press, 1991).

3 See John P. Wright and Paul Potter, eds., *Psyche and Soma: Physicians and Metaphysicians on the Mind-Body Problem from Antiquity to Enlightenment* (Oxford: Oxford University Press, 2000); Danijela Kambaskovic-Sawers, ed., "Conjunctions of Mind, Soul and Body from Plato to the Enlightenment," special issue, *Studies in the History of Philosophy of Mind* 15 (2014).

4 For a history of the process of that institutionalization, see Stéphane Van Damme, *Descartes. Essai d'histoire culturelle d'une grandeur philosophique* (Paris: Presses de Sciences Po, 2002).

5 See Bernard Baertschi, *Les rapports de l'âme et du corps: Descartes, Diderot et Maine de Biran* (Paris: Vrin, 1992); Dennis Des Chene, *Spirits and Clocks: Machine and Organism in Descartes* (Ithaca: Cornell University Press, 2001); François Duchesneau, *Les modèles du vivant de Descartes à Leibniz* (Paris: Vrin, 1998); Peter Hanns Reill, *Vitalizing Nature in the Enlightenment*

(Berkeley: University of California Press, 2005); Ann Thomson, *Bodies of Thought: Science, Religion, and the Soul in the Early Enlightenment* (Oxford: Oxford University Press, 2008).

6 For a (non-exhaustive) database of metaphors for the mind, see Brad Pasanek's "The Mind is a Metaphor" database at http://metaphors.iath.virginia.edu/metaphors.

7 See, for instance, Des Chene, *Spirits and Clocks*; Charles T. Wolfe, "'The brain is a book which reads itself'": Cultured Brains and Reductive Materialism from Diderot to J.J.C. Smart," in *Mindful Æsthetics: Literature and the Science of Mind*, ed. Chris Danta and Helen Groth (New York and London: Bloomsbury, 2013), 73–89.

8 For Réaumur, perhaps the most famous entomologist of the eighteenth century, the category "insect" was capacious enough to include crocodiles. René-Antoine Ferchault de Réaumur, *Mémoires pour servir à l'histoire des insectes*, vol. 1 (Paris: Imprimerie royale, 1734), 58.

9 See Claire Preston, *Bee* (London: Reaktion, 2006); Steven Connor, *Fly* (London: Reaktion, 2006); Katarzyna Michalska and Sergiusz Michalski, *Spider* (London: Reaktion, 2010).

10 Scholars have taken their cue from two works in particular, Jacques Derrida, *The Animal That Therefore I Am*, ed. Marie-Louise Mallet, trans. David Wills (New York: Fordham University Press, 2009); and Giorgio Agamben, *The Open: Man and Animal*, trans. Kevin Attell (Stanford: Stanford University Press, 2004). See also Jane Bennett, *Vibrant Matter: A Political Ecology of Things* (Durham: Duke University Press, 2010); Janelle A. Schwartz, *Worm Work: Recasting Romanticism* (Minneapolis: University of Minnesota Press, 2012); Lisa T. Sarasohn, "'That Nauseous Venomous Insect': Bedbugs in Early Modern England," *Eighteenth-Century Studies* 46.4 (2013): 513–30. Sarasohn seems to have a long-standing interest in worms; see her study of Margaret Cavendish's *Blazing World* with its worm-men in *The Natural Philosophy of Margaret Cavendish: Reason and Fancy during the Scientific Revolution* (Baltimore: Johns Hopkins, 2010), 165–9. I am grateful to Rebecca Bullard for this reference.

11 For a presentation of the debates with extracts of some of the key texts, see Francine Markovits, ed., "L'âme des bêtes," special issue, *Corpus. Revue de philosophie* 16/17 (1991).

12 See, for instance, Tony Nuttall, *A Common Sky: Philosophy and the Literary Imagination* (Berkeley: University of California Press, 1974), 85–6; Dorrit Cohn, *Transparent Minds: Narrative Modes for Presenting Consciousness in Fiction* (Princeton: Princeton University Press, 1978), 3; Stephen Toulmin, "The Inwardness of Mental Life," *Critical Inquiry* 6.1 (1979): 1.

13 Alison Conway has focused on the visual nature of Tristram's fantasy. See *Private Interests: Women, Portraiture, and the Visual Culture of the English Novel, 1709–1791* (Toronto: University of Toronto Press, 2001), 155.

14 The *Discourse* was published along with *The Battle of the Books* and *The Tale of a Tub*. See *A Discourse upon the Mechanical Operations of the Spirit* in *A Tale of a Tub and Other Works*, ed. Marcus Walsh (Cambridge: Cambridge University Press, 2010), 169–87. *The Battle of the Books* famously recasts the quarrel between the Ancients and the Moderns in entomological terms, as that between the spider and the bee. See *A Tale of a Tub and Other Works*, 149–51. For a recent reading of the fable, see Gregory Lynall, *Swift and Science: The Satire, Politics and Theology of Natural Knowledge, 1690–1730* (Basingstoke: Palgrave Macmillan, 2012), 50–68.

15 The etymology of "grub" is from the old English verb to "dig," but it makes for a pun on the word for insect spawn. For the history and geography of literary London, see Pat Rogers, *Grub Street: Studies in a Subculture* (London: Methuen, 1972). It should be noted that in eighteenth-century French as well as English writing, the paid writer or hack attracts manifold entomological insults. See Henri Duranton, ed., *Le pauvre diable: destins de l'homme de lettres au XVIIIe siècle* (Saint-Etienne: Pulications de l'Université de Saint-Etienne, 2006).

16 See Thomas Keymer, *Sterne, the Moderns and the Novel* (Oxford: Oxford University Press, 2002); Melvyn New, "Introduction," in Laurence Sterne, *The Life and Opinions of Tristram Shandy, Gentleman* (London: Penguin, 2003), xxiii–xlix.

17 See Annie Ibrahim, "Maupertuis dans *Le Rêve de D'Alembert*: l'essaim d'abeilles et le polype," *Recherches sur Diderot et sur L'Encyclopédie* 34 (2003): 71–83; Caroline Jacot Grapa, "Le moi-araignée du *Rêve de d'Alembert* de Diderot," *Littérature et médecine: approches et perspectives (XVIe–XIXe siècles)* 24 (2007): 177–98; Colas Duflo, "Le moi-multiple," *Archives de philosophie* 1 (2008): 95–110; Sophie Audidière, Jean-Claude Bourdin, and Colas Duflo, *Encyclopédie du "Rêve de d'Alembert" de Diderot* (Paris: CNRS, 2006).

18 See Preston, *Bee*. For Lucretius, see *On the Nature of the Universe*, a verse translation by Ronald Melville, with an introduction and notes by Don and Peta Fowler (1997; repr. Oxford: Oxford World's Classics, 2008), 60, 62 (book 2, lines 865–73, 926–30).

19 See Jonathan Kramnick, *Actions and Objects from Hobbes to Richardson* (Stanford: Stanford University Press, 2010); Eric Bonabeau, Marco Dorigo, and Guy Théraulaz, *Swarm Intelligence: from Natural to Artificial Systems* (Oxford: Oxford University Press, 1999). Charles T. Wolfe places

D'Alembert's Dream in dialogue with modern neuroscience in "The brain is a book that reads itself."

20 The key text in the theory of extended mind is Andy Clark, *Supersizing the Mind: Embodiment, Action, and Cognitive Extension* (Oxford: Oxford University Press, 2008).

21 See Charles T. Wolfe and Motoichi Terada, "The Animal Economy as Object and Program in Montpellier Vitalism," *Science in Context* 21.4 (2008): 537–79.

22 The network of cross-Channel connections between English and French writers in the eighteenth century is well established; see, for instance, Ann Thomson, Simon Burrows, and Edmond Dziembowski, eds., *Cultural Transfers: France and Britain in the Long Eighteenth Century* (Oxford: Voltaire Foundation, 2010). With particular reference to Sterne, see Lana Asfour, *Laurence Sterne in France* (New York: Continuum, 2008). Diderot was himself a vector for the circulation of English works in France by means of his translations of Stanyan, Robert James, and Shaftesbury, as well as the *Encyclopédie*, which draws on the work of many English philosophers; however, given that so few of Diderot's works, including the *Rêve*, were published in his lifetime, circulating instead to the highly select group of readers of the manuscript journal, *Correspondence littéraire*, his reception in France, let alone in England, was very limited.

23 For machines and automata in English literature, see Leo Braudy, "*Fanny Hill* and Materialism," *Eighteenth-Century Studies* 4 (1970): 21–40; Deidre Lynch, *The Economy of Character: Novels, Market Culture, and the Business of Inner Meaning* (Chicago: University of Chicago Press, 1998); Thomas Keymer, "Mechanism, Materialism and the Novel," in *Literary Milieux: Essays on Text and Context presented to Howard Erskine-Hill*, ed. David Womersley and Richard McCabe (Newark: University of Delaware Press, 2008), 307–33; Joseph Drury, "Haywood's Thinking Machines," *Eighteenth-Century Fiction* 21.2 (2009): 201–28.

24 Laurence Sterne, *The Life and Opinions of Tristram Shandy, Gentleman*, ed. Melvyn New (London: Penguin, 2003), 65–6. All references are to this edition.

25 For instances of the same fantasy in other eighteenth-century writers, see Ann Jessie Van Sant, *Eighteenth-Century Sensibility and the Novel: The Senses in Social Context* (Cambridge: Cambridge University Press, 1993), 60–2.

26 Sterne, *Tristram Shandy*, 65.

27 Christopher Ricks, for instance, focuses his attention instead on the fact that the verb "to take" governs both "character" and "chair." Introduction to *The Life and Opinions of Tristram Shandy, Gentleman*, ed. Melvyn New and

Joan New (1967; repr. New York: Penguin, 1997), xviii. Perhaps Conway nods in their direction when, having quoted the passage in full, she refers to "coarse materiality." *Private Interests*, 155. Fritz Gysin analyses the passage at length in his chapter, promisingly entitled, "Model and Microcosm: Frisks and Gambols in the Dioptrical Beehive," but devotes no time to either bees or maggots. *Model as Motif in Tristram Shandy* (Bern: Francke, 1983), 19–55.

28 See Juliet McMaster, "The Body Inside the Skin: The Medical Model of Character in the Eighteenth-Century Novel," *Eighteenth-Century Fiction* 4.4 (1992): 277–300.

29 The phrase is that of the satirist Ned Ward, quoted in Marjorie Hope Nicolson, *Science and Imagination* (Ithaca: Great Seal Books, 1962), 174.

30 See Daniel Le Clerc's *A Natural and Medicinal History of Worms Bred in the Bodies of Men and other Animals* (London, 1721), first published in Latin as *Historia naturalis et medica latorum lumbricorum intra hominen et alia animalia nascentium* (Geneva, 1715), which drew on Vallisneri's work on human parasites; Gerard de Gols's *A Theologico-philosophical Dissertation concerning Worms in all Parts of Human Bodies* (London, 1727), which draws on Nicolas Andry de Boisregard's *De la génération des vers dans le corps de l'homme* (1700), and refers to Le Clerc. There was also much interest in the marketing of worm-powders designed to cure worms; see, for instance, Pope's satirical poem, "To Mr. John Moore, author of the celebrated Worm-Powder" (1716).

31 In Shadwell's play, *The Virtuoso* (1676), the eponymous type is described by another character as follows: "no man upon the face of the earth is so well seen in the nature of ants, flies, humble-bees, earwigs, millipedes, hog's lice, maggots, mites in a cheese, tadpoles, worms, newts, spiders, and all the noble products of the sun by equivocal generation." Thomas Shadwell, *The Virtuoso*, ed. Marjorie Hope Nicholson and David Stuart Rodes (Lincoln: University of Nebraska Press, 1966), act 3, scene 3.

32 For a useful account of the difference between "equivocal" and "spontaneous" generation in seventeenth- and eighteenth-century writing, see Peter McLaughlin, "Spontaneous versus Equivocal Generation in Early Modern Science," *Annals in the History and Philosophy of Biology* 10 (2005): 79–88.

33 Lucretius, *On the Nature of the Universe*, 61 (book 2, lines 897–901). For studies of the early modern rediscovery of Lucretius, see, for instance, Stephen Greenblatt, *The Swerve: How the World Became Modern* (London: Norton, 2011).

34 For a good account of these, see Marc J. Ratcliff, *The Quest for the Invisible: Microscopy in the Enlightenment* (Farnham: Ashgate, 2009).

35 See Shirley A. Roe, "Voltaire versus Needham: Atheism, Materialism, and the Generation of Life," *Journal of the History of Ideas* 46.1 (1985): 65–87.

36 The best history of these developments is still that to be found in Jacques Roger, *Les sciences de la vie dans la pensée française du XVIIIe siècle: La génération des animaux de Descartes à l'Encyclopédie* (Paris: Albin Michel, 1993), which exists in a partial translation as *The Life Sciences in Eighteenth-Century French Thought* (Stanford: Stanford University Press, 1997).

37 *Samuel Johnson's Dictionary of the English Language*, ed. Alexander Chalmers (London: Studio Press, 1994).

38 The examples quoted in the *OED* are taken from act 3, scene 4 of Fletcher's play, *Women Pleas'd* (1647), and letter 94 of Howell's *A New Volume of Letters* (1647).

39 Samuel Butler, *Characters and Passages from Note-Books*, ed. A.R. Waller (Cambridge: Cambridge University Press, 1908), 90.

40 *The Remaining Medical Works of that Famous and Renowned Physician Dr. Thomas Willis*, trans. S. Pordage (London: T. Dring, C. Harper, J. Leigh, and S. Martyn, 1681), 68. Willis was also interested in the question of the "animal soul"; see his *Two Discourses concerning the Soul of Brutes*, trans. S. Pordage (London: Thomas Dring and John Leigh, 1683). For more on Willis and, notably, his metaphors, see Kathryn Tabb, "'Struck, As It Were, with Madness': Phenomenology and Animal Spirits in the Neuropathology of Thomas Willis," in C.U.M. Smith and H. Whitaker, eds., "Brain, Mind and Consciousness in the History of Neuroscience," special issue, *History, Philosophy and Theory of the Life Sciences* 6 (2014): 43–57.

41 *Vindiciæ Mentis: An Essay of the Being and Nature of Mind, wherein the distinction of mind and body, the substantiality, personality, and perfection of mind is asserted; and the original of our minds, their present, separate, and future state, is freely enquir'd into, in order to a more certain foundation for the knowledge of God, and our selves, and the clearing all doubts and objections that have been, or may be made concerning the life and immortality of our Souls. In a new method.* (London, 1702), 64. Anthony Ossa-Richardson discussed Emes's images, though he referred to them as metaphors, in a paper entitled, "A Parcel of Pipes and Friggling Maggots: Metaphor and the Critique of Materialism in Thomas Eme's *Vindiciæ Mentis*," presented at the conference, "'Thinking Matter': Representations of the Mind-Body Problem," in Oxford at the Maison Française in 2012.

42 Udo Thiel persuasively ascribes the work to Thomas Emes (see *The Early Modern Subject: Self-Consciousness and Personal Identity from Descartes to Hume* (Oxford: Oxford University Press, 2011), 227, note 8.

43 Sterne, *Tristram Shandy*, 6.

44 See John Locke, *An Essay Concerning Human Understanding*, ed. Peter Nidditch (Oxford: Clarendon Press, 1975), 396 (2.33.6). For the usefulness of Locke for understanding Sterne, see W.G. Day, "*Tristram Shandy*: Locke May Not Be the Key," in *Laurence Sterne: Riddles and Mysteries*, ed. V.G. Myer (London: Vision Press, 1984), 75–83; Peter M. Briggs, "Locke's *Essay* and the Tentativeness of *Tristram Shandy*," *Studies in Philology* 82 (1985): 493–520.

45 For an account of Sterne's use of contemporary reproductive theories, see Louis A. Landa, "The Shandean Homunculus: The Background of Sterne's 'Little Gentleman,'" in *Restoration and Eighteenth-Century Literature: Essays in Honour of Alan Dugald McKillop*, ed. Carroll Camden (Chicago: University of Chicago Press, 1963), 49–68. We might note that in the Blondel-Turner controversy about the power of the mother's imagination, Turner describes sperm as "maggots" perhaps to counter his opponent's theory, which accords reproductive priority to the father. See Daniel Turner, *The Force of the Mother's Imagination upon her Fœtus in Utero* (London, 1730), 12; and Marie-Hélène Huet, *Monstrous Imagination* (Cambridge, MA: Harvard University Press, 1993), 63–7.

46 Ibid., 64.

47 For more details, see Lynall, *Swift and Science.*

48 See *A Discourse Concerning the Mechanical Operation of the Spirit*, 179, and Walsh's commentary, 520–1, notes 15, 17, and 19; Clive T. Probyn, "Swift and the Physicians: Aspects of Satire and Status," *Medical History* 18 (1974): 249–61, 254–5; "Swift's Anatomy of the Brain: The Hexagonal Bite of Poetry," *Notes and Queries* 219 (1974): 250–1.

49 There is some debate as to whether those that can are able to do so because each individual atom itself possesses such capacities or because such capacities emerge as a result of their assembling or organizing. See Charles T. Wolfe, "Endowed Molecules and Emergent Organization: The Maupertuis-Diderot Debate," *Early Science and Medicine* 15 (2010): 38–65.

50 *A Discourse*, 179.

51 The references to Lucretius and Bentley are given by Walsh in *A Tale*, 521–2, note 23.

52 Abel Boyer, *The Royal Dictionary, French and English, and English and French* (London, 1711), entry "Magget or Maggot."

53 *A Discourse*, 179.

54 Ibid.

55 As J. Paul Hunter observes, "references to maggotty writing abound in the early century." *Before Novels: The Cultural Contexts of Eighteenth-Century*

English Fiction (London: Norton, 1990), 14. There is no room here to explore Pope's reference to maggots in *The Dunciad* (1728/9), but it should be noted that they are a sign of the way in which Pope's poem draws on Lucretius, as well as Milton: where the latter countered Lucretius's disordered, material universe, in which life in the form of maggots emerged spontaneously from rotting matter, and offered in its place a universe that was no less materialist but in which matter was animated by divine purpose, what Pope offers is an entropic universe, in which Milton's re-ordered matter succumbs to a Lucretian chaos once again in which matter randomly throws up maggots. And in the literary universe that is London, poems are the maggots that are randomly generated out of Grub Street. For more on Pope and Milton, see Sophie Gee, "Milton's Chaos in Pope's London: Material Philosophy and the Book Trade," in *Making Waste: Leftovers and the Eighteenth-Century Imagination* (Princeton: Princeton University Press, 2009), 67–91.

56 Samuel Wesley, *Maggots: Or, Poems on Several Subjects, Never Before Handled; By a Schollar* (London, 1685), 1. The two paratexts make further references to maggots and other insects, such as mosquitos, gnats, lice – the former two are metaphors for critics (n.p.).

57 The comparison between Sterne and Dunton seems to have been available to contemporary readers since, following the success of Sterne's novel, an enterprising publisher reissued Dunton's work with the new title, *The Life, Travels, and Adventures of Christopher Wagstaff, Gentleman, Grandfather to Tristram Shandy* (London: J. Hinxman, 1762).

58 John Dunton, *The Life and Errors of John Dunton, Late Citizen of London, Written by Himself in Solitude, With an idea of a new life; wherein is shewn how he'd think, speak, and act, might he live over his days again: Intermix'd with the New Discoveries the Author has made in his Travels Abroad, And in his Private Conversation at Home. Toegther with the Lives and Characters of a Thousand Persons now Living in London, &c. Digested into Seven Stages, with their Respective Ideas* (London: S. Malthus, 1705), n.p.

59 He mentions Montaigne shortly beforehand (n.p.).

60 See Asfour, *Laurence Sterne in France.*

61 Michael Moriarty, "Figures of the Unthinkable: Diderot's Materialist Metaphors," in *The Figural and the Literal: Problems of Language in the History of Science and Philosophy, 1630–1800*, ed. Andrew E. Benjamin, Geoffrey N. Cantor, and John R.R. Christie (Manchester: Manchester University Press, 1987), 147–75.

62 For a study of this image, see Michel Delon, "La métaphore comme expérience dans le *Rêve de d'Alembert*," in Annie Becq, ed., *Aspects du discours matérialiste en France autour de 1770* (Paris: J. Touzot, 1981).

63 For studies of the spider image, see Georges Poulet, *Les métamorphoses du cercle* (Paris: Plon, 1961), 73–101; available in English translation as *The Metamorphoses of the Circle*, trans. Carley Dawson and Elliot Coleman (Baltimore: Johns Hopkins, 1966), 50–69; Roland Mortier, "Un dieu-araignée?," in *Enlightenment Essays in Memory of Robert Shackleton*, ed. Giles Gaudard Barber and C. Cecil Patrick Courtney (Oxford: Voltaire Foundation, 1988), 223–9; Jacot Grapa, "Le moi-araignée du *Rêve de d'Alembert* de Diderot"; Isabelle Moreau, "L'araignée dans sa toile," in *Les Lumières en movement: la circulation des idées au XVIIIe siècle*, ed. Isabelle Moreau (Lyon: Ecole Normale Supérieure de Lyon, 2009), 199–228.

64 All the names are those of real historical individuals; for Bordeu, see Alexandre Wenger, *Le médecin et le philosophe: Théophile de Bordeu selon Diderot* (Paris: Hermann, 2012). Diderot is fond of including characters in his works that bear his own name, are called "Moi," or who could in some other way easily be (mis)taken for himself.

65 See Denis Diderot, *Le Rêve de d'Alembert*, ed. Colas Duflo (Paris: Garnier Flammarion, 2002), 53.

66 *Rêve*, 85. All translations are mine. Here and below, brackets mark ellipses that are in the original.

67 Ibid.

68 The text is full of moments when characters do not quite seem to know what they are saying or say something that is undermined either by their actions or by later moments in the text; for instance, d'Alembert is unaware he has been dreaming (136), and Mlle de Lespinasse expresses an attachment to her "moi" [self] (99), which the rest of the text works to unsettle. For other ways in which *D'Alembert's Dream* works to undercut inwardness, see Kate E. Tunstall, "Eyes Wide Shut: *Le Rêve de d'Alembert*," in *New Essays on Diderot*, ed. James Fowler (Cambridge: Cambridge University Press, 2011), 141–57.

69 See *Rêve*, 94.

70 See Clark, *Supersizing the Mind*.

71 For a good account of the strange sense of consensus in the text, see Georges Daniel, "Autour du *Rêve de d'Alembert*: réflexions sur l'esthétique de Diderot," *Diderot Studies* 12 (1969): 13–73.

72 *Rêve*, 182.

73 See *Rêve*, 90.

74 Ibid., 83.

75 See, for instance, Duflo, "Le moi-multiple," 98. For a different view, see Tunstall, "Eyes Wide Shut."

76 *Rêve*, 136.

77 Ibid., 137.

78 Ibid.

79 For the history and sociology of science, see, for instance, Steven Shapin, *A Social History of Truth: Civility and Science in Seventeenth-Century England* (Chicago: University of Chicago Press, 1994). There is no space here to consider the questions of adherence, assent, and consent, and of disagreement and dissent. The reference here to the monastery is unlikely not to trouble anyone who has read Diderot's *La Religieuse* [The Nun] (1760), a novel about a woman trying to resist being assimilated into convent life.

80 For a recent set of reflections on the question of authorship in eighteenth-century France, see "Authorship in Eighteenth-Century France," ed. Nicholas Cronk and Joanna Stalnaker, special issue, *Romanic Review* 103.3–4 (2012), and in particular Stalnaker's contribution, "Mademoiselle de Lespinasse's Hand," 276–83.

81 Such a possibility will be familiar to any reader of Diderot's novel, *Jacques le fataliste* [Jacques the Fatalist], in which the narrator often says that "Jacques was saying that his Captain used to say," etc. See Denis Diderot, *Jacques the Fatalist*, trans. David Coward (Oxford: Oxford World's Classics, 2008), 3.

82 Such a claim is made by Jacques Roger, quoted in Caroline Jacot Grapa, *Dans le vif du sujet: Diderot, corps et âme* (Paris: Garnier, 2009), 291. Spiders and swarms of bees are standard images in medical texts of the period, and in philosophical writing that engages with them (see above, note 17). In Maupertuis's *Vénus physique* (1748), there are not only spiders, but also spermatozoa and even silkworms, quoted in Jacot Grapa, *Dans le vif du sujet*, 301.

83 Jacot Grapa, *Dans le vif*, 156–8.

84 He was, of course, also involved in a number of major collective publications, such as the *Encyclopédie* (1750–65) and the *Histoire des Deux Indes* [A History of the Two Indies] (1770); in the former, in particular, his role as author and/or editor is rather unstable, see Marie Leca-Tsiomis, "L'étoile de Diderot: tours et détours de l'auteur," in *Une histoire de la "fonction-auteur" est-elle possible?*, ed. Nicole Jacques-Lefèvre (Saint-Etienne: Université Saint-Etienne, 2001), 141–53.

85 For the literary history of these images, see above, note 9. For studies of intertextuality in Diderot, see Jean Starobinski, "Diderot et la parole des autres," *Critique* 296 (1972): 3–22; Kate E. Tunstall, "Paradoxe sur le portrait: Auto Portrait de Diderot en Montaigne," *Diderot Studies* 30 (2007): 197–210.

86 The comparison runs throughout the poem; for an early instance, see *On the Nature of the Universe*, 26 (book 1, lines 820–9). See Gerard Passannante, *The Lucretian Renaissance: Philology and the Afterlife of a Tradition* (Chicago: University of Chicago Press, 2011).

87 I owe the pun to Douglas R. Hofstadter who asks, "Is the soul more than the hum of its parts?" Daniel Dennett and Douglas R. Hofstadter, *The Mind's I: Fantasies and Reflections on Self and Soul* (New York: Basic Books, 1981), 191.

88 Critics have focused on the image of the machine and overlooked the images of bees and maggots that appear close by. See John Cleland, *Memoirs of a Woman of Pleasure*, ed. Peter Sabor (Oxford: Oxford World's Classics, 2008), 160–4. Such entomological images might be argued to confirm the sense in which Cleland, like La Mettrie, is no Cartesian mechanist, and that he has understood the materialist, vitalist implications of La Mettrie's text. See Ann Thomson, "L'homme-machine: mythe ou métaphore?," *Dix-huitième siècle* 20 (1988): 368–76; Charles T. Wolfe, "'Epicuro-Cartesianism': La Mettrie's Materialist Transformation of Early Modern Philosophy," in *La Mettrie: Ansichten und Einsichten*, ed. Harmut Hecht (Berlin: Berliner Wissenschafts-Verlag, 2004), 75–96.

89 Cyrano de Bergerac, *L'autre monde ou Les états et empires de la Lune* (1657), *Les états et empires du soleil*, ed. Madeleine Alcover (Paris: Champion, 2000), 118. The translation is mine. For more on Cyrano's philosophical and scientific thinking, see Alcover, *La pensée philosophique et scientifique de Cyrano de Bergerac* (Geneva: Droz, 1970).

8 Diderot's Brain

JOANNA STALNAKER

At the end of his life, the ailing philosopher Denis Diderot was still working on a decades-old project that has been called his "second encyclopedia."[1] This was the *Éléments de physiologie*, a work he intended as nothing less than a compendium of all existing knowledge on the operations of the human body and mind. The work was left, apparently unfinished, at Diderot's death in 1784, and its fragmented, partially derivative nature has led some commentators to read it more as a collection of notes for an unrealized project than as a consummate final expression of Diderot's philosophy.[2] Others have called the *Éléments de physiologie* Diderot's philosophical testament, but without addressing what that might mean for our understanding of this work or of Diderot's philosophy in general.[3] I do not mean to suggest here that Diderot realized his ambitions for the *Éléments de physiologie* before he died; we don't know his intentions for the work and we probably never will.[4] I want to propose, however, that in this seemingly unfinished work he gave written form to his vision of the human brain as a vast, dynamic repository for encyclopedic knowledge. Through the form of the work, he also staged the impending loss of his own brain as a living encyclopedia. The *Éléments de physiologie* is thus indeed "something of a swansong," but not simply because it was, along with the *Essai sur les règnes de Claude et de Néron*, one of Diderot's two last works.[5] We should read the *Éléments de physiologie* as Diderot's philosophical testament because in this work he both reflected upon and embodied the end of his philosophical life. Diderot's life as a philosopher was marked by his adherence to materialist philosophy – his belief that nature operated according to a continual recycling and transformation of vital matter – and by his dedication to encyclopedic knowledge as a collective project. Indeed, the *Éléments de physiologie* binds these two aspects of his philosophy together, showing us how new minds formed by the recycling of vital matter continually reinvent new forms of knowledge by integrating and transforming the work of previous minds. It is clear that Diderot wanted to come to some definitive conclusion about philosophy at the end of his life: on the last page of the *Éléments de physiologie*, he summed up his philosophy in a single sentence. But the work as a whole opened a window onto the constantly changing operations of his mind, and its eventual dissolution and recuperation by others. In my reading, the *Éléments de physiologie* takes its meaning from the elaboration of a *form* of philosophical writing that functions as a sort of extended mind, one that encompasses individual thoughts, memories, and projects, but also looks beyond them in acknowledgment of their finitude.

The *Éléments de physiologie* deserves its appellation as Diderot's second encyclopedia in two important respects: first, it synthesized a lifetime of reading in the medical sciences (begun in the 1740s when the young Diderot took courses in anatomy and undertook a translation of the Englishman Robert James's *Medicinal Dictionary*), and second, it aimed to achieve a comprehensive natural history of man based in physiology, psychology, and philosophy.[6] According to Jean Mayer, the first scholar to take Diderot's scientific thought seriously in the 1950s, the *Éléments de physiologie* rivalled and even surpassed the great naturalist Georges-Louis Leclerc, Comte de Buffon's *Histoire naturelle de l'homme*.[7] Unlike Buffon, Diderot was not an experimental scientist, but for Mayer the attentiveness and breadth of his readings allowed him to constitute "a veritable *borrowed experimentation.*"[8] The range of Diderot's sources is astonishing, including, in addition to Buffon, Albrecht von Haller, Julien Offray de La Mettrie, Pierre-Louis Moreau de Maupertuis, Théophile de Bordeu, Jean-Paul Marat, Paul-Joseph Barthez, Marin Cureau de la Chambre, Antoine Le Camus, Robert Whytt, and Charles Bonnet, among many others. In some cases, Diderot used material from his sources to combat their conclusions.[9] But in other cases, notably in the middle section, he borrowed so heavily from his sources that the status of the *Éléments de physiologie* as an original work has been questioned. My reading will combine formal and philosophical analysis to connect this middle section to the two more original parts of the work, to show how the work as a whole functions as an encyclopedic brain even as it contemplates the loss of Diderot's individual brain.[10] I will focus on three aspects of the *Éléments de physiologie* that correspond to its three main sections: first, I will discuss Diderot's physiological theory of death, outlined in his first section on the nature of life and its various forms; second, I will address the derivative nature of the middle section, which was largely borrowed from Haller's writings on the irritability and sensibility of animal tissues and organs; and third, I will consider Diderot's concept of deep memory, which he developed in his third section on the self, consciousness, and memory. Here, Diderot introduced an image of the human brain as a dynamic, encyclopedic repository for a lifetime of sensations and learning. At the same time, he posed the question of what the ultimate destruction of this living repository meant for the practice of philosophy and the continuing advancement of human knowledge.

Death Stops There

In the first part of the *Éléments de physiologie*, entitled "On Beings," Diderot outlined his view of the various life forms found in nature, their organization, and their dissolution in death. Throughout this section he emphasized the provisional character of his contemporaries' knowledge of natural beings, observing that "the manner of classifying natural beings with exactitude can only be the fruit of the successive work of a great number of naturalists: it will be tiresome and very slow. Let us wait and not hurry ourselves to make judgments."[11] The apparent discontinuities between various life forms might simply be the result of as yet undiscovered beings that would allow the naturalist to better perceive the continuous chain of nature; hence Diderot paid special attention to beings he classed as plant-animals, notably the freshwater polyps observed by the Swiss naturalist Abraham Trembley. In his chapter on animals, Diderot rejected the mechanistic view of these animated beings as "hydraulic machines," again emphasizing the extent to which his contemporaries' knowledge of animal movement was provisional: "the laws of movement governing sensitive, animated, organized, living bodies have not even been sketched out yet" (305). Following Haller, Diderot gave great importance to animal sensibility, which he defined as "the quality proper to the animal, which alerts it to the relationship between itself and everything surrounding it" (305). But it was above all with reference to the Hallerian concept of irritability that he introduced his principal concern in this section: the fine line between life and death. As Haller showed in his experiments on cadavers, "certain parts of the body conserve after death, for more or less time, their irritability or individual life" (308–9).[12] This insight into animal physiology paved the way for a fuller discussion of death in which Diderot offered an original synthesis of the views of the French naturalist Buffon, the Montpellier doctor Théophile de Bordeu, and the Scottish physician Robert Whytt.

Diderot's understanding of death was consistent with the gradualist conception of death popularized by Buffon's *Histoire naturelle de l'homme,* published in 1749. According to Buffon, death must be understood not as a singular, catastrophic event, but as a gradual process that gets played out in the body over time. Buffon grounded this speculative theory in empirical studies of the hardening of tree trunks, positing that death was an analogous process of hardening, or ossification, of the body.[13] Although Buffon did not personally contribute to the *Encyclopédie,* passages from the *Histoire naturelle* were frequently included in the work without attribution, as in the Chevalier de Jaucourt's article "Ossification," which reproduced Buffon's theory of death.[14] In the *Éléments de physiologie,* Diderot combined Buffon's theory with a view of the human body he took from Bordeu, according to which various organs work together as a system while also possessing their own individual vitality. As Kurt Ballstadt puts it, "Bordeu viewed the body as a more-or-less loose assembly of organs, hierarchically arranged, in which each vital organ possessed a certain degree of autonomy. … Human life was, for Bordeu, a multi-layered phenomenon. The life of the body as a whole was superimposed over the lives of the organs themselves, which could be viewed as semi-independent systems in their own right."[15] This view informed Diderot's understanding of animal organization, a key concept for eighteenth-century vitalists.[16] For Diderot, the initially fluid animal has sensibility and life in each of its constituent parts, but seems to lack "a sensibility and a life common to the mass" (310). As an animal takes on its organized form, "there is established a general and common sensibility that the organs share diversely" (310). In *Le Rêve de d'Alembert,* Diderot expressed this distinction with an image borrowed from Bordeu's 1751 *Recherches anatomiques sur la position des glandes et sur leur action,* when Dr Bordeu invites Mlle de Lespinasse to imagine the difference between a swarm of bees that appears to act as a whole but is in fact merely joined by contiguity (the animal in its initially fluid state) and a swarm of bees that has been fused to form a continuous whole (the animal in its organized state).[17] It is significant that the distinction between the two swarms of bees appears extremely slight and is even imperceptible to the human eye.

The fine line between contiguity and continuity in Bordeu's bee metaphor informed Diderot's understanding of death as a relative phenomenon. In the *Éléments de physiologie,* he combined the Buffonian view of death as a process of gradual hardening with the Bordeu-inspired notion that the various parts of the body can harden and lose their sensibility at different times, thereby isolating themselves from the whole: "[The sensibility] appears proportional to the progress of hardening; the harder an organ gets, the less sensitive it is. The more quickly it advances towards hardness, the more quickly it loses its sensibility and isolates itself from the system" (310). Thus, for Diderot, death was not only a gradual process, as it was for Buffon, but also a discontinuous process in which various parts of the body became dissociated from the whole each according to its own rhythm.[18] Diderot's conception of death was also influenced by Whytt, who, in *An Essay on the Vital and other Involuntary Motions of Animals*, distinguished between "the general death of the body as a system" and the "particular death of the several parts, which does not happen for some time after."[19] In keeping with this view, Diderot posited various levels of life (and death) in any living organism:

> There are certainly two very distinct lives, even three.
> The life of the entire animal:
> The life of each of its organs.
> The life of the molecule. (310–11)

Animal organization is what allows the various organs and molecules of a living being to work in conjunction with each other. But in death, the collective life of the animal ceases, even if the life of its various parts persists. In fact, Diderot asserted the relativity of death in quite radical terms, claiming that it did not reach the level of the molecule: "The heart, the lungs, the spleen, the hand, almost all the parts of the animal live for some time separated from the whole. Even the head separated from the body looks and lives. There is only the life of the molecule or its sensibility that does not cease. That is one of its essential qualities. Death stops there" (311). The notion that death did not reach the animal on the level of the molecule was crucial to Diderot's materialism, which was vitalist, not in the strict sense of positing a vital substance replacing the soul as the source of life, but in the broader sense that it attributed unending vitality to the primitive elements of nature. This view made it possible that after death, the now contiguous (rather than continuous) molecules of an animal's corpse could be recombined in new forms; as Diderot put it, "How many metamorphoses escape us! I see some that are rather quick: why wouldn't there be others for which the period would be more distant? Who knows what may become of the insensitive molecules of animals after their deaths?" (296). In a similar vein, d'Alembert goes so far as to muse, at the climax of his dream, that to die is merely to change forms: "Alive, I act and I react as a whole … dead, I act and I react as molecules. … So I don't die at all. No, without a doubt, I don't die at all in this sense, neither me, nor anything at all. … To be born, to live and to pass, is to change forms."[20] In a letter to his lover Sophie Volland, written in 1759, Diderot himself mused about the possibility that the most basic elements of his body might one day meld with hers to form a new self centuries after their deaths, in a morbid act of procreation. This passage merits being quoted at length in the original French because it prefigures two crucial aspects of the *Éléments de physiologie*:

> Ceux qui se sont aimés pendant leur vie et qui se font inhumer l'un à côté de l'autre ne sont peut-être pas si fous qu'on pense. Peut-être leurs cendres se pressent, se mêlent et s'unissent ! que scais-je ? Peut-être n'ont-elles pas perdu tout sentiment, toute mémoire de leur premier état. Peut-être ont-elles un reste de chaleur et de vie dont elles jouissent à leur manière au fond de l'urne froide qui les renferme. Nous jugeons de la vie des éléments par la vie des masses grossières ! Peut-être sont-ce des choses bien diverses. On croit qu'il n'y a qu'un polype ! Et pourquoi la nature entière ne seroit-elle pas du même ordre ? lorsque le polype est divisé en cent mille parties, l'animal primitif et générateur n'est plus ; mais tous ses principes sont vivants. O ma Sophie ! il me resteroit donc un espoir de vous toucher, de vous sentir, de vous aimer, de vous chercher, de m'unir, de me confondre avec vous quand nous ne serons plus, s'il y avoit dans nos principes une loi d'affinité, s'il nous étoit réservé de composer un être commun, si je devois dans la suite des siècles refaire un tout avec vous, si les molécules de votre amant dissous avoient à s'agiter, à s'émouvoir et à rechercher les vôtres éparses dans la nature ! Laissez-moi cette chimère, elle m'est douce, elle m'assureroit l'éternité en vous et avec vous.[21]

[Those who loved each other during their lives and are buried next to each other may not be as crazy as we think. Perhaps their ashes press up against each other, mingle together and are united! who knows? Perhaps

> they have not lost all feeling, all memory of their initial state. Perhaps they have a remnant of warmth and life that they enjoy in their own way at the bottom of the cold urn that holds them. We judge the life of elements by that of crude masses! Maybe they are very different things. We think there is only one polyp! And why wouldn't all of nature be of the same order? when the polyp is divided into one hundred thousand parts, the primitive and generative animal is no longer; but all its principles are living. Oh my Sophie, I would then still have some hope of touching you, of feeling you, of loving you, of searching for you, of uniting myself, of blending myself with you, when we are no longer! If only there were a law of affinity for our principles, if only our fate were to compose a single being; if only I were to form a whole with you in the coming centuries; if only the dispersed molecules of your lover were to become agitated, to start moving and searching for yours spread in nature. Leave me this illusion. It is sweet to me. It would guarantee me eternity in you and with you.]

This letter sketches out some of the central ideas of the *Rêve de d'Alembert*, which Diderot wrote a decade later in 1769. But it also helps us to understand the *Éléments de physiologie* in two important respects: first, we see Diderot using the term elements, along with molecules, to refer to the basic building blocks of vital matter ("Nous jugeons de la vie des éléments par la vie des masses grossières!"). This suggests that we should read the title of the *Éléments de physiologie* – which has often troubled scholars both because it is taken from Haller and because it seems to reduce the ambitions of Diderot's work to a mere textbook in physiology – not simply as a Hallerian reference to the fundamental elements of the science of physiology, but as drawing an analogy between the work itself and the elements of vital matter (still alive after death). Second, the letter holds out the tantalizing possibility – more fully developed in the *Éléments de physiologie* – that the elements of the human body may contain some memory of their former state after death. Both of these ideas would be essential to Diderot's image of the brain as a living encyclopedia in the third part of his work, and to his reflection on the fate of his own brain after death.

Diderot's erotic musings about reincarnation in his letter to Sophie Volland might seem more in keeping with the speculative, poetic *Rêve de d'Alembert* than with the more empirically grounded, scientific *Éléments de physiologie*.[22] But in fact it was not unusual for Enlightenment vitalists to attempt to ground theories of reincarnation in the empirical sciences. As Kris Pangburn has shown, the Genevan naturalist Charles

Bonnet (another of Diderot's sources) derived his seemingly mystical theory of palingenesis from detailed, anatomical studies seeking to locate the elusive organ of the human soul.[23] Diderot, however, rejected any notion of the soul as the source of life or unity in the animal: "Life persists in the organs when they are separated from the body. Where then is the soul? What becomes of its unity, its indivisibility? … Why not see sensibility, life, movement as so many properties of matter: since we find these qualities in each portion, each particle of flesh?" (333). Although Diderot did use the term soul in the *Éléments de physiologie*, he understood it not as the immaterial substance of an immortal soul, but simply as another word for the unity of the organized animal: "The animal is a complete *unity*, and it is perhaps this unity that constitutes the soul, the self, consciousness, with the aid of memory" (335). Instead of relying on metaphysical notions, Diderot used social metaphors to characterize the organization, or collective life, of the animal. If life was constituted by an animal's various parts working together collectively, the death of its various parts could be seen as analogous to their retreat from the pleasures and duties of a collective, social life:

> Parts united to the body seem to die, at least as a group: in getting older, the flesh becomes muscular, the fiber hardens, the muscles become tendon-like, the tendon appears to have lost its sensibility, I say appears, because it could still have sensation in itself, without the entire animal knowing it. Who can assure us that there isn't an infinity of sensations that excite and extinguish themselves here? Little by little the tendon slackens, it dries out, it hardens, it ceases to live, at least of the common life of the whole system; perhaps it only isolates itself, separates itself from the society whose pains and pleasures it no longer shares and to which it no longer gives back anything. (311)

What is lost, when a part secedes from the whole, is not necessarily its individual sensibility or vitality, but merely its participation in the collective life of the body. Once again, Diderot emphasized his contemporaries' lack of knowledge concerning the hidden processes of life and death: just as we may not perceive the difference between a contiguous and continuous swarm of bees, we may not perceive the continuing sensibility of organs that have separated themselves from the whole. And just as there are infinitely fine gradations between the world of plants and animals, the fine line between a cadaver and a living animal is much more subtle than we may realize. Death is nothing more than the dissolution of a temporary, contingent organization of living molecules that will enter into new forms in the future.

The social metaphors at work in Diderot's theory of death are also significant in light of his reflections, in the same chapter, on the place of the elderly in society. Whereas in the *Histoire naturelle* Buffon used mortality statistics to attack old age as a prejudice to be eradicated by the rational philosopher, Diderot presented a disabused vision of the illusions of old age and the burden the elderly represent for society:[24]

> The child runs towards death with his eyes closed: the adult man is stationary. The old man gets there with his back turned. The child does not see the term of his life span; the adult man feigns to doubt whether one dies at all; the old man soothes himself, trembling, with hope that is renewed from day to day. It is cruelly impolite to speak of death in the presence of an old man: one honors old age, but one does not love it; even if one gains only respite from the painful duties one gives to a man when he dies, it doesn't take one long to console oneself for his death. It is already saying a lot when one does not secretly rejoice. I was 66 years old when I told myself these truths. (313)

In this passage, we hear a rueful note of Diderot's personal experience of aging. But if we link this passage to his reflections on death as a process of dissociation of parts from the whole, we see an implicit analogy between the exclusion of an old man from the pains and pleasures of society and that of an organ from the living, sensitive body. With respect to the dying body, Diderot insisted on the fact that we cannot perceive the sensibility of an organ after it secedes from the whole; although it may appear dead to us, it may continue to possess its own sensibility and vitality apart from the whole. In keeping with this idea, he suggested in a 1774 letter to the Volland family that, contrary to his expectations, his heart had not hardened with age; quite the contrary: "I may have ten more years at the bottom of my bag. Of these ten years, fluxions, rheumatisms, and all the rest of this troublesome family will occupy two or three; let's try to save the seven others for rest and all the scraps of happiness one can hope for after sixty. That is my project and I hope you will want to second me on it. I thought that the fibers of the heart hardened with age. That is not so at all. I might even say that my sensibility has increased. Everything touches me, everything affects me, I will be the most remarkably weepy old man you have ever known."[25] In both his personal correspondence and his philosophical testament,

Diderot offered his readers a glimpse of how his personal experience of aging was infused with his physiological thinking. Beneath the apparent decline of his body, he perceived a continuing vitality that he expected to survive beyond the grave. He understood his death as marking the end of a particular social cooperation among the elements of his body, but not the ultimate destruction of the underlying vitality that had brought that organization into being.

Bodies of Knowledge

The social metaphors at work in Diderot's discussion of animal organization take on an added significance when one considers the encyclopedic and collaborative dimension of the *Éléments de physiologie*. Of course, this work was not written by a *Société de gens de lettres* as the *Encyclopédie* had been. In a certain sense, it was the most deeply personal of Diderot's works, offering his readers a window onto the workings of his mind. But its derivative nature, especially in the second section, has given it a tenuous status in Diderot's corpus.[26] Indeed, the fact that the second section consists largely of a collage of quotations and paraphrases from Haller's eight-volume *Elementa physiologiae corporis humani* (and its one-volume digest the *Primae lineae physiologiae*) has led some scholars to assert that the final state of the two extant manuscript copies cannot possibly represent Diderot's final intentions for the work. As Aram Vartanian puts it, "It is highly implausible, of course, that Diderot had proposed all along to give, in the *Eléments de physiologie*, what would have been in substance merely a compilation – a sort of *cours abrégé* of Haller, enriched by additions from other specialists, plus an informal commentary of his own."[27] Yet the premise behind this claim is that originality is the overriding value in literary and scientific writing. This premise must be questioned if we are to take seriously the characterization of the *Éléments de physiologie* as Diderot's second encyclopedia, and if we are to take full stock of the social metaphors at work in his theory of death. Perhaps originality was not Diderot's primary concern, or perhaps the originality of the work lies not so much in the exposition of new scientific knowledge as in the elaboration of a form that reflects both his conception of knowledge as a shared, social endeavour *and* his understanding of nature as a constant recycling of vital matter in new forms.

Viewed in this light, the term "elements," as Diderot used it in his 1759 letter to Sophie Volland and in the title of the *Éléments de physiologie*, takes on a special significance, regardless of whether Diderot's age and declining health prevented him from realizing the *Éléments de physiologie* as he might have intended.[28] The fragmentary, note-like form of the work (with numerous intriguing aphorisms followed by "to be meditated upon" or "to be explained") embodies the motif of elements (or vital molecules) that was the basis for Diderot's understanding of life as a continual recycling of vital matter. This form also reflects Diderot's understanding of the quest for encyclopedic knowledge as a collective project. Just as Diderot believed that the sentient molecules of his body could be recombined after his death to form other selves, he believed that the elements of other physiologists' knowledge that exist in a fragmentary form in the *Éléments de physiologie* could be recombined to create new knowledge in the future. This is not to say that Diderot limited himself to the role of compiler. As Mayer observes, "He does with his sources what Socrates did with his interlocutors in Plato's dialogues: he takes from them their own refutation, borrowing from them the facts that are most able to overthrow their theories. Moreover, by confronting opposing doctrines, he manages to achieve a comprehensive view thanks to the richness of his documentation."[29] In other words, Diderot played in the *Éléments de physiologie* a similar role to the one he had prescribed for himself in the *Encyclopédie*, that of the Socratic midwife who helped others give birth to new knowledge. But he sometimes did this by breaking knowledge down into its most basic elements, presenting it in a fragmentary form that could be picked up and incorporated into new forms by other writers in the future. Through its form and its content, the *Éléments de physiologie* reminds its readers that Diderot's knowledge of nature is provisional, that it depends on a collective body of empirical observations that is constantly being expanded and revised, and that comprehensive theories of natural processes always exist in creative tension with the labyrinth of empirical evidence.

Thus the derivative quality of Diderot's middle section, entitled "Elements and Parts of the Human Body," is thematically and formally consistent with his project as a whole. The presence of multiple passages from Haller is not a reason to exclude the *Éléments de physiologie* from Diderot's corpus or to argue that it is less original than his other works. On the contrary, in borrowing so liberally from Haller – but departing from him at significant moments – Diderot underlined his reliance on the body of empirical evidence that was available to him in his time. In keeping with Mayer's notion of a "*borrowed experimentation*," Diderot exposed in his middle section the results of Haller's experiments on the sensibility and irritability of organs, presenting his readers with a series of brief chapters covering topics ranging from muscle fibres to the brain to nerves to glands. He concluded this Hallerian survey of body parts with the organs of generation, paving the way for his own discussion of various competing theories of reproduction, and concluding with a chapter on the human fetus. If he was content to borrow from Haller in presenting the "elements" of the human body – the building blocks for his own evolving knowledge of physiology – he chose to arrange the chapters in such a way as to move from the dissected, isolated parts (taken from Haller) to the generation of a living, organized fetus. This progression should be interpreted in terms of Diderot's preoccupation with animal organization and its dissolution in death, and more broadly in the context of contemporary debates among naturalists such as Buffon and Maupertuis concerning the mysteries of generation. Unlike the more derivative chapters on body parts, Diderot's discussion of generation was not lifted directly from Haller; rather, it offered a dynamic exposition of four competing "systems" of generation, in which he engaged with contemporary theories ranging from Buffon's concept of the interior mould to Maupertuis's claim that particles of organic matter were imbued with qualities such as desire, aversion, and even memory in a way that propelled the process of generation.[30] Thus, the middle section allowed Diderot's readers to witness the constitution of knowledge in parallel with the constitution of a living fetus: we begin with the most basic, unorganized elements of empirical knowledge borrowed from Haller, and move to a more synthetic, organized discussion of generation drawn from a variety of sources. Knowledge comes to appear as something that is itself generated through the contact between various minds. Reading, thinking, and writing are likened to physiological processes involved in the creation of life. The *Éléments de physiologie* thus appears as Diderot's brainchild, a familiar metaphor for works of literature but one that takes on a new resonance in the context of his physiologically informed philosophy.

The Encyclopedic Brain

The third section of the *Éléments de physiologie*, entitled "Phenomena of the Brain," explores the workings of the brain and, by extension, the contours of the self, consciousness, and memory. For François Laplassotte, Diderot's treatment of the brain is symptomatic of the "anticerebralism" of eighteenth-century materialism and the surprising lack of progress in the scientific understanding of the brain from the Renaissance to the early nineteenth century. Laplassotte characterizes Diderot's discussion of the brain as "a long and systematic contestation of the prejudices that accord to this organ an importance that, according to Diderot, it does not deserve in the slightest."[31] It is true that Diderot sometimes downplayed the importance of the brain, calling it "an organ like any other" and "only a secondary organ that would never function without the intervention of other organs" (467). Yet, as Paolo Quintili has observed, Diderot's characterization of the brain as "merely an organ of secretion" in the middle section of *Éléments de physiologie* did not reflect his own views but was simply a transcription of Buffon's conclusions.[32] In his more developed discussion of the brain in his chapter on memory, Diderot went on to contest this view, giving a much more powerful role to this organ as a dynamic site of consciousness and encyclopedic memory. As in the *Encyclopédie*, the reader must compare various parts of the work against each other to perceive Diderot's engagement with different theories of the brain and the genesis of his own theory. By including undigested passages from Haller and Buffon, he presented his readers with the scaffolding of his knowledge, and showed his mind at work as he surveyed various theories and compared them with his own insights.

The third part of the *Éléments de physiologie* is undoubtedly the most original part of the work, and the one in which Diderot took on what one critic has called "the 'big issues' of life in general, and of human life in particular."[33] Central among these was his reflection on the constitution and limits of the self as a part of nature. Diderot gave great importance to memory in the constitution of a unified self, asserting that "memory constitutes the self" (471). But he was especially interested in the various ways the brain filters sensory information to create a unified sense of experience. Like Buffon, who characterized life as a seemingly continuous thread that is broken every time we go to sleep, Diderot suggested that even a single day's experience is punctuated by multiple little nights every time we blink: "It seems that we spend our days in little days and little nights. First of all, night falls every time we close our eyelids. And when doesn't this happen to us? If we don't perceive all these little nights, it is just because we don't pay attention to them" (456). Diderot insisted on the gap between the illusion of continuous perception that our brain creates and the reality of intermittent perceptions. In another striking analogy, he compared the soul (to be understood as another term for the self in the context of Diderot's monist materialism) to a person at a noisy dinner table, who only hears the person next to him: "The soul is amid its sensations like a guest at a tumultuous table, who talks with the person next to him, and does not hear the others" (467). Diderot emphasized the extent to which our brains filter out a unified, continuous sense of experience (a single conversation) amid a cacophony of competing sensations (the tumultuous table). Yet, just as the "little nights" are in fact part of our experience, whether consciously or not, so are the other conversations at the dinner table part of the soul's experience ("The soul is amid *its* sensations").

Diderot's interest in the role played by unnoticed sensations – the conversations *not* attended to at the dinner table – was especially apparent in his chapter on memory, where he developed a concept of something we might call deep memory, by analogy to what scientists today call deep time. This concept of memory was extraordinarily expansive, consisting of an immense memory bank of all the sensations – significantly, even unnoticed sensations – we have absorbed over the course of our lives. In a remarkable sentence that merits being quoted in the original French, Diderot represented the brain as a kind of living encyclopedia:

> Je suis porté à croire, que tout ce que nous avons vu, connu, entendu aperçu, jusqu'aux arbres d'une longue forêt, que dis-je, jusqu'à la disposition des branches, à la forme des feuilles, et à la variété des couleurs, des verts et des lumières ; jusqu'à l'aspect des grains de sable du rivage de la mer, aux inégalités de la surface des flots soit agités par un souffle léger, soit écumeux et soulevés par les vents de la tempête, jusqu'à la multitude des voix humaines, des cris des animaux, et des bruits physiques, à la mélodie et à l'harmonie de tous les airs, de toutes les pièces de musique, de tous les concerts que nous avons entendus, tout cela existe en nous à notre insu. (468–9)

> [I am inclined to believe that everything we have seen, known, heard, noticed, all the way down to the trees of a long forest, which is to say, even to the arrangement of branches, to the form of the leaves and the variety of colors, of greens and lights; down to the aspect of grains of sand on the banks of the sea, to the unevenness of the surface of the waves, whether stirred up by a light breeze, or foaming and whipped up by the winds of a storm, down to the multitude of human voices, of animal cries and of physical noises, to the melody and to the harmony of all the airs, of all the pieces of music, of all the concerts we have heard, all of this exists in us unbeknownst to us.]

What is striking about this sentence, in addition to its expansive, breathing syntax, is how deep into nature and into the self Diderot's conception of deep memory reaches. The human brain appears as an immensely powerful tool for recording and preserving the tiniest details of nature absorbed over an entire lifetime of experience. The encyclopedic reach of memory makes the boundaries between the self and nature appear extremely porous; and by extension, it suggests that the boundaries between individuals may be porous too, since each individual brain reaches so deeply into nature. We find a similar idea at work in *Le Rêve de d'Alembert*, where the philosophical dream is somehow shared by d'Alembert (who dreams it), Mlle de Lespinasse (who writes it down), and Bordeu (who knows its content without having spoken to d'Alembert or seen Mlle de Lespinasse's text). As individual parts, or elements, of nature, the characters in *Le Rêve de d'Alembert* appear to share some sort of collective consciousness or memory. And although Diderot never formulated this idea explicitly, the *Éléments de physiologie* begs the tantalizing question – already raised in his 1759 letter to Sophie Volland – of whether the most basic elements of an animal might not hold some traces of its deep memory after death. This idea might well have been suggested to Diderot by Maupertuis's fanciful theory of generation, in which he speculated that particles of matter "preserve the memory of their former situation that they tend to take up again."[34] This theory allowed for the possibility that the most basic elements of nature – the building blocks of future selves – might contain memories of the former selves they had constituted, and that these memories might play a role in the generation of new selves in the future. In this way, the collective memory that the characters of *Le Rêve de d'Alembert* seem to share might even extend across generations, forming a macro memory for the species as a whole over time.[35]

Diderot even suggested that our deep memory, understood as the unification of a lifetime of sensorial experience, could be recalled to our conscious perception by certain actions: "immense memory is the connection between everything one has been in an instant to everything one has been in the following moment, states that, linked by an action, will recall to a man everything he has sensed during his life. I think every man has this memory. The conclusions are easy to draw" (471). The Proustian dimension of this and other passages in the *Éléments de physiologie* has not escaped Diderot's readers, but the implications of deep memory for Diderot's conception of the self, and especially for his view of aging and death, have not been explored.[36] For Diderot, the true unity of the self lay not in the illusory sense of unity created by the brain's filtering of sensations and memories, but rather in "immense or total memory, [which] is a state of complete unity. Partial memory, state of incomplete unity" (472). Diderot was less interested in conscious memory as the locus of a continuous sense of self than in unconscious memory as a receptacle for the multiple sensations that crowd into our brains and are constantly being filtered to create a continuous sense of perception. This idea takes on a special significance at the end of our lives because, as Diderot put it, "old men remember the past in forgetting the present" (473). Just as he insisted on the possible vitality of an apparently deadened organ, Diderot alluded here to the old man's renewed contact with the deep memory that had previously been inaccessible to him.

Diderot's belief that deep memory preserves some record of all of our sensorial perceptions also led him to posit a deep logic underlying seemingly discontinuous intellectual operations. In the allusive style typical of the *Éléments de physiologie*, he wrote: "Intellectual actions interrupted and picked up again after a long interval; phenomenon to be explained" (465). The specific context in which this remark appears has to do with thoughts or intentions that are interrupted by a medical accident and then resumed at a later date. But Diderot's interest in this kind of mental phenomenon speaks more broadly to the long and discontinuous composition of the *Éléments de physiologie* and, more generally, to the way intellectual projects take shape over time. If our deep memory indeed records everything we have ever seen, heard, learned, noticed (or, presumably, read), this might explain why our thought processes are both more discontinuous than we might expect (ideas and projects can be apparently dropped or stalled for long periods of time) and more continuous (unfinished ideas and projects are picked up later in life; forgotten facts or readings can play an unconscious role in the constitution of knowledge) than we might realize. This idea was reflected in the fragmented, collage-like form of the *Éléments de physiologie*: it is as if Diderot were attempting to reproduce the intermittent form of his perceptions of a lifetime of reading in the physiological and medical sciences. Just as Buffon claimed at the end of his life to have attained a broad, sweeping view of nature in its entirety, Diderot sought to represent, through the form of his last encyclopedic project, his mind as an encyclopedic repository for a lifetime of learning about the body. Given his understanding of knowledge as a collective enterprise, the continuity of intellectual operations over time ultimately reached beyond the limits of his own brain, to enter into conversation with other brains in what we today call an extended mind.

The analogy I am drawing between Diderot's image of the brain and the form of the *Éléments de physiologie* as a literary work finds support in Diderot's own analogy of the brain as a dynamic, living book that contains its own reader within it. I will quote this passage in the original French because its allusive quality makes it difficult to decipher:

> Pour expliquer le mécanisme de la mémoire il faut regarder la substance molle du cerveau comme une masse de cire sensible et vivante, mais susceptible de toutes sortes de formes, n'en perdant aucune de celles qu'elle a reçues et en recevant, sans cesse, de nouvelles qu'elle garde. Voilà le livre. Mais où est le lecteur? Le lecteur c'est le livre même. Car ce livre est sentant, vivant, parlant, ou communiquant par des sons, par des traits, l'ordre des sensations; et comment se lit lui-même? En sentant ce qu'il est et en le manifestant par des sons. (470)

> [To explain the mechanism of memory one must see the soft substance of the brain as a mass of sensitive and living wax, but susceptible to all kinds of forms, never losing any of the forms it has taken and endlessly taking new ones that it preserves. Here is the book. But where is the reader? The reader is the book itself. For this book is sensitive, living, speaking, or communicating through sounds, through features, the order of sensations; and how does it read itself? By feeling what it is and by demonstrating it through sounds.]

Contrary to Laplassotte's claim that Diderot sought to downplay the importance of the brain, this passage highlights his insight into the brain's remarkable combination of dynamic plasticity and permanent record-keeping. Far from denigrating the brain as a minor organ, Diderot seemed to marvel at its capacity to be at once a sensitive, living mass of wax that continually changed shape to record new impressions, and a permanent repository for an entire lifetime of sensations and experiences. As such, the brain is a living book, an ideal encyclopedia that records knowledge even as it changes shape to make room for new forms of knowledge. By containing its reader within it, the book gains the capacity to receive impressions while also reflecting on them to develop self-reflexive consciousness. One might then ask, what corresponds to the internal reader within the encyclopedic brain that is the *Éléments de physiologie*? Is it Diderot himself, who left so many traces of his active mind in the work? Or is it the reader, who must grapple with the discontinuous, fragmentary form of the work, and who is thereby invited to enter into conversation with Diderot's mind even long after his death?

If we take a step back to consider the form of the *Éléments de physiologie* as a whole, a clear parallel emerges between the first and third parts, both of which address in different ways the dissolution of the human body and mind. In the first part, Diderot was concerned with what happens to the elements of the body when they isolate themselves from the whole and are restored to their original place in the broader universe of vital matter. In the third part, he was concerned with the relationship between the unified self (which is constituted by the brain's sensorial filtering) and deep memory (which is constituted by the undifferentiated mass of the sensations). In the first part of the *Éléments de physiologie*, we get a fairly clear sense of what happens to the elements of the body after death: as Diderot had already suggested in the *Rêve de d'Alembert*, sentient molecules will be recycled to create new beings. In the third part, in contrast, we get much less of a sense of how Diderot envisioned what happens to the self (and especially to the mind) upon death. Yet the third part begs the question, since it begins with chapters on sensations, understanding, and memory (which are constitutive of the self) and ends with chapters on organs and illnesses (which contribute to the dissolution of the self in death). In his *Discours sur la poésie dramatique*, written in 1758, Diderot observed that memory alone guaranteed the continuity of the self, given the perpetual renewal of vital matter in the body: "It is only by memory that we are one and the same individual for others and for ourselves. At my age, there may not be remaining to me a single molecule of the body that I brought with me at birth. I do not know the term prescribed for my life span; but when the time comes to give this body back to the earth, it may well not contain a single one of the molecules it now has."[37] But in the *Éléments de physiologie*, Diderot complicated this apparent disjuncture between unified memory and vital matter, proposing that vital matter might itself possess some kind of memory. He did so in part through the form of the work, inventing a visceral form of writing that sought to capture the workings of his mind, even as it signalled the ultimate loss of that mind to the processes of nature.

After the penultimate chapter on illnesses, Diderot concluded the *Éléments de physiologie* with a chapter that departs from strictly physiological matters to take up the classical understanding of philosophy as a means of preparing for death. Here, Diderot proposed two different spiritual exercises in preparation for death. The first relies on the faculty of the imagination, which occupies one of the main chapters of the third part: "A rather common fantasy among living people is to imagine themselves dead, standing next to their corpses and following their funeral convoy. It is a swimmer who sees his clothing hung up on the shore. You men who inspire fear no longer, what will you hear then?" (516). This is a classic Stoic meditation, but it also reflects Diderot's growing uncertainty, in the last years of his life, about the posthumous glory he had imagined for himself in his earlier exchange with the sculptor Étienne Maurice Falconet.[38] Diderot's violent attack on Jean-Jacques Rousseau in the *Essai sur les règnes de Claude et de Néron*, the other major work he wrote in his last years, was inspired in part by his fear that his former friend's autobiographical writings might contain personal revelations that would tarnish his public reputation. Yet in the second spiritual exercise described in the *Éléments de physiologie*, Diderot explicitly rejected any preoccupation with posterity, representing philosophy instead as a means of removing oneself from the concerns of everyday life and the fear of death: "Another apprenticeship of death is philosophy, a habitual and profound meditation that removes us from everything surrounding us and annihilates us. The fear of death, says the Stoic, is a handle by which the strong man grabs us and takes us where he pleases. Break the handle and trick the hand of the strong man" (516). In keeping with the tradition of spiritual exercises, Diderot emphasized the habitual dimension of philosophy as a means of preparing for death. Indeed, this Stoic sentence about the fear of death was one Diderot recycled at least twice in the last years of his life, once in his contributions to the abbé de Raynal's *Histoire des Deux Indes* and once in his *Essai sur les règnes de Claude et de Néron*.[39] Such recycling across works that are so different in tone and content suggests that just as living matter is recycled with the death of each individual, the same sentences must be continually recycled as the philosopher faces death. Thus, Diderot concluded the *Éléments de physiologie*, a work generally seen as unfinished, by condensing his entire philosophy into a single sentence: "There is only one virtue, justice; only one duty, to make oneself happy; only one corollary, not to overestimate life for oneself and not to fear death" (516).

In fact, Diderot's Stoic meditation on the annihilation of the self contains the reverse image of his conception of deep memory. Whereas deep memory unifies a lifetime of sensorial experience and blurs the boundaries between the self and nature, and between the self and others, the Stoic meditation removes us from nature and obliterates the self to better understand its place in nature. For Diderot, the philosophical life was one that tracked deep memory through its encyclopedic attempts to understand nature; but it was also one that saw its own efforts as subject to the eventual annihilation of the self, whereby a lifetime of memories and intellectual pursuits will be restored to their elemental nature, only to be recombined by new selves at some point in the future. In this sense, his philosophical testament offered both his last word on philosophy and his acknowledgment that his writings were only one combinatory possibility in the infinite and ever shifting body of human knowledge.

~

In his preface to the eighth volume of the *Encyclopédie*, published in 1765 as the project was drawing to a close, Diderot reflected bitterly on the many years of his life the work had consumed: "If you add to the years of our life that had already passed when we took on this Work, the years we have given to its execution, you will easily see that we have been alive for more years than are now remaining to us. But we will have earned the reward we expected from our Contemporaries and our descendants, if we cause them to say some day that we have not lived in vain."[40] As Diderot looked back on the struggles he faced as the editor of the *Encyclopédie*, the spectre of a wasted philosophical life loomed large. Nonetheless, he insisted that even if his own days were numbered, the *Encyclopédie* would serve as a bulwark against the eventual destruction of human knowledge: "If a revolution of which the germ is perhaps forming in some unknown region of the earth, or is brewing secretly in the very center of civilized countries, breaks out in due course, overthrows cities, disperses peoples once again and brings back ignorance and shadows; if a single complete copy of this Work is preserved, all will not be lost."[41] In the face of various losses – from the death of the philosopher to the return of the dark ages – the *Encyclopédie* promised a permanent record of the progress of human knowledge. As we have seen, Diderot betrayed a similar preoccupation with the consolidation and preservation of knowledge in his second encyclopedia, the *Éléments de physiologie*. But in this work, it was the brain itself that appeared to defy the passage of time through its remarkable capacity to record an entire lifetime of sensations, including the tiniest details of nature, language, and artistic expression. The vast ambitions of the *Éléments de physiologie* make the work appear as a figuration of Diderot's brain, as an enduring record of an entire lifetime of learning about the body. But the work also stages, through the ordering of its chapters, the eventual dissolution of the individual life of the mind. The final chapters on illness and death, and Diderot's Stoic reflections on the meaning of death for the philosopher, remind us that no matter how powerful the brain is in its capacity to record a lifetime of sensations, it will eventually secede from the whole to be broken down into its most basic elements. The question Diderot left us with, at the end of his life, was whether the traces of his deep memory might not be preserved in the vital molecules of his corpse, and what new forms they might take on in the future. He also left us with a form of philosophical writing that embodied both his highest aspirations for the human brain as a living encyclopedia, and his inscription of his own mortal brain into an extended conversation with other brains that he hoped would continue far into the future.

NOTES

1 Kurt Ballstadt, *Diderot: Natural Philosopher* (Oxford: Voltaire Foundation, 2008), 209. It is not clear exactly how late into his life Diderot continued working on the *Éléments de physiologie*. His biographer, Arthur Wilson, suggests that it was until his death, as indicated by his request in 1780 for the tables of contents of Albrecht von Haller's work and his insistence late in his life on the crucial link between philosophy and medicine. See his *Diderot* (New York: Oxford University Press, 1972), 698–9. Paolo Quintili makes the same claim in his recent critical edition of the *Éléments de physiologie.* See his introduction to *Éléments de physiologie*, by Denis Diderot (Paris: Honoré Champion, 2004), 12. In his chronology of Diderot's life and writings, Raymond Trousson states that he worked on the *Éléments de physiologie* until 1781. See his *Diderot jour après jour: Chronologie* (Paris: Honoré Champion, 2006), 176.

2 See, for example, Aram Vartanian, "The Enigma of Diderot's 'Eléments de physiologie,'" *Diderot Studies* 10 (1968): 288.

3 See, for example, Quintili, introduction to *Éléments,* 70; and Kurt Ballstadt, review of *Éléments de physiologie*, by Denis Diderot, ed. Paolo Quintili, *French Studies: A Quarterly Review* 60:3 (July 2006): 397.

4 On the two extant manuscript copies of the *Éléments de physiologie* and the lost autograph manuscript, see Jean Mayer, introduction to *Éléments de physiologie,* by Denis Diderot (Paris: Librairie Marcel, 1964), xvi–xxix.

Mayer argues convincingly that the Vandeul copy offers the most faithful representation of Diderot's intentions for the work.

5 Ballstadt, review of *Éléments*, 397.

6 See Jean Mayer, *Diderot, homme de science* (Rennes: Imprimerie Bretonne, 1959), 278; and Ballstadt, *Diderot: Natural Philosopher*, 176–8.

7 Mayer, *Diderot, homme de science*, 279; and Mayer, introduction to *Éléments*, lvi.

8 Mayer, introduction to *Éléments*, lv.

9 Ibid., liv.

10 Most interpretations of the *Éléments de physiologie* have paid little or no attention to form. Geoffrey Bremner offers a negative assessment of the structure of the work, seeing it as a sign of the impasse Diderot had reached and of a broader epistemological crisis that could only be resolved in the nineteenth century. See his "Les *Éléments de physiologie* et le sens de la vie," in *Diderot: Les Dernières Années*, ed. Peter France and Anthony Strugnell (Edinburgh: Edinburgh University Press, 1985), 81–91. Needless to say, I do not share Bremner's view that that the *Éléments de physiologie* "n'est pas le livre 'sentant, vivant, parlant' dont il parle dans son chapitre sur la mémoire, mais, d'un côté, un texte où le corps est décrit d'une manière qui rappelle de mécanisme, de l'autre, un commentaire où la vie est évoquée, expliquée, démontrée, mais jamais présente" (91).

11 Denis Diderot, *Éléments de physiologie*, vol. 17 of *Oeuvres complètes*, ed. Jean Varloot with Michel Delon, Georges Dulac, and Jean Mayer (Paris: Hermann, 1987), 296. All subsequent citations refer to this edition and are given in the text.

12 On Haller's experiments and their European reception, see Hubert Steinke, *Irritating Experiments: Haller's Concept and the European Controversy on Irritability and Sensibility, 1750–90* (Amsterdam: Rodopi, 2005).

13 Georges Louis Leclerc de Buffon, *Histoire naturelle, générale et particulière, avec la description du Cabinet du Roy*, vol. 2 (Paris: Imprimerie Royale, 1749), 557–89. On Buffon's treatment of death throughout the *Histoire naturelle*, see my "Buffon on Death and Fossils," *Representations* 115:1 (2011): 21–40.

14 Louis de Jaucourt, "Ossification, s.f. s'ossifier, v. neut. [Physiolog.]," in *Encyclopédie, ou Dictionnaire raisonné des sciences, des arts et des métiers*, ed. Denis Diderot and Jean le Rond d'Alembert, University of Chicago: ARTFL Encyclopédie Project (Winter 2008 edition), ed. Robert Morrissey, http://encyclopedie.uchicago.edu/. The *Encyclopédie*'s borrowings from the *Histoire naturelle* often go unnoticed by scholars; for example, Jacques Chouillet attributes passages on aging from the article "Homme" to Diderot, whereas they were in fact lifted from Buffon's work. See his

"Diderot et la retraite," in France and Strugnell, *Diderot: Les Dernières Années*, 23.

15 Ballstadt, *Diderot: Natural Philosopher*, 180. See also Mayer, introduction to *Éléments*, xxxvii.

16 Jessica Riskin, "Mr. Machine and the Imperial Me," in *The Super-Enlightenment: Daring to Know Too Much*, ed. Dan Edelstein (Oxford: Voltaire Foundation, 2010), 75–94.

17 On Diderot's depiction of Bordeu as a doctor-philosopher in *Le Rêve de d'Alembert* and its relationship to the historical figure and his writings, see Alexandre Wenger, *Le Médecin et le philosophe: Théophile de Bordeu selon Diderot* (Paris: Hermann, 2012). On the bee metaphor, see ibid., 39–40. Maupertuis uses the same image in his *Système de la nature*. See Mary Terrall, *The Man Who Flattened the Earth: Maupertuis and the Sciences in the Enlightenment* (Chicago: University of Chicago Press, 2002), 329.

18 On the relationship of part to whole in Diderot's aesthetics, poetics, and philosophy, see Andrew H. Clark, *Diderot's Part* (Aldershot, UK: Ashgate, 2008).

19 Quoted in Mayer, introduction to *Éléments*, xxxix.

20 Denis Diderot, *Le Rêve de d'Alembert*, vol. 17 of *Oeuvres complètes*, ed. Varloot, 139.

21 Diderot to Louise-Henriette [Sophie] Volland, Grandval, 15 October 1759, in Denis Diderot, *Lettres à Sophie Volland*, ed. André Babelon, vol. 1 (Paris: Editions d'Aujourd'hui, 1978), 110–11. Facsimile of the 1930 Gallimard edition. My thanks to Kate E. Tunstall for calling my attention to this letter.

22 Mayer interprets *Le Rêve de d'Alembert* and the *Éléments de physiologie* in terms of an opposition between speculative philosophy and empirical science. See his *Diderot, homme de science*, 272.

23 Kris Pangburn, "Bonnet's Theory of Palingenesis: An 'Enlightened' Account of Personal Resurrection?," in Edelstein, *Super-Enlightenment*, 191–214. See also François Laplassotte, "Quelques étapes de la physiologie du cerveau du XVIIe au XIXe siècle," *Annales. Histoire, Sciences Sociales* 25 (May–June 1970): 599–613.

24 On Buffon's attempt to eradicate the fear of death in his readers through an analysis of mortality statistics, see my "Buffon on Death and Fossils."

25 Diderot to the Volland family, The Hague, 3 September 1774, in Diderot, *Lettres à Sophie Volland*, vol. 3, 260. Jacques Chouillet discusses this and other letters from Diderot's late years in "Diderot et la retraite," 19–29.

26 The collective project of the *Histoire des Deux Indes* poses similar problems. Franco Venturi has suggested that the scholarly attempts to determine precisely which parts of the *Histoire des Deux Indes* were written by Diderot

risk distorting the anonymous, collective nature of the enterprise as it was perceived by eighteenth-century readers. See Franco Venturi, "La vieillesse de Diderot," *Recherches sur Diderot et sur l'Encyclopédie* 13.1 (1992): 17–18.

27 Vartanian, "Enigma," 288.

28 There is some doubt about whether Diderot even intended this as the title for his work, but I would argue that the meaning he gave to the term elements in his letter to Sophie Volland makes it an especially meaningful title. See Mayer, introduction to *Éléments*, xvii.

29 Mayer, *Diderot, homme de science*, 277.

30 On Maupertuis's theories of generation and heredity, and on Diderot's engagement with them in his *Pensées sur l'interprétation de la nature*, see Terrall, *Man Who Flattened the Earth*, chaps. 7 and 10.

31 Laplassotte, "Quelques étapes," 608–9.

32 Quintili, *Éléments*, 172n20.

33 Ballstadt, review of *Éléments*, 397.

34 Quoted from a review of Maupertuis's *Système de la nature* in Terrall, *Man Who Flattened the Earth*, 324.

35 Terrall draws a suggestive analogy between Diderot's conception of the restless mind of the philosopher and Maupertuis' "inquiétude automate" of material particles: "The philosopher seeks new knowledge in the same way that molecules seek their places, by a kind of restless touching and retouching, trial and error, a 'tatonnement' [*sic*] like that of a blind man's stick. The ideal method involves moving back and forth from sense impressions to reflection, from experiment to theory, in a kind of oscillating exploration." *Man Who Flattened the Earth*, 343.

36 For one mention of the Proustian dimension of Diderot's concept of memory, see Wilson, *Diderot*, 699.

37 Quoted in Chouillet, "Diderot et la retraite," 23.

38 See Elena Russo, "Slander and Glory in the Republic of Letters: Diderot and Seneca Confront Rousseau," *Republics of Letters: A Journal for the Study of Knowledge, Politics, and the Arts* 1 (2009): http://arcade.stanford.edu/rofl/slander-and-glory-republic-letters-diderot-and-seneca-confront-rousseau.

39 Quintili, *Éléments*, 361–2n107.

40 Diderot, "Avertissement," *Encyclopédie*, vol. 8, ARTFL.

41 On the eighteenth-century obsession with the destruction of books and knowledge, see Daniel Rosenberg, "The Library of the Disaster," *Romanic Review* 103:3–4 (2012): 317–29.

Conclusion: Can Aesthetics Overcome Instrumental Reason? The Need for Judgment in Mandeville's *Fable of the Bees*

VIVASVAN SONI

One of the most striking developments on the intellectual landscape of the eighteenth century is the emergence of aesthetic theory as an autonomous realm of inquiry. To be sure, reflection on the arts and their social function, and even on beauty itself, is almost as old as philosophy. But prior to the eighteenth century, the perception of the beautiful was not thought to constitute a distinctive mode of cognition, irreducible to logic, epistemology, or ethics. Of course, the idea that the brave thought-adventurers of the eighteenth century discovered a terra incognita of the mind is implausible.[1] Rather, we must ask ourselves what was there before, and what happened when a particular set of cognitive operations was annexed as properly "aesthetic." Most important, why, at this particular juncture in Western intellectual history, did it come to seem imperative to rescue a distinct realm of the aesthetic from the mass of phenomena? When framed in this way, the problem of the emergence of aesthetics is genuinely puzzling. One way to understand the need for aesthetic theory at this moment is as a response (inadequate at best) to the nascent discourse of empiricism and its radical delegitimization of forms of thinking that are ends-oriented: the kind of thinking Aristotle calls *phrōnēsis* (practical wisdom) and I will call judgment.[2]

Before I explain more fully what I mean by this last claim, it is worth remembering that we *already* have an answer to the question about why the aesthetic emerges at this moment, in the form of the so-called critique of instrumental reason, a critique that remains not just serviceable but necessary and powerful today as we endure the encroachment of marketized forms of thinking into every realm of human endeavour.[3] On this account, the Enlightenment witnesses the emergence and consolidation of a distinctive form of thinking that has come to dominate our modernity, a kind of thinking called "instrumental reason" and associated with the new science. The objections to this form of thinking are manifold: that it is mathematizing and even utilitarian in its orientation, treating all phenomena as quantifiable; that it renders everything equivalent and without distinction; that it is reductive, attempting to explain phenomena from as simplified a set of postulates as possible; that it disenchants the world, voiding it of meaning and human purpose; that it is crassly focused on coordinating means to ends, and allows no room for digression and errancy; and finally, that it seeks to explain all human behaviour, starting from the premise of desire and self-interest, making it impossible to imagine actions that might not be self-interested.[4] If we grant that this nexus of features characterizes instrumental reason, then the aesthetic could be viewed as a supplementary discourse that remedies some if not all of these problems.[5] Perhaps most memorably, the experience of the aesthetic is supposed to attest to our capacity for disinterested contemplation, not governed by the dictates of desire or self-interest. Immanuel Kant describes the experience of the beautiful as that which pleases "without interest,"[6] but as Jerome Stolnitz argued long ago, the concern with disinterested contemplation is already evident in Shaftesbury.[7] In his essay, "Sensus Communis," a text Kant appears to have in mind when he writes about the *sensus communis* or universal voice that we hear in aesthetic perception, Shaftesbury argues against Hobbes's claim that all motivation is reducible to self-interest. He observes that we have a herding instinct that operates alongside our desire for self-preservation, and adduces everyday aesthetic experiences as proof that not everything that pleases is for the sake of self-interest. In other words, aesthetic contemplation appears to foil reductive explanations of behaviour as self-interested by offering evidence of a realm of phenomena in which we take pleasure even when we derive no benefit whatsoever from the encounter.[8]

The aesthetic is also a way of re-enchanting the world. We cannot gaze impassively at a beautiful object; it fills us with a feeling of pleasure as we contemplate it. For Baumgarten, who coined the term "aesthetics," what distinguishes aesthetic representations is that they are "clear and confused,"[9] by which he means the object of the representation can be distinguished from others (clear) but its qualities cannot be specified (confused).[10] The confused character of aesthetic representations means precisely that they resist epistemological clarification, analysis, or quantification, functioning as qualitative experiences of the meaningfulness of the world that cannot be explained further – the famous "je ne sais quoi" that defined aesthetic experiences. In fact, in some early accounts, the aesthetic is tasked precisely with re-animating the world with meaning and purposiveness, with a set of ends or final causes that had been stripped from it when phenomena were explained purely in terms of efficient causation. Thus, in *Spectator* 413, part of the sequence on the "pleasures of the imagination," Addison and Steele explicitly frame their aesthetic arguments as a reflection on final causes,[11] which had been bracketed from consideration in the discourses of empiricism.[12] They explain that beauty generates the purposiveness of sexual desire; greatness (sublimity) motivates us to respect and worship god; and our fascination with novelty is the impetus that drives us to seek knowledge.[13] Hutcheson also finds a tripartite purposiveness to the aesthetic. The epistemological and theological functions of the aesthetic are similar to those found in Addison and Steele, but the sexual impetus of beauty is repurposed as that which spurs us to accumulate wealth.[14] The purposes of sexual reproduction, worshipping god, seeking knowledge, and wanting wealth cannot be made by ourselves, but must be given by naturally conditioned modes of aesthetic perception. The function of aesthetic categories, in these cases, is to restore purposiveness, but to do so as if purpose were simply a given and observable fact within the empiricist framework, rather than acknowledging it as the work of free judgment.

But as soon as we express the function of the aesthetic in this way, we begin to glimpse a problem both with the critique of instrumental reason and with the aesthetic response to it. After all, if the aesthetic works to restore our sense of the purposiveness of the world and our lives in it, to give us goals and ends to pursue, then has it not re-established a kind of instrumentality in our lives? Sexual reproduction serves to propagate the species, reverence for god guarantees our morality or secures our fate in the afterlife, the pursuit of knowledge improves our lot, and the accumulation of wealth is perhaps the most instrumental of all ends. How is the pursuit of ends, however lofty these are, to be distinguished from the crassest forms of instrumentality? Furthermore, if purposiveness and instrumentality had to be re-established by the discourse of the aesthetic, does that not imply that instrumental reason had stripped us of these in the first place, making "instrumental reason" a misnomer? Of course, the most important development in aesthetic theory in the century, Kant's *Critique of Judgment*, which by all accounts establishes aesthetics as an autonomous discipline, radically *de-instrumentalizes* the aesthetic, responding directly to the concern that an aesthetic that gives us purpose is open to the charge of serving merely instrumental ends. For Kant, what we experience, when we judge an object to be beautiful, is a *purposiveness without purpose*: "Beauty is the form of the purposiveness of an object, insofar as it is perceived in it without representation of an end" (*CJ*, 5:236). The beautiful object gives us an inkling of a world filled with meaning, but if we try to specify *what* that meaning is, we fail. Indeed, we *must* fail, or we would destroy the distinctively aesthetic dimension of the experience by judging that a particular purpose was given by our encounter with the object (5:229–30).

Kant's account of beauty certainly rescues the beautiful object from any charge of instrumentality. But this solution is not one that can satisfy us. Rather, it points to a profound problem with the critique of instrumental reason and the aesthetic solution to it, which is still widely in evidence today. I suggested earlier that one of the functions of the aesthetic was to restore purposiveness or ends-orientation to a world that had been stripped of it by instrumental reason. Accounts of the world according to the logic of efficient causation – the entire realm of scientific inquiry is encompassed by this – are written in the language of mathematics. But mathematics has no language for purpose and meaning; it can only express quantitative or logical relationality. Thus, the critique of disenchantment is a very real one, but if we accept that to be true, a twofold puzzle remains. First, in what sense is instrumental reason "instrumental" at all, if it eradicates goals, meanings, purposes, ends, from the world? Second, in what sense is the aesthetic an adequate response to "instrumental reason"? It appears to be caught in a double bind. If it restores purposiveness (Addison and Steele, Shaftesbury, Hutcheson), it re-enchants the world, but opens itself up to the charge that aesthetic objects have been instrumentalized. If it refuses to restore purpose (Kant's "purposiveness without purpose"), it shelters itself from the charge of instrumentality, but appears to collude with the disenchantment of the world – the stripping of ends and purposes from the world – enacted by instrumental reason itself. The problem I am describing here is not just an abstract logical dilemma. It is one aspect of what I call the "crisis of judgment" in the eighteenth century, because part of the work of judgment is to specify, indeed to *fiction*, purposes. Now, to specify a purpose is to articulate some goal or end that we judge worthy or important to attain, and thereafter to discern the means to attain that end. But the very act of specifying ends and the means of attaining them requires us to participate in an instrumental logic, and if we refuse instrumentality because of the problems described above, as aesthetic theory since Kant has often sought to do, we risk complete paralysis, inaction, and the refusal of all commitment. Neither alternative is satisfying, but there does not appear to be another on the horizon. Either we judge according to some instrumental logic that we are forced to follow in lockstep, and whose conclusions are dictated in advance by the premises, or we refuse judgment altogether as the only way of resisting the encroachments of instrumentality. The dialectical dance of instrumentality and aesthetics, as it has played itself out since the late eighteenth century, is but one face of the aporia of judgment that we have inherited from the period.[15]

The problem, it should now be apparent, lies with the very notion that "instrumentality" is to be avoided at all costs. If that were the case, then any and all ends are automatically suspect, and we end up with a radical hermeneutics of suspicion that has dominated contemporary discourses of critical theory. But surely we want to be able to specify defensible ends and purposes that will not fall prey to a critique of instrumental reason? How are we to go about doing this? Are there ends and purposes that are not instrumental, and if so, what distinguishes them from instrumental ends? Or is there a good and bad version of instrumentality, and how would we know the difference? As I have been suggesting, this set of questions, problems, and confusions is internal to the Enlightenment constellation of aesthetic discourse in the eighteenth century because, from Shaftesbury to Kant, one of the ways that aesthetic theory develops is precisely as a critique of "instrumental reason" of the kind proposed by Hobbes, Locke, or Mandeville.[16] But the same set of questions, problems, and confusions can also be found in the "critique of instrumental reason" proposed by Horkheimer. In the rest of this essay, I want to turn first to Horkheimer's critique of instrumental reason. A fresh study of this critique is instructive because it will show that, although Horkheimer reproduces the incoherences of eighteenth-century aesthetics around the ends-orientation described above, he nevertheless accurately diagnoses many of the costs entailed in the shift to "subjective reason" (another name for instrumental reason). Perhaps most surprisingly, we will discover that his response to instrumental or subjective reason is not to purge all ends from reason, but to try and preserve (unsuccessfully) a certain orientation towards ends. I will then turn to Bernard

Mandeville's *Fable of the Bees* to offer a new analysis of what is wrong with "instrumental reason," and to suggest how these problems might be remedied, not through a repudiation of instrumentality but rather through a defence of judgment. Mandeville's *Fable* articulates the most extreme version of a market logic in the period, the very epitome of what Horkheimer wants to critique under the name of "instrumental reason." Yet we will find that there is nothing instrumental about this "instrumental reason." On the contrary, it aims to *abolish* ends-oriented thinking entirely. If there is a problem with Mandeville's market logic, I want to argue, it does not lie in instrumentality at all, but in the elision of the practice of judgment that would allow us to posit and commit to a different set of ends than those assumed in Mandeville's account. Mandeville's *Fable* is especially valuable because it *stages* for us this elision of judgment as very few exemplars of "instrumental reason" do. To complete my own analysis, it would be necessary to give a fuller account of the practice of judgment itself, as Shaftesbury, Fielding, and Austen, among others, do. But, for reasons of space, that will have to be undertaken elsewhere.

~

Horkheimer is one of the architects of the critique of instrumental reason, and while he is certainly prone to the danger I have described of eliding the distinction between ends-oriented reason and instrumental reason, he still manages to preserve something of the distinction in his impressive study, *The Eclipse of Reason*. The first chapter of *Eclipse of Reason* ought to be read in its entirety here, for the exemplary diagnosis it offers, but I will offer a brief synopsis. Horkheimer begins by explaining how a premodern conception of objective reason differs from the subjective reason that comes to displace it in modernity:

> The degree of reasonableness of a man's life could be determined according to its harmony with this totality. Its objective structure, and not just man and his purposes, was to be the measuring rod for individual thoughts and actions. ... *The emphasis was on ends rather than means.* The supreme endeavor of this kind of thinking was to reconcile the objective order of the "reasonable," as philosophy conceived it, with human existence, including self-interest and self-preservation. ... The theory of objective reason did not focus on the co-ordination of behavior and aim, *but on concepts – however mythological they sound to us today* – on the idea

of the greatest good, on the problem of human destiny, and on the way of realization of ultimate goals.[17]

The account might as well be Shaftesbury's from his "Soliloquy" essay, with the reference to "harmony" that is such an important feature of Shaftesbury's analysis, the focus on ends, and the uncomfortable recognition of the fictive ground on which judgments are based ("concepts – however mythological they sound to us today"). The effort to distinguish instrumental reason ("the co-ordination of behavior and aim") from ends-oriented reason ("the idea of the greatest good," etc.) is also in evidence here, but the grounds for this distinction remain opaque. How are the aims towards which behaviour is coordinated in any way different from ends, such as the greatest good? Once we have an end such as the latter, don't we coordinate our actions in such a way as to achieve it? It is precisely the ability to distinguish between these two kinds of ends-oriented action that the critique of instrumental reason promises to deliver without being able to do so. All the same, Horkheimer lucidly diagnoses the problems that arise when "objective reason" is displaced by "subjective reason":

> In the subjectivist view, when "reason" is used to connote a thing or an idea rather than an act, it refers exclusively to the relation of such an object or concept to a purpose, not to the object or concept itself. It means that the thing or idea is good for something else. There is no reasonable aim as such, and to discuss the superiority of one aim over another in terms of reason becomes meaningless. (*ER*, 6)

Although Horkheimer recognizes the effects of the transformation that are underway – the inability of reason or judgment to arbitrate between ends – his description of the subjectivist view risks giving up too much, especially when he attributes the instrumentality of such a view to the linking of object with "purpose." Once again, we must ask how such instrumental purposes differ from concepts of objective reason like "the greatest good" described a page earlier? Horkheimer attributes it to the purposiveness itself, but that will not help us separate instrumental from ends-oriented reason. The ultimate effect of the transition from objective to subjective reason may be summarized as follows:

> In the end, no particular reality can seem reasonable *per se*; all the basic concepts, emptied of their content, have come to be only formal shells. As

> reason is subjectivized, it also becomes formalized. ... If the subjectivist view holds true, thinking cannot be of any help in determining the desirability of any goal in itself. (*ER*, 7; see also 92; Horkheimer and Adorno, *DE*, 88–9)

The problem Horkheimer describes here – the problem of how reason can deliberate about substantive ends rather than being simply a formal, calculative, and algorithmic ratiocination – plagues the modern conception of reason disjoined from any ethical vocation.[18] It is, as Horkheimer sees, a problem of judgment: "Reason has never really directed social reality, but now reason has been so thoroughly purged of any specific trend or preference that it has finally renounced even the task of passing judgment on man's actions and way of life" (*ER*, 9).[19] But the terms in which Horkheimer articulates the problem, that of instrumentality and objective versus subjective reasons, obscures the way to a solution. After all, if thinking were to "help in determining the desirability of any goal in itself," then surely a subject will have articulated some goal, purpose, or aim, and we would be hard-pressed to know how these were any different from the instrumental ends and subjective reason that Horkheimer wants to critique. By blocking the way to an account of ends-oriented reason that differs from instrumental reason, Horkheimer's only recourse will be to the formal and empty notion of reason he impugns, as we will see in a moment.

Despite the proximity of my diagnosis to Horkheimer's (and Adorno's), the critique of instrumental reason does not offer us a helpful way to distinguish between a degraded instrumentality and a valuable, indeed indispensable, orientation towards ends. The reasons are manifold.[20] To begin with, the foundation of the distinction, for Horkheimer, lies in the distinction between objective and subjective reason. Objective reason had the ability to ground substantive ends, whereas subjective reason accepts purposes as arbitrarily given and functions only as a means to those ends. However, Horkheimer recognizes that, under the conditions of modernity, it becomes impossible to return to or credit any conception of objective reason: "Today there is a general tendency to revive past theories of objective reason in order to give some philosophical foundation to the rapidly disintegrating hierarchy of generally accepted values. ... But the transition from objective to subjective reason was not an accident, and the process of development of ideas cannot arbitrarily at any given moment be reversed" (*ER*, 61–2). Thus, when Horkheimer himself has recourse to the notion of instrumentality, which relies on being able to distinguish objective from subjective reason, his indictments can only seem arbitrary, vague, subjective, and ungrounded, as they often do in *Eclipse of Reason*. The distinction between defensible ends and a mere instrumentality becomes elusive, and *all* forms of ends-orientation begin to seem suspect. It is in this way that critical theory turns into a merely negative hermeneutics of suspicion, all too adept at offering a critique of the regnant order but without being able to offer a robust or viable alternative to that order, in spite of its proclaimed allegiance to the *empty idea* of the utopian. Speaking of the practice of critical theory, Horkheimer says: "On the contrary, it is suspicious of the very categories of better, useful, appropriate, productive, and valuable, as these are understood in the present order, and refuses to take them as nonscientific presuppositions about which one can do nothing" ("Traditional and Critical Theory," 207). The qualification "as these are understood in the present order" makes clear that some version of these ends is desirable and necessary, though they must be transformed in some way. But what is wrong with the ends themselves? Is it simply the fact of existing within the present order, in which case the problem does not lie with the ends or instrumentality but with the social order itself? How are the problems with that social order to be judged if not instrumentally, by way of some set of purposes or ends? And how can the ends be transformed to make them more appropriate or defensible? Without any ability to distinguish between instrumental and non-instrumental versions of "better," "productive," and "valuable," the critique threatens to consume any account of ends-orientation as merely instrumental. An example of this excessive critique can be found in the *Dialectic of Enlightenment*, when Adorno and Horkheimer compare the man of science to the dictator: "The man of science knows things in so far as he can make them. In this way their potentiality is turned to his own ends" (9). One wonders what, in the abstract, can be wrong with making and shaping things for our own ends, and how it is even possible to live without doing so. Surely any utopian political project will require precisely this turning of potentialities to our own ends, this remaking of the world to be hospitable to our ends. The anti-utopian tendency of radical critique is clearly visible here. The effect of a critique that will concede no orientation according to ends, a critique that cannot offer a defence of certain ends as preferable to others, is that only formal, abstract, and nonsubstantive uses of reason can be endorsed: "In a historical period like the present true theory is more critical than affirmative, just as the society that corresponds to it cannot be called 'productive'" ("Traditional and Critical Theory," 242). For such a negative dialectics, freedom has to be understood as liberation from purposiveness;[21] a non-instrumentalized thinking becomes an endless reflection on itself;[22] and, concrete suggestions for action become taboo.[23]

The only way beyond these impasses of the critique of instrumental reason is through a robust account of the practice of judgment, of the kind we find in Shaftesbury's remarkable "Soliloquy" essay or the novels of Jane Austen, a task that cannot be undertaken here.[24] Such an account of finite judgment will have to satisfy several conditions. It must allow us to specify substantive ends without recourse to notions such as "objective reason" that are no longer available to us. It must embrace the fictions on which any judgment is founded. (We have seen Horkheimer's discomfort with this.) And yet, the process of judgment, and even the construction of appropriate fictions, must not be construed as arbitrary; it has to be grounded, not in Reason, but in the giving of reasons. The conditions that an account of judgment must satisfy are easy to state, but it is difficult to find a working account that satisfies them. Adorno and Horkheimer often gesture towards the necessity for such an account, although they never articulate one themselves, as the problems with the critique of instrumental reason show. For example, in the *Eclipse of Reason*, Horkheimer speaks of the need to define "the objective goals of society" (175); and in "Traditional and Critical Theory," the practice of critical theory is described as "the unfolding of a single existential judgment" (227; see also 234, 239). The *Dialectic of Enlightenment* offers a more extended discussion of judgment (194–201), and even alludes to Hamlet's hesitation as a sign of thinking in very much the way that Shaftesbury's transformation of Lockean hesitation into soliloquy does: "The person who doubts is already outlawed as a deserter. Since Hamlet, hesitation has been a sign of thinking and humanity for modern thinkers" (205). But beyond these gestures, critical theory offers us no resources for distinguishing an ends-oriented reason from instrumental reason.[25]

~

If Horkheimer's theory gives up too much in its efforts to indict instrumental reason, then we must return to the representatives of instrumental reason with fresh eyes, to discern what is problematic about such reasoning and how we might remedy it. Bernard Mandeville's *Fable of the Bees* is perhaps the most glaring instance of an unchecked market logic and precisely the kind of account we might want to critique under the rubric of "instrumental reason."[26] A close examination of the *Fable* can help us understand why a "critique of instrumental reason" will always miss its mark, compelling us to develop a different diagnosis to explain what is so problematic about a theory like Mandeville's. My own explanation, rather than drawing on any concept of instrumentality, will focus on the elision or evasion of judgment in Mandeville's text, the concerted strategy by which it conceals its own judgments to legitimate market-reasoning.

But even with all the problems mentioned above, why avoid the critique of instrumentality, rather than revising or updating it? The answer quite simply is because, if instrumental reason refers to the kind of rationality that is always oriented towards some goal, that is always seeking to maximize efficiencies and optimize outcomes, that always focuses on coordinating means and ends, that allows no room for errancy and the aleatory in its calculations, that is doggedly "teleological" in its orientation (to use a word that has become anathema in contemporary critical discourse), then Mandeville's theory cannot properly be said to be "instrumental." Like Locke (*Essay* Chapter 2.21), Mandeville wants to understand motivation and action in a way that makes no reference to orientation by ends and judgments about ends.[27] In the second edition of the *Essay*, Locke tells us that he has revised his account significantly, because in the first edition he had mistakenly thought that some notion of the "greater good" served as a motivator for action. Now he has come to realize that desire (or what he calls "uneasiness"), not some idea of the "greater good," motivates us to act. In other words, we act because we are uncomfortable with our present, not because we are enticed by a better future that we can imagine.[28] Mandeville's theory, even more strenuously than Locke's, is designed to put an end to high-minded speculation about the ends appropriate for human action. Desire, or in Mandeville's case "passion," is in effect being liberated to follow its wayward path in the present, as any market must, unshackled from the need to orient itself according to what might be considered "good." As Mandeville explains in the introduction to his remarks: "I believe Man … to be a compound of various Passions, that all of them, as they are provoked and come uppermost, govern him by turns, whether he will or no" (*Fable*, 39). We act as the strongest passion in the psyche dictates, overwhelmed by its force, and not according to some rational calculus of maximization.[29] There is hardly any space for reasoned deliberation or reflection on a course of action here, so from this perspective, there is nothing "reasonable" about instrumental reason, just as there is nothing "instrumental" about it, since action has no end in view. If it is nevertheless appropriate to speak of a certain kind of "rationality" at work here, it is because the passions constitute the psyche as a machine whose motions obey a clear logic of efficient causation. We might describe this by saying that the system is rational but without reason. (When the term "Enlightenment rationality" is being used in a pejorative sense, it is usually some version of this "rationality without reason" that is being impugned.) In this context, Mandeville's qualification that a person is governed by whichever passion is uppermost "whether he will or no" is a surprising one, because it suggests that we might have the possibility to will otherwise than passion dictates, that there is some space in which a deliberative reason might go to work, but elsewhere Mandeville denies this possibility, making the will itself indistinguishable from desire. Mandeville's equivocation can be clearly heard in the following argument: "It is impossible that … mere fallen Man, should act with any other View but to please himself while he has the Use of his organs … There is no difference between Will and Pleasure in one sense, and every Motion made in spite of them must be unnatural and convulsive" (348–9). If there is no distinction between will and pleasure, it is unclear how any "Motion made in spite of them" is even possible, but Mandeville allows the possibility nevertheless. This equivocation opens onto a question that haunts the theory throughout, about whether the account of motivation and action is descriptive (we cannot but act in interested and impassioned ways) or normative (we should act in these ways and not through reasoned deliberation about ends, or we will face deleterious consequences). Indeed, the slippage from one to the other is precisely what enables the theory to make its claims without acknowledging its own acts of judgment.

The "economic" account of motivation offered in the introduction is consistent with Mandeville's analyses in the body of the text. The strong motivating force of any passion can only be overcome by a more powerful force, not through any capacity to hesitate and reflect, a capacity that even Locke had conceded (Mandeville, *Fable*, 75, 202, 207; see also Locke, *Essay*, 242, 254). Thus, for example, courage does not arise from some Stoic process of deliberation about our passions that gains command over fear; it is rather the effect of another passion, anger, that overcomes fear. Nevertheless, Mandeville appears to grant that there is some capacity to reason that is distinct from the passions, even though its status may be precarious because it threatens to unhinge the smooth functioning of the system of the passions. Thus, he characterizes reason as both weaker than the passions even when it is operative, and always in the service of the passions even when it pretends not to be:[30] "For we are ever pushing our Reason which way soever we feel Passion to draw it, and Self-love pleads to all human Creatures for their different Views, still furnishing every individual with Arguments to justify their Inclinations. … His strong Habits and Inclinations can only be subdued by Passions of greater Violence" (333). If the only logic of the psyche is the quantitative one of greater and lesser force, it is unclear why the pleadings of reason should be necessary, so the only function of reason must be a disruptive one in the logic of this system. That is precisely why it must be yoked back into the service of the passions. It is not that the passions need a reasoned accounting to give them more force. They operate just fine on their own. Rather, reason itself must be made to play a useful role in their service if it is not to be an unsettling force in the psychic mechanism. *Reason, not passion, is the anarchic wildcard in the system, the one that threatens to derail the very systematicity of the system by its own unaccountable logic.* There are crucial moments when Mandeville acknowledges that reason empowers us to judge otherwise than the system dictates, but it is precisely this capacity that he must rein in with the claim that reason is weak and invariably risks leading us astray. His strategy is to discredit the prudence of using our judgment to question or second-guess the smooth operation of economic rationality. In the example below, Mandeville, by a clever reversal, himself takes up the position of the one posing ethical objections to the malt liquor trade, only to have his judgment exposed as short-sighted by the "good humour'd" proponent of economic reason: "He would answer, that of this I could be no Judge, because I don't know what vast Benefit they might afterwards be of to the Commonwealth" (93). "Of this I could be no Judge": I should simply follow my self-interest, allow others to follow their self-interest, and not speculate about ends that my reason is too weak to calculate.[31] As long as I refuse to think about the bigger picture – indeed, as long as I do not think at all and am content with computation and calculation – unexpected good effects will follow, in this case through the untold employment opportunities provided by the liquor trade.[32]

It will seem strange to claim that judgment, or *reasoned* deliberation about ends, is the greatest threat to "instrumental reason," but such is clearly the case in Mandeville. However, it will seem stranger yet to accuse Mandeville of bracketing purposes and ends, since his account is undoubtedly one of the most powerfully teleological justifications of the functioning of the market that we possess. Although the subtitle of the text, "Private Vices, Public Benefits," coyly avoids specifying the causal link between the two, contenting itself with a jarring juxtaposition, the argument of the text is that the pursuit of one's self-interest, even when it is clearly vicious, has unintended consequences that redound to the public benefit.[33] In spite of disclaimers to the contrary, the text makes the argument for the unfettering not just of the market but of individuals from any moral strictures (thus making this a *Fable* to end all fables, a fable whose intention is to end the moralizing genre of the fable itself).[34] And it makes this case precisely by appealing to the ends it promises will be attained if we follow its prescriptions, namely the public benefits that will result if everyone acts out of self-love rather than attempting to be good citizens. But we must proceed carefully here. We are so accustomed to a reflexive dismissal of teleological thinking and the ends it posits for history that the nature of the problem becomes obscured. The problem with teleological thinking cannot lie in the fact of positing ends by which to orient our action, because then Mandeville's bracketing of ends to guide action would be precisely the solution we are in search of. Rather, the problem with the teleology of the market (which will become the teleology that guides philosophies of history later in the century, such as Hegel's and Kant's) is at least threefold. First, there can be no deliberation about the end itself, which is assumed to be given and self-evident. This becomes apparent when Mandeville narrows down the capacious meaning of "Benefits" to the narrowly economic one of profit and financial advantage. Second, it is assumed that the end naturally and inevitably emerges from the processes of history or the market, whether we work towards its attainment or not. Third, and most important for our purposes here, there is undoubtedly an end being posited for the system ("Public Benefits"), *but the end cannot be said to motivate the actions of the individuals within the system.*[35] Individuals act for their own local ends ("Private Vices") or, more properly, for no ends at all, simply following the overwhelming logic of their passions and interests. In fact, it is often suggested that the surest way to disrupt the attainment of the end is to work concertedly and consciously towards it. The end must be allowed to emerge, and it will emerge as long as we do not meddle by trying to bring it about, or trying to attain some other end. Actions, on this model, work best to attain the ends of the system when they are oblivious to those ends;

they must, to use a Kantian formulation, be purposive without purpose. To call this reason instrumental, then, when it refuses to consider ends, misses the mark, and makes the aesthetic response to it a replication of the same problem, just as to call this reason "reasonable," misses the mark because instrumental reason disavows the use of deliberative judgment, which threatens to disrupt the well-greased "rationality" of the economy of passions.

Let us return now to the problem with which I opened this essay, namely the aesthetic as an inadequate response to both the threat of the elision of ends and the threat of instrumentalization within empiricism. Neither the response outlined earlier in the century by Hutcheson or Addison and Steele, to find purpose already given in the phenomenal texture of the natural world with the beautiful, the sublime, and the new, nor the Kantian response later in the century, to denude the aesthetic object of purpose to avoid the charge of instrumentality, can satisfy us. If the problem with both empiricism and aesthetic discourse in the eighteenth century is that they are, in their different ways, uncomfortable with the work of making ends, then the adequate "aesthetic" response must be to embrace the labour of judgment by which we fashion or fiction ends for ourselves. If judgment always has an aesthetic component to it, that is not because it has an immediate capacity to discern beauty in objects, but rather because it strives to make ends beautiful, so that they can serve as guides for our actions. This judgment will have to craft or fiction ends for action, and deliberate about alternative ends providing some kind of (provisional) justification for them.[36] The work of judgment, at once deliberative and fictioning, cannot be erased. It occurs every time we act, in the fullest sense of the word. But its place can be concealed. This is precisely what Mandeville seeks to do to ensure the smooth functioning of the system, when he downplays the capacity of reason to intervene in the psychic mechanism, for example, or when he narrows the meaning of "Benefit" without admitting that he is making an evaluative judgment about what counts as a benefit, or when he makes alternatives invisible so they cannot enter into the process of deliberation. But before the machine of the market or the Mandevillian psyche can be set in motion, a judgment has to be made about the ends they will serve. Although most of the *Fable of the Bees* is designed to conceal this work – to make the space of judgment invisible or unavailable to us – Mandeville nevertheless puts the work of judgment on display in the *margins* of the text, in the poetic fable of "The Grumbling Hive" that opens his discourse. It is here that we must be convinced, by a work of fictioning and deliberative judgment, that the market societies of today are preferable to the anti-consumerist republican societies of yore. It is in this prefatory and seemingly marginal discourse, to which the rest of the text is then quite literally an appendix or a set of extended footnotes, that Mandeville makes his own judgment. Let us now examine the process by which this judgment takes place.

Rarely do we think of the work of judgment as relying on fictions. But Aristotle tells us that judgment is about the things that can be otherwise, and to be able to conceive of things as being potentially otherwise than they are requires imagination.[37] It is only appropriate, then, that the judgment that authorizes Mandeville's market system as the preferable choice takes place in the course of a fable. But what is striking is how clear-sighted the fable is about its nearly impossible task: it must convince us to prefer life in a restless, corrupt, pointless, consumerist market society to life in a nearly idyllic republican utopia. To do this, the fable begins with a society of bees who live in a modern commercial economy that is kept functioning by a constitutional monarchy, much like Mandeville's England (*Fable*, 6, 17; see also 116–17). But, dismayed by the fraud and mismanagement necessary to keep their society operational, the bees complain endlessly and wish that they lived in a utopia of honesty and frugality. Finally, the gods, fed up with all their complaining, punish them by making them feel shame, which results in the transformation of their modern commercial economy into a utopia. Perversely, the advent of shame *and the resultant transition to a utopian social order* is portrayed as a biblical Fall: "The very moment [Fraud] departs,/ And Honesty fills all their Hearts;/ There shews 'em, *like th' Instructive Tree*,/ Those Crimes which they're asham'd to see" (27, my emphasis). It may sound implausible to describe the Fall as a fall into *utopia*, since the fable is trying to convince us of the undesirability of the alternative, but the representation of the bees' post-lapsarian society draws explicitly on stock tropes of the utopian tradition. In the new utopian order, lawyers and even laws themselves become obsolete (28); prisons and punishments become unnecessary (28); the quality of medicine improves (29–30); the imperial ambitions of the nation evaporate (32); the only wars undertaken are for the sake of justice and liberty (32); Christian charity comes to dominate social relations (30); and although the economy still uses money, everything has become so cheap that the affordability of goods is simply not an issue (28, 32, 34). Indeed, nature itself appears to be miraculously liberated from its shackles by this transformation: "Still Peace and Plenty reign,/ And every Thing is cheap, tho' plain:/ Kind Nature, free from Gard'ners Force,/ Allows all Fruits in her own Course" (34). Perhaps most important, people seem to live well, rather than pursuing an endless and pointless round of consumption: "Those, that remain'd, grown temp'rate, strive,/ Not how to spend; but how to live" (33). It is this idyllic portrait of utopian life, not some caricature of a starving and straitened premodern life, that Mandeville is calling upon us to reject, in favour of a modern commercial economy:[38]

> Then leave Complaints: Fools only strive
> To make a Great an Honest Hive.
> T'enjoy the World's Conveniences,
> Be fam'd in War, yet live in Ease,
> Without great Vices, is a vain
> EUTOPIA seated in the Brain. (36)

This is the judgment we must make, the "moral" we must draw enabled by the fable itself, and it can only take place in the aesthetic terms of the narrative we are given, not according to some set of empirical criteria. I have said that the work of judgment is at once fictioning and deliberative. It is fictioning because it requires the imagination of this utopian alternative against which we might gauge the advantages and disadvantages of commercial society. It is deliberative because Mandeville, in the course of his fiction, gives us *reasons* to prefer modern consumer society to the utopia, as inadequate as these reasons are. The arguments range from the frivolous to the gravely earnest, but none of them can have the knock-down force of a syllogism, which makes the utopia inconceivable as an alternative, since the choice between the two will always be a judgment we make and a judgment that we can always make differently. Indeed, examining the fable's reasons, it is still difficult to know what dictates the preference for consumer society over the utopia of the fable. Among the silliest of reasons for the preference is the worry that the utopian economy will only produce plain goods, unable to entertain the taste for rarity, luxury, and novelty ("Rarities cannot be had"). The aestheticizing character of the objection is all too apparent here, implicitly appealing to the contemporary aesthetic category of the new. Other concerns centre on the collapse of the commercial economy, from the rise of unemployment within the formal economy of the division of labour (32) to the worry that satisfaction with their lot will prevent people from working (34–5). But as weighty as these objections are, they cannot be sustained on their own terms, since they depend on us accepting the value of the commercial economy itself, which is precisely what the fable is supposed to convince us of. Perhaps the most serious objection is the Schmittian one: the worry that such a utopia would constantly face an existential threat, beset on all sides by foes that would want to eliminate or incorporate it (35). But even the spectre of this existential threat is not sufficient since we can always judge that our continued political life is not worth having if it is denuded of all its value, a judgment unavailable to a Schmittian politics but one that we must preserve nevertheless. As the extreme example of the existential threat shows, the judgment between these two political systems, and indeed these two forms of life, cannot lie in any empirically adduced advantage, whose value can always be called into question. It must lie, rather, in the aesthetic dimension, by which I mean not the unaccountable and dogmatic assertion of value but instead the ends that we fashion and fiction for ourselves and convince others to love. For the utopia, this end is the kind of "living" or "living well" that we can call by its old-fashioned name of happiness ("Not how to spend; but how to live"). But what is the end for which consumer society is instituted? Its end, if we are to judge by the fable's immoral "Moral," is simply itself, not something substantive beyond it: "Then leave Complaints: Fools only strive/ To make a *Great* an honest Hive/ ... / Bare Virtue can't make Nations live/ In *Splendor*" (36–7, my emphasis).[39] Thus, not only are the desiring or passionate agents within this economy motivated by a kind of purposiveness without purpose, but the economy itself, like a work of art, has become its own non-instrumental end, acquiring an autonomy that severs it from the human ends one might have thought it was instituted to subserve.[40] This is why the fable has recourse to the aesthetic language of "greatness" and "splendour" at this point, as a way of convincing us of the economy's autonomous value. Only on these aesthetic terms, only by valuing greatness and splendour over honesty and living well, would we choose the commercial economy over the bees' post-lapsarian utopia. Clearly, then, the opposition of instrumentality and aesthetic autonomy cannot assist us in grasping what is problematic about this situation. The problem is rather taking something to be an end (the economy) over against the kinds of beings that have the ability to make their own ends. The only redress we have in this situation is to insist on our capacity to judge that things might be better otherwise, in other words to fashion different ends for ourselves. It is precisely this capacity that most of the text, with its economistic account of mental functioning, seeks to conceal from us but that glimmers before us here briefly in the opening poem.

So, confronted with the choice between commercial society and the post-lapsarian utopia of the bees, how will we decide? Ultimately, I will have to leave it to your best judgment, but not without first quoting these wise words that preface Mandeville's prefatory fable:

> If laying aside all worldly Greatness and Vain-Glory, I should be ask'd where I thought it was most probable that Men might enjoy true Happiness, I would prefer a small peaceable Society, in which Men neither envy'd nor esteem'd by Neighbours, should be contented to live upon the Natural Product of the Spot they inhabit, to a vast Multitude abounding in Wealth and Power, that should always be conquering others by their Arms Abroad, and debauching themselves by Foreign Luxury at Home. (12–13)

NOTES

1 On the apodictic, axiomatic, and non-dialectical style of argument favoured by modern theorists, see Thomas Pfau, *Minding the Modern: Human Agency, Intellectual Traditions, and Responsible Knowledge* (Notre Dame, IN: University of Notre Dame Press, 2013), 24, 191, 258.

2 See Alasdair C. MacIntyre, *After Virtue: A Study in Moral Theory*, 2nd ed. (Notre Dame, IN: University of Notre Dame Press, 1984); Charles Taylor, *Sources of the Self: The Making of the Modern Identity* (Cambridge, MA: Harvard University Press, 1989). For those who view the Enlightenment as embodying a teleological and instrumental reason, the claim will sound counter-intuitive. This essay is, among other things, an attempt to mediate between the critiques offered by MacIntyre and Taylor and those of Horkheimer's critical theory.

3 Michael J. Sandel shows how, over the last 30 or 40 years, market thinking has crept into areas of social life once thought to be sheltered from it, so that "without quite realizing it, without ever deciding to do so, we drifted from *having* a market economy to *being* a market society." *What Money Can't Buy: The Moral Limits of Markets* (New York: Farrar, Straus and Giroux, 2012), 10. Mandeville's *Fable* clearly marks one of the earliest

moments in the longer history of this conceptual transformation, which Hannah Arendt had also presciently diagnosed in *The Human Condition* (Chicago: University of Chicago Press, 1958).

4 Although the term "instrumental reason" is associated with the Frankfurt School, and I will be taking up Horkheimer's and Adorno's version specifically below, the critique of instrumentalization and instrumentality is widespread in the contemporary humanities, and has arguably been present in some form since Kant's insistence that acting morally requires us to treat others as ends in themselves, rather than as mere means and instruments. One could argue that Derrida's and Levinas's ethics of alterity serve a similar function of refusing the instrumentalization of ethics and human relations. For other recent critiques that seek to address the problem of instrumentality, whether explicitly or not, see Arendt, *Human Condition*; Pfau, *Minding the Modern*; Sandel, *What Money Can't Buy*; Anne-Lise François, *Open Secrets: The Literature of Uncounted Experience* (Stanford: Stanford University Press, 2008); Jacques Rancière, *Aisthesis: Scenes from the Aesthetic Regime of Art*, trans. Zakir Paul (London: Verso, 2013); Vivasvan Soni, *Mourning Happiness: Narrative and the Politics of Modernity* (Ithaca: Cornell University Press, 2010); Vivasvan Soni, "Energy/*Energeia*," in *Fueling Culture*, ed. Patricia Yaeger, Imre Szeman, and Jennifer Wenzel (New York: Fordham University Press, forthcoming); Stefan Collini, *What Are Universities for?* (London: Penguin, 2012).

5 Of course, there are many critiques that insist that the aesthetic cannot remedy these problems, but is caught within them. See, for example, Pierre Bourdieu, *Distinction: A Social Critique of the Judgment of Taste*, trans. Richard Nice (Cambridge, MA: Harvard University Press, 1984). But it is sufficient for my argument that we recognize in aesthetic theories the effort to remedy these problems, whether successful or not.

6 Immanuel Kant, *Critique of the Power of Judgment*, ed. Paul Guyer, trans. Paul Guyer and Eric Matthews (Cambridge: Cambridge University Press, 2000), 5:211. Hereafter cited parenthetically as *CJ*.

7 Jerome Stolnitz, "On the Significance of Lord Shaftesbury in Modern Aesthetic Theory," *Philosophical Quarterly* 11.43 (1961): 100.

8 See Anthony Ashley Cooper, Third Earl of Shaftesbury, *Characteristicks of Men, Manners, Opinions, Times*, 3 vols. (Indianapolis: Liberty Fund, 2001), 1:56–8, 70–1, 85.

9 Alexander Gottlieb Baumgarten, *Reflections on Poetry*, trans. Karl Aschenbrenner and William B. Holther (Berkeley: University of California Press, 1954), 42.

10 Frederick C. Beiser, *Diotima's Children: German Aesthetic Rationalism from Leibniz to Lessing* (Oxford: Oxford University Press, 2009), 38.

11 Joseph Addison and Richard Steele, *The Spectator*, ed. Henry Morley, vol. 2. (London: George Routledge and Sons, 1891), 720.

12 Francis Bacon, *The New Organon*, ed. Lisa Jardine and Michael Silverthorne (Cambridge: Cambridge University Press, 2000), 102; John Locke, *An Essay Concerning Human Understanding*, ed. Roger Woolhouse (London: Penguin, 2004), 234.

13 Addison and Steele, *Spectator*, 720–1.

14 Francis Hutcheson, *An Inquiry into the Original of Our Ideas of Beauty and Virtue in Two Treatises*, ed. Wolfgang Leidhold (Indianapolis: Liberty Fund, 2004), 79, 46–60, 76.

15 See Vivasvan Soni, "Introduction: The Crisis of Judgment," *The Eighteenth Century: Theory and Interpretation* 51.3 (2010): 261–88.

16 For a discussion of the radical opposition, and indeed incommensurability, between these two kinds of theoretical account in the period – the one naturalist, reductionist, and voluntarist, the other neo-Platonic or neo-Stoic in its orientation – see Pfau, *Minding the Modern*, 185–413. Since I discuss Mandeville at length below, it should be noted that Pfau situates Mandeville as unquestionably within the reductionist tradition (249–69), but he is not alone. M.R. Jack also views Mandeville as "a psychologist interested in giving a naturalistic account of ethical phenomena." "Religion and Ethics in Mandeville," in *Mandeville Studies: New Explorations in the Art and Thought of Dr. Bernard Mandeville (1670–1733)*, ed. Irwin Primer (The Hague: Martinus Nijhoff, 1975), 35. See also, Hector Monro, *The Ambivalence of Bernard Mandeville* (London: Clarendon Press, Oxford University Press, 1975), 248; Thomas A. Horne, *The Social Thought of Bernard Mandeville: Virtue and Commerce in Early Eighteenth-Century England* (New York: Columbia University Press, 1978), x, 9, 41, 92; M.M. Goldsmith, *Private Vices, Public Benefits: Bernard Mandeville's Social and Political Thought* (Cambridge: Cambridge University Press, 1985), 50, 77; Louis Dumont, *From Mandeville to Marx: The Genesis and Triumph of Economic Ideology* (Chicago: University of Chicago Press, 1977), 80. Despite Mandeville's claims, in the "Vindication" and elsewhere, that the *Fable* "is a Book of severe and exalted Morality, that contains a strict Test of Virtue" (*The Fable of the Bees; or, Private Vices, Publick Benefits*, ed. F.B. Kaye, vol. 1 [Indianapolis: Liberty Fund, 1988], 404–5. Hereafter cited parenthetically; see also, 229), a claim that some have sought to take at face value (Speck, "Mandeville," 78; Monro, *Ambivalence*, 15), M.M. Goldsmith gives a judicious and compelling account of why the *Fable* has been received as exemplary of the hermeneutics of suspicion

("Mandeville's Pernicious System," in *Mandeville and Augustan Ideas: New Essays*, ed. Charles W.A. Prior [Victoria, BC: English Literary Studies, University of Victoria, 2000], 79–81). Although Monro argues that there are many different Mandevilles, and significant ambiguity in how we read him (*Ambivalence*, 1–2, 23, 261), his description of Mandeville's "comic vision" also confirms the naturalist accounts (261–67).

17 Max Horkheimer, *Eclipse of Reason* (New York: Oxford University Press, 1947), 4–5, my emphasis, hereafter cited parenthetically as *ER*; see also, Max Horkheimer and Theodor Adorno, *Dialectic of Enlightenment*, trans. John Cumming (New York: Continuum, 1972), 104, hereafter cited parenthetically as *DE*.

18 Thomas Pfau, "The Philosophy of Shipwreck: Gnosticism, Skepticism, and Coleridge's Catastrophic Modernity," *Modern Language Notes* 122 (2007): 949–1004.

19 See also Max Horkheimer, "Traditional and Critical Theory," in *Critical Theory: Selected Essays*, trans. Matthew J. O'Connell and others (New York: Continuum, 1972), 202, 208, hereafter cited parenthetically. As Horkheimer explains, the alternative to judgment, to which dialectical social theorists from Mandeville to Hegel will recur, is to abandon the outcome to objective conflict: "Reason has turned them over for ultimate sanction to the conflicting interests to which our world actually seems abandoned" (*ER*, 9). Surprisingly, both Horkheimer and Shaftesbury also adopt this agonistic model in different contexts.

20 One question that I cannot take up here, but needs to be explored further, is what the "instrumental" in instrumental reason refers to: at various times, it is the instrumental use of reason itself; a purely procedural (formal) or non-instrumental use of reason; the instrumental use of persons; or, the instrumental domination of nature.

21 "Even as a negation of that social purposiveness which is spreading through the market, its freedom remains essentially bound up with the premise of a commodity economy" (Horkheimer and Adorno, *DE*, 157).

22 "Enlightenment has put aside the classic requirement of thinking about thought" (Horkheimer and Adorno, *DE*, 25). If critical theory means to restore this gesture of thinking about thought, it is one that can be traced back to Kant's critical project, but especially the inward turn that the Kantian aesthetic subject makes when it issues a judgment that something is beautiful, a judgment that has no content beyond the subject's reflection on its own faculties. See Kant, *CJ*, 5:203.

23 "The author is not trying to suggest anything like a program of action" (Horkheimer, *ER*, vi).

24 For readings of two Austen novels in this vein, see Vivasvan Soni, "Committing Freedom: The Cultivation of Judgment in Rousseau's *Emile* and Austen's *Pride and Prejudice*," *The Eighteenth Century: Theory and Interpretation* 51.3 (2010): 363–87; Soni, "Preface: Jane Austen's Critique of Aesthetic Judgment," in *Jane Austen and the Arts: Elegance, Propriety, and Harmony*, ed. Natasha Duquette and Elisabeth Lenckos (Bethlehem: Lehigh University Press, 2014).

25 On the more widespread withering of this distinction, see Thomas Pfau, "The Letter of Judgment: Practical Reason in Aristotle, the Stoics, and Rousseau," *The Eighteenth Century: Theory and Interpretation* 51.3 (2010): 292.

26 For the specific historical context out of which Mandeville's polemic emerges, see Goldsmith, *Private Vices*; Horne, *Social Thought*; W.A. Speck, "Mandeville and the Eutopia Seated in the Brain," in *Mandeville Studies: New Explorations in the Art and Thought of Dr. Bernard Mandeville (1670–1733)*, ed. Irwin Primer (The Hague: Martinus Nijhoff, 1975). However, as Goldsmith shows, Mandeville's argument casts a much longer shadow across the eighteenth century beyond its immediate context (*Private Vices*, 122; see also Horne, *Social Thought*, 76–95; Dumont, *From Mandeville to Marx*, 63–4). Sandel's recent book makes apparent that the concerns I am addressing in Mandeville's text are still very much with us today (*What Money Can't Buy*). What is most important for my purposes here is not any specific economic theory that Mandeville articulates, but rather his unprecedented defence of the logic of market rationality. On the novelty of Mandeville's defence of the market, one that has well transcended the historical moment of its inception, see Goldsmith, *Private Vices*, 120–59; Dumont, *From Mandeville to Marx*, 61–81. On the emergence of the economy as a conceptual category in this period, see Dumont, *From Mandeville to Marx*, 33–9.

27 Pfau, *Minding the Modern*, 269.

28 See Locke, *Essay*, 233–8.

29 On the passions as the motor of Mandeville's system, see Monro, *Ambivalence*, 265; Horne, *Social Thought*, 18. For an account of the economic logic of passions, and the process by which the passions are rationalized as interests in this period, see Albert O. Hirschman, *The Passions and the Interests: Political Arguments for Capitalism before Its Triumph* (Princeton: Princeton University Press, 1977).

30 See Horne, *Social Thought*, 19; Goldsmith, *Private Vices*, 153.

31 This sense of the weakness of reason in calculating consequences and outcomes persists all the way to Kant, and is one of his reasons for developing a deontological ethics. See Immanuel Kant, *Groundwork of the*

Metaphysics of Morals, in *Practical Philosophy*, trans. and ed. Mary J. Gregor (Cambridge: Cambridge University Press, 1996), 4:395.

32 It is of course no coincidence that, under the conditions of modernity, narcotics come to function as the ideal form of the commodity in so many contexts. For a powerful literary account of this logic that links the emergence of global capitalism to the narcotics trade, see Amitav Ghosh, *Sea of Poppies* (New York: Farrar, Straus and Giroux, 2008) and Amitav Ghosh, *River of Smoke* (New York: Farrar, Straus and Giroux, 2011). For the narcotic logic of modern conceptions of happiness, see Soni, *Mourning Happiness*.

33 Once again, see Goldsmith, "Mandeville's Pernicious System," 75, 79–81, on why it is legitimate to read Mandeville this way despite his disclaimers.

34 It should be noted that Mandeville translated La Fontaine's fables (Horne, *Social Thought*, 26; Goldsmith, *Private Vices*, 29). Of course, Mandeville's *Fable* should not be read as encouraging us to vice. Its key operation, which enables market rationality to take hold, is to decouple market logic from moral questions altogether. See Horne, *Social Thought*, ix, 33, 75; Jack, "Religion and Ethics in Mandeville," 42; Goldsmith, "Mandeville's Pernicious System," 81; Goldsmith, *Private Vices*, 102, 143, 149; Monro, *Ambivalence*, 260; Dumont, *From Mandeville to Marx*, 36, 61, 75, 77–81. As Sandel points out: "This nonjudgmental stance towards values lies at the heart of market reasoning and explains much of its appeal" (*What Money Can't Buy*, 14; see also, 48; Mandeville, *Fable*, 314–15). However, as he shows so well, markets are not necessarily neutral with regard to values, as economic theory claims. They can actually change (diminish, corrupt) the value of the very goods they wish to promote (113–18). Dumont also argues that a certain normativity clings to the market, even though a supposed emancipation from norms is what allows economic rationality to take hold (*From Mandeville to Marx*, 36, 62, 77).

35 See Mandeville, *Fable*, 368; Dumont, *From Mandeville to Marx*, 74.

36 Sandel describes a similar deliberative practice (*What Money Can't Buy*, 112). He also recognizes the importance of ends and judgment (35, 79, 90), but does not focus on the fictionalizing process by which ends are constituted, as I am doing.

37 See Aristotle, *Nicomachean Ethics*, in *The Complete Works of Aristotle: The Revised Oxford Translation*, ed. Jonathan Barnes, vol. 2 (Princeton: Princeton University Press, 1984), 1112a 17–b 11, 1139a 14, 1141b 8–12.

38 See also the description at Mandeville, *Fable*, 232. Because Mandeville's polemic is directed against the utopia, its utopian character is easily missed. Dumont characterizes the fall into utopia this way: "with vice

gone, activity and prosperity disappear and are replaced by sloth, poverty, and boredom in a much reduced population" (*From Mandeville to Marx*, 64).

39 See also Mandeville, *Fable*, 365; Dumont, *From Mandeville to Marx*, 77, 81.

40 On the way that money becomes an end in itself in Mandeville, see Goldsmith, *Private Vices*, 124–6, 137–8. For Dumont, the most important change implied by the establishment of economic rationality is a shift to the "primacy of the relations to things over the relations between men" (*From Mandeville to Marx*, 81; see also 5, 67, 76).

Contributors

David Alvarez is associate professor of English at DePauw University. He has published on Joseph Addison, Mary Astell, and Shaftesbury. His essay in this volume is part of a book project on the passions and religious tolerance in the English Enlightenment.

Alison Conway is professor of English at the University of Western Ontario. She is the author of *Private Interests: Women, Portraiture, and the Visual Culture of the English Novel, 1709–1791* (Toronto 2001) and *The Protestant Whore: Courtesan Narrative and Religious Controversy in England, 1680–1750* (Toronto 2010). Her current book project investigates interfaith marriage and the British eighteenth-century novel.

Sarah Ellenzweig is associate professor of English at Rice University. She is the author of *The Fringes of Belief: English Literature, Ancient Heresy, and the Politics of Freethinking, 1660–1760* (Stanford 2008). Her current book project explores the English novel and the philosophy of motion in the literary culture of the Enlightenment.

Jonathan Kramnick is Maynard Mack Professor of English at Yale University. He is the author of *Actions and Objects from Hobbes to Richardson* (Stanford 2010), and *Making the English Canon: Print-Capitalism and the Cultural Past, 1700–1770* (Cambridge 1999). His next book, under contract with the University of Chicago Press, will be *Paper Minds: Literature and Some Problems of Consciousness*, portions of which have appeared recently in *Critical Inquiry* and elsewhere.

Sara Landreth is assistant professor of English at the University of Ottawa. Her research addresses Restoration and eighteenth-century theories about motion and emotion, and also explores how changing ideas about movement contributed to the origins of our modern disciplinary divide between the arts and the sciences.

Ruth Mack is associate professor of English at the State University of New York at Buffalo and the author of *Literary Historicity: Literature and Historical Experience in Eighteenth-Century Britain* (Stanford 2008). She is at work on a book on eighteenth-century ideas about habit and knowledge.

Mary Helen McMurran is associate professor of English at the University of Western Ontario. She is the author of *The Spread of Novels: Translation and Prose Fiction in the Eighteenth Century* (Princeton 2009). Her current project traces the eighteenth-century reconstruction of the category "pagan" and the nature of religious experience, as well as ideas of spirit and soul, in relation to the period's empiricist and materialist currents.

Vivasvan Soni is associate professor of English at Northwestern University. His book, *Mourning Happiness: Narrative and the Politics of Modernity* (Cornell 2010), won the Modern Language Association Prize for a First Book. He is working on a project that probes the long history of our discomfort with judgment, tracing its genesis in eighteenth-century discourses of empiricism and aesthetics.

Joanna Stalnaker is associate professor in the Department of French at Columbia University. She is the author of *The Unfinished Enlightenment: Description in the Age of the Encyclopedia* (Cornell 2010) and winner of the American Society for Eighteenth-Century Studies Kenshur prize. She is completing a book on the Enlightenment *philosophes*' last works.

Kate E. Tunstall is associate professor of French at the University of Oxford and Fellow of Worcester College. She is the author of *Blindness and Enlightenment. An Essay. With New Translations of Diderot's "Lettre sur les aveugles" and La Mothe Le Vayer's "Of a Man Born Blind"* (Continuum 2011). She is co-translator, with Caroline Warman, of Denis Diderot's *Rameau's Nephew* (2014), which was published in an open-access, multimedia edition and won the 2014 British Society for Eighteenth-Century Studies Digital Prize.

Index

Figures in the text are indicated by a page reference followed by *fig*.

www.ingramcontent.com/pod-product-compliance
Lightning Source LLC
LaVergne TN
LVHW090152080826
844660LV00013B/779/J

* 9 7 8 1 4 4 2 6 5 0 1 1 4 *

www.ingramcontent.com/pod-product-compliance
Lightning Source LLC
LaVergne TN
LVHW090152080826
844660LV00013B/779/J

* 9 7 8 1 4 4 2 6 5 0 1 1 4 *